Why Do You Need This New Edition?

If you're wondering why you should buy this new edition of *Critical Reading, Critical Thinking,* here are four good reasons!

Because listening—like reading and viewing—demands critical thinking skills, this edition includes a new section on **critical listening** (Ch. 3), followed by appropriate activities focusing on analytical listening skills.

New **Listening Springboard Inquiries (LSI)** throughout Parts 2 and 3 encourage you to *listen* critically by sending you to audio files and online sources to hear contemporary voices and by offering thought-provoking questions about what you hear.

③ About one-third of all the **readings and activities, including those in Mastery Tests,** have been replaced with more current content, so you have fresh, compelling topics to read and write about.

④ **Chapter Outcomes** are linked to **MyReadingLab** in Looking Back…Looking Forward features at the end of each chapter, to alert you to additional resources and self-study tools in Pearson's online resource for readers, so you can check your progress in mastering the skills taught in each chapter.

D0162210

PEARSON

Critical Reading, Critical Thinking

Focusing on Contemporary Issues

FOURTH EDITION

Richard Pirozzi (Late)

Gretchen Starks-Martin

ST. CLOUD STATE UNIVERSITY

Julie Bonadonna Dziewisz

JEFFERSON COMMUNITY COLLEGE

Longman

Boston   Columbus   Indianapolis   New York   San Francisco   Upper Saddle River
Amsterdam   Cape Town   Dubai   London   Madrid   Milan   Munich   Paris   Montréal   Toronto
Delhi   Mexico City   São Paulo   Sydney   Hong Kong   Seoul   Singapore   Taipei   Tokyo

This book is dedicated to

David, Steve, and Danny

Sponsoring Editor: Virginia Blanford
Editorial Assistant: Lindsey Allen
Senior Supplements Editor: Donna
  Campion
Marketing Manager: Tom DeMarco
Production Manager: Ellen MacElree
Project Coordination, Interior Design,
  and Electronic Page Makeup:
  Integra Software Services, Inc.
Cover Design Manager: John
  Callahan

Cover Designer: Laura Shaw
Cover Images (clockwise from top left):
  Exactostock/Superstock, © Joseph
  Sohm/GalileoPix, Solent News/
  Rex USA
Photo Researcher: Rona Tuccillo
Senior Manufacturing Buyer: Roy
  Pickering
Printer and Binder: Edwards Brothers
Cover Printer: Lehigh-Phoenix
  Color/Hagerstown

For permission to use copyrighted material, grateful acknowledgment is made
to the copyright holders on pp. 456–458, which are hereby made part of this
copyright page.

Library of Congress Cataloging-in-Publication Data

Pirozzi, Richard C.
Critical reading, critical thinking: focusing on contemporary issues/Richard
Pirozzi (late), Gretchen Starks-Martin, Julie Bonadonna Dziewisz.—4th ed.
    p. cm.
  Includes bibliographical references and index.
  ISBN-13: 978-0-205-83522-5 (alk. paper)
  ISBN-10: 0-205-83522-8 (alk. paper)
  1. Reading (Higher education)   2. Critical thinking.   I. Starks-Martin,
Gretchen.   II. Dziewisz, Julie Bonadonna.   III. Title.
LB2395.3.P56 2010
428.4071'1—dc22

                                                                2010030263

Longman
is an imprint of

www.pearsonhighered.com

ISBN-10:   0-205-83522-8
ISBN-13: 978-0-205-83522-5

Brief Contents

Detailed Contents

PART THREE   CRITICAL READING: EVALUATING WHAT YOU READ 287

Preface

The objective of *Critical Reading, Critical Thinking: Focusing on Contemporary Issues* is to provide students with critical reading and thinking opportunities that are compelling, current, and relevant. The focus on contemporary issues encourages students to engage in reading and thinking about a range of topics that are important in today's world and to apply the skills presented in the text to everyday issues. Each contemporary passage is followed by questions intended to provoke students to use higher-level thinking strategies in responding to the issue.

Critical Reading, Critical Thinking includes vocabulary strategies (in the Eye on Vocabulary features), textbook reading strategies, and guidance in problem solving, using inference, distinguishing purpose and tone, and evaluating electronic texts. Also included are a wide range of quotes, puzzles, images (including photographs, cartoons, and charts and graphs), posters and billboards, Web sites, and other elements of our everyday lives that require critical thinking and reflect current issues and ideas.

■ New to This Edition

This fourth edition maintains its focus on developing students' critical thinking and reading skills while adding a number of fresh features:

- **A new section on critical listening.** Recognizing that listening—like reading and viewing—demands critical thinking skills, we have added a brief section and appropriate activities in Chapter 3 focusing on listening skills.
- **Listening Springboard Inquiries (LSI).** In addition to the Web Site Investigations (WSI) and Crime Scene Investigations (CSI), this edition includes new end-of-chapter exercises throughout Part 2 that encourage students to *listen* critically. These activities send students to audio files and online sources to listen to contemporary voices and offer thought-provoking questions about what they hear.
- **New readings, Activities, and Mastery Tests.** About one-third of all the activities and readings, including those in the Mastery Tests for each chapter, have been replaced with more current content, so instructors have fresh activities to assign.
- **Chapter Outcomes linked to MyReadingLab.** Looking Back... Looking Forward features at the end of each chapter send students to

appropriate content in Pearson's online resource for developmental reading—MyReadingLab—to support their mastery of the chapter's learning objectives.

■ How This Book Is Organized

Critical Reading, Critical Thinking is divided into three parts:

- **Part 1, Back to Basics,** is intended for students who need to brush up on basic skills. Chapter 1 provides a review of vocabulary skills, including a complete overview of basic vocabulary development (using context clues, using word parts, recognizing denotative and connotative meanings, and using glossaries and dictionaries). Chapter 2 offers an overview of basic reading strategies. And Chapter 3, on reading textbooks, includes three popular approaches to textbook reading (SQ4R, concept mapping, and KWL) as well as an extended excerpt from an actual textbook.
- **Part 2, Dealing with Complexity,** presents the approaches to contemporary issues and basic problem solving that underlie the rest of the book.
- **Part 3, Critical Reading: Evaluating What You Read,** offers extensive guidance in advanced critical reading skills, including using inference, distinguishing between facts and opinions, recognizing purpose and tone, and looking at online and visual texts with a critical eye.

■ Features You Will Find in *Critical Reading, Critical Thinking*

Throughout the text, passages on a variety of high-interest contemporary issues reinforce reading, thinking, writing, listening, and oral communication skills. This content is supported by a wide range of features and activities:

- **Chapter Outlines and Chapter Outcomes** open each chapter, offering clear learning goals for the content that follows. **Looking Back ... Looking Forward** features at the end of each chapter link the goals to resources and review materials in Pearson's MyReadingLab.
- Each chapter begins with **Think About It!** and ends with **Think Again!**—features designed to encourage critical thinking by providing stimulating and engaging photographs, puzzles, problems, or quotations, along with accompanying questions and activities.

- At the end of most chapters, **Web Site Investigations** send students online to explore and evaluate relevant issues; **Crime Scene Investigations** and **Sherlock Holmes** puzzles offer engaging and often humorous opportunities for students to test their problem-solving strategies; and the new **Listening Springboard Inquiries** provide chances for students to evaluate oral texts.
- **A wealth of Activities** throughout provide ample review and support for the content covered in each chapter.
- **Mastery Tests** at the end of each chapter allow students to test their learning.
- **Perforated pages** allow both Activities and Mastery Tests to be removed from the book and turned in for grading.

■ Additional Resources

Instructors may access both an Instructor's Manual and a Test Bank created specifically for this book online at Pearson Higher Education's Instructor Resource Center (**www.pearsonhighered.com/educator**).

MyReadingLab (**www.myreadinglab.com**): MyReadingLab combines diagnostics, practice exercises, tests, and powerful assessments to help improve student reading skills and reading level. Student reading skills are improved through a mastery-based format of practice exercises that include objective-based questions, open-ended questions, short-answer questions, combined-skills exercises, and more. Student reading level is assessed through the Lexile framework, the most widely adopted reading measure in use today, which measures both reader ability and text difficulty on the same scale. MyReadingLab allows students to increase their Lexile number and realize their progress over time.

The Pearson Developmental English Package

Pearson is pleased to offer a variety of support materials to help make teaching reading easier on teachers and to help students excel in their coursework. Contact your local Pearson sales representative for more information on pricing and how to create a package.

Acknowledgments

We are indebted to many people who helped in the journey of this book. First and foremost, we acknowledge the inspiration of Richard Pirozzi, without whose expertise in reading and belief that reading must be taught in the context of contemporary issues this book would not have been a reality.

The following reviewers provided valuable suggestions for this new edition of *Critical Reading, Critical Thinking:*

Karen Brown	Wallace Community College
Kate Frost	Arizona State University
Margaret Yobbi	New Jersey Institute of Technology
Levia Dinardo	College of Southern Nevada
Paige Sindt	Arizona State University
Aden B. Hamer	Indiana University of Pennsylvania
Anne Iseda	Jackson Community College
Lynda Wolverton	Polk Community College
Tracy Francis	Durham Technical College

In addition, our colleagues at Pearson Longman were encouraging, creative, and efficient. We particularly are grateful to our original acquisitions editor, Kate Edwards; Ginny Blanford, Senior Sponsoring Editor, who picked up the reins from Kate; Lindsey Allen, our editorial assistant; Ellen MacElree and the production team; and Sarah Burkhart with Elm Street Publishing Services.

Special thanks go to our families for their encouragement and support. They deserve our most heartfelt gratitude for their enthusiasm and patience, which allowed us to focus on this collaborative effort during the revision process.

GRETCHEN STARKS-MARTIN
JULIE BONADONNA DZIEWISZ

PART ONE
BACK TO BASICS

Understanding Vocabulary: A Review

CHAPTER OUTLINE

CHAPTER OUTCOMES

After completing Chapter 1, you should be able to:

- Use context clues to uncover word meanings.
- Use word parts to uncover word meanings.
- Recognize the difference between a word's denotation and connotation.
- Use a glossary to find word meanings.
- Use the dictionary effectively.

Think About It!

Every chapter in this textbook begins with "Think About It!" and ends with "Think Again!" sections. These sections are designed to help you focus on thinking critically. Enjoy them.

Critical thinkers are very careful about observing their surroundings. As a critical thinker, look carefully at the photographs below. There is something strange in each of the scenes. Do you know what it is? Discuss the photographs with your classmates.

1

2

When you looked at the outline and outcomes for this chapter, you might have thought to yourself that some or much of this information is familiar. In fact, you might have the same thought about the next two chapters. At this point in your education, it is important to understand that reviewing will help you make better sense of the kind of reading you are asked to do in college and will serve as a foundation on which to build the advanced critical reading and thinking skills presented in the other chapters.

Throughout this book, you will encounter some very interesting topics that should add to and enrich your educational experience as a college student. You will also encounter passages that may seem difficult and topics that challenge your way of thinking. By mastering the skills and strategies presented in this book, you will be able to tackle a variety of reading levels and think more critically about different issues and topics in this and other college courses.

■ The Power of Words

The difference between **the right word** and the almost right word is the difference between lightning and a lightning bug.

Mark Twain 1835–1910, *American Humorist,* Writer

We use words every day to express ourselves in speaking and in writing. Mark Twain's quote above clearly illustrates how one's *choice* of words can be critical to communication. Sometimes using the wrong word can get us into trouble, embarrass us, or can create a funny situation. For instance, saying that a musician received a standing *elevation*, instead of a standing *ovation*, for an outstanding performance can be funny but also embarrassing if the individual does not know the correct meaning of the words and just uses the wrong word. Words or combinations of words can conjure up different images, feelings, and reactions—and a range of intensity within those emotions. Words can make us laugh, cry, feel angry, create feelings of disgust, and help us to express love. We have all had experience with words in this respect. We may react differently depending upon the situation, conditions, our mood, or experience.

Think about these words or phrases. What ideas or feelings come to your mind?

| war | success | challenge | "you're fired" | "I love you" | soft |
| rejection | "good-bye" | petite | stagger | devour | peace |

Look at these quotes, and discuss what they mean.

"I find that the harder I work, the more luck I seem to have."

—Thomas Jefferson

"I am not afraid of storms, for I am learning how to sail my ship."

—Louisa May Alcott

"Only those who risk going too far can possibly find out how far one can go."

—T.S. Eliot

"You must be the change you want to see in the world."

—Mahatma Gandhi

A large vocabulary is an asset to you as a student and an employee and for your personal life. The more words you know, the more you will understand what you read and hear and then can apply to your speaking and writing. Thus, a greater range of topics will be of interest to you, and you can also project a more interesting background. We all like to be considered intelligent, and a strong vocabulary and appropriate use of words helps to portray ourselves as educated individuals.

As you may already realize, your college education will depend on learning new words. Facing that fact and approaching the task in a systematic way are crucial for several reasons. First, on assignments and tests, instructors will ask you to define key terms used in the particular subject areas. Another reason is that the more words you know, the better you will understand what you read or hear; thus, you will be able to retain information more easily. Also, in a general sense, broadening your vocabulary will enable you to become more effective in your communication skills: reading, writing, listening, and speaking. Not only will you comprehend better, but you will also have more words at your disposal to fulfill your responsibilities as a student. Finally, when you graduate, you will be better equipped to understand and deal with the world around you.

This chapter explores different ways of finding the meanings of unfamiliar words: using the context, recognizing denotation and connotation, using word parts, using a glossary, and using a dictionary. The method you employ will depend upon the given situation and sometimes your personal preference. However, when you are comfortable with *all* the methods, you increase your chances of finding word meanings quickly and efficiently.

■ Using Context Clues

Which of the following is the correct definition of the word *bar?*

1. The legal profession
2. A room or counter where alcohol is served
3. A piece of solid material longer than it is wide
4. Anything that impedes or prevents
5. All of the above

The answer to the question is "All of the above" because the meaning of *bar* depends on how it is used in a sentence. For example, the following sentences all use the word correctly:

1. Jessica was admitted to the *bar* two years after she graduated from law school.
2. After class, the students went to a *bar* to relax and have a few drinks.
3. Hold on to the *bar* so that you don't fall if the subway comes to a sudden stop.
4. The police set up a roadblock to *bar* his escape.

The **context** refers to the surrounding words in a sentence that give a word its specific meaning. Like the word *bar*, many other words have multiple meanings, and you can determine which meaning applies by the way those words are used in a sentence. Thus, you can often use the context to help you figure out the meanings of unfamiliar words without consulting a dictionary.

Various aspects of the context can be used individually or in combination to reveal word meanings, including punctuation, synonyms, antonyms, examples, and general sentence clues.

Punctuation

After introducing a word or term, writers sometimes provide its meaning and set it off through the use of punctuation marks, making the definition easy for readers to recognize. For example, a definition can be introduced with a colon:

> Pedro's general condition deteriorated after the physician discovered that he was suffering from **edema:** the accumulation of fluid in various organs of the body.

edema = the accumulation of fluid in various organs of the body.

The meaning of a word can be set off between commas (or by just one comma if the definition falls at the end of a sentence):

> Lovelock's theory is intricately tied to **cybernetics,** the study and analysis of how information flows in electronic, mechanical, and biological systems.
>
> F. Kurt Cylke Jr., *The Environment,* p. 78

cybernetics = the study and analysis of how information flows in electronic, mechanical, and biological systems

For greater emphasis, dashes can be used instead of commas:

> Regulation increased substantially during the 1970s. By the end of that decade, numerous proposals for **deregulation**—the removal of old regulations— had been made.
>
> Roger LeRoy Miller, *Economics Today,* 9th ed., p. 648

deregulation = the removal of old regulations

Definitions can also be enclosed in parentheses:

> Music consists of three basic elements: **pitch** (melody); **rhythm** (sounds grouped according to a prescribed system); and **timbre** (the qualities of a tone that make a C-sharp sound different, say, on a tuba than on a guitar). From these building blocks, human beings have created rock and roll, rap, sonatas, blues, folk songs, chants, symphonies, jazz, opera, ... the variations are end- less. Where there are human beings, there is music.
>
> Carol Tavris and Carole Wade, *Psychology in Perspective,* p. 575

pitch = melody
rhythm = sounds grouped according to a prescribed system
timbre = the qualities of a tone that make a C-sharp sound different, say, on a tuba than on a guitar

The definition of a term in a foreign language is usually placed in quota- tion marks:

> The *Ceteris Paribus* **Assumption: All Other Things Being Equal.** Everything in the world seems to relate in some way to everything else in the world. It would be impossible to isolate the effects of changes in one variable on another variable if we always had to worry about the many other variables that might also enter the analysis. As in other sciences, economics uses the *ceteris paribus assumption. Ceteris paribus* means "other things constant" or "other things equal."
>
> Roger LeRoy Miller, *Economics Today,* 9th ed., p. 10

ceteris paribus = "other things constant" or "other things equal"

The same is true of a definition taken from an outside source:

> **Affirmative action**—"programs instituted by private and public institutions to overcome the effects of and to compensate for past discrimination"

(Greenberg and Page, 1997, p. 576)—has recently come under attack in many parts of the United States.

affirmative action = programs instituted by private and public institutions to overcome the effects of and to compensate for past discrimination

Synonyms

Writers sometimes use **synonyms**, or words that mean the same or almost the same, to provide you with the meanings of unfamiliar words, as in the following sentence:

First, **psychotropic** or **mood-altering** drugs became increasingly popular among health practitioners, made patients easier to handle and increased their chances of being released.

Richard Sweeney, *Out of Place: Homelessness in America*, p. 69

Psychotropic and **mood-altering** are synonyms. Therefore, psychotropic drugs are drugs that alter or change our mood.

Antonyms

Writers may use **antonyms**, or words that mean the opposite, to help you figure out the meanings of unfamiliar words, as in the following sentence:

Whereas Princess Diana was rather **tall**, Mother Teresa was **diminutive**.
Whereas indicates that a contrast is being drawn between Princess Diana and Mother Teresa. **Tall** and **diminutive** must be antonyms; therefore, *diminutive* means "short" or "small."

Examples

Sometimes writers use familiar examples that *may* be helpful in determining word meanings, as in the following sentence:

The United States, Canada, England, and France are all examples of **autonomous** nations, because they are not controlled by any other governments.
If you have knowledge about some or all of these countries and are aware of what they have in common, perhaps you can figure out that **autonomous** means "independent" or "self-governing."

General Sentence Clues

You may be able to figure out the meaning of an unfamiliar word by study-ing the general sense of the sentence and focusing on the key words used in it, as in the following example:

> The **driver's eyes** were **bloodshot** and his **speech** was **slurred**; the **police officer** quickly concluded that he was **inebriated**.
>
> The sense of the sentence—with the use of the key words **driver, bloodshot** with reference to **eyes, slurred** with reference to **speech**, and **police officer**—is that this is a scene involving a drunken driver and hence that **inebriated** must mean "intoxicated" or "drunk."

ACTIVITY 1

DIRECTIONS: Using the context, try to determine the meanings of the words that appear under the sentences. In each case, be prepared to discuss what clues are present to help you. Many of the sentences are taken from college textbooks.

1. Judy does not talk very much at the staff meetings, but James is quite loquacious.

   loquacious: _____

2. For years, cigarette manufacturers denied that cigarette smoke was carcinogenic even though millions of smokers were dying from lung cancer.

   carcinogenic: _____

3. Adolf Hitler, Fidel Castro, and Saddam Hussein are good examples of infamous leaders.

   infamous: _____

4. Although the movie character James Bond is always involved in "clandestine" or "secret" activities, some intelligence work today is actually accomplished out in the open.

   clandestine: _____

5. Because of his attitude and harsh treatment of women in general, the captain has been called a misogynist by the female officers.

   misogynist: _____

DIRECTIONS: Using the context, determine the meanings of the words that appear after the sentences.

1. They favor government responses to the threat of global warming, the gradual warming of the Earth's atmosphere caused by burning fossil fuels and industrial pollutants.

   Neal Tannahill, *THINK American Government,* p. 92

   global warming: _____

2. With podcasting, consumers can download audio files (podcasts) or video files (vodcasts) via the Internet to an iPod or other handheld device and then listen to or view them whenever and wherever they wish.

   Gary Armstrong and Philip Kotler, *Marketing: An Introduction,* 9th ed., p. 426

   podcasts: _____

   vodcasts: _____

3. When information has little inherent meaning, mnemonic strategies build in meaning by connecting what is to be learned with established words or images.

   Anita Woolfolk, *Educational Psychology,* 10th ed., p. 294

   mnemonic strategies: _____

4. The electoral system affects policymaking because legislators worried about winning reelection focus their energy on pork barrel spending, which are expenditures to fund local projects that are not critically important from a national perspective.

   Neal Tannahill, *THINK American Government,* p. 185

   pork barrel spending: _____

5. Unlike the public Internet, an intranet is a private network that allows authorized company personnel or outsiders to share information electronically in a secure fashion without generating mountains of paper.

   Warren J. Keegan and Mark C Green, *Global Marketing,* 6th ed., p. 172

   intranet: _____

ACTIVITY 3

DIRECTIONS: Using the context, determine the meanings of the words that appear after the sentences.

1. How do you explain a student who struggles to read, write, spell, or learn math, even though he or she does not have intellectual disabilities, emotional problems or educational disadvantages and have normal vision, hearing, and language capabilities? One explanation is that the student has a learning disability.

    Anita Woolfolk, *Educational Psychology,* 10th ed., p. 142

    learning disability: _____

2. Childbirth, or parturition, begins with labor—contractions of the uterine muscles and opening of the cervix—and concludes with delivery—expelling the child and placenta from the vagina.

    George Zgourides, *Human Sexuality,* p. 249

    parturition: _____

    labor: _____

    delivery: _____

3. Both the baby boomers and Gen Xers will one day be passing the reins to the Millennials (also called Generation Y or echo boomers). Born between 1977 and 2000, these children of the baby boomers number 83 million, dwarfing the Gen Xers and larger even than the baby boomer segment.

    Gary Armstrong and Philip Kotler, *Marketing: An Introduction*, 9th ed., p. 72

    Millennials: _____

4. Graphs reveal whether two variables are positively or negatively related. A **positive** (or **direct**) **relationship** exists between two variables if an increase in the value of one variable is associated with an increase in the value of the other variable.

    A **negative** (or **inverse**) **relationship** exists between two variables if an increase in the value of one variable is associated with a reduction in the value of the other variable.

    Paul R. Gregory, *Essentials of Economics,* 4th ed., p. 16

    positive relationship: _____

    inverse relationship: _____

5. Interest groups have generally used two methods to pursue their goals through the judicial process. The first is to initiate suits directly on behalf of a group or class of people whose interests they represent (such suits are commonly referred to as "class actions"). The second method is for the interest group to file a brief as a "friend of the court" (*amicus curiae*) in support of a person whose suit seeks to achieve goals that the interest group is also seeking.

Richard F. Cord et al., *Political Science: An Introduction*

class action: _____

amicus curiae: _____

ACTIVITY 4   DIRECTIONS: *Using the context, determine the meanings of the words that appear after the sentences.*

1. A number of states have enacted legislation to allow gay men and lesbians to form civil unions, legal partnerships between two men or two women that give the couple all the benefits, protections and responsibilities under law that are granted to spouses in a traditional marriage.

Neal Tannahill, *THINK American Government*, p. 375

civil unions: _____

2. Although the shape and size of our bones do not significantly change after puberty, our **bone density,** or the strength of our bones, continues to develop into early adulthood. *Peak bone density* is the point at which our bones are strongest because they are at their highest density. About 90% of a woman's bone density is built by 17 years of age, whereas the majority of a man's bone density is built during his twenties. However, male or female, before we reach the age of 30 years, our bodies have reached peak bone mass, and we can no longer significantly add to our bone density. In our thirties, our bone density remains relatively stable, but by age 40, it begins its irreversible decline.

Janice Thompson and Melinda Manore, *Nutrition: An Applied Approach*, p. 312

bone density: _____

peak bone density: _____

3. The term *ghetto* originated in Venice, where the section of the city in which Jews were required to live was, in late medieval times, called the "borghetto." This word derived from the Italian word *borgo*, which meant "borough," which is a major section of a city. *Borghetto* was the

diminutive form meaning "little borough." Over time the word was shortened to *ghetto,* and its use spread to all European languages. Today the term is often applied to any neighborhood occupied by an ethnic or racial minority.

Rodney Stark, *Sociology*

borgo: _____

borghetto: _____

ghetto: _____

4. If the crime charged is within the jurisdiction of a municipal court, the arrestee may also be asked to make a **plea**, a statement of innocence or guilt, at the initial appearance. For minor crimes this appearance is sometimes called an **arraignment.** The judge then sets a date for trial in municipal court.

Jay S. Albanese, *Criminal Justice,* p. 160

plea: _____

arraignment: _____

5. Within every culture, there is an overall sense of what is beautiful and what is not beautiful, what represents good taste as opposed to tastelessness or even obscenity, and so on. Such considerations are matters of aesthetics. Global marketers must understand the importance of visual aesthetics embodied in the color or shape of a product, label or package.

Warren J. Keegan and Mark C Green, *Global Marketing*, 6th ed., p. 110

aesthetics: _____

ACTIVITY 5

DIRECTIONS: Using the context, determine the meanings of the words that appear after the sentences.

1. Shippers use intermodal transportation—combining two or more modes of transportation. Piggyback describes the use of rail and trucks; fishyback, water and trucks; trainship, water and rail; and airtruck, air and trucks.

Gary Armstrong and Philip Kotler, *Marketing: An Introduction*, 9th ed., p. 315

intermodal transportation: _____

2. You'll need to know fallacies—errors in argument—as both a reader (to spot them) and a writer (to avoid them). The many common fallacies fall into two groups. Some evade the issue of the argument. Others treat the argument as if it were much simpler than it is.

H. Ramsey Fowler et al., *The Little, Brown Handbook,* 8th ed., p. 155

fallacies: _____

3. Many people diet occasionally to lose those three or four extra pounds, and their behavior certainly doesn't qualify as disordered eating. But at some point for some people, those occasional weight-loss diets become habitual, and a cycle of chronic dieting begins. **Chronic dieting** is usually defined as consistently and successfully restricting energy intake to maintain an average or below average body weight (Manore 1996). The chronic dieter is often referred to as a "restrained eater" in the research literature and may be at risk for poor health and nutrition.

Conversely, weight cycling or "yo-yo" dieting occurs when a person who is normal weight or overweight successfully diets to lose weight, then regains the lost weight, and then repeats the cycle all over again (Manore 1996). One reason why weight cyclers are thought to be unsuccessful at maintaining long-term weight loss is their failure to make permanent lifestyle changes in their eating and exercise behaviors.

Janice Thompson and Melinda Manore, *Nutrition: An Applied Approach,* pp. 475–476

chronic dieting: _____

weight cycling: _____

4. The concept of ranking is the basis for one very useful kind of score reported on standardized tests, a percentile rank score. In percentile ranking, each student's raw score is compared with the raw scores of the students in the norming sample. The percentile rank shows the percentage of students in the norming sample that scored at or below a particular raw score.

Anita Woolfolk, *Educational Psychology,* 10th ed., p. 581

percentile rank: _____

5. There are many kinds of ***prosocial behavior***—behavior that benefits others, such as helping, cooperation, and sympathy. Such impulses arise early in life. Researchers agree that young children respond sympathetically to companions in distress, usually before their

second birthday (Hay, 1994; Kochanska, 1993). The term *altruism* is usually reserved for behavior that is aimed at helping others, requires some self-sacrifice, and is not performed for personal gain. Batson and colleagues (1989) believe that we help out of *empathy*— the ability to take the perspective of others, to put ourselves in their place.

Samuel E. Wood, Ellen Green Wood, and Denise Boyd, *Mastering the World of Psychology*, p. 577

prosocial behavior: _____

altruism: _____

empathy: _____

ACTIVITY 6   DIRECTIONS: *Bring to class ten examples of context clues taken from your other text-books, and include the word meanings you were able to figure out using those clues. If you do not have other textbooks at this time, ask your classmates who are using other books to share their examples with you.*

■ Using Word Parts: Roots, Prefixes, Suffixes

Your knowledge of word parts (roots, prefixes, suffixes) can help you de-termine the meanings of unfamiliar words. A root is the basic part, or stem, from which words are derived. For example, the root *tang* means "touch," and the word *tangible* is formed from it. A prefix is a word part or group of letters added *before* a root or word to change its meaning or to create a new word. For instance, if we add the prefix *in*—which means "not"—to *tangible*, we get *intangible*. Thus, we change the meaning from touchable to untouchable. Finally, a suffix is a word part or group of let-ters added *after* a root or word to create another word or to affect the way a word is used in a sentence. As you saw in the example above, the suffix *ible,* meaning "capable of being," can be added to the root *tang* to form *tangible* or *intangible*. Thus, the word *intangible* is made up of the prefix *in* (not), the root *tang* (touch), and the suffix *ible* (capable of being), which add up to the literal meaning "not capable of being touched." The more roots, prefixes, and suffixes that you know, the greater the likelihood that you will be able to use at least some of them to figure out word meanings.

ACTIVITY 7

DIRECTIONS: *Following is a table that lists some of the more common word parts, their meanings, and an example for each. When possible, use the word parts to help you figure out the definitions of the examples that are unfamiliar to you. Write your definitions in the spaces provided. Also try to provide another word for each of the roots, prefixes, and suffixes. If you have difficulty coming up with some of the definitions or examples, your instructor or classmates may help you when this exercise is discussed in class.*

ROOTS

Root	Meaning	Example	Definition	Another Word
aqua	water	aquatic		
audi	hear	audible		
auto	self	autobiography		
bene	good, well	benign		
bio	life	biography		
chron	time	synchronize		
cred	believe	credible		
culp	blame	culprit		
derm	skin	dermatology		
dict, dic	to speak	diction		
geo	earth	geology		
graph	to write	polygraph		
log	speech	dialog		
micro	small	microbiology		
mit, miss	to send	mission		
mort	death	mortal		
path	feeling	sympathy		
ped	foot	pedicure		
phob	fear	claustrophobia		
phon	sound	phonics		
poly	many	polygamy		
port	to carry	transport		
pseud	false	pseudonym		
psych	mind	psychology		
script	to write	Scripture		
spec	to look	spectacles		
therm	heat	hyperthermia		

PREFIXES				
Prefix	Meaning	Example	Definition	Another Word
a–	not, without	atheist		
ante–	before, in front of	anterior		
anti–	against, opposite	antiseptic		
bi–	two	bilingual		
circum–	around	circumference		
col–, com–, con–,	together, with	congregate		
contra–	against	contraception		
de–	away from	deploy		
dis–	not, apart, away	disable		
extra–	more than	extraterrestrial		
hyper–	over	hyperactive		
hypo–	under	hypodermic		
il–	not	illogical		
im–	not	immobile		
in–	not	inoperative		
inter–	between	interstate		
intra–	within	intrastate		
ir–	not	irrational		
mal–	bad	malignant		
mis–	wrong	misadvise		
mono–	one	monologue		
non–	not	nonprofit		
poly–	many	polygon		
post–	after	posterior		
pre–	before	prejudice		
pro–	for	proponent		
re–	back, again	recede		
retro–	backward	retroactive		
semi–	half	semiconscious		
sub–	under	subservient		
super–	over	supernatural		
tele–	far	telescope		

Prefix	Meaning	Example	Definition	Another Word
trans–	across	transfer		
tri–	three	tripod		
un–	not	uncivil		

SUFFIXES				
Suffix	Meaning	Example	Definition	Another Word
–able	capable of	readable		
–ar	relating to	solar		
–en	made of	golden		
–er	person who	adviser		
–ful	full of	plentiful		
–fy	to make	pacify		
–hood	condition	bachelorhood		
–ible	capable of	edible		
–ize	to make	sterilize		
–less	without	penniless		
–logy	study of	sociology		
–ment	state of being	harassment		
–or	person who	conductor		
–ward	direction	westward		

ACTIVITY 8   *DIRECTIONS: Taking your examples from the exercise above, make up sentences in your notebook using each one of them.*

■ Recognizing Word Denotation and Connotation

When learning vocabulary, an important distinction to make is between the denotation and connotation of a word. **Denotation** is the literal or dictionary definition of a word. **Connotations** of a word suggest *other* meanings or ideas. Usually a word's connotation brings with it a specific tone or feeling. Authors will use connotative meanings of words to support their purpose or to establish a specific tone. For example, the denotative meaning of *weak* (according to *Merriam-Webster's Dictionary*) is *lacking strength.* Connotations of the word *weak* are *powerless, feeble, frail, fragile, infirm,* and *decrepit.* Some words can give a positive or negative connotation. For example, if you were to say an individual was powerless, this word would relate a more positive image than if you were to say he or she was feeble. Another example is the word *mistake.* The denotative meaning is *to misunderstand the meaning or intention of.* Connotations or other suggested meanings of the word *mistake* are *misinterpret* and *blunder.* The word *misinterpret* has a positive connotation while *blunder* has a negative one.

ACTIVITY 9

DIRECTIONS: For each word provided, list the denotative meaning and as many connotative meanings as you can think of.

1. Write the denotative meaning of the word *curious.* _____

   List as many connotative meanings as you can for the word *curious.*

   _____

   _____

   _____

2. Write the denotative meaning of the word *talk.* _____

   List as many connotative meanings as you can for the word *talk.*

   _____

   _____

   _____

   _____

3. Write the denotative meaning of the word *walk.* _____

   List as many connotative meanings as you can for the word *walk.*

   _____

   _____

   _____

ACTIVITY 10

DIRECTIONS: For the words below, list as many different connotations as you can think of. Compare your list with those of other students in your class. For example, the word ruin *has many connotations. Some examples are* destroy, wreck, kill, dash, spoil, crush, annihilate, mar, demolish, damage, decay, devastate, waste, disintegrate, destruct.

1. sad _____

2. surprising _____

3. eat _____

4. say _____

5. girl _____

6. story _____

7. rule _____

8. house _____

9. person _____

10. calm _____

ACTIVITY 11

DIRECTIONS: For the words or phases below, list positive and negative connotations. For example, for the word automobile, *positive connotations might be* car *or* vehicle, *and negative connotations might be* lemon *or* junker.

	Positive	Negative
1. helper	_____	_____
2. to look	_____	_____
3. look for	_____	_____
4. erase	_____	_____
5. write	_____	_____
6. be silent	_____	_____
7. forget	_____	_____
8. slow	_____	_____
9. thin	_____	_____
10. unique	_____	_____

ACTIVITY 12

DIRECTIONS: Read the sentences and write new sentences with different connotations. Share your answers with the class and see how many different ideas you can generate. Discuss the sentences and how they imply different meanings.

Example 1:   The man and woman *held* hands.

Different connotations: The man and woman *clutched* hands.

                                 The man and woman *grasped* hands.

                                 The man and woman *shook* hands.

Example 2:   The kite *flew* over the field.

Different connotations: The kite *soared* over the field.

                                 The kite *floated* over the field.

1. Sentence: After school Andre *ate* a snack.

   A different connotation: _____

2. Sentence: Okee *carried* the package.

   A different connotation: _____

3. Sentence: Daniel *wrote* a letter to Joe.

   A different connotation: _____

4. Sentence: Theresa *copied* the paper.

   A different connotation: _____

5. Sentence: The *friendly* female talked to Stephen.

   A different connotation: _____

6. Sentence: That was a *noticeable* mistake.

   A different connotation: _____

7. Sentence: That was an *unimportant* topic.

   A different connotation: _____

8. Sentence: There was *peace* between the two parties.

   A different connotation: _____

9. Sentence: Dena *told* the secret to the others.

   A different connotation: _____

10. Sentence: Joe *questioned* the man about the incident.

    A different connotation: _____

■ Using a Glossary

Glossaries often are found in the back matter—or sometimes within the chapters themselves—of content textbooks dealing with such subjects as business, health, psychology, and sociology. A **glossary** is alphabetized and provides definitions for the most important terms used in the textbook.

Unlike a dictionary, which generally lists several meanings and provides additional important information about each word, a glossary only gives the one meaning that is appropriate for the specific subject matter of that textbook. A glossary also provides definitions for specialized combinations of words generally not found in the dictionary. For example, in the glossary in the back of this text, you will find definitions for *figurative language* and *random thinking*. Although the dictionary does give separate meanings for each of these words, it does not define them when they are used together, as does this particular glossary. In short, glossaries are useful tools because they provide you with a rapid means of finding the appropriate definitions of the most important terms used in a given subject area.

Become familiar with the glossaries in your textbooks to assist you with meanings of specialized terms for the subjects you are studying.

ACTIVITY 13

DIRECTIONS: Find the meanings of the following words using the glossary from this text. Write out the definition.

1. connotation: _____

_____

_____

2. irony: _____

_____

_____

3. paraphrasing: _____

_____

_____

4. tone: _____

_____

_____

5. inference: _____

_____

_____

■ Using the Dictionary

The dictionary is a very valuable tool not only for finding word meanings, but also because it provides additional important information about each word, including correct spelling, pronunciation, part of speech (noun, pronoun, adjective, verb, adverb, conjunction, preposition), various endings, and derivation (origin). The derivation, or etymology, of a word refers to its historical development, including what language it came from.

As you know, the dictionary is alphabetized. At the top of each page, two boldfaced words appear; these are the first and last entries on that page. Thus, if the word you are looking up fits alphabetically between the guide words on a particular page, you can find it there.

Let us look at a typical entry taken from *The Random House Dictionary:*

prim·i·tive (prim' i tiv), *adj* [L. *primitivus,* from *primus,* first] **1** being the first or earliest of the kind **2** characteristic of early ages or of an early state of human development **3** simple or crude—*n* **4** a person or thing that is primitive **5** a naive or unschooled artist—**prim'·i·tive·ly,** *adv*—**prim'·i·tive·ness, prim'·i·tiv'·i·ty,** *n*—**prim'·i·tiv'·ism,** n

The word *primitive* is located on the dictionary page between the guide words **primary accent** and **principle.** Right after the correct spelling of the word comes the pronunciation (in parentheses). Most dictionaries provide a pronunciation key for the symbols that they use, which usually is located either at the front of the dictionary or on the bottom of the individual pages. The next entry tells us the part of speech; *primitive* is an adjective. The derivation of the word—located within the brackets—is Latin from *primitivus,* which comes from *primus,* meaning first. Five definitions follow, the last two of which are for when *primitive* is used as a noun. Finally, the various endings are provided. These endings change the part of speech of the word to an adverb or a noun. Most dictionaries furnish a key that explains the abbreviations used for such things as parts of speech and derivation.

As you can see, dictionaries provide much valuable information about words that can be very useful as you make your way through college. If you do not own a dictionary, purchase one immediately, and refer to it often. In fact, you should buy two dictionaries—an unabridged, hardcover one for use at home and a smaller, paperback one to carry with you while you are at school. Also, the school library has very large dictionaries that come in handy when you are studying there.

ACTIVITY 14   *DIRECTIONS: Use your dictionary to answer the following questions.*

1. Which of the following words would you find on a page with the guide words **narrative–natural?**

narrow	narthex	natural history
nativism	natural gas	nascent
nasalize	narrator	naturalism
narrate	nationwide	natty

2. Find and write down the correct spellings for the following words.

   nationalise: _____   salamandar: _____

   azalia: _____   slouche: _____

   envesion: _____   cognative: _____

3. Write out the pronunciation guide for each of these words.

   chamois: _____   mullah: _____

   kamikaze: _____   concierge: _____

   ubiquitous: _____   retrospect: _____

4. Indicate the parts of speech for the words below.

   confluence: _____   revenue: _____

   insolvable: _____   agreeably: _____

   within: _____   an: _____

5. Provide the derivation for each of the following words.

   terrapin: _____   laudable: _____

   voodoo: _____   geriatrics: _____

   tapioca: _____

6. Give the various endings for these words.

   demolish: _____   asphyxiate: _____

   vibrate: _____   condense: _____

   obfuscate: _____   sage: _____

7. Write out the definitions for the words listed below.

apathy: _____

conservative: _____

liberal: _____

prognosis: _____

zealous: _____

Using Online Dictionaries

Online dictionaries are another source for looking up information relating to word meanings, pronunciation, and spelling. A reliable online dictionary can be a valuable resource, especially when a print dictionary is not available. The convenience of using an online dictionary is popular among college students. Some of the most commonly used and comprehensive online dictionaries are listed below. Many Web sites offer not only an English dictionary but also translations into other languages, a thesaurus, a dictionary of idioms, and links to other dictionary sites. Take a look at these sites so that you can familiarize yourself with the resources available:

Merriam-Webster Online
http://www.m-w.com/

OneLook Dictionary Search
http://www.onelook.com/

Dictionary.com
http://dictionary.reference.com/

Longman Dictionary of Contemporary English (especially for English language learners)
http://www.ldoceonline.com

Cambridge Dictionaries Online
http://dictionary.cambridge.org/

■ Learning and Reviewing Vocabulary Words

Whether you use the context, word parts, a glossary, or the dictionary to find the meanings to the most important words that you encounter in college, it is a good idea to keep a written record of these vocabulary words either in a notebook or on note cards. Writing them down helps you learn, remember, and review them for tests without having to look them up again. In addition to writing down the definitions, always include the sentences in which the words appeared so that you are aware of the context, and indicate which textbooks or other sources they came from.

ACTIVITY 15

Directions: Following the format below, start a vocabulary notebook by recording in your notebook unfamiliar words that you come across while reading your textbooks or various other sources. If you prefer, you may use note cards instead.

Model

NAME OF TEXTBOOK OR OTHER SOURCES

Word	Context	Definition

Example 1

Introduction to Business

Word	Context	Definition
consolidate	It is important for businesses to consolidate (combine) their resources.	combine

Example 2

Western Civilization

Word	Context	Definition
capitulate	Because the army was surrounded and very low on ammunition, the general was forced to capitulate.	give up

ACTIVITY 16

DIRECTIONS: There are several word-a-day sites available online. Choose one of the word-a-day sites listed below and check it daily for the new word, or sign up to have words sent to you via e-mail. For vocabulary practice, Freerice.com, operated through the World Food Program, donates ten grains of rice for every correct vocabulary word. Keep a daily journal of the words, their definitions, and a sentence using the word.

Merriam-Webster Online
http://www.m-w.com

A.Word.A.Day
http://wordsmith.org/awad/

New York Times: The Learning Network
http://learning.blogs.nytimes.com/category/word-of-the-day/

Oxford English Dictionary
http://www.oed.com/

Vocab Vitamins
http://www.vocabvitamins.com/

Dictionary.com
http://dictionary.reference.com/wordoftheday/

World Food Program
http://www.freerice.com

Using Concept Cards

Concept cards look like and are used like flash cards. Information is printed on both sides so that the cards can be used to review terms or concepts related to a particular subject.

The use of concept cards is a strategy that facilitates the process of learning new words or terms. These are best used in courses that emphasize vocabulary and knowledge of related information—concepts. Concept cards, although similar to flash cards, require more than a definition.

For example, on the front of the card list your term or concept and under it write a sentence using the word that helps you to understand the word. On the back, write the definition, use the word in your own sentence, and list any examples or other information that would assist in learning and retaining the word.

Example:
Front of card:

dehydration

<u>Dehydration</u> is a serious health problem that results when fluid excretion exceeds fluid intake.

Definition and sentences from *Nutrition: An Applied Approach*, p. 252 by Janice Thompson and Melinda Manore

Back of card:

Def: dehydration: depletion of body fluid that results when fluid excretion exceeds fluid intake.

Opposite: overhydration—dilution of body fluid that results when water intake or retention is excessive.

See urine color chart in text.

The baby had a fever, so we were careful about providing enough liquids so that she would not become dehydrated.

INVESTIGATION WSI
WEB SITE

CRITICAL READING

The specialized vocabulary you must learn in your content courses is very important. Create a crossword puzzle or make some flashcards for a chapter in one of your textbooks by using the Internet. The following sites create them for you. All you have to do is input the vocabulary information!

www.edhelper.com/crossword.htm [for crossword puzzles]

www.flashcardexchange.com [create your own flashcards]

www.studycell.com/ [create your own mobile flashcards]

LOOKING BACK . . . LOOKING FORWARD

To check your progress in meeting this chapter's learning objectives, log in to www.myreadinglab.com, go to your Study Plan, and click on the Reading Skills tab. Choose Vocabulary from the list of subtopics. Read and view the assets in the Review Materials section, then complete the Practices and Tests in the Activities section. You can check your scores by clicking on the Gradebook tab.

THINK AGAIN!

How can you prove that 3 is half of 8?

AND AGAIN!

Read the three quotes below, and write a paragraph that reflects the meaning of these ideas.

"Maybe all we can hope to do is end up with the right regrets."

Playwright Arthur Miller

"Do the one thing you think you cannot do. Fail at it. Try again. Do better the second time. The only people who never tumble are those who never mount the high wire. This is your moment. Own it."

Oprah Winfrey

"Without continual growth and progress, such words as improvement, achievement, and success have no meaning."

Benjamin Franklin

BOUDOIR

At the end of each chapter in this textbook you will have the opportunity to engage in a CSI puzzle by using your critical thinking skills to solve a picture mystery provided by Lawrence Treat in his book, *Crime and Puzzlement.*

For each mystery:

- first, read the narrative and all the questions
- second, examine the picture carefully
- third, answer the questions in the order they appear and come up with the solution

Amy LaTour's body was found in her bedroom last night, as shown, with her pet canary strangled in its cage. Henry Willy and Joe Wonty, her boyfriends; Louis Spanker, a burglar known to have been in the vicinity; and Celeste, her maid, were questioned by the police.

Wilbur Unisex, who happened to be in the area pursuing the *Heliconius charitonius,* put down his butterfly net and solved the case. Can you?

Questions

1. How was Amy apparently killed? ☐ Shot ☐ Stabbed ☐ Strangled ☐ Beaten

2. Is there evidence of a violent struggle? ☐ Yes ☐ No

3. Was her murderer strong? ☐ Yes ☐ No

4. Was Amy fond of jewelry? ☐ Yes ☐ No

5. Was she robbed? ☐ Yes ☐ No

6. Do you think she had been on friendly terms with her killer? ☐ Yes ☐ No

7. Was the canary strangled before Amy's death? ☐ Yes ☐ No

8. Was this a crime of passion? ☐ Yes ☐ No

9. Did Willy have a motive? ☐ Yes ☐ No

10. Who killed Amy? ☐ Henry Willy ☐ Joe Wonty ☐ Louis Spanker ☐ Celeste

Text and illustration from Lawrence Treat, *Crime and Puzzlement: 24 Solve-Them-Yourself Picture Mysteries* (David R. Godine, Publisher, 1981), pp. 2–3

Boudoir

Name _____   Date _____

MASTERY TEST 1–1

DIRECTIONS: Using the context, write the meanings next to the words that appear after the sentences.

1. Finally, the concept of **social engineering** was born—the belief that *strong governmental leaders, advised by social scientists, could use social science to design a preferred social order.* This notion remains a central ingredient in modern sociological thought.
   Richard P. Appelbaum and William J. Chambliss, *Sociology,* pp. 18–19

   social engineering: _____

   _____

2. Your readers will expect an essay you write to be focused on a central idea, or thesis, to which all the essay's paragraphs, all its general statements and specific information, relate. The thesis is the controlling idea, the main point, the conclusion you have drawn about the evidence you have accumulated. Even if you create a composition on the World Wide Web, you'll have a core idea that governs the links among pages and sites.
   H. Ramsey Fowler et al., *The Little, Brown Handbook,* 8th ed., p. 30

   thesis: _____

3. Communicating via electronic devices, especially facsimile (fax) machines and computerized electronic mail (e-mail), speeds up correspondence but also creates new challenges. For both fax transmissions and e-mail, the standards are the same as for other business correspondence: state your purpose at the outset and write straightforwardly, clearly, concisely, objectively, courteously, and correctly.
   H. Ramsey Fowler and Jane E. Aaron, *The Little, Brown Handbook,* p. 757

   fax: _____

   e-mail: _____

4. When the press secretary announced that the president had "passed away" instead of saying that he had died, he was using a euphemism.

   euphemism: _____

   _____

5. In the late nineteenth and early twentieth centuries, Southern white authorities adopted an array of devices designed to prevent African Americans from exercising

meaningful voting rights. Disfranchisement methods included tests of understanding, literacy tests, the white primary, grandfather clauses and poll taxes. Disfranchisement is the denial of voting rights.

Neal Tannahill, *THINK American Government*, p. 372

disfranchisement: _____

6. You will often have multiple audiences, some *primary* (the people for whom your document is specifically intended) and some *secondary* (other people who may have reason to read all or part of the document). For example, your engineering report may be read by people who need to analyze the details of what you've written and by those who need to know only the conclusions and recommendations. If you know this in advance, you can make decisions about the document that can accommodate both types of readers. For example, you can decide whether it would be better to "front-load" the document ... by putting the recommendations first or to begin with the background discussion.

Kristin R. Woolever, *Writing for the Technical Professions,* pp. 12–13

primary audience: _____

_____

secondary audience: _____

_____

frontload: _____

7. Energy researchers have seized on the potential of plant power as a promising fuel source. One of the oldest energy pathways on the planet is **photosynthesis.** In this process, green plants, algae, and certain bacteria use light energy to make sugar from carbon dioxide and water. During the process, they also produce the oxygen we need to breathe and store an energy source that could help solve the human power problem.

Neil A. Campbell et al., *Biology: Concepts and Connections,* 5th ed., p. 106

photosynthesis: _____

_____

8. Rather than setting a high initial price to skim off small but profitable market segments, some companies use market-penetration pricing. They set a low initial price in order to penetrate the market quickly and deeply—to attract a large number of buyers and win a large market share.

Gary Armstrong and Phillip Kotler, *Marketing: An Introduction*, 9th ed., p. 271

market-penetration pricing: _____

9. "Will I succeed or fail? Will I be liked or laughed at?" Will I be accepted by teachers in this new school?" These predictions are affected by self efficacy—our beliefs about our personal competence or effectiveness in a given area.

Anita Woolfolk, *Educational Psychology,* 10th ed., p. 359

self efficacy: _____

10. Whereas the professor's lecture last night was very clear, her remarks today were ambiguous.

ambiguous: _____

11. Those who oppose capital punishment offer incarceration for life with no chance for parole as an acceptable alternative.

incarceration: _____

12. Demography—the study of populations—reviews the ways populations change in size. Births (natality) and deaths (mortality) account for most changes in a population. The difference between the two rates determines its growth or decline.

Robert Leo Smith and Thomas M. Smith, *Elements of Ecology,* 4th ed., p. 150

demography: _____

natality: _____

13. While some people become addicted to prescription drugs and painkillers, we focus our attention here on **illicit drugs**—those drugs that are illegal to possess, produce, or sell.

Rebecca J. Donatelle, *Health: The Basics,* 4th ed., p. 167

illicit: _____

14. A study of life extends from the global scale of the entire living planet to the microscopic scale of cells and molecules. The biosphere consists of all the environments on Earth that support life … regions of land, bodies of water, and the lower atmosphere. A closer look at one of these environments brings us to the level of an **ecosystem,** which consists of all the organisms living in a particular area, as well as all the nonliving, physical components of the environment with which the organisms interact, such as air, soil, water, and sunlight.

Neil A. Campbell et al., *Biology: Concepts and Connections,* 5th ed., p. 2

ecosystem: _____

_____

15. The major constituent of urine is water. The amount of urine excreted daily by an adult may vary from 500 to 2500 ml (milliliters). The exact amount depends on liquid intake and the amount of water lost through perspiration. Heavy perspiration decreases the volume of urine formed. Coffee, tea, or alcoholic beverages have a diuretic (stimulate formation of urine) effect.

Robert J. Ouellette, *Introductory Chemistry*

constituent: _____

excreted: _____

diuretic: _____

16. A bill is a proposed law. Except for revenue raising bills, which must begin in the House, any bill may be introduced in either chamber. A resolution is a legislative statement of opinion on a certain matter. Resolutions may be introduced in either chamber. A member who introduces a measure in know as its sponsor.

Neal Tannahill, *THINK American Government,* p. 218

bill: _____

resolution: _____

sponsor: _____

17. An unusual type of capitalism is laissez-faire: a term borrowed from the French that means the noninterference of government in the business sector.

laissez-faire: _____

18. Slavery established a ground for the seeds of racism. When, during the late eighteenth century, abolitionists (people who opposed slavery) increasingly denounced the slave trade, advocates of slavery were forced to find new arguments to defend their actions.

Institute for Contemporary Curriculum Development, *Patterns of Civilization: Africa*

abolitionists: _____

advocates: _____

19. Much of the violent crime in the United States is committed by recidivists, and it is simply amazing that our society lets these habitual criminals back on the street.

recidivists: _____

20. The chemist converted the liquid into gas by heating it over a slow flame.

converted: _____

21. Nomads—Bedouins, or desert Arabs—dwelt with their herds in the neighborhood of Mecca.

Sydney Nettleton Fisher, *The Middle East: A History*

Bedouins: _____

22. Urethritis, inflammation of the urethra, is usually an ascending infection. It may be caused by a bacterial or viral infection or by trauma from an indwelling catheter or repeated cystoscopic examinations.

Lillian S. Brunner and Doris S. Suddarth, *Textbook of Medical-Surgical Nursing*

urethritis: _____

23. What was needed was a way to identify the sphere of influence of a city: the area whose inhabitants depend on the central city for jobs, recreation, newspapers, television, and a sense of common community.

Rodney Stark, *Sociology*

sphere of influence: _____

24. All kinds of companies now market online. Click-on companies operate only on the Internet. As the Internet grew, the success of the dot-coms caused existing brick-and-mortar manufacturers and retailers to reexamine how they served their markets.

Gary Armstrong and Philip Kotler, *Marketing: An Introduction*, 9th ed., p. 428

click-on companies: _____

25. Breathing in is called inspiration or inhalation.

Gerard J. Tortora and Nicholas P. Anagnostakos, *Principles of Anatomy and Physiology*

inspiration: _____

26. When negotiations do break down, disagreements between union and management representatives may be settled by mediation—the process of bringing in a third party, called a mediator, to make recommendations for the settlement of differences. The final step in settling union-management differences is arbitration—the process of bringing in an impartial third party, called an arbitrator, who renders a binding decision in the dispute. The impartial third party must be acceptable to the union and to management, and his or her decision is legally enforceable. In

essence, the arbitrator acts as a judge, making a decision after listening to both sides of the argument.

Louis E. Boone and David L. Kurtz, *Contemporary Business*

mediation: _____

arbitration: _____

27. The physicians decided to treat the cancer with radiation rather than drugs. This change in treatment plans was for the purpose of palliation: to relieve the pain without curing.

palliation: _____

28. Since the time of John Locke, David Hume, David Hartley, and other British philosophers of the 1660s and 1700s, association (the linking of sensations or ideas) has been regarded as central to all thought processes.

James W. Kalat, *Introduction to Psychology*

association: _____

29. The term "triage" was first described in the *Annals of Military Medicine* as the process of sorting the sick and wounded on the basis of urgency and type of condition presented so that the patient can be properly routed to the appropriate medical area. It is, therefore, right that triage be used in the emergency situations encountered daily in the streets.

J. A. Young and Dean Crocker, *Principles and Practice of Respiratory Therapy*

triage: _____

30. When the fort was enveloped by the enemy on all sides, it was only a matter of time before it fell.

enveloped: _____

Name _____ Date _____

MASTERY TEST 1–2

DIRECTIONS: Using word parts, try to figure out the meanings of the words listed below.

1. aquanaut: _____

   _____

   _____

2. inaudible: _____

   _____

   _____

3. biology: _____

   _____

   _____

4. antechamber: _____

   _____

   _____

5. circumscribe: _____

   _____

   _____

6. contradiction: _____

   _____

   _____

7. monosyllable: _____

_____

_____

8. telepathy: _____

_____

_____

9. immortal: _____

_____

_____

10. phobia: _____

_____

_____

11. polysyllable: _____

_____

_____

12. hypothermia: _____

_____

_____

13. malcontent: _____

_____

_____

14. hyperextend: _____

_____

_____

15. bisect: _____

_____

_____

16. substandard: _____

_____

_____

17. pathology: _____

_____

_____

18. dictation: _____

_____

_____

19. impediment: _____

_____

_____

20. transcription: _____

_____

_____

Name _____ Date _____

MASTERY TEST 1–3

A. Directions: *Using the partial glossary on pages 43–46, answer the following questions.*

1. A "run-on sentence" can also be referred to as a _____ sentence.

2. An example of an "acronym" is _____

3. Another word for "trite expressions" is _____

4. Provide an example of a "dangling modifier." _____

_____

_____

5. What is a "search engine"? _____

_____

_____

6. To "upload" is to _____

_____

_____

7. What is the difference between "abstract" and "concrete" words? _____

_____

_____

8. A word's "denotation" can be found in the _____

9. Define "sentence fragment" and provide an example. _____

_____

_____

10. A "database" is a collection and organization of _____

B. DIRECTIONS: Answer the following questions by using the dictionary page on page 47.

1. Name the guide words. _____

2. Write out the pronunciation illustration for the word "patulous." _____

3. What is the part of speech of the word "patrician"? _____

4. Name the various endings of the word "patrol." _____

   _____

   _____

5. What is the meaning of the word "patrimony"? _____

   _____

   _____

6. "Patrol wagon" is also called _____

7. What is the derivation of the word "patriot"? _____

   _____

   _____

8. Another name for "Pauli exclusion principle" is _____

   _____

   _____

9. List the words that have more than one entry. _____

   _____

   _____

10. Another spelling of "patronize" is _____

Glossary

This glossary defines terms of grammar, rhetoric, literature, and Internet research.

absolute phrase   A phrase consisting of a noun or pronoun plus the *-ing* or *-ed* form of a verb (a participle): *Our accommodations arranged, we set out on our journey. They will hire a local person, other things being equal.* An absolute phrase modifies a whole clause or sentence (rather than a single word), and it is not joined to the rest of the sentence by a connector.

abstract and concrete   Two kinds of language. Abstract words refer to ideas, qualities, attitudes, and conditions that can't be perceived with the senses: *beauty, guilty, victory.* Concrete words refer to objects, persons, places, or conditions that can be perceived with the senses: *Abilene, scratchy, toolbox.* See also *general and specific.*

acronym   A pronounceable word formed from the initial letter or letters of each word in an organization's title: NATO (North Atlantic Treaty Organization).

active voice   See *voice.*

adjectival   A term sometimes used to describe any word or word group, other than an adjective, that is used to modify a noun. Common adjectivals include nouns (*wagon train, railroad ties*), phrases (*fool on the hill*), and clauses (*the man that I used to be*).

adjective   A word used to modify a noun (*beautiful morning*) or a pronoun (*ordinary one*). Nouns, some verb forms, phrases, and clauses may also serve as adjectives: *book sale; a used book; sale of old books; the sale, which occurs annually.* (See *clauses, prepositional phrases,* and *verbals and verbal phrases.*)

Adjectives come in several classes

A descriptive adjective names some quality of the noun: *beautiful morning, dark horse.*

A limiting adjective narrows the scope of a noun. It may be a possessive (*my, their*); a demonstrative adjective (*this train, these days*); an interrogative adjective (*what time? whose body?*); or a number (*two boys*).

A proper adjective is derived from a proper noun: *French language, Machiavellian scheme.*

courseware   A program for online communication and collaboration among the teacher and students in a course.

critical thinking, reading, and writing   Looking beneath the surface of words and images to discern meaning and relationships and to build knowledge.

cumulative (loose) sentence   A sentence in which modifiers follow the subject and verb: *Ducks waddled by, their tails swaying and their quacks rising to heaven.* Contrast *periodic sentence.*

> **dangling modifier**   A modifier that does not sensibly describe anything in its sentence.
>
> **Dangling**   *Having arrived late*, the concert had already begun.
>
> **Revised**   Having arrived late, *we found that* the concert had already begun.

data   In argument, a term used for *evidence*. See *evidence.*

database   A collection and organization of information (data). A database may be printed, but the term is most often used for electronic sources.

declension   A list of the forms of a noun or pronoun, showing inflections for person (for pronouns), number, and case.

demonstrative adjective   See *adjective.*

demonstrative pronoun   See *pronoun.*

denotation   The main or dictionary definition of a word. Contrast *connotation.*

dependent clause   See *clause.*

derivational suffix   See *suffix.*

description   Detailing the sensory qualities of a thing, person, place, or feeling.

purpose   For a writer, the chief reason for communicating something about a topic to a particular audience. Purposes are both general (usually explanation or persuasion) and specific (taking into account the topic and desired outcome).

quotation   Repetition of what someone has written or spoken. In direct quotation (direct discourse), the person's words are duplicated exactly and enclosed in quotation marks: *Polonius told his son, Laertes, "Neither a borrower nor a lender be."* An indirect quotation (indirect discourse) reports what someone said or wrote but not in the exact words and not in quotation marks: *Polonius advised his son, Laertes, not to borrow or lend.*

rational appeal   See *appeals.*

reciprocal pronoun   See *pronoun.*

reflexive pronoun   See *pronoun.*

rhetoric   The principles for finding and arranging ideas and for using language in speech or writing to achieve the writer's purpose in addressing his or her audience.

rhetorical question   A question asked for effect, with no answer expected. The person asking the question either intends to provide the answer or assumes it is obvious: *If we let one factory pollute the river, what does that say to other factories that want to dump wastes there?*

run-on sentence   See *fused sentence.*

sans serif   See *serifs.*

search engine   A computer program that conducts Internet searches from keywords or directories.

secondary source   A source reporting or analyzing information in other sources, such as a critic's view of a work of art or a sociologist's summary of others' studies. Contrast *primary source.*

second person   See *person.*

sentence   A complete unit of thought, consisting of at least a subject and a predicate that are not introduced by a subordinating word. Sentences can be classed on the basis of their structure in one of four ways. A simple sentence contains one main clause: *I'm leaving.* A compound sentence contains at least two main clauses: *I'd like to stay, but I'm leaving.* A complex sentence contains one main clause and at least one subordinate clause: *If you let me go now, you'll be sorry.* A compound-complex sentence contains at least two main clauses and at least one subordinate clause: *I'm leaving because you want me to, but I'd rather stay.*

sentence fragment   A sentence error in which a group of words is set off as a sentence even though it begins with a subordinating word or lacks a subject or a predicate or both.

Fragment	She lost the race. *Because she was injured.* [*Because,* a subordinating conjunction, makes the italicized clause subordinate.]
Revised	She lost the race because she was injured.
Fragment	He could not light a fire. *And thus could not warm the room.* [The italicized word group lacks a subject.]
Revised	He could not light a fire. Thus *he* could not warm the room.

sentence modifier   An adverb or a word or word group acting as an adverb that modifies the idea of the whole sentence in which it appears rather than any specific word: *In fact, people will always complain.*

server   A computer that links other computers in a network. Servers transfer data and store files.

setting   The place where the action of a literary work happens.

sexist language   Language expressing narrow ideas about men's and women's roles, positions, capabilities, or value.

signal phrase   Words that indicate who is being quoted: *"In the future,"* *said Andy Warhol, "everyone will be world-famous for fifteen minutes."*

simile   See *figurative language*.

simple predicate   See *predicate*.

simple sentence   See *sentence*.

simple subject   See *subject*.

simple tense   See *tense*.

thesis   The central, controlling idea of an essay, to which all assertions and details relate.

thesis statement   A sentence or more that asserts the central, controlling idea of an essay and perhaps previews the essay's organization.

transitional expression   A word or phrase, such as *thus* or *for example*, that links sentences and shows the relations between them. The error known as a comma splice occurs when two main clauses related by a transitional expression are separated only by a comma.

transitive verb   A verb that requires a direct object to complete its meaning.

trite expressions (clichés)   Stale expressions that dull writing and suggest that the writer is careless or lazy.

two-word verb   A verb plus a preposition or adverb that affects the meaning of the verb *jump off, put away, help out*.

uniform resource locator (URL)   An address for a source on the World Wide Web, specifying protocol (the standard for transferring data and files), domain (the computer, or server, housing the source), and path (the location and name of the source).

unity   The quality of an effective essay or paragraph in which all parts relate to the central idea and to each other.

upload   To transfer data or files from your local computer to another computer.

variety   Among connected sentences, changes in length, structure, and word order that help readers see the importance and complexity of ideas.

verb   A word or group of words indicating the action or state of being of a subject. The inflection of a verb and the use of helping verbs with it indicate its tense, mood, voice, number, and sometimes person. See separate listings for each aspect and *predicate*.

H. Ramsey Fowler et al., *The Little, Brown Handbook*, 8th ed., pp. 943, 950, 963, 964, 967

dependence of wives and children, and the reckoning of descent and inheritance in the male line; *broadly* : control by men of a disproportionately large share of power **2** : a society or institution organized according to the principles or practices of patriarchy

pa·tri·cian \pə-ˈtri-shən\ *n* [ME *patricion,* fr. AF *patrician,* fr. L *patricius,* fr. *patres* senators, fr. pl. of *pater* father — more at FATHER] (15c) **1** : a member of one of the original citizen families of ancient Rome **2 a** : a person of high birth : ARISTOCRAT **b** : a person of breeding and cultivation — **patrician** *adj*

pa·tri·ci·ate \-ˈtri-shē-ət, -ˌāt\ *n* (ca. 1656) **1** : the position or dignity of a patrician **2** : a patrician class

pat·ri·cide \ˈpa-trə-ˌsīd\ *n* (1593) **1** [L *patricida,* fr. *patr-* + *-cida* -cide] : one who murders his or her own father **2** [LL *patricidium,* fr. L *patr-* + *-cidium* -cide] : the murder of one's own father — **pat·ri·cid·al** \ˌpa-trə-ˈsī-dᵊl\ *adj*

pat·ri·lin·eal \ˌpa-trə-ˈli-nē-əl\ *adj* (1904) : relating to, based on, or tracing descent through the paternal line ‹a ~ society›

pat·ri·mo·ny \ˈpa-trə-ˌmō-nē\ *n* [ME *patrimoine, patrimonie,* fr. AF *patremoine,* fr. L *patrimonium,* fr. *patr-, pater* father] (14c) **1 a** : an estate inherited from one's father or ancestor **b** : anything derived from one's father or ancestors : HERITAGE **2** : an estate or endowment belonging by ancient right to a church — **pat·ri·mo·ni·al** \ˌpa-trə-ˈmō-nē-əl\ *adj*

pa·tri·ot \ˈpā-trē-ət, -ˌät, *chiefly Brit* ˈpa-trē-ət\ *n* [MF *patriote* compatriot, fr. LL *patriota,* fr. Gk *patriōtēs,* fr. *patria* lineage, fr. *patr-, patēr* father] (1605) : one who loves his or her country and supports its authority and interests

pa·tri·ot·ic \ˌpā-trē-ˈä-tik, *chiefly Brit* ˌpa-\ *adj* (1757) **1** : inspired by patriotism **2** : befitting or characteristic of a patriot — **pa·tri·ot·i·cal·ly** \-ti-k(ə-)lē\ *adv*

pa·tri·ot·ism \ˈpā-trē-ə-ˌti-zəm, *chiefly Brit* ˈpa-\ *n* (ca. 1726) : love for or devotion to one's country

Patriots' Day *n* (1897) : the third Monday in April observed as a legal holiday in Maine and Massachusetts in commemoration of the battles of Lexington and Concord in 1775

pa·tris·tic \pə-ˈtris-tik\ *also* **pa·tris·ti·cal** \-ti-kəl\ *adj* (ca. 1828) : of or relating to the church fathers or their writings

pa·tris·tics \-tiks\ *n pl but sing in constr* (1847) : the study of the writings and background of the church fathers

Pa·tro·clus \pə-ˈtrō-kləs, -ˈträ-\ *n* [L, fr. Gk *Patroklos*] (15c) : a Greek hero and friend of Achilles slain by Hector at Troy

[1]**pa·trol** \pə-ˈtrōl\ *n* (1664) **1 a** : the action of traversing a district or beat or of going the rounds along a chain of guards for observation or the maintenance of security **b** : the person performing such an action **c** : a unit of persons or vehicles employed for reconnaissance, security, or combat **2** : a subdivision of a Boy Scout troop or Girl Scout troop

[2]**patrol** *vb* **pa·trolled; pa·trol·ling** [F *patrouiller,* fr. MF, to tramp around in the mud, fr. *patte* paw — more at PATTEN] *vi* (1691) : to carry out a patrol ~ *vt* : to carry out a patrol of — **pa·trol·ler** *n*

pa·trol·man \pə-ˈtrōl-mən\ *n* (1867) : one who patrols; *esp* : a police officer assigned to a beat

patrol wagon *n* (1887) : PADDY WAGON

pa·tron \ˈpā-trən, *for 6 also* pa-ˈtrōⁿ\ *n* [ME, fr. AF, fr. ML & L; ML *patronus* patron saint, patron of a benefice, pattern, fr. L, defender, fr. *patr-, pater*] (14c) **1 a** : a person chosen, named, or honored as a special guardian, protector, or supporter **b** : a wealthy or influential supporter of an artist or writer **c** : a social or financial sponsor of a social function (as a ball or concert) **2** : one that uses wealth or influence to help an individual, an institution, or a cause **3** : one who buys the goods or uses the services offered esp. by an establishment **4** : the holder of the right of presentation to an English ecclesiastical benefice **5** : a master in ancient times who freed his slave but retained some rights over him **6** [F, fr. MF] : the proprietor of an establishment (as an inn) esp. in France **7** : the chief male officer in some fraternal lodges having both men and women members — **pa·tron·al** \ˈpā-trə-nᵊl; *Brit* pə-ˈtrō-nᵊl, pa-\ *adj*

pa·tron·age \ˈpa-trə-nij, ˈpā-\ *n* (14c) **1** : ADVOWSON **2** : the support or influence of a patron **3** : kindness done with an air of superiority **4** : business or activity provided by patrons ‹the new branch library is expected to have a heavy ~› **5 a** : the power to make appointments to government jobs esp. for political advantage **b** : the distribution of jobs on the basis of patronage **c** : jobs distributed by patronage

pa·tron·ess \ˈpā-trə-nəs\ *n* (15c) : a woman who is a patron

pa·tron·ise *Brit var of* PATRONIZE

pa·tron·ize \ˈpā-trə-ˌnīz, ˈpa-\ *vt* **-ized; -iz·ing** (1589) **1** : to act as patron of : provide aid or support for **2** : to adopt an air of condescension toward : treat haughtily or coolly **3** : to be a frequent or regular customer or client of — **pa·tron·i·za·tion** \ˌpā-trə-nə-ˈzā-shən, pa-\ *n* — **pa·tron·iz·ing·ly** \ˈpā-trə-ˌnī-ziŋ-lē, ˈpa-\ *adv*

patron saint *n* (1717) **1** : a saint to whose protection and intercession a person, a society, a church, or a place is dedicated **2** : an original leader or prime exemplar

pat·ro·nym·ic \ˌpa-trə-ˈni-mik\ *n* [ultim. fr. Gk *patronymia* patronymic, fr. *patr-* + *onyma* name — more at NAME] (1612) : a name derived from that of the father or a paternal ancestor usu. by the addition of an affix — **patronymic** *adj*

pa·troon \pə-ˈtrün\ *n* [F *patron* & Sp *patrón,* fr. ML *patronus,* fr. L, patron] (1743) **1** *archaic* : the captain or officer commanding a ship **2** [D, fr. F *patron*] : the proprietor of a manorial estate esp. in New York orig. granted under Dutch rule but in some cases existing until the mid-19th century

pat·sy \ˈpat-sē\ *n, pl* **pat·sies** [perh. fr. It *pazzo* fool] (1903) : a person who is easily manipulated or victimized : PUSHOVER

pat·ten \ˈpa-tᵊn\ *n* [ME *patin,* fr. AF, fr. *pate* paw, hoof, fr. VL **patta,* of imit. origin] (14c) : a clog, sandal, or overshoe often with a wooden sole or metal device to elevate the foot and increase the wearer's height or aid in walking in mud

[1]**pat·ter** \ˈpa-tər\ *vb* [ME *patren,* fr. *paternoster*] *vt* (14c) : to say or speak in a rapid or mechanical manner ~ *vi* **1** : to recite prayers (as paternosters) rapidly or mechanically **2** : to talk glibly and volubly **3** : to speak or sing rapid-fire words in a theatrical performance — **pat·ter·er** \-tər-ər\ *n*

[2]**patter** *n* (1758) **1** : a specialized lingo : CANT; *esp* : the jargon of criminals (as thieves) **2** : the spiel of a street hawker or of a circus barker **3** : empty chattering talk **4 a (1)** : the rapid-fire talk of a comedian **(2)** : the talk with which an entertainer accompanies a routine **b** : the words of a comic song or of a rapidly spoken usu. humorous monologue introduced into such a song

[3]**patter** *vb* [freq. of [3]*pat*] *vi* (1611) **1** : to strike or pat rapidly and repeatedly **2** : to run with quick light-sounding steps ~ *vt* : to cause to patter

[4]**patter** *n* (1844) : a quick succession of light sounds or pats

[1]**pat·tern** \ˈpa-tərn\ *n* [ME *patron,* fr. AF, fr. ML *patronus*] (14c) **1** : a form or model proposed for imitation : EXEMPLAR **2** : something designed or used as a model for making things ‹a dressmaker's ~› **3** : an artistic, musical, literary, or mechanical design or form **4** : a natural or chance configuration ‹frost ~*s*› ‹the ~ of events› **5** : a length of fabric sufficient for an article (as of clothing) **6 a** : the distribution of shrapnel, bombs on a target, or shot from a shotgun **b** : the grouping made on a target by bullets **7** : a reliable sample of traits, acts, tendencies, or other observable characteristics of a person, group, or institution ‹a behavior ~› ‹spending ~*s*› **8 a** : the flight path prescribed for an airplane that is coming in for a landing **b** : a prescribed route to be followed by a pass receiver in football **9** : TEST PATTERN **10** : a discernible coherent system based on the intended interrelationship of component parts ‹foreign policy ~*s*› **11** : frequent or widespread incidence ‹a ~ of dissent› ‹a ~ of violence› ***syn*** see MODEL — **pat·terned** \-tərnd\ *adj* — **pat·tern·less** *adj*

[2]**pattern** *vt* (ca. 1586) **1** *dial chiefly Eng* **a** : MATCH **b** : IMITATE **2** : to make, adapt, or fashion according to a pattern **3** : to furnish, adorn, or mark with a design ~ *vi* : to form a pattern

pat·tern·ing \ˈpa-tər-niŋ\ *n* (1862) **1** : decoration, composition, or configuration according to a pattern **2** : physical therapy esp. for neurological impairment based on a theory holding that repeated manipulation of body parts to simulate normal motor developmental activity (as crawling or walking) promotes neurological development or repair

pat·ty *also* **pat·tie** \ˈpa-tē\ *n, pl* **patties** [F *pâté* pâté] (1710) **1** : a little pie **2 a** : a small flat cake of chopped food ‹a hamburger ~› **b** : a small flat candy ‹a peppermint ~› **3** : PATTY SHELL

pat·ty–cake \ˈpa-tē-ˌkāk\ *or* **pat–a–cake** \ˈpa-də-ˌkāk, ˈpat-ə-\ *n* [fr. the opening words of the rhyme] (1889) : a game in which two participants (as mother and child) clap their hands together to the rhythm of an accompanying nursery rhyme

pat·ty·pan \ˈpa-tē-ˌpan\ *n* [*pattypan* pan for baking patties] (1900) : a roundish summer squash having a scalloped edge — called also *cymling*

patty shell *n* (1909) : a shell of puff pastry made to hold a creamed meat, fish, or vegetable filling

pat·u·lous \ˈpa-chə-ləs\ *adj* [L *patulus,* fr. *patēre* to be open — more at FATHOM] (1616) : spreading widely from a center ‹a tree with ~ branches›

pat·zer \ˈpät-sər, ˈpat-\ *also* **pot·zer** \ˈpät-\ *n* [prob. fr. G *Patzer* bungler, fr. *patzen* to blunder] (1959) : an inept chess player

pau·ci·ty \ˈpȯ-sə-tē\ *n* [ME *paucite,* fr. L *paucitat-, paucitas,* fr. *paucus* little — more at FEW] (15c) **1** : smallness of number : FEWNESS **2** : smallness of quantity : DEARTH

Paul \ˈpȯl\ *n* [L *Paulus,* fr. Gk *Paulos*] (bef. 12c) : an early Christian apostle and missionary and author of several New Testament epistles

Paul Bun·yan \-ˈbən-yən\ *n* (1925) : a giant lumberjack of American folklore

Pau·li exclusion principle \ˈpau̇-lē-\ *n* [Wolfgang *Pauli*] (1926) : EXCLUSION PRINCIPLE — called also *Pauli principle*

Pau·line \ˈpȯ-ˌlīn\ *adj* (1817) : of or relating to the apostle Paul, his epistles, or the doctrine or theology implicit in his epistles

Paul·ist \ˈpȯ-list\ *n* (ca. 1883) : a member of the Roman Catholic Congregation of the Missionary Priests of St. Paul the Apostle founded by I. T. Hecker in the U.S. in 1858

pau·low·nia \pȯ-ˈlō-nē-ə\ *n* [NL, fr. Anna *Pavlovna* †1865 Russ. princess] (1843) : any of a genus (*Paulownia*) of Chinese trees of the snapdragon family; *esp* : one (*P. tomentosa*) widely cultivated for its panicles of fragrant violet flowers

paunch \ˈpȯnch, ˈpänch\ *n* [ME, fr. AF **panche, pance,* fr. L *pantic-, pantex*] (14c) **1 a** : the belly and its contents **b** : POTBELLY **2** : RUMEN

paunchy \ˈpȯn-chē, ˈpän-\ *adj* **paunch·i·er; -est** (1598) : having a potbelly — **paunch·i·ness** *n*

pau·per \ˈpȯ-pər\ *n* [L, poor — more at POOR] (1516) **1** : a person destitute of means except such as are derived from charity; *specif* : one who receives aid from funds designated for the poor **2** : a very poor person — **pau·per·ism** \-pə-ˌri-zəm\ *n*

pau·per·ize \ˈpȯ-pə-ˌrīz\ *vt* **-ized; -iz·ing** (1834) : to reduce to poverty — **pau·per·i·za·tion** \ˌpȯ-pə-rə-ˈzā-shən\ *n*

pau·piette \pō-ˈpyet\ *n* [F *paupiette,* fr. It *polpetta* meat croquette, dim. of *polpa* pulp, flesh, fr. L *pulpa*] (1889) : a thin slice of meat or fish wrapped around a forcemeat filling

[1]**pause** \ˈpȯz\ *n* [ME, fr. L *pausa,* fr. Gk *pausis,* fr. *pauein* to stop] (15c) **1** : a temporary stop **2 a** : a break in a verse **b** : a brief suspension of the voice to indicate the limits and relations of sentences and their parts **3** : temporary inaction esp. as caused by uncertainty : HESITATION **4 a** : the sign denoting a fermata **b** : a mark (as a period or comma) used in writing or printing to indicate or correspond to a pause of voice **5** : a reason or cause for pausing (as to reconsider) ‹a thought that should give one ~› **6** : a function of an electronic device that pauses a recording

[2]**pause** *vb* **paused; paus·ing** *vi* (15c) **1** : to stop temporarily **2** : to linger for a time ~ *vt* : to cause to pause : STOP

pa·vane \pə-ˈvän, -ˈvan\ *also* **pa·van** *same or* ˈpa-vən\ *n* [MF *pavane,* fr. It dial. *pavana,* fr. fem. of *pavano* of Padua, fr. *Pava* (Tuscan *Padova*) Padua] (1535) **1** : a stately court dance by couples that was introduced from southern Europe into England in the 16th century **2** : mu-

\ə\ abut \ᵊ\ kitten, F table \ər\ further \a\ ash \ā\ ace \ä\ mop, mar
\au̇\ out \ch\ chin \e\ bet \ē\ easy \g\ go \i\ hit \ī\ ice \j\ job
\ŋ\ sing \ō\ go \ȯ\ law \ȯi\ boy \th\ thin \t͟h\ the \ü\ loot \u̇\ foot
\y\ yet \zh\ vision, beige \k, ⁿ, œ, ue, ʸ\ *see* Guide to Pronunciation

2

Understanding What You Read: A Review

CHAPTER OUTLINE

Distinguishing Topics, Main Ideas, Major Details, and Minor Details

> Unstated Main Ideas

Recognizing Patterns of Organization

> Simple Listing of Facts

> Time Sequence

> Comparison and Contrast

> Cause and Effect

Uncovering the Central Message of a Longer Selection

Summarizing and Paraphrasing

CHAPTER OUTCOMES

After completing Chapter 2, you should be able to:

- Distinguish topics main ideas, major details, and minor details.
- Recognize patterns of organization (simple listing of facts, time sequence, comparison and contrast, and cause and effect).
- Uncover the central message of a longer selection.
- Summarize and paraphrase the most important points of a selection or chapter.

Think About It!

Look carefully at the photographs. What is the topic of the photographs? What is the overall message the author is communicating about the topic of each photograph? Discuss the photographs with your classmates.

■ Distinguishing Topics, Main Ideas, Major Details, and Minor Details

In addition to uncovering word meanings, being able to differentiate among topics, main ideas, major details, and minor details is an extremely important skill because it contributes to a much better understanding of what you are reading. Read the following paragraph; then answer the question "What is this about?"

One way to recover the past is through music. Popular songs not only provide insight into attitudes and beliefs but also quickly convey the mood and feelings of an era. Through their lyrics, songwriters express the hopes and fears of a people and the emotional tone of an age. Consider, for example, the powerful message conveyed in the Democratic party adoption of "Happy Days Are Here Again" as a campaign theme during the Great Depression. The decline of pop music and the rise of rock and roll in the 1950s tells historians a great deal about the mood of that period. Similarly, the popularity of both folk music and rock in the 1960s provides another way of following social change in that turbulent decade.

Gary B. Nash and Julie Roy Jeffrey, The American People, 5th ed., p. 976

If your answer to the question was "music," you are correct: Virtually all of the sentences in the paragraph deal with that particular topic. The **topic** is the subject of a given paragraph, and it can usually be expressed in a word or phrase that can serve as a title.

Now reread the same paragraph, and try to answer the following question: "What is the overall message the writer is communicating about the topic?" The answer to that question can be found in the first sentence, which states: "One way to recover the past is through music." That sentence is the **main idea** of the paragraph because it lets you know in a general sense what the writer wants to say about the topic, and it sums up all or most of the remaining sentences. In fact, the main idea always mentions the topic, which explains why the main idea—when it is stated—is also referred to as the **topic sentence.** The rest of the paragraph then consists of **details** that provide more information in order to make the main idea clearer.

Not all details, however, are of equal importance. Some lend direct support to the main idea and are called **major details.** Others, called **minor details**, lend direct support to the major details but only indirect support to the main idea. In other words, major details explain main ideas more specifically, and minor details explain the major details more specifically. For instance, the second and third sentences in the paragraph on music are the major details because they support the main idea directly by telling you specifically how or why the past can be recovered through music. In short, they supply more information to help make the main idea clearer. The remaining sentences are minor details that further explain the major details by providing very specific examples. Look again at the paragraph, reprinted here, and take note of the topic, main idea, major details, and minor details.

Topic: Music

Main idea at the beginning

<u>One way to recover the past is through music.</u> Popular songs not only provide insight into attitudes and beliefs but also quickly convey the mood and feelings of an era. Through their lyrics, songwriters express the hopes and fears of a people and the emotional ⎤ **Major details**

tone of an age. Consider, for example, the powerful message conveyed in the Democratic party adoption of "Happy Days Are Here Again" as a campaign theme during the Great Depression. The decline of pop music and the rise of rock and roll in the 1950s tells historians a great deal about the mood of that period. Similarly, the popularity of both folk music and rock in the 1960s provides another way of following social change in that turbulent decade.

Minor details

It is very important for you, as a reader, to be aware of the main idea of every paragraph that you encounter, because the main idea sums up the other sentences and focuses on the overall message that the writer is trying to convey about a given topic. Details give you additional information that make it easier for you to understand the main idea.

When the main idea is stated, as in the example on music, it can be found anywhere in a paragraph—at the beginning, at the end, or somewhere in between. In addition, sometimes a paragraph will have a main idea expressed in more than one sentence. Look at the following examples, and pay particular attention to the topics, main ideas, major details, and minor details, which have been labeled for you.

Topic: Insect species

Main idea at the beginning

The total number of insect species is greater than the total of all other species combined. About a million insect species are known today, and researchers estimate that at least twice this many exist (mostly in tropical forests) but have not yet been discovered. Insects have been prominent on land for the last 400 million years. They have been much less successful in aquatic environments; there are only about 20,000 species in freshwater habitats and far fewer in the sea.

Main idea

Major detail

Minor details

Neil A. Campbell et al., *Biology: Concepts and Connections,*
5th ed., p. 382.

Topic: Violence

Main idea at the end

Throughout U.S. history, various groups that believed the government would not respond to their needs have resorted to some form of violence. Analyzing fifty-three U.S. protest movements, William Gamson (1975) found that 75 percent of the groups that used violence got what they wanted, compared with only 53 percent of those that were nonviolent. Violence, it seems, can pay off.

Minor detail

Major detail

Main idea

Alex Thio, *Sociology: A Brief Introduction,* 4th ed., p. 369

Topic: Sexual abuse of children

Children usually experience strong short-term reactions to being sexually abused but are often too confused or frightened to tell. They feel upset, helpless, frightened, and guilty; if physically injured, the pain experienced makes them particularly fearful of future contacts. The child's experience of abuse can be minimized or exacerbated by a nonabusing significant adult's management of the event. Parents

Minor details

Main idea

Main idea somewhere in between

(nonabusers) who handle the event as an unfortunate but not devastating experience and who can reassure the child that he or she is in no way to blame reduce the impact on the child significantly. On the other hand, the impact of the event may be very much intensified by the parents' negating, angry, and hostile responses. Parents —Major details

often react so strongly and negatively out of their own feelings of anger, powerlessness, and (too often) denial that they cannot focus constructively on the child, thus isolating the child and providing inadequate help to prevent long-term consequences. —Minor detail

Kay Johnston Starks and Eleanor S. Morrison, *Growing Up Sexual,* p. 183

Topic: Anti-drug education

Twenty or thirty years ago, high school health and safety courses may have mentioned some of the hazards of sustained alcohol abuse but with that exception, drug education would not have been found in the high school curriculum. —Minor detail

Main idea expressed in more than one sentence

Today, one would be hard-pressed to find a single school in America that does not offer anti-drug education as part of its basic curriculum. —Main idea Usually, anti-drug programming begins in the elementary grades and intensifies in junior high and high —Major detail

school. In addition to school-based programs, the Partnership for a Drug-Free America and other advocacy groups have sponsored national anti-drug media campaigns targeted mainly at youth —Main idea ("This is your brain. This is your brain on drugs"). Contemporary youth are bombarded with messages about the evils of drugs and exhortations to avoid their use. If American children watch as much television as alleged, the average teenager is exposed to anti-drug messages several times each day. —Major details

James D. Wright and Joel A. Devine, *Drugs as a Social Problem,* p. 51

Occasionally, certain phrases and words, such as "in short," "in brief," "in summary," "in fact," "clearly," "thus," "yes," and "as these examples show," introduce the main idea. Be on the lookout for them. Major and minor details are sometimes preceded by the words "for example" or "for instance" because details generally are examples or instances of something. Look carefully for the main idea directly above those words! Finally, simple lists of sentences that begin with such words as "first," "second," "third," and "finally" are often major details, and you usually can find the main idea just before the first item on those lists. A simple listing of facts is a common pattern of organization.

Unstated Main Ideas

Sometimes a paragraph will consist of just details with no topic sentence or stated main idea. However, that does not mean that there is no overall message regarding the topic. It is simply unstated and therefore cannot be found in the paragraph. When that occurs, the details should point you in the direction of the message, which you can then put into your own words. Look at this example:

> The average American consumer eats 21 pounds of snack foods in a year, but people in the West Central part of the country consume the most (24 pounds per person), whereas those in the Pacific and Southeast regions eat "only" 19 pounds per person. Pretzels are the most popular snack in the mid-Atlantic area, pork rinds are most likely to be eaten in the South, and multigrain chips turn up as a favorite in the West. Not surprisingly, the Hispanic influence in the Southwest has influenced snacking preferences—consumers in that part of the United States eat about 50 percent more tortilla chips than do people elsewhere.
>
> Adapted from Michael R. Solomon, *Consumer Behavior*, 5th ed., 2002, Prentice-Hall, p. 184, and reprinted in K. McWhorter, *Reading across the Disciplines*, 2nd ed., 2005, Pearson Longman, p. 49

The topic of the paragraph has to do with snack foods that Americans eat. Although no sentence expresses the overall message regarding the topic, a number of details provide examples. The average American eats 21 pounds of snack food in a year. People in the West Central part of the United States eat the most. People in the Pacific and Southeast regions consume the least. Pretzels are popular in the mid-Atlantic area. Pork rinds are popular in the South. Multigrain chips are the favorite in the West. And tortilla chips are consumed in the Southwest. If you take all of these details together and look for one general idea, it would be "Americans differ in their preferences for snack foods according to where they live."

Every paragraph has a topic or subject and an overall message about the topic that is expressed as the main idea. When there is no stated main idea, remember to consider carefully what most or all of the major details in a paragraph have in common, which should then help you figure out the unstated main idea. Remember that major details further explain main ideas, while minor details provide more information about major details. Whether the main idea is stated or not, be sure to come away from each paragraph that you read with the overall message clearly in mind.

What is the unstated main idea of the ad for Earth Share on the next page? Discuss your ideas and thoughts with your classmates.

How can you help protect
the prairie and the penguin?

Simple. Visit www.earthshareca.org and learn how the world's leading
environmental groups are working together under one name. And how easy it is
for you to help protect the prairies and the penguins and the planet.

One environment. One simple way to care for it.
www.earthshareca.org

Ad
Council

Earth Share
OF CALIFORNIA

ACTIVITY 1

DIRECTIONS: For each of the passages that follow, find and label the topic, the main idea, and the major details. If the main idea is unstated, write it out in your own words after the passage. Remember that the topic is the answer to the question "What is this about?" and the main idea answers the question "What is the overall message the writer is communicating about the topic?" Also keep in mind that the major details are major because they lend direct support to the main idea.

1

Cutting-edge technology is now being used to improve customer service in the food service industry. The person taking your order at a fast-food drive-thru may not be in the restaurant—in fact, he or she may not even be in the state and could possibly be in another country. Several McDonald's restaurants in Colorado, Minnesota, and Missouri process orders through a centralized facility in Colorado, and other fast-feeders such as Hardee's and Carl's Jr. are joining in. High-speed data connections and voice-over-Internet protocol technology, or VoIP, enable businesses to outsource this task so that workers can concentrate on preparing the food and filling orders accurately. Some systems take temporary digital images of customers or cars placing orders so that workers can avoid mix-ups and speed up service. Domino's Pizza uses Internet technology for order placements and is launching a text-message ordering system for registered customers. Sit-down restaurants are also experimenting with table-side phone ordering and are placing credit/debit swipes at customers' fingertips. In Asia, customers routinely use their smart phones or palm computers to place an order from anywhere, and we will see this technology in the United States in the near future. Customers must be careful, however, because professional order takers are better at up-selling (that is, getting customers to order more-expensive options) and increasing the average order size.

Gary Armstrong and Philip Kotler, *Marketing: An Introduction,* 9th ed., pp. 32–33

2

One of the greatest benefits of studying psychology is that you learn not only how the brain works in general but also how to use yours in particular—by thinking critically. **Critical thinking** is the ability and willingness to assess claims and to make objective judgments on the basis of well-supported reasons. It is the ability to look for flaws in arguments and to resist claims that have no supporting evidence. Critical thinking, however, is not merely negative thinking. It also fosters the ability to be *creative and constructive*—to come up with various possible explanations for events, think of implications of research findings, and apply new knowledge to a broad range of social and personal problems. You can't separate critical thinking from creative thinking, for it is only when you question *what is* that you can begin to imagine *what can be.*

Carol Tavris and Carole Wade, *Psychology in Perspective,* p. 10

3

It would be nice if everything we said was understood exactly as intended. Unfortunately, this is not the case. Messages are filtered by listeners' attitudes, values, and beliefs; consequently, changes in their meaning may occur. Someone who distrusts others and is skeptical of what people say, for example, will interpret the words "I like you a lot" differently from someone who is more trusting. A skeptic might think, "He doesn't really mean that, he's only saying it to get on my good side." A more trusting person will accept the message and treat it as a genuine expression of affection. The difference in interpretation between what the "speaker said" and what the "receiver heard" is called the interpersonal gap. Other examples include:

Lisa: "I'm really feeling angry. That's the last time I want to see you do that."

Manuel's interpretation: She is always blaming me for things. I wish she would stop.

Jasmine's interpretation: It was my fault. She is right. I'll try to do things differently in the future.

Courtney's interpretation: She's got to be kidding. What I did could not be that important.

Anthony F. Grasha, *Practical Applications of Psychology*, p. 259

4

Who discovered America? This is not as easy a question to answer as one might think. The first human beings to set foot on the continents of North and South America came from Asia. Perhaps 80,000 years ago they settled an area stretching from northeastern Siberia through the Aleutian islands in Alaska. Scholars refer to the region as "Beringia," named after the explorer Vitus Bering. Most of the area is now submerged beneath the Bering Strait and adjacent waters. During the Ice Age, however, when more precipitation was trapped on land as snow or ice, the ocean was far shallower, exposing much of the ocean bed. During this period, some of the people of "Beringia" moved in search of game and green grass to what is now the North American continent. Almost certainly the settlers of the Americas, the ancestors of the modern Indians, were unaware that they were entering "new" territory. So we must look elsewhere (and much later in time) for the "discoverer" of America as we use that word.

Probably the first European to reach America was a Norseman, Leif Ericson. He ventured before the day of the compass into the void of the North Atlantic and, around the year 1000, reached the shores of Labrador. Yet Ericson's discovery passed practically unnoticed for centuries, and to most modern inhabitants of the New World he lives only in legend.

John A. Garraty and Mark C. Carnes, *The American Nation,* 10th ed., p. 3

5

We need relationships with others to know that we are truly alive. While we strive for positive relationships with our friends, family, and significant others, we sometimes find ourselves in relationships that result in an emotional roller coaster. While negative relationships may cause us distress, intimate relationships that have gone bad can send us in a downward spiral emotionally and physically. How can we ensure that the relationship in which we are investing our time, energy, and emotion is a healthy one? What are the characteristics of a healthy relationship? How do our relationships contribute to our overall health and well-being?

Rebecca J. Donatelle, *Health: The Basics,* 4th ed., p. 96

6

Why is the air in cities so polluted from automobile exhaust fumes? When automobile drivers step into their cars, they bear only the private costs of driving. That is, they must pay for the gas, maintenance, depreciation, and insurance on their automobiles. But they cause an additional cost, that of air pollution, which they are not forced to take account of when they make the decision to drive. Air pollution is a cost because it causes harm to individuals—burning eyes, respiratory ailments, and dirtier clothes, cars, and buildings. The air pollution created by automobile exhaust is a cost that individual operators of automobiles do not yet bear directly. The social cost of driving includes all the private costs plus at least the cost of air pollution, which society bears. Decisions made only on the basis of private costs lead to too much automobile driving or, alternatively, to too little money spent on the reduction of automobile pollution for a given amount of driving. Clean air is a scarce resource used by automobile drivers free of charge. They will use more of it than they would if they had to pay the full social costs.

Roger LeRoy Miller, *Economics Today*, p. 761

7

Marketing to children has always been controversial. Indeed, in the 1970s, the Federal Trade Commission considered prohibiting all advertising to children, and in some other countries it is illegal to advertise to children. Now, with the child obesity rate in the United States greater than 18 percent and predicted to exceed 20 percent in just a few years, there is pressure on marketers, in general, and food marketers, in particular, to curb their marketing practices to children. Studies report that children view more than 20 food ads each day with over 90 percent of them promoting high-fat, high-sugar products. The marketing concept focuses on satisfying customers' needs and wants, but are marketers crossing the line when they cater to younger consumers' wants for products that may counter parental wishes or that may be unhealthy?

Gary Armstrong and Philip Kotler, *Marketing: An Introduction*, 9th ed., p. 33

8

For years it was believed that our natural resources were free goods which, although wasted and exploited, would be replenished by nature. This nation did not recognize that it was destroying the ability of nature to maintain a balanced ecological system. Today many of our lakes and streams are too polluted to support plant and fish life. In strip-mine areas, the wasted land lies barren. Energy sources that took nature thousands of years to create are consumed within minutes. As indicated by these few examples, a realistic program of environment and energy conservation should be adopted by every business.

Raymond E. Glos et al., *Business: Its Nature and Environment*

9

What, then, are the realities? There is a distinction which it is important to make in any discussion of Islam. The word "Islam" is used with at least three different meanings, and much misunderstanding can arise from the failure to distinguish between them. In the first place, Islam means the religion taught by the Prophet Muhammad and embodied in the Muslim revelation known as the Qur'ån. In the second place, Islam is the subsequent development of this religion through tradition and through the work of the great Muslim jurists and theologians. In this sense it includes the mighty structure of the Sharï'a, the holy law of Islam, and the great corpus of Islamic dogmatic theology. In the third meaning, Islam is the counterpart not of Christianity but rather of Christendom. In this sense Islam means not what Muslims believed or were expected to believe but what they actually did—in other words, Islamic civilization as known to us in history. In discussing Muslim attitudes on ethnicity, race, and color, I shall try to deal to some extent at least with all three but to make clear the distinction between them.

Bernard Lewis, *Race and Slavery in the Middle East*

10

As a young child growing up in Brooklyn, New York, during the 1940s, I experienced firsthand the effects of relative poverty and discrimination. In the schools I attended, a common perception was that my culture and language were inferior. I spoke only Spanish when I entered first grade, and I was immediately confronted with the arduous task of learning a second language while my developed native language was all but ignored. Almost 50 years later, I still remember the frustration of groping for English words I did not know to express thoughts I could say very capably in Spanish. Equally vivid are memories of some teachers' expectations that my classmates and I would not do well in school because of our language and cultural differences. This explains my fourth-grade teacher's response when mine was the only hand to go up when she asked whether anybody in the class wanted to go to college. "Well, that's okay," she said, "because we always need people to clean toilets."

Sonia Nieto, *Affirming Diversity*, 3rd ed., p. 1

ACTIVITY 2 DIRECTIONS: *Using your other textbooks, find examples of paragraphs with the types of main ideas that we have discussed. Find a variety with topic sentences in the beginning, at the end, and somewhere in between. Also look for examples of paragraphs with a main idea expressed in more than one sentence and ones that have unstated main ideas. If you do not have other textbooks at this time, ask your classmates who are using other books to share their textbooks with you.*

■ Recognizing Patterns of Organization

Look carefully at this sequence of numbers:

16–1–20–20–5–18–14–19   1–18–5   8–5–12–16–6–21–12

Does this mean anything to you? Can you see a message? Probably not. What if you were told that each number corresponds to a letter in the alphabet, numbered in order from 1 to 26? Is that better? After a few minutes, you should be able to figure out that the message is "Patterns are helpful"!

Once you determine the arrangement or pattern of something, the message is much easier to understand. Have you ever heard someone say, "I am starting to see a pattern here?" That comment usually means that several pieces of similar information are enabling the person to come to a particular conclusion. For example, if Jonathan has consistently arrived late for psychology class during the first three weeks of the semester, his instructor would see a pattern and might conclude that Jonathan is not a very responsible student. Again, patterns can be useful by adding meaning to given situations.

Writers often help readers recognize important details by arranging them in a certain way. These arrangements of details are called **patterns of organization**, and there are four major ones: **simple listing of facts, time sequence, comparison and contrast**, and **cause and effect.** When reading material is organized using one or more of these patterns, you will more easily see not only details but also the main idea. Or the main idea may tip you off to the presence of a specific pattern of organization. So it is a two-way process. Let us take a look at each of the patterns.

Simple Listing of Facts

This pattern involves a list of details that could include the causes, characteristics, examples, or types of something. Writers will often use **transition words** such as the following to help you recognize this pattern:

also, another, examples, factors, finally, following, in addition, last, list, many, numbers (first, second, etc.), other, part, several, types, next, moreover, further, furthermore

Determining the main idea can also be of help, because it will let you know exactly what is being listed. Look at the following example:

> The Internet is a powerful tool for advertisers. Click-through rates are one measure of effectiveness. Another trend is paid search advertising. New products and services spawned by the digital revolution include: broadband, which permits transmission of streaming media over the Internet; mobile commerce (m-commerce) which is made possible by Wi-Fi, Bluetooth, WiMax, and other forms of wireless connectivity; telematics and global positioning systems (GPS); and short message service (SMS). Smart phones are creating new markets for mobile music downloads, including ringtones, truetones, and full-track music files; they can also be used for mobile gaming and Internet phone service using VoIP.
>
> Warren J. Keegan and Mark C. Green, *Global Marketing*, 6th ed., p. 480

Notice how the main idea, "The Internet is a powerful tool for advertisers," covers a number of products, which you may or may not be familiar with. The main idea is in the first sentence. The list of products uses transition words such as *one measure, another trend, including*, and *also*. The list also includes punctuation such as the colon and the semicolon to let you know there will be a list of Internet advertising trends.

Another example of a simple listing of facts or details does not have the main idea in the first sentence. Read the following example:

> America can be fairly called a "drug culture" in the sense that nearly everyone uses drugs of one sort or another. When we are ailing, we expect to be given some drug that will make us feel better. If we have trouble sleeping, we take sleeping medications, whether over-the-counter or prescribed. If we feel anxious, we want anti-anxiety drugs, and if we feel depressed, we seek antidepressants. If we want sex without the risk of pregnancy, we take "the pill." Millions of us get "up" with caffeine and come "down" with alcohol. It has even been argued that mood-altering drugs satisfy an *innate* human need to suspend ordinary awareness, a need much like sexual tension that "arises spontaneously from within, builds to a peak, finds relief, and dissipates" (Weil, 1972: 22). The use of drugs to make one feel better or to solve one's problems, whatever they might be, is deeply entrenched in our culture and our expectations.
>
> James D. Wright and Joel A. Devine, *Drugs as a Social Problem*, p. 2

In this example, the main idea is stated in both the first and last sentences, which convey just about the same overall message. Writers will sometimes repeat the same—or close to the same—main idea in the first and last sentences of a paragraph, which makes it easier to spot. All the rest of the sentences in the paragraph are major details that list the kinds of drugs people take and their reasons for taking them. Although there is no numbering, you are helped to recognize the presence of the list by the repetition of the words *when we* and *if we*.

Time Sequence

This pattern involves details placed in the order in which they occur in time. Transition words often found in time sequence include these:

after, before, beginning, dates, finally, first, last, later, next, once, prior, repeat, steps, then, thereafter, times of day, when, year, previously, now, following, immediately, while, during, often, until, soon

Historical and other material with dated events or times of the day are the most obvious place to find this pattern, as in the following example:

> The population of the United States has been shifting to the South and the West, the region known as the Sunbelt, and away from the Northeast and Midwest, the Frostbelt. In 1970, a majority of the nation's population, 52 percent, lived in the Frostbelt. The population has subsequently shifted steadily to the South and West. In 2000, 58 percent of Americans lived in the Sunbelt. The Sunbelt population is growing because of relatively higher birthrates in the region, immigration from abroad, and intrastate migration from the Frostbelt.
>
> Neal Tannahill, *THINK American Government*, p. 22

Once again, the main idea is stated in the first sentence, which informs you that the time sequence organizes details that illustrate how "the population has shifted." The *dates* make it easy to identify the major details that directly support the overall message.

This pattern can also include the steps in a process, directions, or anything else that is accomplished in a definite time order, as in the example below:

> In courtship, a male and female loon swim side by side while performing a series of displays. (1) The courting birds frequently turn their heads away from each other. (In sharp contrast, a male loon defending his territory often charges at an intruder with his beak pointed straight ahead.) (2) The birds then dip their beaks in the water, and (3) submerge their heads and necks. Prior to copulation, the male invites the female onto land by (4) turning his head backward with his beak held downward. There, (5) they copulate.
>
> Neil A. Campbell et al., *Biology: Concepts and Connections*, 5th ed., p. 716.

The main idea is stated in the first sentence, which tells you that "In courtship, a male and female loon swim side by side while performing a series of displays." That sentence, along with the transition words *series,* *then,* and *prior,* lets you know that behavior is being traced that must be accomplished in a definite sequence. The rest of the sentences, with the exception of the one in parentheses, are major details that trace the steps in the process. Although the major details are numbered, the pattern of organization here is time sequence rather than a simple listing of facts because the steps in the process must be done in that order. In other words, Step 1 must be accomplished before Step 2, Step 2 must be accomplished before Step 3, Step 3 must be accomplished before Step 4, and Step 4 must be accomplished before Step 5. With a simple listing, the items on a given list are not in any specific time order. This is the key difference between those two patterns.

Comparison and Contrast

This pattern organizes details that deal with the similarities (comparison) and differences (contrast) between persons, events, ideas, or things. Transition words that are often found with comparison and contrast include these:

> alike, between, common, commonalities, compare, contrast, debate, difference, disagree, distinction, distinguish, like, likeness, on the other hand, same, similarity, unlike, whereas

Also, the main idea usually tells you exactly what is being compared or contrasted. Read the following example:

1   Think of all the ways that human beings are alike. Everywhere, no matter what their backgrounds or where they live, people love, work, argue, dance, sing, complain, and gossip. They rear families, celebrate marriages, and mourn losses. They reminisce about the past and plan for the future. They help their friends and fight with their enemies. They smile with amusement, frown with displeasure, and glare in anger. Where do all these commonalities come from?

2   Think of all the ways that human beings differ. Some of us are extroverts, always ready to throw a party, make a new friend, or speak up in a crowd; others are shy and introverted, preferring the safe and familiar. Some are trailblazers, ambitious and enterprising; others are placid, content with the way things are.

Some take to book learning like a cat to catnip; others don't do so well in school but have lots of street smarts and practical know-how. Some are overwhelmed by even the most petty of problems; others, faced with severe difficulties, remain calm and resilient. Where do all these differences come from?

Carol Tavris and Carole Wade, *Psychology in Perspective,* p. 83

The first paragraph deals with how human beings are similar as stated by the main idea: "Think of all the ways that human beings are alike." The transition words *alike* and *commonalities* help you recognize the pattern. All of the remaining sentences, with the exception of the last one, are major details that directly support the overall message by giving examples of similarities. The main idea of the second paragraph—"Think of all the ways that human beings differ"—tells you that it is concerned with how human beings are different, and the transition words *differ* and *differences* are also revealing. Again, the rest of the sentences in the paragraph, except the last one, are major details that directly support the overall message by providing examples of differences.

Do you notice that there is an additional pattern of organization in both paragraphs? There is also a simple listing of facts. The repetition of the word *they* in the first paragraph and *some* and *others* in the second one gives strong indication that lists are present. As you can see, writers sometimes use a *combination of patterns,* which is very helpful to you, because it gives you more than one opportunity to recognize important details and thus better understand what you are reading.

Cause and Effect

This pattern organizes details that present causes or reasons along with their effects or results. In other words, this pattern explains why something has happened. For example, if one of your classmates asked you how you got an A+ on the last history test (*effect*), you might proceed to explain that you attended all classes (*cause*), took down every word the professor said (*cause*), read all the assignments (*cause*), and studied on a daily basis (*cause*). In essence, you would be using the cause-and-effect pattern to give the reasons why you earned such a high grade.

Transition words to look for when this pattern is present include these:

affects, because, brings out, cause, consequences, contributed, create, effect, leads to, reaction, reason, result, therefore, whereas, due to, accordingly, since, if...then, thus

Sometimes the causes are stated first, as in the following example:

> During the late 1980s, news articles, TV shows, and radio commentaries proclaimed that the nation was facing a shortage of scientists. The growth in high-tech industries was going to create demands for scientists and engineers that would not be met. The government even suggested that this shortage would endanger national security. The result was an increase in the number of students seeking postgraduate education, especially doctoral degrees in engineering, the sciences, mathematics, and computer science. For example, in 1981–1982, a total of 2,621 Ph.D.s were granted in engineering; by 1991–1992, the number had more than doubled, to 5,488. Similar, though less dramatic, increases were seen in the number of doctorates awarded in the sciences and mathematics.
>
> Roger LeRoy Miller, *Economics Today,* p. 77

The first three sentences in the paragraph provide causes:

- "During the late 1980s, news articles, TV shows, and radio commentaries proclaimed that the nation was facing a shortage of scientists."
- "The growth in high-tech industries was going to create demands for scientists and engineers that would not be met."
- "The government even suggested that this shortage would endanger national security."

The fourth sentence states the effect:

- "The result was an increase in the number of students seeking postgraduate education, especially doctoral degrees in engineering, the sciences, mathematics, and computer science."

More specific information, which directly supports the effect, is found in the remaining sentences, preceded by the words *for example.* Notice the two transition words *create* and *result,* which help you recognize the pattern. The main idea, which for the most part is unstated, would read something like this: "There was an increase in the number of students seeking postgraduate education in engineering, sciences, mathematics, and computer science as a result of national concern in the late 1980s that there was a serious shortage of scientists and engineers."

This pattern sometimes presents effects first, followed by causes, as in the following example:

> People became homeless for a variety of reasons. Some started life in seriously disturbed families. Others fell prey to alcohol and drugs. Still others had

health or learning problems that eroded the possibility of a stable life. For millions of working Americans, homelessness was just a serious and unaffordable illness away. Though many Americans initially regarded the homeless as "bag ladies, winos, and junkies," they gradually came to realize that the underclass category included others as well.

Gary B. Nash and Julie Roy Jeffrey, The American People, 5th ed., p. 1013

The first sentence—"People became homeless for a variety of reasons"— has the transition word *reasons* and also lets you know that *homelessness* is the effect. Causes are presented in the second, third, and fourth sentences, which are the major details:

- "Some started life in seriously disturbed families."
- "Others fell prey to alcohol and drugs."
- "Still others had health or learning problems that eroded the possibility of a stable life."

Did you notice a second pattern of organization? Right again! The words *some, others,* and *still others* indicate that the causes are also organized in a simple listing of facts. When you read, recognizing one or more than one pattern of organization enables you to focus on important information and thus helps you comprehend better.

ACTIVITY 3

Directions: In the following passages, find the main ideas, patterns of organization, and the most important details organized by the patterns. Write your answers and share them as instructed by your professor. Be prepared to discuss the transition words that helped you identify the patterns.

1

1   If you follow tennis, you know that John McEnroe was famous for his on-court antics and spectacular temper tantrums; he was the bad boy of the tennis circuit. Once, when McEnroe noticed a small microphone that could pick up what the players were saying, he walked over and hit it with his racquet, breaking a string. Then he strolled to the sidelines and got a new racquet. There was no penalty for this little episode. In fact, it seemed to work to his advantage: He got all charged up for the game, while his opponent's performance suffered from the interruption. McEnroe also received plenty of attention from fans and the media, who loved him or loved to hate him.

2   In contrast, Bjorn Borg, another tennis champion, was controlled and civilized on the court. "Once I was like John [McEnroe]," he told a reporter. "Worse. Swearing and throwing rackets. Real bad temper. Ask anyone who knew me in

Sweden then, 10 or 11 years ago. Then, when I was 13, my club suspended me for six months. My parents locked my racket in a cupboard for six months. Half a year I could not play. It was terrible. But it was a very good lesson. I never opened my mouth on the court again. I still get really mad, but I keep my emotions inside" (quoted in Collins, 1981).

Carol Tavris and Carole Wade, *Psychology in Perspective*, p. 211

2

"Junk mail!" We all know what it is, but have you ever considered the environmental impact of all that unsolicited mail? The Department of the Environment estimates that Americans spend more than $320 million per year to dispose of junk mail. Approximately 42 billion pieces of unsolicited mail are delivered annually, representing 41 pounds of junk mail per adult each year. More than 100 million trees are cut down and 28 billion gallons of water are used each year to feed our junk mail addiction. Statistics such as these have lead some consumers and communities to fight back. For example, the San Francisco and Santa Barbara areas of California started a "Stop Junk Mail" campaign and provide useful tips for consumers at www.stopjunkmail.org. The United States is not the only concerned country. British environment minister David Miliband has declared a "war on junk mail" and has threatened legislation forcing direct marketers to go to an opt-in model of mailing. Charities responded that this was simply "hair-brained lunacy." The direct-mail industry in the United Kingdom is already reeling from a government mandate that 30 percent of delivered direct mail in 2006 be recycled, amounting to proving that more than 600,000 pieces had been recycled by direct marketers by the end of that year.

Gary Armstrong and Philip Kotler, *Marketing: An Introduction*, 9th ed., p. 446

3

A lecture hall, for example, provides lots of opportunity to listen but very few opportunities to respond. Research shows that such settings promote a **one-way communication** pattern in which the teacher talks and students, for the most part, listen. For example, 70 percent of the time in a typical college classroom is spent with the teacher talking. Of the remaining time in a class period, students spend about 15 percent of it either responding to questions or asking questions and 15 percent remaining silent (Bonwell and Eison, 1991). When snuggling close to someone you care about, you and your partner have opportunities to talk and to listen. Thus, a **two-way communication** pattern is established.

Anthony F. Grasha, *Practical Applications of Psychology*, p. 262

4

American blacks were deeply involved in the Revolution. In fact, the conflict provoked the largest slave rebellion in American history prior to the Civil War. Once the war was under way, blacks found a variety of ways to turn events to their own advantage. For some, this meant applying revolutionary principles to their own lives and calling for their personal freedom. For others, it meant seeking liberty behind English lines or in the continent's interior.

Gary B. Nash and Julie Roy Jeffrey, *The American People*, p. 201

5

1   The extraordinary popularity of sports in the postwar period can be explained in a number of ways. People had more money to spend and more free time to fill. Radio was bringing suspenseful, play-by-play accounts of sports contests into millions of homes, thus encouraging tens of thousands to want to see similar events with their own eyes.

2   There had been great athletes before, such as Jim Thorpe, a Sac and Fox Indian, who won both the pentathlon and the decathlon at the 1912 Olympic Games, made Walter Camp's All-America football team in 1912 and 1913, then played major league baseball for several years before becoming a pioneer founder and player in the National Football League. But what truly made the 1920s a Golden Age was the emergence of a remarkable collection of what today would be called "superstars."

John A. Garraty, *A Short History of the American Nation*, p. 423

ACTIVITY 4

DIRECTIONS: *In the following passages, find the main ideas, patterns of organization, and the most important details organized by the patterns. Write your answers as instructed by you professor. Be prepared to discuss the transition words that helped you identify the patterns.*

1

Second Life is a virtual world launched in 2003 by Linden Labs in San Francisco, California. It boasts more than nine million inhabitants who connect for fun and to escape. Registered members create online digital alter egos called avatars, and now users can actually speak to each other. The currency is called Linden dollars, with $1 equal to about 270 Linden dollars. Users can purchase land in Second Life to start a business or build a home. The world started with 64 acres but now has more than 65,000 acres as it expanded to meet users' demand. Second Life is not the only virtual world. Approximately $200 million of real money moves through virtual worlds overall. Second Life is more adult oriented but there are other worlds, such as Habbo and Nictropolis, targeted to children. Marketers see opportunities for research and promotion in virtual worlds. Useful insights into consumer preferences and behavior can be gleaned from observing virtual behavior, but some skeptics claim this might not be valid due to consumers not being themselves in these worlds. However, marketers such as IBM, Sony, Adidas, Pontiac, Kraft, and Coca-Cola have a strong presence, much like product placement in other forms of media. Kraft launched 70 new products in a virtual supermarket and found that consumers do go grocery shopping in their fantasy world and that they do read product information.

Gary Armstrong and Philip Kotler, *Marketing: An Introduction,* 9th ed., p. 380

2

Collective behavior is relatively spontaneous, unorganized, and unpredictable social behavior. It contrasts with *institutionalized behavior,* which occurs in a well-organized, rather predictable way. Institutionalized behavior is frequent and routine. Every weekday, masses of people hurry to work. On every campus, groups of students walk to classes. These predictable patterns of group action are basically governed by social norms and are the bedrock of social order. Collective behavior, however, operates largely outside the confines of these conventional norms.

Alex Thio, *Sociology: A Brief Introduction,* 4th ed., p. 438

3

The aspect of the physical environment that places the greatest constraint on organisms is climate. Climate is one of those terms we use loosely. In fact, people sometimes confuse climate with weather. **Weather** is the combination of temperature, humidity, precipitation, wind, cloudiness, and other atmospheric conditions at a specific place and time. **Climate** is the long-term average pattern of weather. We can describe the local, regional, or global climate.

Robert Leo Smith and Thomas M. Smith, *Elements of Ecology,* p. 31

4

Did you know that within three months after the Pilgrims landed at Plymouth Rock, half of them had died from malnutrition and illness because of the harsh conditions they encountered? Some of the surviving Pilgrims gave up and returned with the *Mayflower* when it sailed back across the Atlantic. The remaining Pilgrims struggled with famine. After three years of enduring conditions bordering on starvation, and after some Pilgrims became so desperate that they took to stealing from the others, the colonists began to reconsider a key method they had adopted in an effort to promote their new society. This was the practice of "farming in common," which entailed pooling what they produced and then rationing this "common property" in equal allotments. Following much thought and discussion, the colonists decided instead to parcel the *land* equally among families, who could then either consume or trade all fruits of their labors. This change in the Pilgrims' incentive structure worked wonders. Soon they had such bountiful harvests that they decided to have a day of thanksgiving—the forerunner of the modern American Thanksgiving holiday.

Roger LeRoy Miller, Economics Today, p. 760

5

The rate of weathering depends on the type of rock and on environmental conditions. Geologists define three major types of rock: igneous, sedimentary, and metamorphic. **Igneous rocks** are formed by the cooling of volcanic flows, surface or subterranean. The properties of these rocks depend on the rate and temperature at which they form. **Sedimentary rocks** are formed by the deposition of mineral particles (sediments). The properties of sedimentary rocks depend on the type of sediment from which they are formed. Some sediments are of biological origin; for example, shells of ocean invertebrates may fall to the sea floor. **Metamorphic rocks** are either igneous or sedimentary rocks that have been altered by heat and the pressure of overlying rock.

Robert Leo Smith and Thomas M. Smith, Elements of Ecology, 4th ed., p. 97

ACTIVITY 5   *DIRECTIONS: Using your other textbooks, find examples of passages that illustrate the four patterns of organization that we have discussed. If you do not have other textbooks at this time, ask your classmates who are using other books to share their textbooks with you.*

◼ Uncovering the Central Message of a Longer Selection

To this point, we have been discussing using context to find word meanings; distinguishing main ideas, major details, and minor details; and recognizing patterns of organization in paragraphs. All of these skills, of course, can be applied to selections or passages that include several paragraphs. Examples are articles, essays, textbook sections, and chapters.

Just as every paragraph has a main idea, every longer selection also has a main idea that gives the central message of all of the paragraphs within that selection. The **central message** represents the specific aspect of the topic that the writer wishes to discuss, and it is supported by the information in the selection, including the main ideas of the individual paragraphs and most, if not all, of the details. Patterns of organization can help you uncover the central message by directing you to the most important details.

Once again, it is important to determine first what the topic is by answering the question "What is this about?" Most longer selections will have a title or a heading to help you determine the topic. If there is no title or heading, you can usually figure out the topic by reading the selection carefully, concentrating particularly on sentences near the beginning, which will often mention the subject matter. Once you have determined the topic, you identify the central message by answering the question "What is the central message that the writer is communicating about the topic?"

The main idea of a longer selection can be stated or unstated, as is the case with main ideas in paragraphs. When the main idea is stated, it can usually be found somewhere within the first few paragraphs or the last few paragraphs. When it is unstated, a very careful reading of the selection will usually enable you to figure out the overall main idea. Read the following example, determine the topic, and see if you can identify the main idea by answering the question "What is the central message that the writer is communicating about the topic?"

The Greening of Aging

1   It's summer in upstate New York, the sun is shining, and it's time to make hay. Bill Thomas, medical doctor, gentleman farmer, and deep thinker, heads out to take the year's first cutting. His is a "mixed power" farm, which means that the tractor shares the load with a pair of massive 1-ton workhorses. Thomas takes the reins, clucks his tongue, and sets out across the field.

2   Perhaps because of his vantage point, here among the plants and living creatures of Summer Hill, a 258-acre working farm in Sherburne, N.Y., this Harvard-trained doctor doesn't look at organizations and search for the efficiency of a machine, but instead imagines the nurturing possibilities of a garden. He's brought this perspective to a most unlikely domain—the world of nursing homes. As a medical director at an upstate New York nursing home in the early 90's, Thomas moved dogs, cats, birds, and plants into a facility and radically shifted the focus from delivering scheduled institutional care to providing for the dignity and emotional well-being of the residents. Called the Eden Alternative, the project was a success and allowed Thomas to create a nonprofit that now lists 300 Eden Home conversions in America and an additional 200 overseas.

3   Thomas is now on to his next big thing: The Green House Project. The first Green Houses were constructed in Tupelo, Mississippi, in 2003. Now that an intensive evaluation has documented their success, Thomas has teamed up with the Robert Wood Johnson Foundation to replace more than 100 nursing homes nationwide with clusters of small, cozy houses, each sheltering eight to ten residents in private rooms, with private bathrooms and an open kitchen. In other words, a place like home.

4   With his startling common-sense ideas and his ability to persuade others to take a risk, this creative and wildly exuberant 46-year old country doctor has become something of a culture changer—reimagining how Americans will approach aging in the 21st century. And with 35 million Americans over 65—a number that will double by 2030—that takes a big imagination indeed.

5   Thomas, the ultimate ideas man, has handed off the day-to-day operation of the Green House Project to trusted associates and has begun focusing on what might be the closest project yet to his heart, Eldershire, a multigenerational "intentional community" that he plans to build on his property in Summer Hill. In the past, he has struggled to translate the world of Summer Hill into nursing homes. With Eldershire, the home will become another part of his growing garden.

From Caroline Hsu, "The Greening of Aging," *U.S. News & World Report*, June 19, 2006. Copyright 2006 U.S. News & World Report, L.P. Reprinted with permission.

The heading of the passage lets you know that the topic deals with "aging." The first paragraph introduces you to a concept of "back to the old days" of farming. This selection uses a simple listing of facts and a time sequence organizational pattern. The second paragraph describes how Bill Thomas has applied that concept to nursing homes. Details describe the success of this concept. He moved animals and plants into the home. The unstated main idea would be that Thomas applied the concept of a garden to nursing home facilities.

The third paragraph expands on this idea by describing the Green House project. The object is to make the nursing facility a place like "home." So the main idea could be: Bill Thomas is changing the concept of nursing home facilities to make them more like home.

The last two paragraphs describe Thomas's vision and his new Eldershire project, using supporting details to show the need for more retirement facilities. These paragraphs reinforce the main idea of the passage.

Let's look at another example. As you read the selection, notice how the information is structured. Think carefully about the topic, the supporting details, and the central message of the whole passage.

Wireless Worries: Cell Phones and Risks to Health

1   In less than a decade, cell phones have become a household staple, with the number of subscribers skyrocketing from 16 million in 1994 to over 110 million today and still rising by 1 million per month.

2   Although cell phones have become commonplace, their use continues to spur controversy, particularly regarding questions of potential health risk. While the cell phone

industry assures consumers that phones are safe, a former industry research director, Dr. George Carlo, argues that past studies have not provided conclusive evidence of safety and we do not know the effects of cell phone usage on future generations. He observed, "This is the first generation that has put relatively high-powered transmitters against the head, hour after hour, day after day."

3   Are increases in the prevalence of brain tumors and other neurological conditions in the last decade related to cell phone use? At high power levels, radiofrequency energy (the energy used in cell phones) can rapidly heat biological tissue and cause damage, such as burns. However, cell phones operate at power levels well below the level at which such heating occurs. Many countries, including the United States and most of Europe, follow standards set by the Federal Communications Commission (FCC) for radiofrequency energy based on research by several scientific groups. These groups identified a whole-body *specific absorption rate (SAR)* value for exposure to radiofrequency energy. Four watts per kilogram was identified as a threshold level of exposure at which harmful biological effects may occur. The FCC requires wireless phones to comply with a safety limit of 1.6 watts per kilogram.

4   The U.S. Food and Drug Administration (FDA), the World Health Organization, and other major health agencies agree that the research to date has not shown radiofrequency energy emitted from cell phones to be harmful. However, they also point to the need for more research and caution that, because cell phones have only been widely used for less than a decade and no long-term studies have been done, there is not enough information to say they are risk-free. Three large, case-control studies and one large cohort study have compared cell phone use among brain cancer patients and individuals free of brain cancer. Key findings from these studies indicate that:

5   Brain cancer patients did not report more cell phone use overall than controls. In fact, for unclear reasons, most of the studies showed a lower risk of brain cancer among cell phone users.

6   None of the studies showed a clear link between the side of the head on which the cancer occurred and the side on which the phone was used.

7   There was no correlation between brain tumor risk and dose of exposure, as assessed by duration of use, date since first subscription, age at first subscription, or type of cell phone used.

8   However, these studies are not conclusive, and preliminary results from smaller, well-designed studies have continued to raise questions. A recent Swedish study found higher risk of a benign brain tumor among adults who had used analog cell phones (which produce higher exposure levels than their digital counterparts) for at least ten years. At the moment, the biggest risk from cell phones appears to come from using them while driving, with a corresponding increase in vehicle crashes. However, if you prefer to err on the side of caution, follow these hints to lower your risk:

9   Use lighter- or dash-mounted phones or headphones/ear buds when driving. This not only keeps your hands free, but, if subsequent studies indicate a health risk, you will have minimized your exposure to radiofrequency energy. Exposure levels drop dramatically with distance.

10   Limit cell phone usage. Use land-based phones whenever possible.

11   Check the SAR level of your phone. Purchase one with a lower level if yours is near the FCC limit.

Rebecca J. Donatelle, *Health: The Basics*, 7th ed., p. 450, © 2007. Reprinted by permission of Pearson Education, Inc., Upper Saddle River, New Jersey.

The heading of the selection lets you know that the topic is the risks to health and wireless cell phones. The first paragraph emphasizes the prevalence of cell phones. The second paragraph brings up the central message of the effect of cell phone usage and potential health risks.

Paragraph three gives details of the SAR rate of phones and paragraphs four through seven give details of some of the research studies. Paragraph eight is a key one because it states the central message that the studies are not conclusive and further research is needed. However, there is evidence that cell phone use can cause car crashes. The selection concludes with three suggestions for lowering the risk of cell phone use.

The organizational pattern of this selection is a simple listing of facts; the selection states the central message and then provides evidence. As you can see, uncovering the topic and central message of a selection is very useful because it requires that you focus on the most important information. That focus should help you derive more meaning from textbook material and other kinds of reading. It will also help you master the approach to contemporary issues discussed in Chapter 4 by enabling you to determine what is at issue, distinguish among opposing viewpoints, and arrive at an informed personal viewpoint.

ACTIVITY 6

DIRECTIONS: *Find the topic and central message for each of the selections that follow by answering the questions "What is this about?" and "What is the central message that the writer is communicating about the topic?" Remember to look carefully at main ideas within the paragraphs and at any patterns of organization that may be present, because they will help you focus on the most important information.*

1

1   As consumers become more and more comfortable with computer and digital technologies, many companies are placing information and ordering machines—called *kiosks* (in contrast to vending machines, which dispense actual products)—in stores, airports, and other locations. Kiosks are popping up everywhere these days, from self-service hotel and airline check-in devices to in-store ordering kiosks that let you order merchandise not carried in the store.

2   In-store Kodak, Fuji, and HP kiosks let customers transfer pictures from memory sticks, mobile phones, and other digital storage devices, edit them, and make high-quality color prints. Kiosks in Hilton hotel lobbies let guests view their reservations,

get room keys, view prearrival messages, check in and out, and even change seat assignments and print boarding passes for flights on any of 18 airlines. Outdoor equipment retailer REI has at least four Web-enabled kiosks in each of its 63 stores that provide customers with product information and let them place orders online. Kiosks in Target stores link to articles from *Consumer Reports* magazine, and Mazda dealers let customers use kiosks to research car and truck values through Kelly Blue Book.

3   Business marketers also use kiosks. For example, Dow Plastics places kiosks at trade shows to collect sales leads and to provide information on its 700 products. The kiosk system reads customer data from encoded registration badges and produces technical data sheets that can be printed at the kiosk or faxed or mailed to the customer. The system has resulted in a 400 percent increase in qualified sales leads.

Gary Armstrong and Philip Kotler, *Marketing: An Introduction,* 9th ed., ɔ. 425, © 2009. Reprinted by permission of Pearson Education, Inc., Upper Saddle River, New Jersey.

2

1   It was Michael's first day at the university. Besides feeling a little overwhelmed, he was concerned about obtaining the right signatures from the right advisors, dealing with the financial aid office, locating the right buildings, and finding his classrooms. During orientation week, Michael had also found registering for classes to be a nightmare. Long lines. Short tempers. And he couldn't get into all the classes he wanted, at least not at convenient times. Michael certainly didn't relish the thought of being in class at 8:00 every week-day morning.

2   Michael had signed up for some of the usual courses: Math, History, Art Appreciation, English, and Human Sexuality. These classes sounded interesting, but the idea of also taking Human Sexuality really appealed to him: "Taking a sex class is going to be a breeze! I'm already an expert. I probably won't even have to open the book. I can look for dates. X-rated videos. Sexy stories. Way to go, Mike! At least I'll have one 'easy A' this semester!"

3   If you're like Michael, your initial expectation of a course in human sexuality might be to watch sex education films, listen to people talk about their sex lives, and follow the instructor's discussion of sexual activities you've already experienced. You may see the class as a way of meeting potential sexual partners or maintaining a good grade point average. If you already think of yourself as a sexual expert, you may even consider this course a less than valuable way to spend your time.

4   You'll soon realize, however, that studying human sexuality involves much more than just reading stimulating sexual case studies and watching videos. You'll encounter a great deal of new material. You'll spend time rethinking your values and attitudes about sexuality. The differing viewpoints of your classmates will at times challenge your beliefs about what is acceptable. You'll come to view human sexuality for what it is—a beautiful and integral, but complex, part of life.

George Zgourides, *Human Sexuality,* pp. 2–3

3

High-tech Solution for Surgical Snafu

1   In the leap of faith that is surgery, one can only hope everyone in the operating room gets the sponge count right. In a rare complication of about 3,000 of the 40 million surgeries performed in the United States each year, somebody forgets something inside someone. The majority of those items are surgical gauze sponges.

2   In a study in the *Archives of Surgery* journal, a new technique was reported where a sponge tagged with radio-frequency identification was left inside the cavity. Before the patient's wound was closed, one surgeon passed a hand-held, wand-like scanning device over the patient. The sponge was correctly pinpointed and within three seconds the sponge was found and removed.

3   This study shows that the solution to this type of medical mistake could be technological. Dr. Atul Gawande, a surgeon at Boston's Brigham and Women's Hospital, says, "At first, you think, 'How stupid could nurses and doctors be? This is a problem of negligence.' But if you've ever had to count 52 cards in a deck, you know that once in a while you get it wrong."

4   There's an especially high chance someone will get the count wrong after a catastrophe such as a car accident, when seconds count in saving lives. Dr. Gawande found that what put patients at risk are emergency situations, mid-surgery changes in the operating plan, and obesity.

5   Scissors, scalpels, needles and pins are also left behind in an estimated 1,000 surgeries a year. But metal, at least, can be detected in an X-ray. It's the soft stuff, such as a cotton swabs, that are more likely to be left inside a patient.

6   Other technologies to catch wayward surgical hardware and soft fabrics are being tested. This includes sponges with bar codes or ones implanted with tiny bits of metal that will respond to metal detectors.

4

Today's Athletes Owe Everything to Ali

He Took a Stand and Lost Much of His Career. Would Anyone Do That Now?

MAX WALLACE

1   This weekend, the nation's newspapers are caught up in two separate events. While the news sections focus on the 25th anniversary of the end of the

Vietnam War, the sports pages are dissecting last night's heavyweight championship fight between Lennox Lewis and Michael Grant.

2   But 33 years ago this week, Vietnam and the world of boxing loudly converged on both the front page and the sports page when Muhammad Ali refused to be inducted into the United States Army.

3   Ordinarily, such anniversaries offer little more than a chance for reflective nostalgia. But this one may present a long-overdue opportunity to reassess the legacy of Ali and the broader impact of the modern athlete on society.

4   Before Ali came along, the history of American boxing had mirrored the social and political currents of the day. When Jack Johnson became the first African-American heavyweight champion in 1908, his victory was widely considered a blow to white supremacy and declared by *The New York Herald* "an event more calamitous than the San Francisco earthquake."

5   Subsequent Johnson victories set off race riots in American cities. The novelist Jack London publicly implored the former champion Jim Jeffries to come out of retirement to "restore the title to White America." After Johnson was persecuted by the government and subsequently run out of the country, white boxers simply refused to fight blacks for more than a generation.

6   When Joe Louis came along 30 years later in a new era of condescending tolerance toward blacks, his handlers counseled him to act docile, humble and obedient—a "credit to his race." America accepted Louis, even admired him, and his meek image was to become the expected model for African-Americans for another quarter century. Once Louis outlived his usefulness, his mob handlers discarded him and he died penniless.

7   Ali was also determined to be a credit to his race. But for him, those words had a very different meaning than they did for Joe Louis.

8   The seeds of the revolution Ali led were planted in February 1964 when Cassius Clay defeated the heavily favored Sonny Liston to win his first heavyweight championship.

9   The following day, Clay, bolstered by his mentor Malcolm X, stepped in front of a room of journalists to declare his conversion to the Nation of Islam. After fielding hostile questions, he voiced the words that would become his lifelong anthem and would forever change the world of sports: "I don't have to be what you want me to be."

10   His affiliation with the Black Muslims, and subsequent name change, made him a national pariah and outraged many of the country's leading sportswriters, who were stunned by an athlete who dared to voice a political opinion. As a result, most of America's sports pages continued to refer to Ali by what he called his "slave name," Cassius Clay.

11   But if his religious conversion inspired petty revenge, this paled in comparison to what came next.

12   In 1966, J. Edgar Hoover and the American government, paranoid about Ali's influence on young blacks, decided that the easiest way to keep a troublemaker in line would be to keep him under the watchful eye of Uncle Sam for two years. Although Ali had already been declared ineligible for military service, the Army changed its eligibility standards, and suddenly Ali was targeted for induction.

13   When the notice came as he was training for his next bout, Ali uttered the phrase that would earn him a place as the most despised man in America: "I ain't got no quarrel with the Vietcong. No Vietcong ever called me nigger."

14   Ali's words set off a firestorm, earning him vicious condemnation throughout much of the news media and the country.

15   Widespread protests against the Vietnam War had not yet begun, but with that one phrase, Ali articulated the reason to oppose the war for a generation of young Americans, and his words served as a touchstone for the racial and antiwar upheavals that would rock the 60's. Ali's example inspired Martin Luther King Jr.— who had been reluctant to alienate the Johnson administration and its support of the civil-rights agenda—to voice his own opposition to the war for the first time.

16   Ali, claiming conscientious objector status, instinctively understood that America had no business in Vietnam where, in the words of Stokely Carmichael, "Black folks are fighting a war against yellow folks so that white folks can keep a land they stole from red folks."

17   The government offered Ali the same opportunity given to Joe Louis in World War II. He could fight exhibitions for the troops and keep his title without seeing a battlefield. But Ali refused, saying, "I'd be just as guilty as the ones doing the killing."

18   Within minutes of his induction refusal on April 28, 1967, the New York State Athletic Commission stripped him of his title, declaring his actions "detrimental to the best interests of boxing," despite having granted licenses to more than 200 murderers, rapists and other convicted felons over the years. Ali's most serious offense was a traffic violation two years earlier.

19   He was convicted of draft evasion and sentenced to five years in prison, a sentence subsequently overturned by the Supreme Court, after Ali endured four years in internal exile and a legal battle tougher than fighting Liston, Joe Frazier and George Foreman combined. He lost millions of dollars and the peak years of his career. Through it all, he declared, "My principles are more important than the money or my title."

20   When he finally regained his title seven years later and emerged as a world-wide icon, he spent most of his time and money outside the ring fighting for economic justice and human rights. His example was cited by Arthur Ashe, Billie Jean King and others as they fought their own battles to change the face of sports and society.

21   The sports sociologist Harry Edwards argues that Ali's actions paved the way for the unparalleled influence of Michael Jordan and other present-day superstars.

"Before Ali," Edwards said, "black athletes were merely 20th-century gladiators in the service of white society."

22   And how have today's superstar athletes carried on Ali's legacy of principles over profit? By shilling running shoes made under sweatshop conditions in Third World countries, including Vietnam. By demonstrating a consistent example of greed and bad behavior. And by pretending the world outside sports does not exist.

23   It is time to measure athletes for more than just their athletic accomplishments and to hold them accountable for their behavior outside the arena, to recognize their significant impact on a large segment of society. Today's generation needs sports heroes whose principles and aspirations extend beyond the next pair of Air Nikes.

24   Today, Ali—despite his Parkinson's syndrome—spends more than 200 days a year on the road as a roving ambassador for human rights and as a spokesman for the Jubilee 2000 campaign to cancel Third World debt. Now a traditional Muslim, he regularly denounces the anti-Semitism of Louis Farrakhan, the leader of the movement he once belonged to.

25   It's time to make Muhammad Ali, not today's two-dimensional corporate pitchmen, the standard by which all athletes are judged.

ACTIVITY 7

DIRECTIONS: *Find the topic and central message of the following poem, remembering to answer the questions "What is this about?" and "What is the central message that the writer is communicating about the topic?"*

A Quiet House in the Suburbs

MARK HILLRINGHOUSE

I'm the only one home
until the mail arrives and the kids return
from school. Sunlight falls on my face
as yet unshaved. The lazy and the industrious
5   live in two separate worlds. Day laborers and
commuters go their separate ways.
I'm blessed to have blue skies and summer
clouds in October. The leaves turn golden
and shimmer in the light breeze.
10   Without a burning desire it is impossible
to write great poems. I should pay bills
and organize bank statements but spend

my time listening to birds and sipping coffee.
A screened porch,
15   a half-finished house,
an old Chevy—a salary
that only gets me through three weeks of the month
though I am not starving or unclothed.
I don't bother keeping up appearances.
20   I pursue my daydreams in quiet
passing one day after another reading poems.
I know I should rake and weed but let nature
take over. Human affairs have little to do
with this world: from ancient times
25   politics and government have not changed.
People still suffer poverty and despair.
But here on this porch mornings and evenings,
I forget my chores and clear a space for dreaming.
The squirrels chatter and busy themselves for winter,
30   the crows fight for scraps of leftover food,
fallen leaves cover my yard and driveway.
I have not swept, I have not washed or prepared dinner,
I will do nothing all day.

■ Summarizing and Paraphrasing

If you truly understand reading material, you should be able first to interpret it, then to condense or shorten it, and finally to put it into your own words. When you condense information, you are *summarizing* the main points by using many of the writer's own terms. Putting the information into your own words is called *paraphrasing*—a skill you use when writing out unstated main ideas. In short, paraphrasing involves rewording or substituting your own words—not your opinions—for the author's, except for certain key terminology essential to the meaning of the material. We often use both summarizing and paraphrasing in our everyday lives. For example, when you try to explain to someone what happened in class or what a particular movie or television program was about, you are summarizing and paraphrasing. In those instances, you generally use your own words to provide a short description without relating, word for word, everything that occurred.

Given the vast amount of information normally presented in a typical college reading assignment, you need to find a way to reduce the information to manageable proportions. Summarizing and paraphrasing, when you do it correctly, should make textbook material easier to learn and remember. To summarize you must be able to pick out the most important information usually found in main ideas, major details, and context definitions. Underlining and highlighting with a marker are techniques that help you focus better by getting you more actively involved in your reading, while enabling you to separate the information you need for your summary.

Underlining and highlighting are very useful for several reasons. First, the physical act forces you to be more attentive, thereby aiding your concentration; you are less likely to daydream or fall asleep. Second, in determining what you should underline or highlight, you first must evaluate carefully what you are reading, which results in better comprehension. Third, because underlining and highlighting involve increased concentration, thought, and evaluation, they help you remember. Finally, when done properly, underlining and highlighting help you to locate quickly only the most important information when you review; you need not read the material in its entirety again. In short, make it a habit to underline or highlight with a marker, particularly when you are dealing with textbook material.

The major problem with underlining and highlighting is that students sometimes do too much, finding it difficult to determine what is important. You can avoid this problem by concentrating only on the information you find in main ideas, major details, and context definitions. Use patterns of organization and context clues to help you locate them.

After underlining or highlighting and then summarizing material, you can attempt to paraphrase it. To do this correctly, you must understand fully what the writer is saying; otherwise, you may omit important information and lose some of the meaning. For example, look at the passage that follows:

There are three types of noise that can block communication. The first, external noise, includes those obvious things that make it difficult to hear, as well as many other kinds of distractions. For instance, too much cigarette smoke in a crowded room might make it hard for you to pay attention to another person, and sitting in the rear of an auditorium might make a speaker's remarks unclear. External noise can disrupt communication almost anywhere in our model—in the sender, channel, message, or receiver.

The second type of noise is physiological. A hearing disorder is probably the most obvious type of physiological barrier, although many more exist. Consider, for instance, the difficulty you experience as a listener when you are suffering from a cold or are very tired. In the same way you might speak less when you have a sore throat or a headache.

Psychological noise refers to forces within the sender or receiver that make these people less able to express or understand the message clearly. For instance, an outdoorsman might exaggerate the size and number of fish caught in order to convince himself and others of his talents. In the same way, a student might become so upset upon learning that she failed a test that she would be unable (perhaps unwilling is a better word) to clearly understand where she went wrong.

Notice how the main idea and the details (some of which are organized by the simple listing pattern of organization) have been underlined to make them stand out. A summary of the passage would read something like the following:

> External, physiological, and psychological noise can block communication. External noise, which includes distractions that make it difficult to hear, can disrupt communication in the sender, channel, message, or receiver. There are many physiological barriers, such as a hearing disorder. Psychological noise refers to forces within the sender or receiver that make these people less able to express or understand the message.

Although the information has been condensed, many of the writer's words have been repeated, which by itself does not necessarily mean that true understanding has taken place. Therefore, if we were to go one final step and paraphrase the passage, we might end up with something like the following:

> Outside distractions, physical problems, and mental factors can all interfere with communication. Distractions can disrupt the sender, channel, message, or receiver. Any kind of a physical disorder, such as a hearing or speaking problem, makes it difficult to communicate. Finally, forces within the mind of the sender or receiver can have a negative effect on a message.

As you can see, very few of the writer's words have been used to paraphrase the passage, but the most important information has been included through the use of other, perhaps more familiar, terms. The ability to paraphrase demonstrates a more complete understanding of whatever you are reading because you are able to translate the material into words that are more meaningful to you, which should make the information easier to learn and remember.

Until this point the skills of summarizing and paraphrasing have been separated for purposes of discussion. However, you may want to combine them as they become more familiar to you. For example, look at the following passage, paying particular attention to the sentences that have been underlined:

One of the first women to make a career in psychology was Mary Calkins. When Henry Durant founded Wellesley College in 1870, he decided to hire only women to teach the all-female student body. But he could find no woman with an advanced degree in psychology. Finally, in 1890, he hired a bright young woman, Mary Calkins, who had a B.A. degree in classics, to teach psychology, promising that he would pay for her graduate education in psychology. Then the problem was to find a graduate program that would accept a female student. After much debate and stiff resistance, nearby Harvard University finally agreed to let her attend graduate classes, although at first it would not allow her to register officially as a student. In 1895, when she passed the final examination for the Ph.D. degree, one of her professors remarked that she had performed better on the examination than had any other student in the history of the department.

The Harvard administration, however, was still unwilling to grant a Ph.D. degree to a woman. It suggested a compromise. It would grant her a Ph.D. degree from Radcliffe College, the recently established women's undergraduate college associated with Harvard. She refused, declaring that to accept the compromise would violate the high ideals of education. She never gave in, and neither did Harvard. Although Mary Calkins never received a Ph.D. degree, she became a pioneer in psychological research, inventing a technique of studying memory, known as the paired-associates method, that is still used today.

James W. Kalat, *Introduction to Psychology*

Remember that the goal here is to first reduce the amount of information by eliminating unimportant material. So concentrating on the topic, main ideas, major details, and context definitions is crucial. Next, the information should be translated into the reader's own words—except those words used by the writer that are crucial to the meaning of the passage. A summary that has been paraphrased could possibly look like the following:

Henry Durant founded Wellesley College in 1870 and hired Mary Calkins to teach psychology. Because she did not have a degree in that field, she tried to get into a graduate program. After much resistance because she was a woman, Harvard agreed to have her attend classes. Although she passed the Ph.D. exam with a performance that was the best ever, Harvard refused to give her the degree because she was a woman. Instead it offered to have Radcliffe College, which was an undergraduate woman's college associated with Harvard, grant her the degree. She refused to accept the offer and never received her Ph.D. However, she still contributed to the field by inventing a way of studying memory called the paired-associates method that is still used today.

Notice how only certain key words, such as the names of the schools, the names of individuals, and specialized terms such as "paired-associates method," are included. Nevertheless, the information is condensed and different words are used without losing the basic meaning of the passage. Thus, the material should be easier to understand, learn, and remember. Make it a practice to underline or highlight and then summarize and paraphrase your reading assignments whenever you can.

In this textbook, you can practice your underlining, highlighting, summarizing, and paraphrasing skills, particularly when distinguishing among opposing viewpoints and rationales as part of the approach to contemporary issues introduced in Chapter 4. Also, at the end of this and all the remaining chapters there is "Looking Back," which asks you to summarize or paraphrase the most important points you learned from the chapter and determine how they can be put to use in other classes. Because of the importance of these skills, take advantage of the opportunities provided to practice them.

ACTIVITY 8

Directions: Underline or highlight the most important information in the short story that follows and then summarize and/or paraphrase. Share your work as instructed by your professor.

The Tell-Tale Heart

Edgar Allan Poe

1   TRUE!—nervous—very, very dreadfully nervous I had been and am; but why *will* you say that I am mad? The disease had sharpened my senses—not destroyed—not dulled them. Above all was the sense of hearing acute. I heard all things in the heaven and in the earth. I heard many things in hell. How, then, am I mad? Hearken! and observe how healthily—how calmly I can tell you the whole story.

2   It is impossible to say how first the idea entered my brain; but once conceived, it haunted me day and night. Object there was none. Passion there was none. I loved the old man. He had never wronged me. He had never given me insult. For his gold I had no desire. I think it was his eye! Yes, it was this! He had the eye of a vulture—a pale blue eye, with a film over it. Whenever it fell upon me, my blood ran cold; and

so by degrees—very gradually—I made up my mind to take the life of the old man, and thus rid myself of the eye for ever.

3   Now this is the point. You fancy me mad. Madmen know nothing. But you should have seen *me*. You should have seen how wisely I proceeded—with what caution—with what foresight—with what dissimulation I went to work! I was never kinder to the old man than during the whole week before I killed him. And every night, about midnight, I turned the latch of his door and opened it—oh, so gently! And then, when I had made an opening sufficient for my head, I put in a dark lantern, all closed, closed, so that no light shone out, and then I thrust in my head. Oh, you would have laughed to see how cunningly I thrust it in! I moved it slowly—very, very slowly, so that I might not disturb the old man's sleep. It took me an hour to place my whole head within the opening so far that I could see him as he lay upon his bed. Ha!—would a madman have been so wise as this? And then, when my head was well in the room, I undid the lantern cautiously—oh, so cautiously—cautiously (for the hinges creaked)—I undid it just so much that a single thin ray fell upon the vulture eye. And this I did for seven long nights—every night just at midnight—but I found the eye always closed; and so it was impossible to do the work; for it was not the old man who vexed me, but his Evil Eye. And every morning, when the day broke, I went boldly into the chamber, and spoke courageously to him, calling him by name in a hearty tone, and inquiring how he had passed the night. So you see he would have been a very profound old man, indeed, to suspect that every night, just at twelve, I looked in upon him while he slept.

4   Upon the eighth night I was more than usually cautious in opening the door. A watch's minute hand moves more quickly than did mine. Never before that night, had I *felt* the extent of my own powers—of my sagacity. I could scarcely contain my feelings of triumph. To think that there I was, opening the door, little by little, and he not even to dream of my secret deeds or thoughts. I fairly chuck-led at the idea; and perhaps he heard me; for he moved on the bed suddenly, as if startled. Now you may think that I drew back—but no. His room was as black as pitch with the thick darkness (for the shutters were close fastened, through fear of robbers), and so I knew that he could not see the opening of the door, and I kept pushing it on steadily, steadily.

5   I had my head in, and was about to open the lantern, when my thumb slipped upon the tin fastening, and the old man sprang up in bed, crying out—"Who's there?"

6   I kept quite still and said nothing. For a whole hour I did not move a muscle, and in the meantime I did not hear him lie down. He was still sitting up in the bed listening;—just as I have done, night after night, hearkening to the death watches in the wall.

7   Presently I heard a slight groan, and I knew it was the groan of mortal terror. It was not a groan of pain or of grief—oh, no!—it was the low stifled sound that arises from the bottom of the soul when overcharged with awe. I knew the sound well. Many a night, just at midnight, when all the world slept, it has welled up from my own bosom, deepening, with its dreadful echo, the terrors that distracted me. I say I knew it well. I knew what the old man felt, and pitied him, although I chuckled at heart. I knew that he had been lying awake ever since the first slight noise, when he had turned in the bed. His fears had been ever since growing upon him. He had been trying to fancy them causeless, but could not. He had been saying to himself—"It is nothing but the wind in the chimney—it is only a mouse crossing the floor," or "it is merely a cricket which has made a single chirp." Yes, he had been trying to comfort himself with these suppositions: but he had found all in vain. *All in vain;* because Death, in approaching him had stalked with his black shadow before him, and enveloped the victim. And it was the mournful influence of the unperceived shadow that caused him to feel—although he neither saw nor heard—to *feel* the presence of my head within the room.

8   When I had waited a long time, very patiently, without hearing him lie down, I resolved to open a little—a very, very little crevice in the lantern. So I opened it—you cannot imagine how stealthily, stealthily—until, at length a single dim ray, like the thread of the spider, shot from out the crevice and fell full upon the vulture eye.

9   It was open—wide, wide open—and I grew furious as I gazed upon it. I saw it with perfect distinctness—all a dull blue, with a hideous veil over it that chilled the very marrow in my bones; but I could see nothing else of the old man's face or person: for I had directed the ray, as if by instinct, precisely upon the damned spot.

10   And have I not told you that what you mistake for madness is but overacuteness of the senses?—now, I say, there came to my ears a low, dull, quick sound, such as a watch makes when enveloped in cotton. I knew *that* sound well, too. It was the beating of the old man's heart. It increased my fury, as the beating of a drum stimulates the soldier into courage.

11   But even yet I refrained and kept still. I scarcely breathed. I held the lantern motionless. I tried how steadily I could maintain the ray upon the eye. Meantime the hellish tattoo of the heart increased. It grew quicker and quicker, and louder and louder every instant. The old man's terror *must* have been extreme! It grew louder, I say, louder every moment!—do you mark me well? I have told you that I am nervous: so I am. And now at the dead hour of the night, amid the dreadful silence of that old house, so strange a noise as this excited me to uncontrollable terror. Yet, for some minutes longer I

refrained and stood still. But the beating grew louder, louder! I thought the heart must burst. And now a new anxiety seized me—the sound would be heard by a neighbour! The old man's hour had come! With a loud yell, I threw open the lantern and leaped into the room. He shrieked once—once only. In an instant I dragged him to the floor, and pulled the heavy bed over him. I then smiled gaily, to find the deed so far done. But, for many minutes, the heart beat on with a muffled sound. This, however, did not vex me; it would not be heard through the wall. At length it ceased. The old man was dead. I removed the bed and examined the corpse. Yes, he was stone, stone dead. I placed my hand upon the heart and held it there many minutes. There was no pulsation. He was stone dead. His eye would trouble me no more.

12   If still you think me mad, you will think so no longer when I describe the wise precautions I took for the concealment of the body. The night waned, and I worked hastily, but in silence. First of all I dismembered the corpse. I cut off the head and the arms and the legs.

13   I then took up three planks from the flooring of the chamber, and deposited all between the scantlings. I then replaced the boards so cleverly, so cunningly that no human eye—not even *his*—could have detected anything wrong. There was nothing to wash out—no stain of any kind—no blood-spot whatever. I had been too wary for that. A tub had caught all—ha! ha!

14   When I had made an end of these labours, it was four o'clock—still dark as midnight. As the bell sounded the hour, there came a knocking at the street door. I went down to open it with a light heart,—for what had I *now* to fear? There entered three men, who introduced themselves, with perfect suavity, as officers of the police. A shriek had been heard by a neighbour during the night; suspicion of foul play had been aroused; information had been lodged at the police office, and they (the officers) had been deputed to search the premises.

15   I smiled,—for *what* had I to fear? I bade the gentlemen welcome. The shriek, I said, was my own in a dream. The old man, I mentioned, was absent in the country. I took my visitors all over the house. I bade them search—search *well*. I led them, at length, to *his* chamber. I showed them his treasures, secure, undisturbed. In the enthusiasm of my confidence, I brought chairs into the room, and desired them *here* to rest from their fatigues, while I myself, in the wild audacity of my perfect triumph, placed my own seat upon the very spot beneath which reposed the corpse of the victim.

16   The officers were satisfied. My *manner* had convinced them. I was singularly at ease. They sat, and while I answered cheerily, they chatted of familiar things. But, ere long, I felt myself getting pale and wished them gone. My head ached, and I fancied a ringing in my ears: but still they sat and still they chatted. The ringing became more distinct:—it continued and became more distinct: I talked more freely to get rid of the feeling: but it continued and gained definiteness—until, at length, I found that the noise was *not* within my ears.

17   No doubt I now grew *very* pale;—but I talked more fluently, and with a heightened voice. Yet the sound increased—and what could I do? It was *a low, dull, quick sound—much such a sound as a watch makes when enveloped in cotton.* I gasped for breath—and yet the officers heard it not. I talked more quickly—more vehemently; but the noise steadily increased. I arose and argued about trifles, in a high key and with violent gesticulations; but the noise steadily increased. Why *would* they not be gone? I paced the floor to and fro with heavy strides, as if excited to fury by the observations of the men—but the noise steadily increased. Oh God! what *could* I do? I foamed—I raved—I swore! I swung the chair upon which I had been sitting, and grated it upon the boards, but the noise arose over all and continually increased. It grew louder—louder—*louder!* And still the men chatted pleasantly, and smiled. Was it possible they heard not? Almighty God!—no, no! They heard!—they suspected!—they *knew!*—they were making a mockery of my horror!—this I thought, and this I think. But anything was better than this agony! Anything was more tolerable than this derision! I could bear those hypocritical smiles no longer! I felt that I must scream or die! and now—again!—hark! louder! louder! louder! *louder!*

18   "Villains!" I shrieked, "dissemble no more! I admit the deed!—tear up the planks! here, here!—it is the beating of his hideous heart!"

Tales of Mystery and Imagination, pp. 17–21

CRITICAL READING

Do you have an opinion about a current issue or controversy? What are the pros and cons of this issue? Investigate with YouTube (www.youtube.com), and find two videos that demonstrate a pro and a con about an issue that you have an opinion about. Some suggestions might be "dangers of Facebook," "radiation and cell phones," or video game violence." Share your videos with the class as instructed by your professor.

THE FAIR EVANGELINE

Remember to follow these steps:

- first, read the narrative and all the questions
- second, examine the picture carefully
- third, answer the questions in the order they appear, and come up with the solution

Have fun!

The Admirable Farragut was not only a talented painter, but one of the fastest who ever lived: He could complete a portrait in five minutes. His all-time record was a landscape done in 2 minutes and 36 ^{11}/100 seconds.

In fact, his only shortcoming was that his amours went almost as fast as his brush, often with disastrous results. But no other tragedy approached that of the Fair Evangeline, whose body was found in a shallow grave one moonlit night.

"I expected to meet her at a ruined house on the shores of Lake Rembrandt," the Admirable Farragut told my cousin Phoebe, to whom he tried to sell the painting which is reproduced here. "Unfortunately," he said, "she never arrived, but while waiting, I painted this landscape exactly the way I saw it, including a figure a mile away from me and highlighted by the moonlight reflected from the lake. After I'd finished, I picked up my field glasses and focused on the figure, which I could then see clearly. He was digging a grave, and to my surprise I recognized him. He was—but his name escapes me at the moment, except that it's the same last name as his wife's, the Fair Evangeline, whose last name is—Good Grief! She never told me!"

The husband in question, C. Starrs, was an astronomer of note. He told my cousin Phoebe he'd been wandering around Lake Rembrandt in the hope of sighting a new comet. When the police questioned him, Starrs said, "I saw the man who was digging the grave, and I recognized him as the Admirable Farragut."

After that, Starrs refused to speak, except to make a brief statement. "The Admirable Farragut," he said, "is a lousy painter."

My cousin Phoebe agreed, but didn't press the matter. Instead, she pointed out that the case hinged on proving which of the two men was a liar, of which there was no doubt.

Whom did she accuse, and why?

Questions

1. Is there any evidence to support the Admirable Farragut's statement?   ☐ Yes   ☐ No
2. Is there any evidence to support C. Starr's statement?   ☐ Yes   ☐ No
3. Does the painting itself contain any evidence indicating the time when the grave digger was at work?   ☐ Yes   ☐ No
4. Did the Admirable Farragut have a possible motive?   ☐ Yes   ☐ No
5. Did C. Starrs have a possible motive?   ☐ Yes   ☐ No
6. Where was Farragut standing when he painted the picture? _____
7. Who killed the Fair Evangeline? _____

Text and illustration from Lawrence Treat, *Crime and Puzzlement—My Cousin Phoebe: 24 Solve-Them-Yourself Picture Mysteries* (Henry Holt and Co., 1991) pp. 7–8

The Fair Evangeline

LOOKING BACK . . . LOOKING FORWARD

To check your progress in meeting this chapter's learning objectives, log in to www.myreadinglab.com, go to your Study Plan, and click on the Reading Skills tab. Choose the appropriate chapter topics (Main Ideas, Supporting Details, Patterns of Organization, Outlining and Summarizing) from the list of subtopics. Read and view the assets in the Review Materials section, then complete the Practices and Tests in the Activities section. You can check your scores by clicking on the Gradebook tab.

THINK AGAIN!

What is the topic of these two photos? Identify the central message implied in these photos.

1

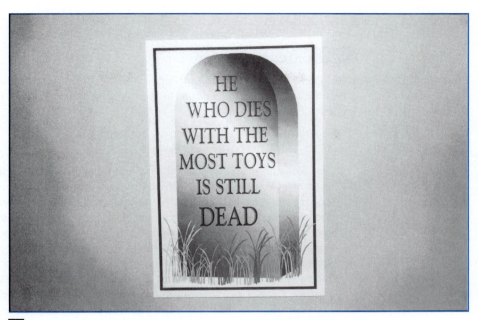

2

Name _____ Date _____

MASTERY TEST 2–1

DIRECTIONS: Write out the main idea for each of the following selections. Write out your thinking in how you came to your conclusion(s). Your instructor will give you feedback to your responses.

1

Many people report that speaking in front of an audience is their number-one fear. Even many experienced and polished speakers have some anxiety about delivering an oral presentation, but they use this nervous energy to their advantage, letting it propel them into working hard on each presentation, preparing well in advance, and rehearsing until they're satisfied with their delivery. They know that once they begin speaking and concentrate on their ideas, enthusiasm will quell anxiety. They know, too, that the symptoms of anxiety are usually imperceptible to listeners, who cannot see or hear a racing heart, upset stomach, cold hands, and worried thoughts. Even speakers who describe themselves as nervous usually appear confident and calm to their audiences.

H. Ramsey Fowler et al., *The Little, Brown Handbook,* 8th ed., pp. 923–924

Main idea: _____

_____

_____

2

The term "technical profession" applies to a broad spectrum of careers in today's changing workplace where technology is making astonishingly rapid advances and boundaries between companies, countries, and continents are blurring and jobs are being redefined. In the past, the term "technical" conjured up an image of a male engineer with his T-square and slide rule, who made his living by his prowess at mathematical calculations. Today the computer has replaced the slide rule, and the technical professionals include an expanding cast of characters: women as well as men, engineers and scientists of all types, computer programmers, MIS professionals, technicians, laboratory personnel, biotechnical workers—anyone whose job entails working with specialized skills and knowledge in the hands-on fields of science, engineering, and technology.

Kristin R. Woolever, *Writing for the Technical Professions,* p. 1

Main idea: _____

_____

_____

3

For most people, choosing a spouse has never been an inexpensive or easy activity. Not long ago, some people were arguing that the institution of marriage was dying. Yet recent statistics show that the opposite is true: The percentage of Americans getting married has increased. Spouse selection is clearly an activity that most people eventually choose to engage in. A variety of considerations are involved. For example, the ease or difficulty of obtaining a divorce may have an effect on how spouses are chosen; so may the factor called love. Is there a rational, economic reason why individuals prefer a marriage in which there is mutual love? To answer this question, you need to know about the nature of economics.

Roger LeRoy Miller, *Economics Today*, p. 3

Main idea: _____

_____

_____

4

Firearms-related violence is a major societal issue in the United States. More than 300,000 violent crimes involving firearms are committed each year, killing nearly 30,000 people and injuring another 80,000, costing more than $100 billion for medical, security, and legal services. Although gun sales are legal, most crimes are committed using weapons obtained through diverted sales. The distribution channel for this product is multitiered, with manufacturers selling to wholesale distributors that sell to dealers who sell to the public. Several federal, state, and local laws regulate the sale of firearms. The federal enforcement agency is the Bureau of Alcohol, Tobacco, Firearms, and Explosives (known as the ATF or BATF). Firearms are sold to the public by BATF-licensed dealers, known as federal firearms licensees (FFLs). The FFLs must follow laws and safeguards, selling firearms only to individuals who are considered legal purchasers (for example, over 18 years of age, not a convicted criminal, not mentally defective). However, the major channels for firearms diversion include gun shows, straw man purchases (that is, a legal purchaser buys a gun on behalf of someone who cannot legally buy one), theft, nonstore FFLs (also known as "basement bandits" or "car trunk dealers"), unlicensed sellers, and corrupt FFLs. Gun control advocates, public safety groups, and several municipal governments have launched lawsuits against manufacturers, distributors, and dealers, claiming that industry members are not doing enough to stop diverted sales.

Gary Armstrong and Philip Kotler, *Marketing: An Introduction*, 9th ed., p. 319

Main idea: _____

_____

_____

5

Currently, 25 nations suffer from chronic water shortages. The number of countries affected by such shortages is expected to increase to at least 90 within ten years. International tension over water availability is increasing rapidly. Currently there are 155 rivers and lakes shared by two or more countries. More than 30 are shared by three countries and 20 are shared by dozens of countries. United Nations estimates suggest that there is a real danger of war erupting in at least 10 areas around the world as a direct result of international competition over water resources. Shortages do not stem from the disappearance of water. The nature of the planet's hydrologic cycle is such that, for the most part, the total supply of freshwater never increases or diminishes. Shortages stem from population growth, misuse and waste, the latter two frequently making water unfit for human consumption.

F. Kurt Cylke Jr., *The Environment,* p. 58

Main idea: _____

_____

_____

6

The environmental movement is a child of the sixties that has stayed its course. Where other manifestations of that decade of protest—pacifism, the counter-culture and the civil rights struggle—have either lost out or lost their way, the green wave shows no sign of abating. The environmental movement has refused to go away and, some would say, refused to grow up, retaining the vigor and intensity but also the impatience and intolerance of an ever-youthful social movement. Alone among the movements of the sixties, it has gained steadily in power, prestige and, what is perhaps most important, public appeal.

Ramachandra Guha, *Environmentalism: A Global History,* p. 1

Main idea: _____

_____

_____

7

All relationships involve a degree of risk. However, without the risk of friendships, intimacy, and shared experiences, most of us would not grow, would not be sufficiently stimulated, and life would hold no excitement. Those of us who choose to take risks—who let ourselves feel, love, and express our deepest emotions—are vulnerable to great love as well as great unhappiness. Taking a look at our intimate and non-intimate relationships, components of our sexual identity, our gender roles, and our sexual orientation may help us better understand who we are in our life and our relationships. Ultimately, this understanding will prepare us to make healthful, responsible, and satisfying decisions about our relationships and sexuality.

Rebecca J. Donatelle, Health: The Basics, 4th ed., p. 96

Main idea: _____

_____

_____

8

What is the particular problem you have to resolve? Defining the problem is the critical step. The accurate definition of a problem affects all the steps that follow. If a problem is defined inaccurately, every other step in the decision-making process will be based on that incorrect point. A motorist tells a mechanic that her car is running rough. This is a symptom of a problem or problems. The mechanic begins by diagnosing the possible causes of a rough-running engine, checking each possible cause based on the mechanic's experience. The mechanic may find one problem—a faulty spark plug. If this is the problem, changing the plug will result in a smooth-running engine. If not, then a problem still exists. Only a road test will tell for sure. Finding a solution to the problem will be greatly aided by its proper identification. The consequences of not properly defining the problem are wasted time and energy. There is also the possibility of hearing "What, that again! We just solved that problem last month, or at least we thought we did."

Joseph T. Straub and Raymond F. Attner, Introduction to Business

Main idea: _____

_____

_____

9

Many reasons have been advanced to account for nonreporting of crime. Some victims of rape and assault fear the embarrassment of public disclosure and interrogation by the police. Increasingly, evidence reveals that much violence occurs between persons who know each other—spouses, lovers, relatives—but the passions of the moment take on a different character when the victim is asked to testify against a family member. Another reason for nonreporting is that lower socioeconomic groups fear police involvement. In some neighborhoods, residents believe that the arrival of the law for one purpose may result in the discovery of other illicit activities, such as welfare fraud, housing code violations, or the presence of persons on probation or parole. In many of these same places the level of police protection has been minimal in the past, and residents feel that they will get little assistance. Finally, the value of property lost by larceny, robbery, or burglary may not be worth the effort of a police investigation. Many citizens are deterred from reporting a crime by unwillingness to become "involved," go to the station house to fill out papers, perhaps go to court, or to appear at a police lineup. All these aspects of the criminal process may result in lost workdays and in the expense of travel and child care. Even then, the stolen item may go unrecovered. As these examples suggest, multitudes of people feel that it is rational not to report criminal incidents because the costs outweigh the gains.

George F. Cole, *The American System of Criminal Justice*

Main idea: _____

_____

_____

10

Imagine you are standing before an enormous clock on which the hands tick away the years of the earth's history. The clock is set so that 24 hours represent the nearly 5-billion-year history of our planet. On this cosmic scale, a single second equals nearly 60,000 years; a single minute, 3.5 million years. The first life on earth—the simple one-celled organisms that emerged in the oceans some 2.5 to 3.5 billion years ago—do not make their appearance until at least 7 hours on the clock have passed by. The dinosaurs appear at about the twenty-third hour; they walk the planet for less than 42 minutes, then disappear forever. On this 24-hour clock, the first humanlike creatures appear during the last 2 minutes (4.5 million years ago), and *Homo sapiens* emerges in the last 4 seconds, some 250,000 years ago. What we call human history has barely appeared at all. Written languages, cities, and agriculture, which date back some 12,000 years, emerge only in the last quarter second, representing not even a tick.

On a planetary scale, human beings are very recent arrivals indeed, and what we proudly refer to as human history barely registers. Yet, although we arrived only an instant ago, we have certainly made our presence known. Our population has exploded a thousandfold during the last 17 seconds on the planetary clock, from five million people before written language heralded the dawn of human history to nearly six billion people today. Within 40 years, another five billion people will be added to our crowded planet. Human beings already occupy every corner of the earth, crowding out other forms of plant and animal life. Thanks to modern science, technology, and industry, each of us today is capable of consuming a vastly greater amount of the planet's limited resources than were our prehistoric ancestors. The damage to our planet caused by this explosion in the population is one of the major global issues facing the world today.

P. Appelbaum and William J. Chambliss, *Sociology,* p. 4

Main idea: _____

_____

_____

Name _____ Date _____

MASTERY TEST 2–2

DIRECTIONS: *Identify the pattern of organization for each of the following passages.*

1

Managing stress is not unlike training to participate in any sport. Those who are healthy are in good physical condition, get proper amounts of rest, and eat a healthy diet typically perform well. Such individuals have the physical endurance and strength to handle the stresses of the event. In much the same way, we need "to be in shape" to handle the demands and challenges of daily living. People who are physically fit become fatigued less easily; they remain alert to cope with the demands placed upon them; their immune systems are stronger; they possess more energy for handling events in their lives; and they are less susceptible to illnesses.

Anthony F. Grasha, *Practical Applications of Psychology*, p. 413

Pattern of organization: _____

2

The overhead door installation has caused delays and cost overruns for the HOTCELL chamber operation. The door motor terminal strip was not labeled, and the terminals were not consistent. This required significant time for the electrical contractor to troubleshoot and complete accurate terminations. The overhead door installer was not able to provide assistance, since he had no way of knowing how they were factory wired. In addition, at least one motor was factory wired incorrectly, which was corrected by the electrical contractor. The door limit switch and safety edges have had to be periodically reset on frequent failures of operation. The door seals have also been a problem. In addition, the wall panels have had to be returned because of a lack of fit at the joints.

Kristin R. Woolever, *Writing for the Technical Professions*, p. 316

Pattern of organization: _____

3

1   Although it was easy to romanticize the West, that region lent itself better to the realistic approach. Almost of necessity, novelists writing about the West described coarse characters from the lower levels of society, and dealt with crime and violence. It would have been difficult indeed to write a genteel romance about a mining camp. The outstanding figure of western literature, the first great American realist, was Mark Twain.

2   Twain, whose real name was Samuel L. Clemens, was born in 1835. He grew up in Hannibal, Missouri, on the banks of the Mississippi. After having mastered the printer's trade and worked as a riverboat pilot, he went west to Nevada in 1861. Soon he was publishing humorous stories about the local life under the *nom de plume* Mark Twain. In 1865, while working in California, he wrote "The Celebrated Jumping Frog of Calaveras County," a story that brought him national recognition. A tour of Europe and the Holy Land in 1867–1868 led to the writing of *The Innocents Abroad* (1869), which made him famous.

John A. Garraty, *A Short History of the American Nation*, p. 342

Pattern of organization: _____

4

Rebates are a guarantee by firms to reimburse consumers directly for the purchase of a product, subject to certain conditions. Technically, the term has the same meaning as **refund,** except that *rebate* is used for durables and *refund* for nondurables. The typical conditions for a rebate are the mailing in of (1) the refund voucher, (2) a proof of purchase from the product container or package and (3) the sales receipt. The rebate is similar to the coupon. Thus much of our discussion about coupons would apply to rebates. However, rebates differ from coupons in one important way: they require much greater effort to redeem.

Gerard F. Tellis, *Advertising and Sales Promotion Strategy*, p. 282

Pattern of organization: _____

5

Economics is a social science that employs the same kinds of methods used in other sciences, such as biology, physics, and chemistry. Like these other sciences, economics uses models, or theories. Economic **models,** or **theories,** are simplified representations of the real world that we use to help us understand, explain, and predict economic phenomena in the real world. There are, of course, differences between sciences. The social sciences—especially economics—make little use of laboratory methods in which changes in variables can be explained under controlled conditions. Rather, social scientists, and especially economists, usually have to examine what has already happened in the real world in order to test their models, or theories.

Roger LeRoy Miller, *Economics Today*, p. 9

Pattern of organization: _____

6

1   Illegal immigration is controversial. Critics charge that undocumented workers drive down wages for American citizens while overcrowding schools and hospital emergency rooms. They argue that unauthorized immigrants undermine the

nation's cultural integrity because they create cultural enclaves that resemble their home countries instead of learning English and adopting the customs of the United States. The opponents of illegal immigration favor tighter border controls, strict enforcement of immigration laws, and punishment for American citizens who provide unauthorized immigrants with jobs, housing, health care, and other services.

2   Immigration advocates contend that the United States benefits from immigration, even illegal immigration. They argue that undocumented workers take jobs that citizens do not want and that they pay more in taxes than they receive in government services. An influx of hard-working, well-motivated manual workers enhances the competitiveness of American industry and provides additional jobs for citizens as managers. The defenders of immigration believe that today's immigrants enrich the nation's culture just as did earlier waves of immigrants from Great Britain, Germany, Ireland, Italy, and Poland. Furthermore, the proponents of immigration contend that most recent immigrants are quick to learn English and eager to become citizens so they can participate in the nation's political life. Immigration advocates believe that the United States should grant legal status to undocumented workers who have helped build the nation's economy while enacting a realistic immigration system to enable foreign workers to enter the country legally to find jobs.

Neal Tannahill, *THINK American Government*, p. 20

Pattern of organization: _____

7

1   Economics provides powerful tools to analyze the real world. The large issues, such as inflation, unemployment, the business cycle, economic growth, and balance of international payments, attract the most attention. They influence presidential elections, when we buy new cars and homes, whether we are laid off from jobs, and whether we view the future with optimism or pessimism. The study of the economy in the large is called **macroeconomics.** Macroeconomics treats the economy as a whole. It studies the determinants of total output and its growth, total employment and unemployment, and the general movement in prices.

2   Economists study the small issues as well—how individual businesses behave in different competitive environments; how we choose to use our time; how prices of individual commodities are determined; whether a farmer plants wheat or rye. Although these routine decisions seemingly have a less dramatic effect, they determine the way we live our daily lives. The small issues determine how our television sets and automobiles are built; the prices we pay for cable television; whether soft drinks are sweetened with sugar or corn syrup; whether shoe leather is cut by hand or lasers; and whether the prices of airline tickets rise or fall. This study of the economy in the small is called **microeconomics.** Microeconomics looks at the behavior of the economy's small parts—business firms and households.

Paul R. Gregory, *Essentials of Economics*, p. 3

Pattern of organization: _____

8

1   Humans are strongly attracted to the seashore. Travel brochures show scenic, empty sandy beaches and pristine shore vegetation. Rarely do they show the real picture: crowded beaches backed by strands of hotels, boardwalks, and shops. Recreational and commercial development of seashores, along with intensive seasonal human use, has had a long-term impact on intertidal ecosystems, the severity of which will increase as human populations grow.

2   This use has had serious effects on intertidal wildlife, especially that of sandy shores. Beach-nesting birds such as the piping plover *(Charadrius melodus)* and the least tern *(Sterna antillarum)* are so disturbed by bathers and dune buggies that both species are in danger of extinction. Other terns and shore birds are subjected to competition for nest sites and to egg predation by rapidly growing populations of large gulls that are highly tolerant of humans and thrive on human garbage. Sea turtles and the horseshoe crab *(Limulus polyphemus)*, dependent on sandy beaches for nesting sites, find themselves evicted and are declining rapidly for that reason.

3   Habitat destruction is only one aspect of human impact on intertidal ecosystems. Another is pollution. Seashore cottages use septic tanks that drain into sandy soil; commercial developments drain all sorts of wastes into the ground; and coastal cities and small towns pour raw sewage into shallow waters off the coast.

4   Each incoming tide brings into the beaches feces-contaminated water that makes beaches unhealthy for humans and wildlife alike. Tides also carry in old fishing lines, plastic debris and other wastes, and blobs of oil, all hazardous to humans and wildlife.

Robert Leo Smith and Thomas M. Smith, *Elements of Ecology,* p. 506

Pattern of organization: _____

9

1   Tobacco harms public health and should be strictly regulated. Studies indicate that smoking claims more than 400,000 lives and smoking-related healthcare costs exceed $75 billion annually. According to the BBC, smokers take more sick time than nonsmokers, and smokers are considerably less productive. Regulating tobacco products will help reduce these public costs.

2   The tobacco settlement holds cigarette makers accountable for past actions. The tobacco settlement forced cigarette makers to admit their culpability and their responsibility to rectify the effects of past practices. Cigarette makers must pay out $206 billion to help smokers quit, to provide health care to current and ex-smokers, and to reimburse the states for health care expenditures for tobacco related diseases.

3   The tobacco settlement is an example of regulation through the cooperation of private and public institutions. The tobacco settlement calls for the cigarette industry to provide funds for "smoking cessation programs, healthcare, education, and programs

benefiting children"; and to limit its marketing in order to prevent America's youth from taking up smoking.

4   On the other hand, tobacco products are legal and consumers are responsible for their choices. Cigarettes are legal and the choice is freely made. Industries and businesses should not be held responsible for the actions of individuals who choose to use their products. The tobacco industry should not be required to pay for public healthcare costs.

5   To force an industry to provide public benefits for the results of this freely made choice is a *de facto* tax. This is an impermissible encroachment of government on the private sphere. Constitutional theory holds that taxes should be raised and spent by elected legislative assemblies-not by deals cut between lawyers and state attorneys general.

Neal Tannahill, *THINK American Government,* p. 320

Pattern of organization: _____

10

1   **Sexually transmitted infections (STIs)** have been with us since our earliest recorded days on earth. In spite of our best efforts to eradicate them, prevent them, and control their spread, they continue to increase, affecting millions more Americans than previously thought, according to the first new STI estimate in a decade. Today, there are more than 20 known types of STIs. Once referred to as "venereal diseases" and then "sexually transmitted diseases," the most current terminology is believed to be broader in scope and more reflective of the number and types of these communicable diseases. More virulent strains and more antibiotic-resistant forms spell trouble for at-risk populations in the days ahead.

2   Several reasons have been proposed to explain the present high rates of STIs. The first relates to the moral and social stigma associated with these infections. Shame and embarrassment often keep infected people from seeking treatment. Unfortunately, these people usually continue to be sexually active, thereby infecting unsuspecting partners. People who are uncomfortable discussing sexual issues may also be less likely to use and/or ask their partners to use condoms as a means of protection against STIs and/or pregnancy.

3   Another reason proposed for the STI epidemic is our casual attitude about sex. Bombarded by media hype that glamorizes easy sex, many people take sexual partners without considering the consequences. Others are pressured into sexual relationships they don't really want. Generally, the more sexual partners a person has, the greater the risk for contracting an STI.

4   Ignorance about the infections themselves and an inability to recognize actual symptoms or to acknowledge that a person may be asymptomatic yet still have the infection are also factors behind the STI epidemic.

Rebecca, J. Donatelle, *Health: The Basics,* 4th ed., pp. 328–329

Pattern of organization: _____

Name _____   Date _____

DIRECTIONS: *Write out the central message for each of the following selections.*

1

Damon Conquered Stuttering Problem

ANTHONY MCCARRON

1   He seems made to stand in front of a television camera—glib, rock-star handsome with a ready smile and a helluva player too. He is a spokesman for Puma, has talked teammates through complicated labor negotiations as the Red Sox union representative and is the darling of post game interviews.

2   But speaking didn't used to be so easy for Yankee outfielder Johnny Damon. For several years as a child, Damon stuttered so badly he was afraid to introduce himself. Sometimes there was cruel teasing from other kids.

3   Damon vividly remembers going to the movies as a youth and trying to pay child's prices. When clerks saw his man-sized frame—by the time he was 12, he was 6-1, 185 pounds—they thought he was kidding. When they heard him stutter as he tried to explain that he was big for his age, they thought he was lying.

4   "My mind was going a thousand miles an hour and my mouth would say whatever came to it," Damon recalled. "I slowed down, took my time, connected my words and got better. Now I'm talking in front of millions of people a day. At times, there are some slight hesitations, but I feel like I've overcome it. I just roll with it and feel like I've come a long way."

5   Words "kind of lock up" when a person stutters, said Jane Fraser, the president of the Stuttering Foundation of America. About three million Americans stutter, about 1 percent of the population. Around 5 percent of children stutter at some point, though most outgrow it.

6   There are plenty of famous people who have battled stuttering, including sports stars such as Tiger Woods, Bill Walton, and Kenyon Martin. Winston Churchill and Marilyn Monroe dealt with it, too.

7   "A lot of kids work their way out of stuttering by being good at sports," Fraser said. "I think that sports analogies help kids who stutter. You've got to work on your speech. We tell kids, 'Don't think someone who can hit a baseball is an expert because they just do it five minutes a day.' That's something we like to share with teens and their eyes get all big."

8   Now Damon is so smooth, interviews with him turn into magazine cover stories. He has signed a contract with Puma to pitch that company's gear in television and print ads. "I always thought I had a stuttering problem and people would stay away.

But I guess because I overcame it, I tend to draw people into me and people want to hear me speak now," Damon said. "And that's pretty amazing."

Adapted from Anthony McCarron, "Speaking of Damon. Former Stutterer Now Talks Good Game," *New York Daily News*, July 13, 2006, Sports Section, p. 61. © New York Daily News, L.P. Used with permission.

Central message: _____

_____

_____

2

New Twist in Light Bulbs

Mary Beth Breckenridge

1   Compact fluorescent bulbs—those swirled, energy-efficient light bulbs—have been in the news a lot lately as people look for ways to save money and save the planet. In Australia, the government announced it's phasing out sales of incandescent bulbs in favor of eco-friendly fluorescents. A California legislator has proposed a ban on incandescents in that state. And Wal-Mart is in a yearlong campaign to encourage each of its 100 million regular customers to buy a compact fluorescent bulb.

2   It's not that environmentalists think this odd-looking gizmo holds the single answer to high energy bills or global warming. It's just that they see it as a simple yet effective way to make a difference. Compact fluorescent lamps, often called CFLs, use much less energy than the familiar incandescent bulbs. CFLs typically use one-fourth to one-third the electricity of incandescent bulbs. A good bulb will also last six to ten times as long—around five years with typical use.

3   Environmental advocates also urge us to consider the wider impact. The federal government says that if every U.S. household changed one incandescent light bulb to an Energy Star CFL, enough electricity would be saved to light 2.5 million homes, and the reduction in greenhouse-gas emissions would equal the amount produced by almost 800,000 cars.

4   Some people complain of headaches and eyestrain from fluorescent lighting because of the way light flickers rapidly in the bulb, a result of the nature of alternating electrical current and the way fluorescent lighting is produced. The flicker is so fast that the eye can't see it, but some people still sense it.

5   Newer CFLs are designed to address that problem. They use an electronic ballast—the part of the bulb that controls the electrical supply. It greatly speeds the flicker to the point that it is imperceptible.

6   CFLs are not without drawbacks. Brands differ in longevity, energy use and the quality of light they produce. In addition, CFLs contain small amounts of mercury and must be handled as hazardous waste.

Mary Beth Breckenridge, "New Twist in Light Bulbs," *Akron Beacon Journal*, March 10, 2007, p. E1. Reprinted with permission of the Akron Beacon Journal and Ohio.com.

Central message: _____

_____

_____

3

Kipling and I

JESÚS COLÓN

1   Sometimes I pass Debevoise Place at the corner of Willoughby Street...I look at the old wooden house, gray and ancient, the house where I used to live some forty years ago...

2   My room was on the second floor at the corner. On hot summer nights I would sit at the window reading by the electric light from the street lamp which was almost at a level with the windowsill.

3   It was nice to come home late during the winter, look for some scrap of old newspaper, some bits of wood and a few chunks of coal, and start a sparkling fire in the chunky fourlegged coal stove. I would be rewarded with an intimate warmth as little by little the pigmy stove became alive puffing out its sides, hot and red, like the crimson cheeks of a Santa Claus.

4   My few books were in a soap box nailed to the wall. But my most prized possession in those days was a poem I had bought in a five-and-ten-cent store on Fulton Street. (I wonder what has become of these poems, maxims and sayings of wise men that they used to sell at the five-and-ten-cent stores?) The poem was printed on gold paper and mounted in a gilded frame ready to be hung in a conspicuous place in the house. I bought one of those fancy silken picture cords finishing in a rosette to match the color of the frame.

5   I was seventeen. This poem to me then seemed to summarize, in one poetical nutshell, the wisdom of all the sages that ever lived. It was what I was looking for, something to guide myself by, a way of life, a compendium of the wise, the true and the beautiful. All I had to do was to live according to the counsel of the poem and follow its instructions and I would be a perfect man—the useful, the good, the true human being. I was very happy that day, forty years ago.

6   The poem had to have the most prominent place in the room. Where could I hang it? I decided that the best place for the poem was on the wall right by the entrance to

the room. No one coming in and out would miss it. Perhaps someone would be interested enough to read it and drink the profound waters of its message…

7   Every morning as I prepared to leave, I stood in front of the poem and read it over and over again, sometimes half a dozen times. I let the sonorous music of the verse carry me away. I brought with me a handwritten copy as I stepped out every morning looking for work, repeating verses and stanzas from memory until the whole poem came to be part of me. Other days my lips kept repeating a single verse of the poem at intervals throughout the day.

8   In the subways I loved to compete with the shrill noises of the many wheels below by chanting the lines of the poem. People stared at me moving my lips as though I were in a trance. I looked back with pity. They were not so fortunate as I who had as a guide to direct my life a great poem to make me wise, useful and happy.

9   And I chanted:
If you can keep your head when all about you
Are losing theirs and blaming it on you…
If you can wait and not be tired by waiting,
Or being lied about, don't deal in lies,
Or being hated don't give way to hating…
If you can make one heap of all your winnings;
And risk it on one turn of pitch-and-toss,
And lose, and start again at your beginnings…

10   "If—," by Kipling, was the poem. At seventeen, my evening prayer and my first morning thought. I repeated it every day with the resolution to live up to the very last line of that poem.

11   I would visit the government employment office on Jay Street. The conversations among the Puerto Ricans on the large wooden benches in the employment office were always on the same subject. How to find a decent place to live. How they would not rent to Negroes or Puerto Ricans. How Negroes and Puerto Ricans were given the pink slips first at work.

12   From the employment office I would call door to door at the piers, factories and storage houses in the streets under the Brooklyn and Manhattan bridges. "Sorry, nothing today." It seemed to me that that "today" was a continuation and combination of all the yesterdays, todays and tomorrows.

13   From the factories I would go to the restaurants, looking for a job as a porter or dishwasher. At least I would eat and be warm in a kitchen.

14   "Sorry"… "Sorry"…

15   Sometimes I was hired at ten dollars a week, ten hours a day including Sundays and holidays. One day off during the week. My work was that of three men: dishwasher, porter, busboy. And to clear the sidewalk of snow and slush "when you have nothing else to do." I was to be appropriately humble and grateful not only to the owner but to everybody else in the place.

16   If I rebelled at insults or at a pointed innuendo or just the inhuman amount of work, I was unceremoniously thrown out and told to come "next week for your pay." "Next week" meant weeks of calling for the paltry dollars owed me. The owners relished this "next week."

17   I clung to my poem as to a faith. Like a potent amulet, my precious poem was clenched in the fist of my right hand inside my secondhand overcoat. Again and again I declaimed aloud a few precious lines when discouragement and disillusionment threatened to overwhelm me.

If you can force your heart and nerve and sinew
To serve your turn long after they are gone…

18   The weeks of unemployment and hard knocks turned into months. I continued to find two or three days of work here and there. And I continued to be thrown out when I rebelled at the ill treatment, overwork and insults. I kept pounding the streets looking for a place where they would treat me half decently, where my devotion to work and faith in Kipling's poem would be appreciated. I remember the worn-out shoes I bought in a secondhand store on Myrtle Avenue at the corner of Adams Street. The round holes in the soles that I tried to cover with pieces of carton were no match for the frigid knives of the unrelenting snow.

19   One night I returned late after a long day of looking for work. I was hungry. My room was dark and cold. I wanted to warm my numb body. I lit a match and began looking for some scraps of wood and a piece of paper to start a fire. I searched all over the floor. No wood, no paper. As I stood up, the glimmering flicker of the dying match was reflected in the glass surface of the framed poem. I unhooked the poem from the wall. I reflected for a minute, a minute that felt like an eternity. I took the frame apart, placing the square glass upon the small table. I tore the gold paper on which the poem was printed, threw its pieces inside the stove and, placing the small bits of wood from the frame on top of the paper, I lit it, adding soft and hard coal as the fire began to gain strength and brightness.

20   I watched how the lines of the poem withered into ashes inside the small stove.

A Puerto Rican in New York and Other Sketches, 1982, International Publishers Co., Inc.

Central message: _____

_____

_____

4

1   Mankind has engaged in gambling for many centuries. Archeologists have unearthed six-sided dice dating from around 3000 B.C. Ancient Egyptians played a game resembling backgammon. On the Indian subcontinent more than 3500 years ago, there were public and private gambling houses, dice games, and betting on fights between animals. Farther east, Asian cultures also have a rich and long tradition of gambling. As cultural artifacts, playing cards had their primitive origins in Asia. When Europeans

arrived in North America, they found that the native peoples had been gambling in a variety of ways for centuries. Of course, the European settlers and colonists were no strangers to gambling themselves. They brought with them a penchant for gambling in various forms, including card-playing, dice games, and lotteries. Even the Puritan settlers played cards.

2   Much of America's Revolutionary War was funded from lottery proceeds. Likewise, several of the young nation's new universities, including Columbia, Yale, and Princeton, were founded with substantial financial assistance from lotteries. America's connection to gambling has continued throughout its Civil War, two World Wars, and the emergence of Nevada as the icon of "Las Vegas-style" gambling.

3   Today, gambling has gone global. This seems logical, given gambling's prevalence through time around the world. The Internet Age is creating new opportunities for gamblers as well as challenges for those wanting to limit the spread of gambling and access to it. No longer is it necessary to physically travel to a casino or horse track to place bets on blackjack, sporting events, and horse racing. "Virtual" casinos have sprung up to engage the gambler in online gaming opportunities. In the 1990s, online casinos proliferated as Internet entrepreneurs sought to satisfy the worldwide demand for online gaming. These companies were based outside the United States because of questions about the legality of such an activity under state and federal law. Many of these companies, including Gibraltar-based Party Gaming Plc and 888 Holdings Plc, are publicly traded corporations.

4   Despite its long history of gambling, the United States has also engaged in strict regulation of the industry. The surge in Internet gaming triggered efforts to ban such activity, and to prosecute those who are the principals of the so-called offshore online casinos. This regulatory action has angered governments in various countries, especially smaller countries where the online casinos are based. One country, Antigua and Barbuda (Antigua), filed a claim with the WTG in 2004 arguing that U.S. laws and policies pertaining to online gambling violate the terms of a fair trade agreement known as the General Agreement on Trade in Services (GATS).

5   Antigua claimed that the United States discriminated against foreign suppliers of "recreational services," including Internet gaming. The claim was based on the following argument: Even as it maintains a number of federal laws that prohibit offshore Internet gaming, the United States exempts off-track betting on horse races over the Internet from these same federal laws. According to the suit, this situation benefits domestic interests at the expense of offshore casinos.

Warren J. Keegan and Mark C. Green, *Global Marketing*, 6th ed., p. 169.

Central message: _____

_____

_____

Name _____   Date _____

DIRECTIONS: *Underline or highlight the most important information in each of the passages that follow and then summarize and/or paraphrase them as instructed by your professor.*

1

Conflict Interaction

1   As do most things in life, conflict offers a mixture of the good, the bad, and the uncertain. On the positive side, conflicts allow us to air important issues, they produce new and creative ideas, they release built-up tension. Handled properly, conflicts can strengthen relationships; they may lead groups and organizations to re-evaluate and clarify goals and missions; and they can also initiate social change to eliminate inequities and injustice. These advantages suggest that conflict is normal and healthy, and they underscore the importance of understanding and handling conflict properly.

2   But, perhaps more familiar is the negative side of conflict. Heated exchanges spiral out of control, resulting in frustration, tension, hard feelings, and, ultimately, more conflict. Low-grade family conflicts, prosecuted through criticism, arguments, nagging, and verbal abuse, not only distance parents from children and husbands from wives, but also lower self-esteem and create problems that may follow people through their entire lives. Additionally, conflicts are sometimes violent, not only between strangers, but also in the workplace and within the family. Sometimes **not** being able to start a conflict is the source of frustration. If one friend persistently denies that a problem exists or changes the subject when it comes up, the other cannot discuss the things that are bothering her, and the friendship suffers. The various negative experiences we all have with conflict are reinforced in the media, where it often seems that the only effective way to solve problems is to shoot somebody.

3   Conflicts also bring uncertainty. As we will see, the great "unpredictables" in life often center around how interactions will go. Conversations, meetings, conflicts all have in common the fact that they may suddenly turn in unexpected directions. Indeed, the uncertainties that arise in conflicts often cause them to turn in negative directions.

Joseph P. Folger et al., *Working Through Conflict,* p. 1

2

Compulsory Voting in Australia

1 Compulsory voting is the legal requirement that citizens participate in national elections. It is a low-cost, efficient remedy to the problem of low turnout. Voter participation rates are almost 20 percent higher in nations with compulsory voting than they are in other democracies. Almost everyone votes in Australia, a nation that has had compulsory voting since 1924. For example, voter turnout was 94 percent in the 2004 national election.

2 The Australian Election Commission (AEC) enforces the nation's compulsory voting law. The AEC sends a "please explain" letter to people who fail to vote in a particular election. Election no-shows can either pay a fine or offer an explanation. If the AEC decides that the explanation is valid, it can waive the fine. The courts settle disputes between the AEC and individual non-voters over the validity of excuses. The proportion of Australians fined for failing to vote never exceeds 1 percent of the electorate.

3 Political scientists believe that compulsory voting strengthens political parties. Because parties do not have to devote resources to turning out the vote, they can focus on persuasion and conversion. Compulsory voting builds party loyalty. Survey research in Australia finds that most Australian voters express firm and longstanding commitments to a party. You have read that lower-income people are less likely to vote than middle-income citizens. So, compulsory voting also benefits political parties representing the working-class interests more than those representing middle- and upper-income voters because lower-income people are less likely to vote than middle-income citizens.

Neal Tannahill, *THINK American Government*, p. 109

3

Getting the Most Out of Your Textbooks: A Review

CHAPTER OUTLINE

CHAPTER OUTCOMES

After completing Chapter 3, you should be able to:

- Overview a textbook.
- Preview a textbook chapter.
- Use reading and study strategies to effectively read textbook material.

Think About It!

Look carefully at the two photos below. What do these photos say about popular products on the market? Do you agree or disagree with the way each product is portrayed in the photograph? Discuss your answers with your classmates.

1 *The Surgeon General warns that smoking is a frequent cause of wasted potential and fatal regret.*

I was raised to believe that milk was part of a healthy diet. Then I discovered that to increase production, many dairy companies inject cows with hormones and antibiotics that we end up drinking. And that cows are kept "artificially" pregnant so they'll produce more milk all year long. So I scrapped my milk mustache for a soy one. It's healthier for me AND the cows. WHY MILK? Try soy instead.

2

■ Overviewing Your Textbooks

If you were to move to a new town, one of your chief concerns would be getting to know your way around as quickly and efficiently as possible. You would want to become familiar with your neighborhood in order to locate the nearest bank, the best store for food shopping, the movie theaters, the hospital, the post office, and any other establishments that are important or helpful to you. By accomplishing this task at the very beginning, you would feel more secure and comfortable with your new surroundings, and it would save you time by enabling you to get places faster.

As a college student, at the beginning of every semester, you should get to know your way around your new textbooks as quickly and efficiently as possible. Other than instructors, textbooks are the most important sources of information that you use in most of your courses. Thus, you want to become very familiar with them in order to save time and feel secure and comfortable when reading them. You accomplish this through the use of **overviewing**, which is a quick method of getting acquainted with textbooks.

Overviewing involves **skimming**, or quickly glancing over, the front and back parts of a textbook in order to find out what it is about, how it is organized, and what aids to understanding are offered to help you comprehend the information better. **Aids to understanding**, or **learning aids**—which make it easier to use your textbooks—could include appendices, bibliographies, glossaries, graphic aids, indexes, objectives, outlines, prefaces, previews, questions, reference sources, summaries, tables of contents, and vocabulary lists.

At the very least, the front pages of a textbook usually include a title page, table of contents, and preface. As you know, the **title page** tells you what the book is about in addition to providing the name of the author, the publishing company, and the edition. The back of the title page gives the copyright date or the date of publication of that particular edition of the book so that you know whether you are dealing with material that is current. After the title page, you will most often find the **table of contents**, which is a blueprint of the entire book's organization. It lists not only the section and chapter titles but also all the main headings in each chapter. In short, the table of contents tells you more specifically what the textbook is about and helps you understand how the chapter headings are related to one another. For example, if headings such as "Anxiety Disorders," "Schizophrenia," "Anger," and "Depression" are listed under a larger heading such as "Understanding Emotional Disorders," you would recognize immediately that the four subheadings are all examples of emotional disorders. Recognizing these kinds of connections or relationships would help make it easier to understand the chapter when you read it later on.

The **preface**, which generally comes after the table of contents, is also referred to as an introduction. Sometimes it is divided into "To the Instructor" and "To the Student" sections, or it may be a combination of both. Regardless of how it is structured or for whom it is written, the preface is valuable because it usually gives the author's purpose for writing the textbook, lists the features that make the book noteworthy, tells how the book is organized to help the reader, and lists and explains the aids to understanding. All of this information lets you know what you should accomplish as a result of reading the book and what is provided by the writer to help you to use it more efficiently. Although the table of contents shows what is included in the back part of a textbook, you should take a quick look for yourself.

The back pages of a textbook almost always include an alphabetically arranged **index**, which gives page locations for very specific information. Sometimes the index is divided into name and subject sections, which makes it easier to use. As you know from the discussion in Chapter 1, an alphabetically arranged **glossary** is also often found in the back, and it provides definitions of either individual words or combinations of words that fit the context of a given text. Many of those combinations of words will not even be found in a dictionary. For example, the glossary in a biology textbook defines *neutral variation* as "genetic variation that provides no apparent selective advantage for some individuals over others." Although the dictionary provides separate definitions for *neutral* and *variation,* it does not define them in combination. Thus glossaries give the meanings for specialized terms. They are also quicker to use than a dictionary because you do not have to search through a long list of definitions to find the specific one that fits the subject matter.

A **bibliography** contains sources used by the author to write the book and is often supplemented by a list of **reference sources** or **suggested readings.** It may be located at the back of a textbook or at the end of each chapter. **Credits** and **notes** are sometimes listed as well. They are all useful if research is necessary in order to read further on a given topic or when having to write a paper. On occasion, you can also find an **appendix** that includes supplementary or additional information such as definitions, experiments, maps, or diagrams that can prove helpful in understanding the subject matter of the textbook.

Overviewing takes only a short time, but it is well worth the effort. The sooner you become familiar with a textbook, the better your chances of reading it faster and with much more understanding. Furthermore, your awareness of all the aids to understanding included in the book by the writer should make the whole experience easier and more rewarding—and these elements come in very handy when studying for exams.

ACTIVITY 1

DIRECTIONS: Overview the front and back of this textbook. As instructed by your professor, answer the overview questions. Be prepared to discuss where you found your answers to the questions.

Overview Questions

1. What is the textbook about?

2. Who are the authors?

3. What is the edition?

4. What is the name of the publishing company?

5. What is the date of publication?

6. What are the two types of contents listed in this book?

7. How many chapters are in the book?

8. What can be found in the back of the book?

9. What is the author's purpose for writing the book? Where did you find this information?

10. What are the major features?

11. In the index, how many entries are under "skimming"?

12. What textbook reading strategies are included?

13. What is a "value word"?

14. What is "unbiased"?

15. What is the difference between a "prefix" and a "suffix"?

16. What is an "antonym"?

17. What is the name of the article written by Ron Kaufman?

18. What is the name of the book written by Paul R. Gregory?

19. What does *f* indicate in the index pages?

20. On what page can you find "negative connotation"?

ACTIVITY 2

DIRECTIONS. Do an overview of one of the textbooks you are using in another course, and write a few paragraphs in which you discuss what you learned from your overview. If you do not have other textbooks at this time, ask your classmates who are using other books to share their paragraphs with you.

■ Previewing Textbook Chapters

Suppose you are invited to a party this Saturday night in an unfamiliar part of your state, and you are very excited about going because all your friends will be there. Unfortunately, you are working until 9 P.M. that night, which means that you have to travel alone and arrive late for the affair. When Saturday night comes around, you certainly would not get into your car and drive around aimlessly trying to find the party. Not only would you waste time and gas, but there is a real chance you would never arrive! Instead, you would have found out specifically where the party is, the best way to get there, and approximately how long the trip is going to take you. Furthermore, when getting directions, you would have asked for landmarks like traffic lights, service stations, and other structures to help guide your way. In short, you would have tried to become familiar with the route so that you could get to your destination as quickly and efficiently as possible.

We can apply the same principle to reading textbook chapters. Before starting an assignment, you should find out where you are going by familiarizing yourself with the material as much as possible. Not only will it ultimately save time and effort to do this, but it will result in much better comprehension because you know where you are going and what to look for along the way. The process by which you become acquainted with a textbook chapter is called **previewing.** Like overviewing, previewing involves skimming or quickly glancing over the material to determine what you will be reading about, how the information is organized, and what aids to understanding are provided to help you with the task.

When previewing a textbook chapter, proceed through the following steps:

1. Take note of the title, which tells you the topic of the chapter. Once again, it is the answer to the question "What is this about?"

2. Check the length of the chapter so that you can gauge how long it will take you to read. While you are at it, try to get an idea of how difficult the material is, because that also affects the time it will take you to get through it. The purpose here is for you to prepare yourself psychologically for the task and come up with a schedule for its completion, which could involve dividing up the assignment.

3. Check to see whether there are objectives, goals, or outcomes at the beginning of the chapter. They tell you exactly what you are expected to know when you finish reading it, so they can serve as your personal study goals.

4. Skim the first several paragraphs, which are often an introduction to the main points to be covered and sometimes present the central message of the entire chapter.

5. Skim the last several paragraphs, which could serve as a summary of the most important information including, once again, the central message of the chapter. Keep in mind that writers sometimes provide a more formal summary or review in a separate section at the end of a chapter, which makes it easy to recognize.

6. Skim the major and minor chapter headings so that you become aware of the topics covered and how they are related to one another. As noted earlier, it is important to note connections between major and minor headings.

7. Look carefully at the **graphic aids,** which include charts, graphs, maps, pictures, and tables. They illustrate important information mentioned in the context of the textbook and often sum up major points made by the writer. Pay particular attention to the **captions** or **titles** and any explanations that appear over, under, or alongside the graphic aids, because you want to find out what they are about and be aware of the information that they stress. In short, no matter what graphic aid you encounter, you should always be able to answer the following two questions: "What is this graphic aid about?" and "What are the major points stressed?"

8. Check whether there are questions within or at the end of the chapter. Because they also focus on the major points, you should keep any questions in mind and try to answer them as you read. At the very least, the questions can serve as guides to direct your reading to the most valuable information.

9. Take note of any other aids to understanding offered in the chapter, such as exercises, outlines, previews, vocabulary lists, or boldfaced and italicized vocabulary defined in context or in the margins. All of these aids can help make your reading more meaningful.

After you have completed your preview of a chapter, take a few moments to think carefully about what you have learned. As you read the chapter, remember what you have discovered from your preview so that you can focus on the most important information. Although it only takes a short time, previewing is an excellent way to get acquainted with textbook material. That familiarity will pay off later on by enabling you to read quicker and with much more understanding.

ACTIVITY 3

Directions: Chapter 4 in this textbook contains very important information that will be used throughout the rest of the book. Familiarize yourself with that chapter by previewing it, and then answer the preview questions and write a few paragraphs about what you learned in your notebook.

Preview Questions

1. What is the chapter about?
2. How long will it take you to read it?

3. Are there objectives, goals, or outcomes at the beginning of the chapter that can serve as your personal study goals?

4. Is an introduction or a summary provided?

5. What is the central message of the entire chapter?

6. How many major and minor headings are there? Name them.

7. How many characteristics of critical thinking are there?

8. Are any graphic aids provided? If so, what are they about? What major points do they stress?

9. Are there questions within or at the end of the chapter?

10. What other aids to understanding are offered in the chapter that can help make your reading more meaningful?

Essay

Write a few paragraphs in which you discuss what you learned from your preview of the chapter and how your preview will help you read the chapter more quickly and with greater understanding.

ACTIVITY 4

DIRECTIONS: *Preview the following chapter from an educational psychology textbook, and write a few paragraphs in which you discuss what you learned from your preview.*

MODULE

13

Girls and Boys: Differences in the Classroom

By the time you have finished this module, you should be able to answer the following questions:

- What are the distinctions between sexual identity and gender-role identity?
- What is the school's role in the development of gender differences?
- Are there sex-related differences in cognitive abilities?

WHAT WOULD YOU SAY?

You are interviewing for a job in a 2nd/3rd grade in an affluent district. After a few questions, the principal asks, "Do you believe that boys and girls learn differently?" How would you answer? ■

While I was proofreading this very page for a previous edition, riding cross-country on a train, the conductor stopped beside my seat. He said, "I'm sorry, dear, for interrupting your homework, but do you have a ticket?" I had to smile at his (I'm sure unintended) sexism. I doubt that he made the same comment to the man across the aisle who was writing on his legal pad. Like racial discrimination, messages of sexism can be subtle.

In this section, we examine the development of two related identities that can be the basis for discrimination—sexual identity and gender-role identity. We particularly focus on how men and women are socialized and the role of teachers in providing an equitable education for both sexes.

Sexual Identity

Connect and **Extend** to the **Research**

See the Spring 2004 issue of *Theory Into Practice* on "Sexual Identities and Schooling" (Vol. 43, No. 2). Guest Editors: Mollie V. Blackburn and Randal Donelson.

The word *gender* usually refers to traits and behaviors that a particular culture judges to be appropriate for men and for women. In contrast, *sex* refers to biological differences (Brannon, 2002; Deaux, 1993). **Sexual identity** includes gender identity, gender-role behaviors, and sexual orientation (Patterson, 1995). *Gender identity* is a person's self-identification as male or female. Gender-role behaviors are those behaviors and characteristics that the culture associates with each gender, and *sexual orientation* involves the person's choice of a sexual partner. Relations among these three elements are complex. For example, a woman may identify herself as a female (gender-identity), but behave in ways that are not consistent with the gender role (play football), and may be heterosexual, bisexual, or homosexual in her orientation. So sexual identity is a complicated construction of beliefs, attitudes, and behaviors.

Sexual Orientation

During adolescence, about 8% of boys and 6% of girls report engaging is some same-sex activity or feeling strong attractions to same-sex individuals. Males are more likely than females to experiment with same-sex partners as adolescents, but females are more likely to experiment later, often in college. Fewer adolescents actually have a homosexual or bisexual orientation—about 4% of adolescents identify themselves as gay (males who chose male partners), lesbian (females who chose female partners), or bisexual (people who have partners of both sexes). This number increases to about 8% for adults (Savin-Williams & Diamond, 2004; Steinberg, 2005).

Scientists debate the origins of homosexuality. Most of the research has been with men, so less is known about women. Evidence so far suggests that both biological and social factors are involved. For example, sexual orientation is more similar for identical twins than for fraternal twins, but not all identical twins have the same sexual orientation (Berk,

Sexual identity A complex combination of beliefs and orientations about gender roles and sexual orientation.

Cluster 5: Culture and Community

Woolfolk, *Educational Psychology* 10th ed., pp. 192–200

2005). There are quite a few models describing the development of sexual orientation. Most focus on how adolescents develop an identity as gay, lesbian, or bisexual. Generally, the models include the following or similar stages (Berk, 2005; Yarhouse, 2001):

- *Feeling different*—Beginning around age 6, the child may be less interested in the activities of other children who are the same sex. Some children may find this difference troubling and fear being "found out." Others do not experience these anxieties.
- *Feeling confused*—In adolescence, as they feel attractions for the same sex, students may be confused, upset, lonely, unsure of what to do. They may lack role models and try to change to activities and dating patterns that fit heterosexual stereotypes.
- *Acceptance*—As young adults, many of these youth sort through sexual orientation issues and identify themselves as gay, lesbian, or bisexual. They may or may not make their sexual orientation public, but might share the information with a few friends.

The problem with phase models of identity development is that the identity achieved is assumed to be final. Actually, newer models emphasize that sexual orientation can be flexible, complex, and multifaceted; it can change over the lifetime. For example, people may have dated or married opposite-sex partners at one point in their lives, but have same-sex attractions or partners later in their lives, or vice versa (Garnets, 2002).

Parent and teachers are seldom the first people to hear about the adolescent's sexual identity concerns. But if a student does seek your counsel, Table 13.1 has some ideas for reaching out.

TABLE 13.1

Reaching Out to Help Students Struggling with Sexual Identity
These ideas come from the *Attic Speakers Bureau*, a program of The Attic Youth Center, where trained peer educators reach out to youth and youth-service providers in schools, organizations, and health-care facilities.

Reaching Out

If a lesbian, gay, bisexual, or transgender youth or a youth questioning his or her own sexual orientation should come to you directly for assistance, remember the following simple, 5-point plan:

LISTEN It seems obvious, but the best thing that you can do in the beginning is allow that individual to vent and express what is going on in his or her life.

AFFIRM Tell them, "You are not alone."—this is crucial. A lot of LGBTQ youth feel isolated and lack peers with whom they can discuss issues around sexual orientation. Letting them know that there are others dealing with the same issues is invaluable. This statement is also important because it does not involve a judgment call on your part.

REFER You do not have to be the expert. A referral to someone who is trained to deal with these issues is a gift you are giving to that student, not a dismissal of responsibility.

ADDRESS Deal with harassers—do not overlook issues of verbal or physical harassment around sexual orientation. It is important to create and maintain an environment where all youth feel comfortable and welcome.

FOLLOW-UP Be sure to check in with the individual to see if the situation has improved and if there is anything further you may be able to do.

There are also some things that you as an individual can do to better serve LGBTQ youth and youth dealing with issues around sexual orientation:

- Work on your own comfortability around issues of sexual orientation and sexuality.
- Get training on how to present information on sexual orientation effectively.
- Dispel myths around sexual orientation by knowing facts and sharing that information.
- Work on setting aside your own personal biases to better serve students dealing with issues around sexual orientation and sexuality.

Source: From Figure 3. Copyright © The Attic Speakers Bureau and Carrie E. Jacobs, Ph.D. Reprinted with permission.

Recognizing gender schemas as potential barriers to success may allow children's choices to become less gender driven. The 2002 film, *Bend It Like Beckham,* in which a teenaged girl from a traditional Indian family aspires to succeed as a professional soccer player, explores how society and different cultures define appropriate activities for girls and boys.

Gender-Role Identity

Connect and **Extend**
to the **Research**

For a lively debate on the termi-
nology of gender and sex, see the
March 1993 issue of *Psychological
Science.*

Gender-role identity is the image each individual has of himself or herself as masculine or feminine in characteristics—a part of self-concept. Erikson and many other earlier psychologists thought that identifying your gender and accepting gender roles were straightforward; you simply realized that you were male or female and acted accordingly. But today, we know that some people experience conflicts about their gender identity. For example, transsexuals often report feeling trapped in the wrong body; they experience themselves as female, but their biological sex is male or vice versa (Berk, 2005; Yarhouse, 2001).

How do gender-role identities develop? As early as age 2, children are aware of gender differences—they know whether they are girls or boys and that mommies are girls and daddies are boys. It is likely that biology plays a role. Very early, hormones affect activity level and aggression, with boys tending to prefer active, rough, noisy play. By age 4, children have a beginning sense of gender roles—they believe that some toys are for boys (trucks, for example) and some are for girls (dolls) and that some jobs are for girls (nurse) and others are for boys (police officer) (Berk, 2005). Play styles lead young children to prefer same-sex play partners with similar styles, so by age 4, children spend three times as much play time with same-sex playmates as with opposite-sex playmates; by age 6, the ratio is 11 to 1 (Benenson, 1993; Maccoby, 1998). Of course, these are averages and individuals do not always fit the average. In addition, many other factors—social and cognitive—affect gender-role identity.

Parents are more likely to react positively to assertive behavior on the part of their sons and emotional sensitivity in their daughters (Brody, 1999; Fagot & Hagan, 1991). Through their interactions with family, peers, teachers, and the environment in general, children begin to form **gender schemas**, or organized networks of knowledge about what it means to be male or female. Gender schemas help children make sense of the world and guide their behavior (see Figure 13.1). So a young girl whose schema for "girls" includes "girls play with dolls and not with trucks" or "girls can't be scientists" will pay attention to, remember, and interact more with dolls than trucks, and she may avoid science activities (Berk, 2005; Leaper, 2002; Liben & Signorella, 1993).

Gender-role identity Beliefs
about characteristics and behaviors associated with one sex as
opposed to the other.

Gender schemas Organized networks of knowledge about what it
means to be male or female.

Cluster 5: Culture and Community

FIGURE 13.1

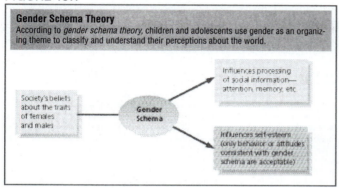

Gender Schema Theory
According to *gender schema theory*, children and adolescents use gender as an organizing theme to classify and understand their perceptions about the world.

Society's beliefs about the traits of females and males → Gender Schema →

Influences processing of social information— attention, memory, etc.

Influences self-esteem (only behavior or attitudes consistent with gender schema are acceptable)

Gender-Role Stereotyping in the Preschool Years

Different treatment of the sexes and gender-role stereotyping continue in early childhood. Researchers have found that boys are given more freedom to roam the neighborhood, and they are not protected for as long a time as girls from potentially dangerous activities such as playing with sharp scissors or crossing the street alone. Parents quickly come to the aid of their daughters, but are more likely to insist that their sons handle problems themselves. Thus, independence and initiative seem to be encouraged more in boys than in girls (Brannon, 2002; Fagot, Hagan, Leinbach, & Kronsberg, 1985).

And then there are the toys! Walk through any store's toy section and see what is offered to girls and boys. Dolls and kitchen sets for girls and toy weapons for boys have been with us for decades, but what about even more subtle messages? Margot Mifflin went shopping for a toy for her 4-year-old that was not gender-typed and found a Wee Waffle farm set. Then she discovered that "the farmer plugged into a round hole in the driver's seat of the tractor, but the mother—literally a square peg in a round hole—didn't" (Mifflin, 1999, p. 1). But we cannot blame the toy makers alone. Adults buying for children favor gender-typed toys and fathers tend to discourage young sons from playing with "girl's" toys (Brannon, 2002).

By age 4 or 5, children have developed a gender schema that describes what clothes, games, toys, behaviors, and careers are "right" for boys and girls—and these ideas can be quite rigid (Brannon, 2002). Many of my student teachers are surprised when they hear young children talk about gender roles. Even in this era of great progress toward equal opportunity, a preschool girl is more likely to tell you she wants to become a nurse than to say she wants to be an engineer. After she had given a lecture on the dangers of sex stereotyping in schools, a colleague of mine brought her young daughter to her college class. The students asked the little girl, "What do you want to be when you grow up?" The child immediately replied, "A doctor," and her professor/mother beamed with pride. Then the girl whispered to the students in the front row, "I really want to be a nurse, but my Mommy won't let me." Actually, this is a common reaction for young children. Preschoolers tend to have more stereotyped notions of sex roles than older children, and all ages seem to have more rigid and traditional ideas about male occupations than about what females do (Berk, 2005).

Gender Bias in the Curriculum

During the elementary school years, children continue to learn about what it means to be male or female. Unfortunately, schools often foster these **gender biases** in a number of

Gender biases Different views of males and females, often favoring one gender over the other.

Connect and **Extend**
to **PRAXIS II**™
Gender Bias (IV, B4)
There has been much debate in
the news media over possible gender bias in schools. What can you
as a teacher do to reduce or eliminate gender bias and its effects?

ways. Most of the textbooks produced for the early grades before 1970 portrayed both males and females in stereotyped roles. Publishers have established guidelines to prevent these problems, but it still makes sense to check your teaching materials for stereotypes. For example, even though children's books now have an equal number of males and females as central characters, there still are more males in the titles and the illustrations, and the characters (especially the boys) continue to behave in stereotypic ways. Boys are more aggressive and argumentative, and girls are more expressive and affectionate. Girl characters sometimes cross gender roles to be more active, but boy characters seldom show "feminine" expressive traits (Brannon, 2002; Evans & Davies, 2000). Videos, computer programs, and testing materials also often feature boys more than girls (Meece, 2002).

Another "text" that students read long before they arrive in your classroom is television. Remember the commercial count break I asked you to take earlier? (No—you can't take another one here.) A content analysis of television commercials found that White male characters were more prominent than any other group. Even when only the actor's voice could be heard, men were 10 times more likely to narrate commercials. And the same pattern of men as the "voice of authority" on television occurred in the United Kingdom, Europe, Australia, and Asia. Women were more likely than men to be shown as dependent on men and often were depicted at home (Brannon, 2002). So, before and after going to school, students are likely to encounter texts that overrepresent males.

Sex Discrimination in Classrooms

There has been quite a bit of research on teachers' treatment of male and female students. You should know, however, that most of these studies have focused on White students, so the results reported in this section hold mostly for White male and female students. One of the best-documented findings of the past 25 years is that teachers have more overall interactions and more negative interactions, but not more positive interactions, with boys than with girls (Jones & Dindia, 2004). This is true from preschool to college. Teachers ask more questions of males, give males more feedback (praise, criticism, and correction), and give more specific and valuable comments to boys. As girls move through the grades, they have less and less to say. By the time students reach college, men are twice as likely to initiate comments as women (Bailey, 1993; Sadker & Sadker, 1994). The effect of these differences is that from preschool through college, girls, on the average, receive 1,800 fewer hours of attention and instruction than boys (Sadker, Sadker, & Klein, 1991). Of course, these differences are not evenly distributed. Some boys, generally high-achieving White students, receive more than their share, whereas high-achieving girls receive the least teacher attention.

The imbalances of teacher attention given to boys and girls are particularly dramatic in math and science classes. In one study, boys were questioned in science class 80% more often than girls (Baker, 1986). Teachers wait longer for boys to answer and give more detailed feedback to the boys (Meece, 2002; Sadker & Sadker, 1994). Boys also dominate the use of equipment in science labs, often dismantling the apparatus before the girls in the class have a chance to perform the experiments (Rennie & Parker, 1987).

Stereotypes are perpetuated in many ways, some obvious, some subtle. Boys with high scores on standardized math tests are more likely to be put in the high-ability math group than girls with the same scores. Guidance counselors, parents, and teachers often do not protest at all when a bright girl says she doesn't want to take any more math or science courses, but when a boy of the same ability wants to forget about math or science, they will object. More women than men are teachers, but men tend to be the administrators, coaches, and advanced math and science teachers. In these subtle ways, students' stereotyped expectations for themselves are reinforced (Sadker & Sadker, 1994).

Connect and **Extend**
to the **Research**
See Latham, A. S. (1998). Gender
differences on assessments. *Educational Leadership, 55*(4), 88–89.

Sex Differences in Mental Abilities

Only 23% of the scientists and engineers and just 10% of the physicists in the United States are women, even though women earn about half of the bachelor's degrees in chemistry, biology, and mathematics and about 20% of the bachelor's degrees in physics and engineering (Angier & Chang, 2005; Bleeker & Jacobs, 2004). But let's not overlook the boys. There are areas when boys lag behind girls. For example, women earn 30% more bachelor's degrees overall than men and 50% more master's degrees. And African American women now earn twice as many college degrees as African American men (Hulbert, 2005). The International Comparisons in Fourth-Grade Reading Literacy: Findings from the Progress in International Reading Literacy Study (Mullis, Martin, Gonzalez, & Kennedy, 2003) revealed that in 34 countries, 4th grade boys scored below girls in reading literacy. Are these differences due to ability, interest, culture, social pressure, discrimination . . . ? Let's see if we can make sense of this issue.

From infancy through the preschool years, most studies find few differences between boys and girls in overall mental and motor development or in specific abilities. During the school years and beyond, psychologists find no differences in general intelligence on the standard measures—these tests have been designed and standardized to minimize sex differences. However, scores on some tests of specific abilities show sex differences. For example, from elementary through high school, girls score higher than boys on tests of reading and writing, and fewer girls require remediation in reading (Berk, 2005; Halpern, 2000). But academically gifted boys in the United States perform better than girls on advanced mathematics tests. In 2001, twice as many boys as girls scored over 700 on the math SATs, but boys also were more likely than girls to get all the answers wrong (Angier & Chang, 2005). In fact, the scores of males tend to be more variable in general, so there are more males than females with very high *and* very low scores on tests (Berk, 2005; Willingham & Cole, 1997). There also are more boys diagnosed with learning disabilities, ADHD, and autism. Diane Halpern (2004) summarized the research:

> Females and males show different average patterns of academic achievement and scores on cognitive ability tests. Females obtain higher grades in school, score much higher on tests of writing and content-area tests on which the questions are similar to material that was learned in school, attain a majority of college degrees, and are closing the gap in many careers that were traditionally male. By contrast, males score higher on standardized tests of mathematics and science that are not directly tied to their school curriculum, show a large advantage on visuospatial tests (especially those that involve judgments of velocity and navigation through three-dimensional space), and are much more knowledgeable about geography and politics. (p. 135)

There is a caution, however. In most studies of sex differences, race and socioeconomic status are not taken into account. When racial groups are studied separately, African American females outperform African American males in high school mathematics; there is little or no difference in the performance of Asian American girls and boys in math or science (Grossman & Grossman, 1994; Yee, 1992). And girls in general tend to get higher grades than boys in mathematics classes (Halpern, 2004). Also, international studies of 15-year-olds in 41 countries show no sex differences in mathematics for half of the countries tested. In fact, in Iceland, girls significantly outperformed boys on all the math tests, just as they usually do on their national math exams (Angier & Chang, 2005).

What is the basis for the differences? The answers are complex. For example, males on average are better on tests that require mental rotation of a figure in space, prediction of the trajectories of moving objects, and navigating. Some researchers argue that evolution has favored these skills in males (Buss, 1995; Geary, 1995, 1999), but others relate these skills to males' more active play styles and to their participation in athletics (Linn & Hyde, 1989; Newcombe & Baenninger, 1990; Stumpf, 1995). The cross-cultural comparisons suggest that much of the difference in mathematics scores comes from learning, not biology. And studies showing that adults rated a math paper attributed to "John T. McKay" a full point higher on a 5-point scale than the same paper attributed to "Joan T. McKay" suggests that discrimination plays a role as well (Angier & Chang, 2005).

Connect and **Extend**
to **PRAXIS II™**
Cultural and Gender Differences in the Classroom (III, B)
What are the sources of possible miscommunication between students and teachers in the classroom because of cultural or gender differences? Identify steps a teacher can take to minimize such problems.

Module 13: Girls and Boys: Differences in the Classroom

Connect and **Extend**
to Your **Teaching Portfolio**
Sadker, D. (1998). Gender equity:
Still knocking at the classroom
door. *Educational Leadership*,
56(7), 22–27. Special section
on Gender Equity, *Phi Delta
Kappan*, Vol. 84, No. 3, 2002,
pp. 235–245.

Eliminating Gender Bias

There is some evidence that teachers treat girls and boys differently in mathematics classes. For example, some elementary school teachers spend more academic time with boys in math and with girls in reading. In one study, high-school geometry teachers directed most of their questions to boys, even though the girls asked questions and volunteered answers more often. Several researchers have found that some teachers tend to accept wrong answers from girls, saying, in effect, "Well, at least you tried." But when boys give the wrong answer, the teachers are more likely to say, "Try harder! You can figure this out." These messages, repeated time and again, can convince girls that they just aren't cut out for mathematics ("Girls' Math Achievement," 1986; Horgan, 1995). If you are like a few of the student teachers I have supervised who "really hate math," please don't pass this attitude on to your students. You may have been the victim of sex discrimination yourself. The *Guidelines* provide additional ideas about avoiding sexism in your teaching. Some are taken from Rop (1997/1998).

Some popular authors have argued that boys and girls learn differently and that schools tend to reward the passive, cooperative behaviors of girls (Gurian & Henley, 2001). Other people believe that schools "shortchange" girls and "fail to be fair" (American Association of University Women [AAUW], 1991; Sadker & Sadker, 1995). The *Point/Counterpoint* examines these issues.

Guidelines: Avoiding Sexism in Teaching

Check to see if textbooks and other materials you are using present an honest view of the options open to both males and females.

EXAMPLES

1. Are both males and females portrayed in traditional and nontraditional roles at work, at leisure, and at home?
2. Discuss your analyses with students, and ask them to help you find sex-role biases in other materials—magazine advertising, TV programs, news reporting, for example.

Watch for any unintended biases in your own classroom practices.

EXAMPLES

1. Do you group students by sex for certain activities? Is the grouping appropriate?
2. Do you call on one sex or the other for certain answers—boys for math and girls for poetry, for example?
3. Monitor your metaphors. Ask students to "tackle the problem" and also to "cook up a solution."

Look for ways in which your school may be limiting the options open to male or female students.

EXAMPLES

1. What advice is given by guidance counselors to students in course and career decisions?
2. Is there a good sports program for both girls and boys?
3. Are girls encouraged to take advanced placement courses in science and mathematics? Boys in English and foreign languages?

Use gender-free language as much as possible.

EXAMPLES

1. Do you speak of "law-enforcement officer" and "mail carrier" instead of "policeman" and "mailman"?
2. Do you name a committee "head" instead of a "chairman"?

Provide role models.

EXAMPLES

1. Assign articles in professional journals written by female research scientists or mathematicians.
2. Have recent female graduates who are majoring in science, math, engineering, or other technical fields come to class to talk about college.
3. Create electronic mentoring programs for both male and female students to connect them with adults working in areas of interest to the students.

Make sure all students have a chance to do complex, technical work.

EXAMPLES

1. Experiment with same-sex lab groups so girls do not always end up as the secretaries, boys as the technicians.
2. Rotate jobs in groups or randomly assign responsibilities.

What if you witness sexism as a student teacher? See this site for ideas: http://www.tolerance.org/teach/magazine/features.jsp?p=0&is=36&ar= 563#

Point/Counterpoint

Do Boys and Girls Learn Differently?

AS WE HAVE SEEN, there are a number of documented sex differences in mental abilities. Do these translate into different ways of learning and thus different needs in the classroom?

POINT **Yes, boys and girls learn differently.**

Since at least the 1960s, there have been questions about whether schools serve boys well. Accusations that schools were trying to destroy "boys culture" and forcing "feminine, frilly content" on boys caused some public concern (Connell, 1996).

Discrimination against girls has ended, the argument runs. Indeed, thanks to feminism, girls have special treatment and special programs. Now, what about the boys? It is boys who are slower to learn to read, more likely to drop out of school, more likely to be disciplined, more likely to be in programs for children with special needs. In school it is girls who are doing better, boys who are in trouble—and special programs for boys that are needed. (Connell, 1996, p. 207)

In their book, *Boys and Girls Learn Differently*, Michael Gurian and Patricia Henley (2001) make a similar argument that boys and girls need different teaching approaches. Reviewing the book, J. Steven Svoboda (2001) writes:

Our schools seem to be creating overt depression in girls and covert depression in boys. Through violence, male hormones and brains cry out for a different school promoting closer bonding, smaller classes, more verbalization, less male isolation, better discipline, and more attention to male learning styles. Most of all, boys need men in their schools. (90% of elementary teachers are female.) They need male teachers, male teaching assistants, male volunteers from the parents or grandparents, and older male students. Peer mentoring across grades helps everybody involved.

For girls, Gurian and Henley recommend developing their leadership abilities, encouraging girls to enjoy healthy competition, providing extra access to technology, and helping them understand the impact of the media on their self-images.

COUNTERPOINT **No, differences are too small or inconsistent to have educational implications.**

Many of Gurian and Henley's claims about sex differences in learning are based on sex differences in the brain. But John Bruer (1999) cautions that

Although males are superior to females at mentally rotating objects, this seems to be the only spatial task for which psychologists have found such a difference. Moreover, when they do find gender differences, these differences tend to be very small. The scientific consensus among psychologists and neuroscientists who conduct these studies is that whatever gender differences exist may have interesting consequences for the scientific study of the brain, but they have no practical or instructional consequences.

In fact, there are boys who thrive in schools and boys who do not; girls who are strong in mathematics and girls who have difficulties; boys who excel in languages and those who do not. There is some evidence that the activities used to teach math may make a difference for girls. Elementary age girls may do better in math if they learn in cooperative as opposed to competitive activities. Certainly, it makes sense to balance both cooperative and competitive approaches so that students who learn better each way have equal opportunities (Fennema & Peterson, 1988).

It also makes sense to offer a variety of ways to learn, so that all students have access to the important outcomes of your teaching. Your attitude and encouragement may make the difference for students, male or female, who need a persuasive boost to believe in themselves as writers, or mathematicians, or painters, or athletes.

WHAT DO YOU THINK?
Vote online at www.mylabschool.com

MODULE 13 | SUMMARY TABLE

Sexual Identity

(pp. 192–199)

What are the stages for achieving a sexual orientation for gay and lesbian youth? Stages of achieving a sexual orientation for gay and lesbian students can also follow a pattern from

discomfort to confusion to acceptance. Some researchers contend that sexual identity is not always permanent and can change over the years.

What is gender-role identity and how do gender-role identities develop? Gender-role identity is the image each individual has of himself or herself as masculine or feminine in characteristics—a part of self-concept. Biology (hormones) plays a role, as does the differential behavior of parents and teachers toward male and female children. Through their interactions with family, peers, teachers, and the environment in general, children begin to form gender schemas, or organized networks of knowledge about what it means to be male or female. Research shows that gender-role stereotyping begins in the preschool years and continues through gender bias in the school curriculum and sex discrimination in the classroom. Teachers often unintentionally perpetuate these problems.

Are there sex differences in cognitive abilities? Some measures of achievement and SAT tests have shown sex-linked differences, especially in verbal and spatial abilities and mathematics. Males seem to be superior on tasks that require mental rotation of objects and females are better on tasks that require acquisition and use of verbal information. Research on the causes of these differences has been inconclusive, except to indicate that academic socialization and teachers' treatment of male and female students in mathematics classes do play a role. Teachers can use many strategies for reducing gender bias.

Sexual identity A complex combination of beliefs and orientations about gender roles and sexual orientation.

Gender-role identity Beliefs about characteristics and behaviors associated with one sex as opposed to the other.

Gender schemas Organized networks of knowledge about what it means to be male or female.

Gender biases Different views of males and females, often favoring one gender over the other.

MODULE 13 CHECK YOURSELF

Date: _____   Name: _____

Write the letter of the correct definition beside the word.

1. _____ Gender-role identity

2. _____ Androgynous

3. _____ Gender schemas

4. _____ Gender biases

   a. Having some typically male and typically female characteristics apparent in one individual
   b. An individual's image of himself or herself as masculine or feminine
   c. Beliefs about characteristics and behaviors associated with one sex as opposed to the other
   d. Organized networks of knowledge about what it means to be male or female

5. The term gender refers to

   a. Biological differences
   b. Characteristics associated with being masculine or feminine
   c. Traits and behaviors that a particular culture judges to be appropriate for men and for women
   d. All of the above

6. What age group has the most stereotyped notion of sex roles?

   a. Early adolescents
   b. Elementary school children
   c. Preschool children
   d. Adolescents

7. True or false: _____ Teachers interact with boys more than with girls.

8. True or false: _____ If guidance counselors do not protest when a bright girl says she doesn't want to take any more math or science classes, it may be an example of gender bias.

9. True or false: _____ There is clear documentation suggesting that biological differences between boys and girls are the cause of achievement discrepancies in math.

10. True or false: _____ In this age of political correctness, teachers do not need to check teaching materials for stereotypes. Textbook companies remove all biased information from their materials.

REFLECT One day you notice that the males are doing most of the talking in your 8th grade classes. Just out of curiosity, you start to note each day how many girls and boys make contributions and ask questions. You are really surprised to see that your first impression was correct. What would you do to encourage more participation by your female students?

(Answers on page A1)

■ Reading a Textbook Chapter Critically: Questions and Answers

In this textbook, you have several opportunities to participate in "Crime Scene Investigation." When detectives investigate a real crime, they ask such questions as "When did the criminal activity occur?" "Are there any clues?" "Who was involved?" "Are there any witnesses?" "What were the possible motives?" Answers to these and questions like them enable detectives to piece together information so that they can solve the crime.

As a student, before you go into a test situation, you always ask your instructor questions to find out what the test will cover, what kind of test it will be, how many questions will be on it, and how many points each will be worth. The information gathered from the answers to those questions helps you to prepare more efficiently for the test and receive a higher grade for your efforts.

The importance of asking questions also applies to reading, as you saw in Chapter 2, when we discussed how to find the topic, main idea, details, and central message. Furthermore, in this chapter, questions were used to gather information for overviewing and previewing purposes. In the remaining chapters, you will be answering questions that help focus and improve your understanding and require that you evaluate or critically read material from various sources. Thus, questioning has a very important role to play when it comes to dealing with textbooks and other kinds of reading as well.

How, then, do you actually apply **critical reading** to a textbook chapter? As you may have guessed, it involves the use of questions. When we discussed overviewing and previewing, we emphasized the importance of major and minor chapter headings because they make you aware of the topics covered and how the topics are related. Headings are generally highlighted in boldface or in colored type to stress their importance to the reader. *By simply turning those headings into questions, you are focusing your attention on the most important information in a textbook chapter and evaluating that information to answer your questions.* Sometimes writers actually provide headings that are already in question form, which makes your job even easier. Nevertheless, when you have to make headings into questions yourself, you can do so through the use of words often found in questions, such as *who, when, what, where, how,* and *why.* For example, look at the following headings and their corresponding questions.

Heading	*Question*
Booker T. Washington	Who was Booker T. Washington?
The Best Time to Study	When is the best time to study?
Physical Needs	What are physical needs?

The Cradle of Civilization	Where was the cradle of civilization?
Preventing Accidents	How do you prevent accidents?
The Need for Love	Why do we need love?

Sometimes it is very important to develop a question that relates a minor heading to a major one in order to understand how they are connected or related to each other. For instance, if the minor heading "Genetic Factors" is found under the major heading "The Development of Emotions" in a given chapter, then an appropriate question would read something like "What are genetic factors, and how do they contribute to the development of emotions?" By asking a question like this, you are focusing not only on the meaning of genetic factors but also on their relationship to the development of emotions. Certainly, that is what the textbook writer wants you to do.

When answering the questions that you have developed, you should always look for the central message of each chapter section and be aware of main ideas, patterns of organization, and context definitions. Although we have already discussed them at length in Chapters 1 and 2, it should be stressed again here that they are all extremely important because they provide the information with which to answer your questions. As discussed in Chapter 2, it is a very good idea to underline or highlight with a marker the information contained in main ideas, patterns of organization, and context definitions to separate it from the other material.

To review, underlining or highlighting is a useful technique that contributes to better comprehension because it requires that you evaluate carefully when deciding what information needs to be separated from the rest. That makes you into a more active, attentive reader, which is also an aid to concentration. Finally, this skill makes it easier to review the important information that you have separated in each section of a chapter without having to go back to reread everything. In short, underlining, highlighting, marking up, and even writing in your textbooks will help you to become a much more involved reader.

Carefully read the chapter section that follows. Make the heading into a question, and then answer your question by using the information provided in the passage. Pay particular attention to the sentences that have been underlined.

1   **Isolate and Locate the Source of the Problem** This means finding the part of the environment that is most likely responsible for the issue. A source can be one of three things. *First, the source of a problem might be other people in your life.* An organization I once consulted with was having trouble keeping its staff washrooms clean. They were used by staff and visitors. Management issued

washroom keys to its staff and had visitors use a public washroom in the building. Unfortunately, the washrooms remained as messy as ever. The problem was incorrectly linked with visitors and not members of the organization. Once this was called to the staff's attention and washroom rules were discussed with people, the appearance of the washrooms improved.

2   *Second, the source of a problem might be some object in your environment.* A neighbor's car radio went out whenever he approached a local radio station. He complained to the station manager that its equipment was causing his radio to malfunction. As far as the radio station manager knew, my neighbor was the only person with this problem. Thus, it seemed unlikely that the radio station's equipment was in some way responsible. He had one of his technicians check my neighbor's radio. The technician found a loose wire that apparently turned the radio off when it was jarred by potholes in the street near the station. Those same potholes jarred the radio back into operation. Properly locating the problem led to a solution.

3   *The third source of a problem might be a relationship.* Whenever we have an interpersonal problem, a natural tendency is to blame the other person. "It couldn't be my fault," we might think to ourselves. Interpersonal problems are much easier to resolve when the relationship is viewed as the source.

4   A former neighbor and his wife, for example, used to argue over who would take the garbage out to their garbage cans, located in their backyard. One would think this would be a simple problem to solve. At the very least, the chore could be rotated. Unfortunately, whatever strategy they chose, one of them would inevitably break the deal. Each blamed the other for being absentminded, stubborn, and purposely irritating. They eventually entered counseling for other problems in their marriage and discovered that the techniques they employed to manipulate and control each other interfered with their relationship. Their therapist pointed out that the garbage became a symbol for "who is the garbage person in this relationship" and, by implication, the low-status person in the marriage. The source of the issue was not the garbage per se, but unresolved control and authority issues in their relationship.

Anthony F. Grasha, *Practical Applications of Psychology,* p. 91

If the question you developed from the heading reads something like "How or where do you isolate and locate the source of the problem?" you are correct. You never know for sure whether you have asked the right question until you have at least skimmed the material. However, just the process of thinking about possible appropriate questions forces you from the very beginning to carefully consider the information in front of you. For example, you might have been tempted to make up questions using the words *who, when,* or *why,* but a quick look at the section indicates that the information provides a better answer to a *how* or *where* question.

Hence by trying to decide the best question to ask, you have already begun evaluating the section, which makes for much better comprehension in the long run.

You probably noticed that the first two sentences present the central message, and the major details—which are italicized—are organized into a simple listing-of-facts pattern. Together, they provide the answer to our question:

> Finding the part of the environment that is most likely responsible for the issue involves one of three things: other people in your life, some object in your environment, or a relationship.

Once again, we see the importance of recognizing central messages and patterns of organization, because they contain the most valuable information. You should always be on the lookout for the central messages. The rest of the section consists of minor details that relate various examples designed to make the material clearer.

Reading a textbook chapter with a questioning mind helps focus your attention on the most important information. Furthermore, it makes you into a more active reader, who is thinking carefully about the chapter material in order to find answers. That in turn leads to greater concentration, improved comprehension, and a much better chance of remembering what you have read. In fact, all of the skills that we have discussed in this chapter and Chapters 1 and 2 are designed to help you deal more effectively with textbooks. As a result, the experience with your textbooks should be more meaningful and worthwhile. Take the time to use and improve on these skills as you continue with your education. Your efforts should enable you to increase your learning and achieve higher grades. That is a very good return for your hard work.

ACTIVITY 5

DIRECTIONS: *The following passages are taken from various textbook chapters. For each of the passages, turn the heading into a question and answer it by using the central message and any main ideas, context definitions, and patterns of organization that may be present. Underline or highlight the most important information before writing out the answers.*

1

Marriage as an Exercise in Self-Interest

1   A number of couples, however, remain married for decades even when they know that their marriages are imperfect. To outsiders looking at such a married couple and observing one spouse silently suffering for years while the other spouse

continually behaves in some socially unacceptable manner, the rationality of the marriage can be hard to fathom. To an economist, this makes the institution of marriage an especially interesting case study of human choice.

2   Throughout history, literally billions of people have chosen to be married and to put up with the faults of their matrimonial partners. Why do they do this? One reason that economists have offered is that spouses show consideration for their marriage partners in the hope or expectation that the favor will be returned. This is self-interest at work. In addition, by entering into and staying faithful to a marriage, one spouse establishes a reputation with the other. By honoring their commitment to the marriage, they show more broadly that they are not afraid of commitments. This gives both a greater incentive to trust each other when they make joint financial decisions. By pooling their resources, both marriage partners can thereby make themselves better off than they would be alone. This is also an example of people responding in a self-interested way to incentives they face.

Roger LeRoy Miller, Economics Today, 1999–2000 ed., p. 14

2

Women's Rights in Saudi Arabia

1   Women in Saudi Arabia have limited legal rights. Under Saudi law, which is based on a conservative interpretation of Islam, women are socially and legally dependent on their male guardians—their fathers at birth and their spouses upon marriage. Women cannot even have their own legal identity cards. Their names are added to their father's identify card when they are born and transferred to their husband's identity card when they marry. As a result, a woman cannot travel, purchase property, or enroll in college without the written permission of a male relative.

2   The Saudi government encourages women to be stay-at-home mothers. Women must cover themselves fully in public and wear a veil. They cannot attend classes with men or work with men. Women's education is aimed at making women better wives and mothers. Women cannot study law or become pilots. Instead, they are directed toward occupations deemed suitable for their gender, such as teaching in a girls' school. Women are not allowed to vote or to drive a vehicle. Women who fail to conform to societal norms are subject to harassment by the religious police. They may be arrested, imprisoned, and even caned.

3   Nonetheless, Saudi Arabia has a women's rights movement. Many Saudi women are aware of the status of women in other countries, including Muslim countries, because of the Internet, satellite TV, and travel abroad, and they are demanding better treatment. Young Saudi women in particular, who are better educated than most of the older women, are challenging their

society's conservative interpretation of Islam. They are demanding access to education and employment opportunities.

4   The Saudi government has made some concessions to women's rights. Women are now permitted to stay in a hotel alone without the presence of a male relative. Even though some leading universities continue to admit only men, women now constitute a majority of university students. The Saudi government is also reportedly considering lifting the ban against women driving.

Neal Tannahill, *THINK American Government*, p. 346

3

Proteins Contribute to Cell Growth, Repair, and Maintenance

The proteins in our body are dynamic, meaning that they are constantly being broken down, repaired, and replaced. When proteins are broken down, many amino acids are recycled into new proteins. Think about all of the new proteins that are needed to allow an embryo to develop and grow. In this case, an entirely new human body is being made! In fact, a newborn baby has more than ten trillion body cells.

Even in the mature adult, our cells are constantly turning over, meaning old cells are broken down and parts are used to create new cells. In addition, cellular damage that occurs must be repaired in order to maintain our health. Our red blood cells live for only three to four months then are replaced by new cells that are produced in our bone marrow. The cells lining our intestinal tract are replaced every three to six days. The "old" intestinal cells are treated just like the proteins in food; they are digested and the amino acids absorbed back into the body. The constant turnover of proteins from our diet is essential for such cell growth, repair, and maintenance.

Janice Thompson and Melinda Manore, *Nutrition: An Applied Approach*, p. 204

4

Why We Sleep

1   One likely function of sleep is to provide a "time out" period, so that the body can restore depleted reserves of energy, eliminate waste products from muscles, repair cells, strengthen the immune system, or recover physical abilities lost during the day. The idea that sleep is for physical rest and recuperation accords with the undeniable fact that at the end of the day we feel tired and crave sleep. Though most people can function fairly normally after a day or two of sleeplessness, sleep deprivation that lasts for four days or longer is quite uncomfortable. In animals,

forced sleeplessness leads to infections and eventually death (Rechtschaffen et al., 1983), and the same may be true for people. There is a case on record of a man who, at the age of 52, abruptly began to lose sleep. After sinking deeper and deeper into an exhausted stupor, he developed a lung infection and died. An autopsy showed he had lost almost all of the large neurons in two areas of the thalamus that have been linked to sleep and hormonal circadian rhythms (Lugaresi et al., 1986).

2   Nonetheless, when people go many days without any sleep, they do not then require an equal period of time to catch up; one night's rest usually eliminates all symptoms of fatigue (Dement, 1978). Moreover, the amount of time we sleep does not necessarily correspond to how active we have been; even after a relaxing day on the beach, we usually go to sleep at night as quickly as usual. For these reasons, simple rest or energy restoration cannot be the sole purpose of sleep.

3   Many researchers believe that sleep must have as much to do with brain function as with bodily restoration. Even though most people still function pretty well after losing a single night's sleep, mental flexibility, originality, and other aspects of creative thinking may suffer (Horne, 1988). Chronic sleepiness can impair performance on tasks requiring vigilance or divided attention, and it can lead to automotive and industrial accidents (Dement, 1992; Roehrs et al., 1990). Laboratory studies and observations of people participating in "wake-athons" have shown that after several days of sleep loss, people become irritable and begin to have hallucinations and delusions (Dement, 1978; Luce & Segal, 1966).

4   The brain, then, needs periodic rest. Researchers are trying to find out how sleep may contribute to the regulation of brain metabolism, the maintenance of normal nerve-cell activity, and the replenishment of neurotransmitters. It is clear, however, that during sleep, the brain is not simply resting. On the contrary, most of the brain remains quite active, as we are about to see.

Carol Tavris and Carole Wade, *Psychology in Perspective*, pp. 162–163

5

What Is Deviance?

1   Deviance is generally defined as any act that violates a social norm. But the phenomenon is more complex than that. How do we know whether an act violates a social norm? Is homosexuality deviant—a violation of a social norm? Some people think so, but others do not. There are at least three factors involved in determining what deviance is: time, place, and public consensus or power.

2   First, what constitutes deviance varies from one historical period to another. Nearly 2,000 years ago, the Roman empress Messalina won a bet with a friend by publicly having a prolonged session of sexual intercourse with twenty-five men. At the time, Romans were not particularly scandalized, though they were

quite impressed by her stamina (King, 1985). Today, if a person of similar social standing engaged in such behavior, we would consider it extremely scandalous.

3   Second, the definition of deviance varies from one place to another. A polygamist (a person with more than one spouse) is a criminal in the United States but not in Saudi Arabia and other Muslim countries. Prostitution is illegal in the United States (except in some counties in Nevada) but legal in Denmark, Germany, France, and many other countries. As a married man, President Clinton got into hot water for having an affair, but married leaders in China are fully expected to have girl-friends (Rosenthal, 1998).

4   Third, whether a given act is deviant depends on public consensus. Murder is unquestionably deviant because nearly all societies agree that it is. In contrast, drinking alcoholic beverages is generally not considered deviant. Public consensus, however, usually reflects the vested interests of the rich and powerful. As Marx would have said, the ideas of the ruling class tend to become the ruling ideas of society. Like the powerful, the general public tends, for example, to consider bank robbery a serious crime but not fraudulent advertising, which serves the interests of the powerful.

5   In view of these three determinants of deviant behavior, we may define **deviance** more precisely as an act considered by public consensus, or by the powerful at a given time and place, to be a violation of some social rule.

Alex Thio, *Sociology: A Brief Introduction*, 4th ed., pp. 148–149

ACTIVITY 6   *DIRECTIONS: Read the section called "Gender Role Identity" from the textbook on educational psychology, which you will find on pages 118–126. Turn the heading into a question and answer it by using the central message and any main ideas, context definitions, and patterns of organization that may be present. Underline or highlight the most important information before writing out the answers.*

■ Textbook Reading Strategies: SQ4R, Concept Mapping, and KWL

Successful college students all across the country use strategies to help them read their assignments effectively and efficiently. An important component in making the best use of time when reading college textbooks is to be actively engaged. As previously mentioned, highlighting or underlining key ideas and concepts, making comments or notations in textbooks, and taking notes are some of the ways to keep active. Other more formal and methodical activities involve the use of a reading and study strategy such as SQ4R (Survey, Question, Read, Record, Recall, Review), Concept Mapping, or KWL (What I **K**now, What I **W**ant to Know, What I **L**earned).

SQ4R

SQ4R is the most commonly recommended reading strategy because it has been utilized by college students since the 1940s, when it was first developed by Frank Robinson at Ohio State University. Over the years, there have been several modifications to this method. Here we introduce one that we feel best meets the needs of students as they encounter a range of textbook materials: SQ4R using the Cornell note-taking format.

Before beginning to read, format your paper for the Cornell note-taking method by drawing a vertical line $2\frac{1}{2}$ inches from the left side of the paper, from the top to 2 inches above the bottom of the paper. Then draw a horizontal line across the bottom from this 2-inch location. It should look like this:

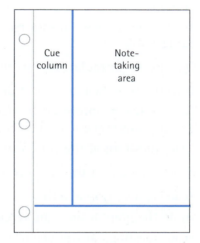

You will write your questions and notes on the right side of the vertical line. Jot down the page number from the text that corresponds with your question on the left side of the line. The page number will assist you in quickly checking the text when you need more information.

As you do the *survey* step of SQ4R, you also complete the *question* step. You will list your questions (and page numbers) and leave a few or several lines blank so that you have space to record your answers during the *read* and *record* steps. So what you will end up with, after surveying and questioning, are several sheets of paper with your questions and blank lines.

You should only write on one side of the paper as you list your questions so that you have additional room for notes, explanations, diagrams, and so on if necessary.

Keeping active as you read helps you remember and learn the material. As you read a section at a time, focus on answering the questions, and write down the answers. When you have completed the process, you will have a greater understanding of the reading, have increased retention of the material, and will also have a study guide for the chapter. If you read the material and complete an SQ4R *before* your instructor lectures on the chapter, you will be able to take notes more easily because you already have several notes. You will also comprehend more of any new material because you have read with focus and intent and were active during the reading process.

Survey – examine before reading to get an overview of the information to be covered

1. Read learning objectives and introductory paragraphs.
2. Read titles, headings, and subheadings.
3. Look at any visuals and their captions such as pictures, charts, graphs, or maps.
4. Read over review questions, chapter summaries, and concluding paragraphs.

Question – formulate and write questions as you survey the material

1. Turn the title, headings, and/or subheadings into questions.
2. Turn terms or important concepts that are bolded or in italics into questions as you encounter them.
3. Read questions at the end of the chapters or after each subheading.

Read – search for the answers to the questions you have developed

1. Read each section at a time.
2. Study the graphic aids and reread captions under pictures, graphs, etc.
3. Read questions at the beginning and/or at end of chapters and study guides that may be available.
4. Note italicized or bold-printed words or phrases and define these terms.

Record – look for and write down answers to the questions

1. As you read each section, write down answers to the questions to headings, subheads, terms, etc.
2. Answer questions at the beginning and/or at the end of chapters and study guide questions.
3. In the margins, record any comments, notations, or additional questions that you may have.

Recall or Recite – read your notes a section at a time and recall the questions

1. Answer the questions without looking, but refer to the text when, and as often as, necessary.

2. Do not go on to the next section until you are able to recite the answers without looking back.

3. Recite the definitions of key terms and concepts.

p. 142	What are styles of conflict?

p. 143	What is nonassertive behavior?

p. 143	What is direct aggression?

p. 144	What is indirect aggression?

See "Crazymaker" chart, p. 145–146

p. 147	What is assertion?

Review

1. Upon completion of reading, skim the chapter, and read your notes. Then check your retention of the material by reciting and quizzing yourself.

2. Short daily reviews (5–10 minutes) are an important component of learning and remembering material and should be a key part of your study habits.

p. 142
 	
Communication styles
Ex. Problem
w/neighbor barking
dog
	What are styles of conflict?
	• 4 ways people act when needs aren't met
	  1) nonassertive behavior
	  2) direct aggression
	  3) indirect aggression
	  4) assertion

p. 143
 	
Ex. Ignor dog; say dog
doesn't bother →
 	
Ex. Wait for dog to die;
wait for neighbor to
realize problem; wait
for neighbor to move →
	What is nonassertive behavior? √ I'm not OK: You're OK
	• 2 ways nonasserters manage conflict
	(Both ways might make you angry and resentful)
	  1) ignore their need or deny problems exists
	  2) realize needs not being met but accept situation—take no action

p. 143 Ex. abusive confrontation w/neighbor about dog →	**What is direct aggression?** √ I'm OK: You're not OK • Usual result—behavior such as anger, defensiveness, hurt, humiliation • Build self up at other's expense—hostility could result in more problems w/neighbor

p. 144
See "Crazymaker" chart
p. 145–146 →
(17 conflict
behaviors of George
Bach)
Ex. complain →
anonymously to city
pound and then express
sympathy; or complain to
neighborhood so maybe
they would confront
neighbor w/dog; or tell
neighbor w/dog about
neighborhood you just
left w/noisy dogs.
	What is indirect aggression? √ I'm OK: You're not OK (but I'll let you think you are)
	"Crazymaking" behaviors occur when people have resentment, anger or rage but not willing to express directly
	• send aggressive messages in subtle, indirect ways and show front of kindness
	• the targets can react with aggressive behavior or retreat w/hurt feelings
	Shortcomings of indirect aggression
	  1) crazymaking won't work—neighbor misses point or gets point and refuses to do anything
	  2) indirect aggression might work for short term but long range other issues could come up—neighbor bad mouths you
	  3) denies people involved a chance to build honest relationships

p. 147 Ex. if dog barking is persistent, go to neighbor and explain problem; discuss desire for solution to satisfy all.	**What is assertion?** √ I'm OK: You're OK • assertive people handle conflicts by expressing needs, thoughts and feelings clearly and directly and believe of possibility to solve problems to benefit all • maintains respect for self and others • may have some feelings of discomfort but after feel better
See "Styles and Conflict" chart pg. 195 for approach to others √; decision making; response of others; success pattern	These are 4 communication styles of conflict. People engage in a variety of ways when their needs are not met or have encountered a conflict.

Concept Mapping

Concept mapping is a textbook reading strategy that utilizes categorization and organization of material in a visual picture. In this study-reading strategy, you draw diagrams to show the relationship between a topic and its ideas. These diagrams, or maps, can take different forms. You can draw them in any way that makes sense to you in describing the relationship of ideas. A concept map is like a visual outline and is an effective tool in determining which information is important and in reviewing for tests.

The following is a concept map of a section of Chapter 3. When using the concept-mapping process:

- first, identify the main topic
- then, identify the major supporting details related to the topic
- finally, branch out to the minor points from those major details

Concept Map

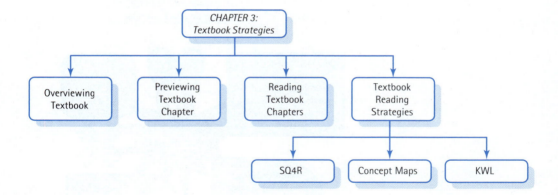

You can use concept maps to create a visual representation of textbook concepts. This can help you see and study the connections among ideas. Study the following two concept maps actually created by students for anthropology and political science courses:

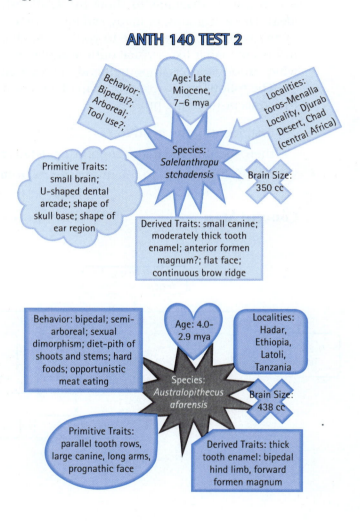

ANTH 140 TEST 2

Behavior: Bipedal?; Arboreal; Tool use?;

Age: Late Miocene, 7–6 mya

Localities: toros-Menalla Locality, Djurab Desert, Chad (central Africa)

Primitive Traits: small brain; U-shaped dental arcade; shape of skull base; shape of ear region

Species: *Salelanthropu stchadensis*

Brain Size: 350 cc

Derived Traits: small canine; moderately thick tooth enamel; anterior formen magnum?; flat face; continuous brow ridge

Behavior: bipedal; semi-arboreal; sexual dimorphism; diet-pith of shoots and stems; hard foods; opportunistic meat eating

Age: 4.0-2.9 mya

Localities: Hadar, Ethiopia, Latoli, Tanzania

Species: *Australopithecus afarensis*

Brain Size: 438 cc

Primitive Traits: parallel tooth rows, large canine, long arms, prognathic face

Derived Traits: thick tooth enamel: bipedal hind limb, forward formen magnum

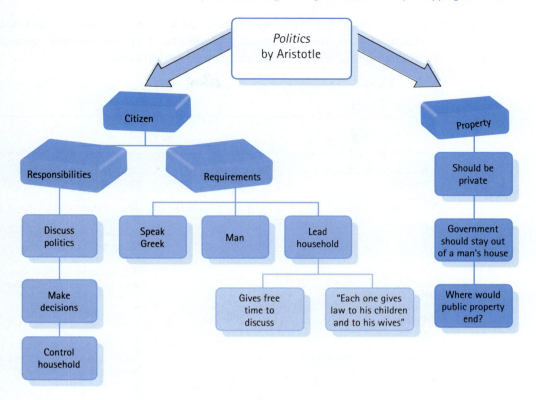

KWL (What I *K*now, What I *W*ant to Know, What I *L*earned)

KWL is a strategy developed by Donna Ogle (1986) that is widely used to help students improve reading comprehension. This strategy requires students to access their prior knowledge; establish a purpose for reading as they determine what information they want to know about the topic; and identify what they learned while reading.

For the *K,* or What I *K*now step, you consider what you already know about the topic. You then write down statements that demonstrate an understanding of the topic.

For the next step, *W,* or What I *W*ant to Know, you write down questions that you have about the topic. This sets the focus and purpose for reading.

The third step, *L,* or What I *L*earned, requires you to monitor your comprehension by recording answers to your questions to additional information you discovered while reading. Go back to the K step and determine if your knowledge about the topic was correct. Make any necessary corrections or modifications to those original statements. Any unanswered questions should be highlighted so they can be addressed in class.

Topic: Gravity

K	W	L
It keeps us from floating around.	What is gravity?	Gravity is the force that pulls objects toward Earth.
It makes things fall.	Why is there less gravity on the moon?	The amount of gravity there depends on the masses of the objects involved. The moon is a lot less massive than the earth, so there is less gravity on the moon than there is on Earth.
There is less gravity on the moon.	How did Newton discover gravity?	
Isaac Newton discovered gravity.	What determines how fast something will fall to the ground? (*teacher question*)	Air resistance determines how fast something will fall to the ground.

Adapted from Jennifer Conner, URL: http://www.indiana.edu/~1517/KWL.htm

ACTIVITY 7

DIRECTIONS: *The textbook selections that follow are longer than those in Activity 5. In addition, they contain both major and minor headings and also include graphic aids. Read "Styles of Conflict" using the SQ4R method. Check your questions with those generated in the sample. Read and answer the questions for the SQ4R, and check the completed SQ4R with what you have developed. For the selection "Self-Awareness," create a concept map, and for "Smokeless Tobacco," develop a KWL chart. You may also use the sample chapter from the educational psychology text for any of these strategies.*

1

Styles of Conflict

1   There are four ways in which people can act when their needs aren't met. Each one has very different characteristics, as we can show by describing a common problem. At one time or another almost everyone has been bothered by a neighbor's barking dog. You know the story: every passing car, distant siren, pedestrian, and

falling leaf seems to set off a fit of barking that leaves you unable to sleep, socialize, or study. By describing the possible ways of handling this kind of situation, the differences between nonassertive, directly aggressive, indirectly aggressive, and assertive behavior should become clear.

Nonassertive Behavior

2   There are two ways in which nonasserters manage a conflict. Sometimes they ignore their needs. Faced with the dog, for instance, a nonassertive person would try to forget the barking by closing the windows and trying to concentrate even harder. Another form of denial would be to claim that no problem exists—that a little barking never bothered anyone. To the degree that it's possible to make problems disappear by ignoring them, such an approach is probably advisable. In many cases, however, it simply isn't realistic to claim that nothing is wrong. For instance, if your health is being jeopardized by the cigarette smoke from someone nearby, you are clearly punishing yourself by remaining silent. If you need to learn more information from a supervisor before undertaking a project, you reduce the quality of your work by pretending that you understand it at all. If you claim that an unsatisfactory repair job is acceptable, you are paying good money for nothing. In all these and many more cases simply pretending that nothing is the matter when your needs continue to go unmet is clearly not the answer.

3   A second nonassertive course of action is to acknowledge your needs are not being met but simply to accept the situation, hoping that it might clear up without any action on your part. You could, for instance, wait for the neighbor who owns the barking dog to move. You could wait for the dog to be run over by a passing car or to die of old age. You could hope that your neighbor will realize how noisy the dog is and do something to keep it quiet. Each of these occurrences is a possibility, of course, but it would be unrealistic to count on one of them to solve your problem. And even if by chance you were lucky enough for the dog problem to be solved without taking action, you couldn't expect to be so fortunate in other parts of your life.

4   In addition, while waiting for one of these eventualities, you would undoubtedly grow more and more angry at your neighbor, making a friendly relationship between the two of you impossible. You would also lose a degree of self-respect, since you would see yourself as the kind of person who can't cope with even a common everyday irritation. Clearly, nonassertion is not a very satisfying course of action—either in this case or in other instances.

Direct Aggression

5   Where the nonasserter underreacts, a directly aggressive person overreacts. The usual consequences of aggressive behaviors are anger and defensiveness or hurt and humiliation. In either case aggressive communicators build themselves up at the expense of others.

6   You could handle the dog problem with direct aggression by abusively confronting your neighbors, calling them names and threatening to call the dogcatcher the next time you see their hound running loose. If the town in which you live has a leash law, you would be within your legal rights to do so, and thus you would gain your goal of bringing peace and quiet to the neighborhood. Unfortunately, your direct aggression would have other, less productive consequences. Your neighbors and you would probably cease to be on speaking terms, and you could expect a complaint from them the first time you violated even the most inconsequential of city ordinances. If you live in the neighborhood for any time at all, this state of hostilities isn't very appealing.

Indirect Aggression

7   In several of his works psychologist George Bach describes behavior that he terms "crazymaking." Crazymaking occurs when people have feelings of resentment, anger, or rage that they are unable or unwilling to express directly. Instead of keeping these feelings to themselves, the crazymakers send these aggressive messages in subtle, indirect ways, thus maintaining the front of kindness. This amiable façade eventually crumbles, however, leaving the crazymaker's victim confused and angry at having been fooled. The targets of the crazymaker can either react with aggressive behavior of their own or retreat to nurse their hurt feelings. In either case indirect aggression seldom has anything but harmful effects on a relationship.

8   You could respond to your neighbors and their dog in several crazymaking, indirectly aggressive ways. One strategy would be to complain anonymously to the city pound and then, after the dog has been hauled away, express your sympathy. Or you could complain to everyone else in the neighborhood, hoping that their hostility would force the offending neighbors to quiet the dog or face being a social outcast. A third possibility would be to strike up a friendly conversation with one of the owners and casually remark about the terrible neighborhood you had just left, in which noisy dogs roamed the streets, uncontrolled by their thoughtless owners. (Or perhaps you could be more subtle and talk about noisy children instead!)

9   There are a number of shortcomings to such approaches as these, each of which illustrate the risks of indirect aggression. First, there is the chance that the crazymaking won't work: the neighbors might simply miss the point of your veiled attacks and continue to ignore the barking. On the other hand, they might get your message clearly, but either because of your lack of sincerity or out of sheer stubbornness they might simply refuse to do anything about the complaining. In either case it's likely that in this and other instances indirect aggression won't satisfy your unmet need.

10   Even when indirect aggression proves successful in the short run, a second shortcoming lies in its consequences over the longer range. You might manage

to intimidate your neighbors into shutting up their mutt, for instance, but in winning that battle you could lose what would become a war. As a means of revenge, it's possible that they would wage their own campaign of crazymaking by such tactics as badmouthing things like your sloppy gardening to other neighbors or by phoning in false complaints about your allegedly loud parties. It's obvious that feuds such as this one are counterproductive and outweigh the apparent advantages of indirect aggression.

Crazymakers: Indirect Aggression

1. What's your conflict style? To give you a better idea of some unproductive ways you may be handling your conflicts, we'll describe some typical conflict behaviors that can weaken relationships. In our survey we'll follow the fascinating work of George Bach, a leading authority on conflict and communication.

2. Bach explains that there are two types of aggression—clean fighting and dirty fighting. Either because they can't or won't express their feelings openly and constructively, dirty fighters sometimes resort to "crazymaking" techniques to vent their resentments. Instead of openly and caringly expressing their emotions, crazymakers (often unconsciously) use a variety of indirect tricks to get at their opponent. Because these "sneak attacks" don't usually get to the root of the problem, and because of their power to create a great deal of hurt, crazymakers can destroy communication. Let's take a look at some of them.

3. **The Avoider**   The avoider refuses to fight. When a conflict arises, he'll leave, fall asleep, pretend to be busy at work, or keep from facing the problem in some other way. This behavior makes it very difficult for the partner to express his feelings of anger, hurt, etc., because the avoider won't fight back. Arguing with an avoider is like trying to box with a person who won't even put up his gloves.

4. **The Pseudoaccommodator**   The pseudoaccommodator refuses to face up to a conflict either by giving in or by pretending that there's nothing at all wrong. This really drives the partner, who definitely feels there's a problem, crazy and causes him to feel both guilt and resentment toward the accommodator.

5. **The Guiltmaker**   Instead of saying straight out that she doesn't want or approve of something, the guiltmaker tries to change her partner's behavior by making him feel responsible for causing pain. The guiltmaker's favorite line is "It's O.K., don't worry about me …" accompanied by a big sigh.

6. **The Subject Changer**   Really a type of avoider, the subject changer escapes facing up to aggression by shifting the conversation whenever it approaches an area of conflict. Because of his tactics, the subject changer and his partner never have the chance to explore their problem and do something about it.

7. **The Distracter**   Rather than come out and express his feelings about the object of his dissatisfaction, the distracter attacks other parts of his partner's life. Thus he never has to share what's really on his mind and can avoid dealing with painful parts of his relationships.

8. **The Mind Reader**   Instead of allowing her partner to express his feelings honestly, the mind reader goes into character analysis, explaining what the

other person really means or what's wrong with the other person. By behaving this way the mind reader refuses to handle her own feelings and leaves no room for her partner to express himself.

9. **The Trapper** The trapper plays an especially dirty trick by setting up a desired behavior for her partner, and then when it's met, attacking the very thing she requested. An example of this technique is for the trapper to say, "Let's be totally honest with each other," and then when the partner shares his feelings, he finds himself attacked for having feelings that the trapper doesn't want to accept.

10. **The Crisis Tickler** This person almost brings what's bothering him to the surface, but he never quite comes out and expresses himself. Instead of admitting his concern about the finances, he innocently asks, "Gee, how much did that cost?" dropping a rather obvious hint but never really dealing with the crisis.

11. **The Gunnysacker** This person doesn't respond immediately when she's angry. Instead, she puts her resentment into her gunnysack, which after a while begins to bulge with large and small gripes. Then, when the sack is about to burst, the gunnysacker pours out all her pent-up aggressions on the overwhelmed and unsuspecting victim.

12. **The Trivial Tyrannizer** Instead of honestly sharing his resentments, the trivial tyrannizer does things he knows will get his partner's goat—leaving dirty dishes in the sink, clipping his fingernails in bed, belching out loud, turning up the television too loud, and so on.

13. **The Joker** Because she's afraid to face conflicts squarely, the joker kids around when her partner wants to be serious, thus blocking the expression of important feelings.

14. **The Beltliner** Everyone has a psychological "beltline," and below it are subjects too sensitive to be approached without damaging the relationship. Beltlines may have to do with physical characteristics, intelligence, past behavior, or deeply ingrained personality traits a person is trying to overcome. In an attempt to "get even" or hurt his partner, the beltliner will use his intimate knowledge to hit below the belt, where he knows it will hurt.

15. **The Blamer** The blamer is more interested in finding fault than in solving a conflict. Needless to say, she usually doesn't blame herself. Blaming behavior almost never solves a conflict and is an almost surefire way to make the receiver defensive.

16. **The Contract Tyrannizer** This person will not allow his relationship to change from the way it once was. Whatever the agreements the partners had as to roles and responsibilities at one time, they'll remain unchanged. "It's your job to... feed the baby, wash the dishes, discipline the kids, ..."

17. **The Kitchen Sink Fighter** This person is so named because in an argument he brings up things that are totally off the subject ("everything but the kitchen sink"): the way his partner behaved last New Year's eve, the unbalanced checkbook, bad breath—anything.

18. **The Withholder** Instead of expressing her anger honestly and directly, the withholder punishes her partner by keeping back something—courtesy, affection, good cooking, humor, sex. As you can imagine, this is likely to build up even greater resentments in the relationship.

19. **The Benedict Arnold** This character gets back at his partner by sabotage, by failing to defend him from attackers, and even by encouraging ridicule or disregard from outside the relationship.

11   In addition to these unpleasant possibilities, a third shortcoming of indirect aggression is that it denies the people involved a chance of building any kind of honest relationship with each other. As long as you treat your neighbors as if they were an obstacle to be removed from your path, there's little likelihood that you'll get to know them as people. While this thought may not bother you, the principle that indirect aggression prevents intimacy holds true in other important areas of life. To the degree that you try to manipulate friends, they won't know the real you. The fewer of your needs you share directly with your coworkers, the less chance you have of becoming true friends and colleagues. The same principle holds for those people you hope to meet in the future. Indirect aggression denies closeness.

Styles of Conflict

	NONASSERTIVE	DIRECTLY AGGRESSIVE	INDIRECTLY AGGRESSIVE	ASSERTIVE
Approach to Others	I'm not O.K., You're O.K.	I'm O.K., You're not O.K.	I'm O.K., You're not O.K. (But I'll let you think you are.)	I'm O.K. You're O.K.
Decision Making	Let others choose	Choose for others. They know it.	Chooses for others. They don't know it.	Chooses for self.
Response of Others	Disrespect, guilt, anger, frustration	Hurt, defensiveness, humiliation	Confusion, frustration, feelings of manipulation	Mutual respect
Success Pattern	Succeeds by luck or charity of others.	Beats out others.	Wins by manipulation.	Attempts "no lose" solutions.

From *The Assertive Woman*, 4th Edition © 2002 by Stanlee Phelps and Nancy Austin. Reproduced by permission of Impact Publishers®, P.O. Box 6016, Atascadero, CA 93423, USA, www.impactpublishers.com. Further reproduction prohibited.

Assertion

12   Assertive people handle conflicts skillfully by expressing their needs, thoughts, and feelings clearly and directly, but without judging others or dictating to them. They have the attitude that most of the time it is possible to resolve problems to everyone's satisfaction. Possessing this attitude and the skills to bring it about doesn't guarantee that assertive communicators will always get what they want, but it does give them the best chance of doing so. An additional benefit of such an approach is that whether or not it satisfies a particular need, it maintains the self-respect of both the asserters and those with whom they interact. As a result, people who manage their conflicts assertively may experience feelings of discomfort

while they are working through the problem. They usually feel better about themselves and each other afterward—quite a change from the outcomes of no assertiveness and aggression.

13   An assertive course of action in the case of the barking dog would be to wait a few days to make sure that the noise is not just a fluke. If things continue in the present way, you could introduce yourself to your neighbors and explain your problem. You could tell them that although they might not notice it, the dog often plays in the street and keeps barking at passing cars. You could tell them why this behavior bothers you. It keeps you awake at night and makes it hard for you to do your work. You could point out that you don't want to be a grouch and call the pound. Rather than behaving in these ways, you could tell them that you've come to see what kind of solution you can find that will satisfy both of you. This approach may not work, and you might then have to decide whether it is more important to avoid bad feelings or to have peace and quiet. But the chances for a happy ending are best with this assertive approach. And no matter what happens, you can keep your self-respect by behaving directly and honestly.

2

Self-Awareness

Your **self-awareness** represents the extent to which you know yourself. Understanding how your self-concept develops is one way to increase your self-awareness: The more you understand about why you view yourself as you do, the more you will understand who you are. Additional insight is gained by looking at self-awareness through the Johari model of the self, or your four selves (Luft, 1984).

Your Four Selves

Self-awareness is neatly explained by the model of the four selves, the **Johari window**. This model, presented…[on page 149], has four basic areas, or quadrants, each of which represents a somewhat different self. The Johari model emphasizes that the several aspects of the self are not separate pieces but are interactive parts of a whole. Each part is dependent on each other part. Like that of interpersonal communication, this model of the self is transactional.

The Open Self

The *open self* represents all the information, behaviors, attitudes, feelings, desires, motivations, and ideas that you and others know. The type of information included here might range from your name, skin color, and sex to your age, political and religious affiliations, and financial situation. Your open self will vary in size, depending on the situation you're in and the person with whom you're interacting. Some

	Known to Self	Not Known to Self
Known to Others	**Open Self** Information about yourself that you and others do know	**Blind Self** Information about yourself that you don't know but that others do know
Not Known to Others	**Hidden Self** Information about yourself that you know but others don't know	**Unknown Self** Information about yourself that you don't know and that others do not know

The Johari Window

Visualize this model as representing your self. The entire model is of constant size, but each section can vary, from very small to very large. As one section becomes smaller, one or more of the others grows larger. Similarly, as one section grows, one or more of the others must get smaller. For example, if you reveal a secret and thereby enlarge your open self, this shrinks your hidden self. Further, this disclosure may in turn lead to a decrease in the size of your blind self (if your disclosure influences other people to reveal what they know about you but that you have not known). How would you draw your Johari window to show yourself when interacting with your parents? With your friends? With your college instructors? The name Johari, by the way, comes from the first names of the two people who developed the model, Joseph Luft and Harry Ingham.

Source: Joseph Luft, *Group Processes: An Introduction to Group Dynamics,* 3rd ed. Mountain View, CA: Mayfield, p. 60. Copyright © 1984 by Joseph Luft. Reproduced with permission of The McGraw-Hill Companies.

people, for example, make you feel comfortable and supported; to them, you open yourself wide, but to others you may prefer to leave most of yourself closed.

Communication depends on the degree to which you open yourself to others and to yourself (Luft, 1969). If you don't allow other people to know you (thus keeping your open self small), communication between you and others becomes difficult, if not impossible. You can communicate meaningfully only to the extent that you know others and yourself. To improve communication, work first on enlarging the open self.

The Blind Self

The *blind self* represents all the things about yourself that others know but of which you're ignorant. These may vary from the relatively insignificant habit of saying "You Know," rubbing your nose when you get angry, or having a distinct body odor, to things as significant as defense mechanisms, fight strategies, or repressed experiences.

Some people have a very large blind self; they seem totally oblivious to their faults and sometimes (though not as often) to their virtues. Others seem overly eager to have a small blind self. They seek therapy at every turn and join every self-help group. Some believe they know everything there is to know about themselves, that they have reduced the blind self to zero. Most of us lie between these extremes.

Communication and interpersonal relations are generally enhanced as the blind self becomes smaller. But be careful of trying to help someone else "discover" his or her blind self. This could cause serious problems. Such a revelation might trigger a breakdown in defenses; it might force people to admit their own jealousy or prejudice when they're not psychologically ready to deal with such information. Such revelations are best dealt with cautiously or under the guidance of trained professionals.

The Hidden Self

The *hidden self* contains all that you know of yourself and of others that you keep secret. In any interaction, this area includes everything you don't want to reveal, whether it's relevant or irrelevant to the conversation. At the extremes, we have the overdisclosers and the underdisclosers. The overdisclosers tell all. They tell you their marital difficulties, their children's problems, their financial status, and just about everything else. The underdisclosers tell nothing. They talk about you but not about themselves.

The problem with these extremes is that individuals don't distinguish between those who should and those who shouldn't be privy to such information. They also don't distinguish among the types of information they should or should not disclose. The vast majority of people, however, keep certain things hidden and disclose others; they make disclosures to some people and not to others. They're *selective* disclosers.

The Unknown Self

The *unknown self* represents truths about yourself that neither you nor others know. The existence of this self is inferred from a number of sources. Sometimes it's revealed through temporary changes brought about by special experimental conditions such as hypnosis or sensory deprivation. Sometimes this area is revealed by certain projective tests or dreams. Mostly, however, it's revealed by the fact that you're constantly learning things about yourself that you didn't know before (things that were previously in the unknown self)—for example, that you become defensive when someone asks you a question or voices disagreement, or that you compliment others in the hope of being complimented back.

Joseph A. DeVito, *The Interpersonal Communication Book*, 11th ed., pp. 58–59

3

Smokeless Tobacco

1   Smokeless tobacco is used by approximately 5 million U.S. adults. Most users are teenage (20 percent of male high school students) and young adult males, who are often emulating a professional sports figure or a family member. There are two types of smokeless tobacco—chewing tobacco and snuff. Chewing tobacco comes in the form of loose leaf, plug, or twist. Chewing tobacco contains tobacco leaves treated with molasses and other flavorings. The user places a "quid" of tobacco in the mouth between the teeth and gums and then sucks or chews the quid to release the nicotine. Once the quid becomes ineffective, the user spits it out and inserts another. Dipping is another method of using chewing tobacco. The dipper takes a small amount of tobacco and places it between the lower lip and teeth to stimulate the flow of saliva and release the nicotine. Dipping rapidly releases the nicotine into the bloodstream.

2   Snuff can come in either a dry or moist powdered form or sachets (tea bag-like pouches) of tobacco. The most common placement of snuff is inside the cheek. In European countries, inhaling dry snuff is more common than in the United States.

Risks of Smokeless Tobacco

3   Smokeless tobacco is just as addictive as cigarettes due to its nicotine content. There is nicotine in all tobacco products, but smokeless tobacco contains more nicotine than do cigarettes. Holding an average-sized dip or chew in your mouth for 30 minutes gives you as much nicotine as smoking four cigarettes. A two-can-a-week snuff dipper gets as much nicotine as a one-and-a-half-pack-a-day smoker.

4   One of the major risks of chewing tobacco is **leukoplakia,** a condition characterized by leathery white patches inside the mouth produced by contact with irritants in tobacco juice. Smokeless tobacco contains 10 times the amount of cancer-producing substances found in cigarettes and 100 times more than the Food and Drug Administration allows in foods and other substances used by the public. Between 3 and 17 percent of diagnosed leukoplakia cases develop into oral cancer. Users of smokeless tobacco are 50 times more likely to develop oral cancers than are nonusers. Warning signs of oral cancers include: lumps in the jaw or neck area; color changes or lumps inside the lips; white, smooth, or scaly patches in the mouth or on the neck, lips, or tongue; a red spot or sore on the lips or gums or inside the mouth that does not heal in two weeks; repeated bleeding in the mouth; difficulty or abnormality in speaking or swallowing.

5   The lag time between first use and contracting cancer is shorter for smokeless tobacco users than for smokers because absorption through the gums is the most efficient route of nicotine administration. A growing body of evidence suggests that long-term use of smokeless tobacco also increases the risk of cancer of the larynx, esophagus, nasal cavity, pancreas, kidney, and bladder. Moreover, many smokeless tobacco users eventually "graduate" to cigarettes.

6   Chewers and dippers do not face the specific hazards associated with heat and smoke, but they do run other tobacco-related risks. The stimulant effects of nicotine may create the same circulatory and respiratory problems for chewers as for smokers. Chronic smokeless tobacco use also results in delayed wound healing, peptic ulcer disease, and reproductive disturbances.

7   Smokeless tobacco also impairs the senses of taste and smell, causing the user to add salt and sugar to food, which may contribute to high blood pressure and obesity. Some smokeless tobacco products contain high levels of sodium (salt), which also contributes to high blood pressure. In addition, dental problems are common among users of smokeless tobacco. Contact with tobacco juice causes receding gums, tooth decay, bad breath, and discolored teeth. Damage to both the teeth and jawbone can contribute to early loss of teeth. Users of all tobacco products may not be able to use the vitamins and other nutrients in food effectively. In some cases, vitamin supplements may be recommended by a physician.

Rebecca J. Donatelle, *Health: The Basics*, 4th ed., p. 208, © 2001. Reprinted by permission of Pearson Education, Inc., Upper Saddle River, New Jersey.

ACTIVITY 8   DIRECTIONS: *Complete an SQ4R on a textbook section in another subject area. Be sure you follow the format for developing questions that help you focus on the reading. It would be most beneficial to you if you select a chapter in preparation for an upcoming assignment or test.*

ACTIVITY 9   DIRECTIONS: *Make a concept map for read a chapter in a textbook from another course. It would be most beneficial to you if you select a chapter in preparation for an upcoming assignment or test.*

ACTIVITY 10   DIRECTIONS: *Using a reading assignment from another course, develop a KWL to facilitate learning the topic.*

■ Listening in College and Beyond

In addition to requiring that we read textbooks, college classes require that we learn to listen effectively. Our communication skills involve listening, speaking, reading, and writing. Throughout our daily lives we communicate with others using all four of these modalities. Look at the following diagram. Think about and discuss the reciprocal skills: listening and speaking; reading and writing. How do you use these skills on a daily basis? Think about and discuss the receptive skills: listening and reading. Think about and discuss the productive skills: speaking and writing. How do you use these skills on a daily basis? Thinking and viewing—nonverbal skills—relate to and encompasses all of these skills.

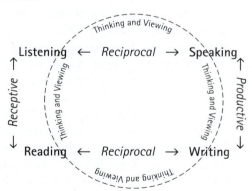

Did you ever stop to think that *silent* and *listen* use the same letters? That should tell us something: Be silent so that you can listen! *Listening* and *hearing* are not the same thing. Listening is one of the most important communication skills because, as a life skill, we listen for a variety of purposes and tasks and apply that to obtain information and be successful. Besides listening to comprehend, listening involves the ability to detect purpose and tone and to judge certain information and situations.

ACTIVITY 11 DIRECTIONS: *Types of listening are: informative, appreciative, relational, critical, and discriminative. Discuss with your class examples of and situations for each:*

- Informative listening: listening to understand
  Examples:
- Appreciative listening: listening for enjoyment
  Examples:
- Relational listening: listening to maintain or improve a relationship
  Examples:
- Critical listening: listening and thinking about an issue to understand, evaluate (judge), analyze (break apart information), synthesize (create or put together)
  Examples:
- Discriminative listening: listening to detect and construct meaning with regard to the speaker's tone, pitch, and volume
  Examples:

What is effective listening? Discuss this with your class.

_____

_____

What is the meaning of this quote? Discuss with your class.

"We were given two ears but only one mouth, because listening is twice as hard as talking."

_____

_____

We know that it is important to develop good listening strategies appropriate for the task. Think about and write down the *bad habits* that you may have that impede good listening and a solution to assist you in improving this behavior so that you can improve your skills to become a better listener.

_____   _____

_____   _____

_____   _____

_____   _____

_____   _____

ACTIVITY 12

DIRECTIONS: Go to www.mindtools.com *and under* communication skills *in the menu, click on* active listening.

Read the information on active listening and jot down the key ideas here:

_____

_____

_____

_____

_____

List the key elements for active listening and be prepared to discuss in class.

_____

_____

_____

_____

_____

DIRECTIONS: Go to www.google.com *and do a search for* effective college listening skills. *Choose a site that looks interesting to you and list components for effective listening. Put a star by those components you need to further develop to become a more efficient and effective listener.*

URL _____

Effective Listening Components:

_____   _____

_____   _____

_____   _____

_____   _____

_____   _____

LOOKING BACK ... LOOKING FORWARD

To check your progress in meeting this chapter's learning objectives, log in to http://www.myreadinglab.com, go to your *Study Plan*, and click on the *Reading Skills* tab. Choose *Reading Textbooks* from the list of subtopics.

Read and view the assets in the *Review Materials* section, then complete the *Practices* and *Tests* in the *Activities* section. Then go back to *Reading Skills*, click on *Active Reading Strategies*, and repeat the process. You can check your scores by clicking on the *Gradebook* tab.

THINK AGAIN!

The following paragraphs are part of a graphic aid taken from a textbook chapter. Can you figure out the point or central message of all three stories taken together?

Picture These Scenes

1   A little league batter leaves the on-deck circle and enters the batter's box. The kid looks kind of scrawny, so you don't expect much, until you notice the gaze of determination and concentration in the batter's eyes and the coach's confident stance. The pitcher winds up, throws—and the kid swings, the bat cracks, and the ball sails sharply over the left-fielder's head. The kid rounds second to third, stares down the third baseman, and executes a perfect slide. Then the batter turns, takes off her cap and lets her long hair fall free, and flashes her winning smile at her third-base coach.

2   The nurse wipes the sweat from the surgeon's brow. The hip replacement surgery is going well, and the saw buzzes in the hand of the skillful surgeon as it is carefully moved through the pelvic bone. The work is demanding and physical. The nurse is adept at handing the surgeon each instrument at exactly the right moment; they have worked together before and make a good team. Now it is time to close, and as the nurse prepares the sutures for the surgeon, a brief smile breaks out. "I am good at what I do," the nurse thinks to himself as he once again reaches over to wipe the surgeon's brow. The surgeon smiles in gratitude, grateful that she has such dedicated and able professionals working with her.

3   Robin undresses, feeling nervous and apprehensive, and then feels silly. After all, the photographer is a professional and has probably seen a thousand naked bodies, so what is one more? All that work in the weight room, the aerobics—why not show off, after all the work it took to get a such a tight body? "I should be proud," Robin thinks, slipping into the robe thoughtfully provided by the photographer. Once exposed to the lights of the studio, Robin gets another pang of doubt but dismisses it and drops the robe. The photographer suggests a seated pose, and Robin strikes it, but he drops his hands to cover his genitals. "Move your hands to your knees, please," the photographer says gently. After all, she is a professional and knows how to put her models at ease.

Janell L. Carroll and Paul Root Wolpe, *Sexuality and Gender in Society*, p. 162

CRITICAL READING

There are textbook study and reading strategies other than those discussed in this chapter. Investigate the Web and see if you can find another strategy that might work for you. Develop a brochure where you give instructions on how to use this new strategy and present it to your classmates. Some examples of other techniques are listed below. However, you are encouraged to be creative and find your own! Try Google.com or YouTube.com to look for textbook reading strategies that might help you.

Purdue University, Indiana—How Can I Organize My Textbook Reading?
http://www.cla.purdue.edu/asc/studentsupport/handouts/

Rio Salado College's Plan, Do, Review
http://www.riosalado.edu/library/tutorials/studySkills/Pages/textbookStrategy.aspx

University of St. Thomas, MN—The "MURDER" study system
 http://www.studygs.net/murder.htm

University of Texas
http://www.utexas.edu/student/utlc/learning_resources/

University of Victoria
http://www.coun.uvic.ca/learning/reading-skills/comprehension.html

LISTENING SPRINGBOARD INQUIRY

Your instructor will select and assign a current podcast, radio message, or video for you to listen to. You may need to subscribe to a site (free) or download special free software (like iTunes or Media Player) in order to listen to these. Or, go to your computer lab and ask the technician if the computers on campus are equipped with this software.

Take notes while you listen to the message. Who are the individuals in the selection and what is their title or position?

_____

_____

What is the main idea of the message?

_____

_____

What are the keys points of the message?

_____

_____

Information on podcasts can be found at http://www.apple.com/itunes/podcasts/
Other sites that have podcasts, Internet radio, or videos:

Public Broadcast Station
http://www.pbs.org/

PublicRadioFan.com
http://www.publicradiofan.com/podcasts.html

BBC
http://www.bbc.co.uk/radio/

Podcast Directory
http://www.podcastdirectory.com/

Digital Podcast
http://www.digitalpodcast.com/

Social Innovation Conversations
http://sic.conversationsnetwork.org/

WNYC
http://www.wnyc.org/podcasting/

WITNESS, THE CAT

Remember to follow these steps:
- first, read the narrative and the question
- second, examine the picture carefully
- third, answer the question and come up with the solution

Have fun!

At 5 P.M. Dixie Tittlemouse, club stewardess at the Sappy Mill Country Club, knocked on the door of the Bon-kei* room. Alarmed when nobody answered, she banged away until Ulrica van Stamen finally staggered over, slid back the bolt, and managed to drag open the door. Upon entering the room, Dixie saw what you see in the sketch. She immediately noticed the empty frame and exclaimed (she was French), "Ah, pauvre Pierre Auguste!"

Unfortunately, the only witness, dead or alive, as to who had stolen the missing Renoir, was Dilly the cat—a club favorite because its meow was a perfect C major, and it could walk along the top of a tennis net without falling. The painting had been appraised at $2 million.

Dixie had some difficulty in waking Ulrica's companions, who were seated counterclockwise from the right: Anthony Adipose, Vera Cruse, and Felonius Winkleman. All four were club members and experienced poker players. But they had known each other only slightly before they'd sat down at the card table. They played for moderate stakes and were comfortably pickled in alcohol when Felonius suggested strip poker. Ulrica exclaimed, "Wow! I hope I lose!" Vera checked a couple of her zippers, and Anthony leered at the two women and said, "My deal." In due course, all four admitted that they'd passed out and consequently could contribute nothing relevant to the theft of the Renoir.

Later on, after a diligent search, the police admitted that they were unable to locate the painting. My Cousin Phoebe, who happened to have stopped at the club for a few rounds of golf after school, knew better and reconstructed the crime. Can you?

*Bon-kei is the Japanese art of miniature landscape using tiny props.

Questions

1. Were all four people apparently drunk? ☐ Yes ☐ No
2. Was the painting hidden in the room, and if so, where? ☐ Yes ☐ No

_____

3. Could a drunken person have cut the picture from its frame? ☐ Yes ☐ No
4. Could a fifth person have entered the room during the night without the knowledge of any of the poker players? ☐ Yes ☐ No
5. Did the cat either eat, drink, or go to the bathroom at the bon-kei? ☐ Yes ☐ No
6. Why do you think the cat fell?

_____

7. Who stole the Renoir?

_____

Text and illustration from Lawrence Treat, *Crime and Puzzlement—My Cousin Phoebe: 24 Solve-Them-Yourself Picture Mysteries* (Henry Holt & Co., 1991) pp. 11–12.

Witness, the Cat

Name _____   Date _____

MASTERY TEST 3-1

Directons: Fill in the blanks and answer the questions.

1. The method used to get acquainted with a new textbook is called

    _____

2. The method used to familiarize yourself with a textbook chapter is called

    _____

3. Questions, reference sources, and summaries are examples of

    _____ aids.

4. A textbook's organization can be seen in the
    a. index
    b. bibliography
    c. glossary
    d. all of the above
    e. none of the above

5. The preface is important because
    a. it gives the author's purpose
    b. lists features
    c. explains the aids to understanding
    d. all of the above
    e. none of the above

6. Page locations for very specific information can be found in the
    a. index
    b. preface
    c. table of contents
    d. appendix
    e. none of the above

7. A _____ provides definitions of words or combinations of words that fit the context of a given textbook.

8. Supplementary or additional information, such as maps and diagrams, can be found in the
    a. table of contents
    b. preface
    c. appendix
    d. index
    e. none of the above

9. For research purposes, it is useful to consult
    a. the bibliography
    b. a list of general reference sources

   c. footnotes
   d. a list of suggested readings
   e. all of the above

10. A _____ contains sources used by the author to write the textbook.

11. The _____ states the topic of a given textbook chapter.

12. You can determine exactly what you are expected to know in a chapter and also set personal study goals by looking at the
   a. objectives
   b. goals
   c. outcomes
   d. all of the above
   e. none of the above

13. _____ aids include charts, graphs, maps, pictures, and tables.

14. _____ or titles let you know what a graphic aid is about.

15. The _____ message of a chapter can sometimes be found in the first or last paragraph.

16. You can plan how to tackle a reading assignment by checking the length and difficulty of a chapter. True or false?

17. Questions at the end of a chapter can help direct your reading to the most valuable information. True or false?

18. Turning _____ into questions helps you focus your attention and evaluate the most important information in a chapter.

19. Underlining or highlighting textbook information is a useful technique that enables you to
   a. comprehend better
   b. review more quickly
   c. concentrate better
   d. all of the above
   e. none of the above

20. The words _____, _____, _____, _____, _____, and _____ should be used to make questions out of chapter headings.

Name _____   Date _____

MASTERY TEST 3-2

DIRECTIONS: *For the two textbook selections that follow, complete one of the following strategies previously introduced: SQ4R, concept mapping, or KLW.*

1

Guidelines for Evaluating Sources

Determine relevance:

- Does the source devote some attention to your topic?
- Where in the source are you likely to find relevant information or ideas?
- Is the source appropriately specialized for your needs? Check the source's treatment of a topic you know something about, to ensure that it is neither too superficial nor too technical.
- How important is the source likely to be for your writing?

Judge reliability:

- How up to date is the source? If the publication date is not recent, be sure that other sources will give you more current views.
- Is the author an expert in the field? Look for an author biography, look up the author in a biographical reference, or try to trace the author over the Internet.
- What is the author's bias? Check biographical information or the author's own preface or introduction. Use book review indexes or citation indexes to learn what others have written about the author or the source.
- Whatever his or her bias, does the author reason soundly, provide adequate evidence, and consider opposing views?

Evaluating Electronic Sources

To a great extent, the same critical reading that serves you with print sources will help you evaluate online sources, too (see the box). But online sources can range from scholarly works to corporate promotions, from government-sponsored data to the self-published rantings of crackpots. To evaluate an online source, you'll first need to figure out what it is.

- *Checking the electronic address.* Look for an abbreviation that tells you where the source originates: edu (educational institution), gov (government body), org (nonprofit organization), mil (military), or com (commercial organization). With a source coming from compex.com, you should assume that the contents reflect the company's commercial purposes (although the information may still be helpful). With a source coming from harvard.edu, you can assume that the contents are more scholarly and objective (although you should still evaluate the information yourself).

- *Determining authorship or sponsorship.* Many sites list the person(s) or group(s) responsible for the site. A Web site may provide links to information about or other work by an author or group. If not, you can refer to a biographical dictionary or conduct a keyword search of the Web. You should also look for mentions of the author or group in your other sources.

  Often you will not be able to trace authors or sponsors or even identify them at all. For instance, someone passionate about the rights of adoptees might maintain a Web site devoted to the subject but not identify himself or herself as the author. In such a case, you'll need to evaluate the quality of the information and opinions by comparing them with sources you know to be reliable.

Guidelines for Evaluating Online Sources

- Check the electronic address for an idea of where the source originates.
- Determine who is responsible for the site.
- Gauge the purpose of the site: to build knowledge? to sell something? to create fear? to achieve another goal?
- Evaluate a Web site as a whole, considering its design, its readability, and the value of its links.

- Weigh contributions to discussion groups by putting them in the context of other contributions. Drop sources whose authors will not answer your direct questions.
- Check for references or links to reliable sources, watching especially for balance.
- Compare online sources with tested mainstream sources.

- *Gauging purpose.* Inferring the purpose of an online source can help you evaluate its reliability. Some sources may seem intent on selling ideas or products. Others may seem to be building knowledge—for instance, by acknowledging opposing views either directly or through links to other sites. Still others may seem determined to scare readers with shocking statistics or anecdotes.

- *Evaluating a Web site as a whole.* Consider both the design and the readability of a Web site and the nature of its links. Is the site thoughtfully designed, or is it cluttered with irrelevant material and graphics? Is it carefully written or difficult to understand? Do the links help clarify the purpose of the site—perhaps leading to scholarly sources or, in contrast, to frivolous or indecent sites?

- *Weighing the contributions to discussion groups.* You need to read individuals' contributions to discussion groups especially critically because they are unfiltered and unevaluated. Even on a discussion list, whose subscribers are likely to be professionals in the field, you may find wrong or misleading data and skewed opinions. With the more accessible Web forums and newsgroups, you should view postings with considerable skepticism.

  You can try to verify a contribution to a discussion group by looking at other contributions, which may help you confirm or refute the questionable posting, and by communicating directly with the author to ask about his or her background and publications. If you can't verify the information from a discussion group and the author doesn't respond to your direct approach, you should probably ignore the source.

- *Checking for references or links to reliable sources.* An online source may offer as support the titles of sources that you can trace and evaluate—articles in periodicals, other online sources, and so on. A Web site may include links to these other sources.
  Be aware, however, that online sources may refer you only to other sources that share the same bias. When evaluating both the original source and its references, look for a fair treatment of opposing views.

- *Comparing online and other sources.* Always consider online sources in the context of other sources so that you can distinguish singular, untested views from more mainstream views that have been subject to verification.

H. Ramsey Fowler and Jane E. Aaron, The Little, Brown Handbook, 8th ed., pp. 669–672

2

Constitutional Principles

To understand the American Constitution, we must study the principles behind it. Let's look in detail at some of the constitution's most important themes.

Representative Democracy

A **democracy** is a system of government in which the people hold ultimate political power. Although the framers of the Constitution favored a government that would answer to the people, they did not want to give too much power to majority opinion. The framers were particularly wary of **direct democracy**, which is a political system in which the citizens vote directly on matters of public concern. The framers of the Constitution worried that ordinary citizens lacked the information to make intelligent policy decisions. They feared that direct democracy would produce policies reflecting hasty, emotional decisions rather than well-considered judgments.

The framers also worried that direct democracy would enable a majority of the people to enact policies that would silence, disadvantage, or harm the minority point of view, thus producing a **tyranny of the majority,** which is the abuse of the minority by the majority. The danger of majority rule is that the majority may vote to adopt policies that unfairly disadvantage the minority. The challenge for the framers of the Constitution was to create a form of government that would provide for majority rule while protecting the rights and liberties of minorities.

Instead of a direct democracy, the framers created a **representative democracy** or a **republic,** which is a political system in which citizens elect representatives to make policy decisions on their behalf. The framers believed that elected representatives would act as a buffer between the people and government policies. Representatives would be more knowledgeable than ordinary citizens about policy issues. They would also be more likely than the general public to recognize the legitimate interests of different groups in society and to seek policy compromises designed to accommodate those interests.

To further guard against the tyranny of the majority, the framers provided that some policy actions could be taken only with the consent of a **supermajority,** a voting margin which is greater than a simple majority. Constitutional amendments must be proposed by two-thirds of the members of both the House and the Senate and ratified by three-fourths of the states. Treaties must be approved by two-thirds of the Senate. Presidential vetoes can be overridden only by a two-thirds vote of each chamber of Congress. Executive and judicial officials can be removed from office only by a two-thirds vote of the Senate. In each of these cases, a simple majority of 50 percent plus one does not prevail. Instead, policy actions require the support, or at least acceptance, of a supermajority of two-thirds or more.

Rule of Law

The **rule of law** is the constitutional principle that holds that the discretion of public officials in dealing with individuals is limited by the law. The very existence of a written constitution implies the rule of law, but certain constitutional provisions deserve special notice. In Article I, Section 9, the Constitution guarantees the privilege of the writ of *habeas corpus* except in cases of invasion, rebellion, or threat to public safety. A **writ of** *habeas corpus* is a court order requiring that government authorities either release a person held in custody or demonstrate that the person is detained in accordance with law. *Habeas corpus* is designed to prevent arbitrary arrest and imprisonment. The Constitution protects Americans from being held in custody by the government unless they are charged and convicted in accordance with the law.

The Constitution prohibits the passage of bills of attainder and *ex post facto* laws. A **bill of attainder** is a law declaring a person or a group of persons guilty of a crime and providing for punishment without benefit of a judicial proceeding. An *ex post facto* law is a retroactive criminal statute that operates to the disadvantage of accused persons. It makes a crime out of an act that was not illegal when it was committed.

Due process of law is the constitutional principle holding that government must follow fair and regular procedures in actions that could lead to an individual's suffering loss of life, liberty, or property. In both the Fifth and Fourteenth Amendments, the Constitution provides that neither Congress (the Fifth Amendment) nor the states (the Fourteenth Amendment) may deprive any person of "life, liberty, or property, without due process of law." Due process of law generally protects individuals from the arbitrary actions of public officials. Before individuals may be imprisoned, fined, or executed, they must be given their day in court in accordance with law. Among other rights, the Constitution guarantees accused persons the right to a speedy, public trial by an impartial jury, the right to confront witnesses, and the right to legal counsel.

Neal Tannahill, *THINK American Government,* pp. 40–43

Name _____   Date _____

MASTERY TEST 3–3

Directions: Pretend that you are in the following situation:

You have been dating a person for the past year and have become very attached. Recently, another person has shown great interest in and started to pursue the person you have been dating, who apparently is very flattered by the extra attention.

Think about how you would handle this conflict situation. Now, based on the textbook passage "Styles of Conflict," which you focused on in Activity 7, identify *your* style of conflict.

_____

_____

_____

_____

_____

_____

_____

HOLMES

SHERLOCK

SHERLOCK HOLMES AND DR. WATSON

Arthur Conan Doyle's fictional detective, Sherlock Holmes, is probably the greatest critical thinker of all time. This semester, you and a classmate will be given the opportunity to play Sherlock Holmes and his loyal companion, Dr. Watson. By putting your minds together, you will attempt to solve the case in "The Adventure of the Three Students."

Be sure to take good notes because at the end of each part of this textbook, the two of you will answer questions concerning the case, which ideally will lead you to the identity of the culprit. As a start, you and your partner should read the first part of the short story and then answer the questions that follow it. Write the answers in your notebooks. Have fun!

The Return of Sherlock Holmes

The Adventure of the Three Students: Part One

A. Conan Doyle

1   It was in the year '95 that a combination of events, into which I need not enter, caused Mr. Sherlock Holmes and myself to spend some weeks in one of our great University towns, and it was during this time that the small but instructive adventure which I am about to relate befell us. It will be obvious that any details which would help the reader to exactly identify the college or the criminal would be injudicious and offensive. So painful a scandal may well be allowed to die out. With due discretion the incident itself may, however, be described, since it serves to illustrate some of those qualities for which my friend was remarkable. I will endeavour in my statement to avoid such terms as would serve to limit the events to any particular place, or give a clue as to the people concerned.

2   We were residing at the time in furnished lodgings close to a library where Sherlock Holmes was pursuing some laborious researches in early English charters—researches which led to results so striking that they may be the subject of one of my future narratives. Here it was that one evening we received a visit from an acquaintance, Mr. Hilton Soames, tutor and lecturer at the College of St. Luke's. Mr. Soames was a tall, spare man, of a nervous and excitable temperament. I had always known him to be restless in his manner, but on this particular occasion he was in such a state of uncontrollable agitation that it was clear something very unusual had occurred.

3   "I trust, Mr. Holmes, that you can spare me a few hours of your valuable time. We have had a very painful incident at St. Luke's, and really, but for the happy chance of your being in the town, I should have been at a loss what to do."

4   "I am very busy just now, and I desire no distractions," my friend answered. "I should much prefer that you called in the aid of the police."

5   "No, no, my dear sir; such a course is utterly impossible. When once the law is evoked it cannot be stayed again, and this is just one of those cases where, for the

credit of the college, it is most essential to avoid scandal. Your discretion is as well known as your powers, and you are the one man in the world who can help me. I beg you, Mr. Holmes, to do what you can."

6   My friend's temper had not improved since he had been deprived of the congenial surroundings of Baker Street. Without his scrapbooks, his chemicals, and his homely untidiness, he was an uncomfortable man. He shrugged his shoulders in ungracious acquiescence, while our visitor in hurried words and with much excitable gesticulation poured forth his story.

7   "I must explain to you, Mr. Holmes, that to-morrow is the first day of the examination for the Fortescue Scholarship. I am one of the examiners. My subject is Greek, and the first of the papers consists of a large passage of Greek translation which the candidate has not seen. This passage is printed on the examination paper, and it would naturally be an immense advantage if the candidate could prepare it in advance. For this reason great care is taken to keep the paper secret.

8   "To-day about three o'clock the proofs of this paper arrived from the printers. The exercise consists of half a chapter of Thucydides. I had to read it over carefully, as the text must be absolutely correct. At four-thirty my task was not yet completed. I had, however, promised to take tea in a friend's rooms, so I left the proof upon my desk. I was absent rather more than an hour.

9   "You are aware, Mr. Holmes, that our college doors are double—a green baize one within and a heavy oak one without. As I approached my outer door I was amazed to see a key in it. For an instant I imagined that I had left my own there, but on feeling in my pocket I found that it was all right. The only duplicate which existed, so far as I knew, was that which belonged to my servant, Bannister, a man who has looked after my room for ten years, and whose honesty is absolutely above suspicion. I found that the key was indeed his, that he had entered my room to know if I wanted tea, and that he had very carelessly left the key in the door when he came out. His visit to my room must have been within a very few minutes of my leaving it. His forgetfulness about the key would have mattered little upon any other occasion, but on this one day it has produced the most deplorable consequences.

10   "The moment I looked at my table I was aware that someone had rummaged among my papers. The proof was in three long slips. I had left them all together. Now I found that one of them was lying on the floor, one was on the side table near the window, and the third was where I had left it."

11   Holmes stirred for the first time.

12   "The first page on the floor, the second in the window, the third where you left it," said he.

13   "Exactly, Mr. Holmes. You amaze me. How could you possibly know that?"

14   "Pray continue your very interesting statement."

15   "For an instant I imagined that Bannister had taken the unpardonable liberty of examining my papers. He denied it, however, with the utmost earnestness, and I am convinced that he was speaking the truth. The alternative was that someone passing had observed the key in the door, had known that I was out, and had entered to look at the papers. A large sum of money is at stake, for the scholarship is a very valuable one, and an unscrupulous man might very well run a risk in order to gain an advantage over his fellows.

16   "Bannister was very much upset by the incident. He had nearly fainted when we found that the papers had undoubtedly been tampered with. I gave him a little brandy and left him collapsed in a chair while I made a most careful examination of the room. I soon saw that the intruder had left other traces of his presence besides the rumpled papers. On the table in the window were several shreds from a pencil which had been sharpened. A broken tip of lead was lying there also. Evidently the rascal had copied the paper in a great hurry, had broken his pencil, and had been compelled to put a fresh point to it."

17   "Excellent!" said Holmes, who was recovering his good-humour as his attention became more engrossed by the case. "Fortune has been your friend."

18   "This was not all. I have a new writing-table with a fine surface of red leather. I am prepared to swear, and so is Bannister, that it was smooth and unstained. Now I found a clean cut in it about three inches long—not a mere scratch, but a positive cut. Not only this, but on the table I found a small ball of black dough, or clay, with specks of something which looks like sawdust in it. I am convinced that these marks were left by the man who rifled the papers. There were no footmarks and no other evidence as to his identity. I was at my wits' ends, when suddenly the happy thought occurred to me that you were in the town, and I came straight round to put the matter into your hands. Do help me, Mr. Holmes! You see my dilemma. Either I must find the man or else the examination must be postponed until fresh papers are prepared, and since this cannot be done without explanation there will ensue a hideous scandal, which will throw a cloud not only on the college, but on the University. Above all things I desire to settle the matter quietly and discreetly."

19   "I shall be happy to look into it and to give you such advice as I can," said Holmes, rising and putting on his overcoat. "The case is not entirely devoid of interest. Had anyone visited you in your room after the papers came to you?"

20   "Yes; young Daulat Ras, an Indian student who lives on the same stair, came in to ask me some particulars about the examination."

21   "For which he was entered?"

22   "Yes."

23   "And the papers were on your table?"

24   "To the best of my belief they were rolled up."

25   "But might be recognised as proofs?"

26   "Possibly."

27   "No one else in your room?"

28   "No."

29   "Did anyone know that these proofs would be there?"

30   "No one save the printer."

31   "Did this man Bannister know?"

32   "No, certainly not. No one knew."

33   "Where is Bannister now?"

34   "He was very ill, poor fellow. I left him collapsed in the chair. I was in such a hurry to come to you."

35   "You left your door open?"

36   "I locked up the papers first."

37   "Then it amounts to this, Mr. Soames, that unless the Indian student recognised the roll as being proofs, the man who tampered with them came upon them accidentally without knowing that they were there."

38   "So it seems to me."

39   Holmes gave an enigmatic smile.

40   "Well," said he, "let us go round. Not one of your cases, Watson—mental, not physical. All right; come if you want to. Now, Mr. Soames—at your disposal!"

41   The sitting-room of our client opened by a long, low, latticed window on to the ancient lichen-tinted court of the old college. A Gothic arched door led to a worn stone staircase. On the ground floor was the tutor's room. Above were three students, one on each story. It was already twilight when we reached the scene of our problem. Holmes halted and looked earnestly at the window. Then he approached it, and, standing on tiptoe with his neck craned, he looked into the room.

42   "He must have entered through the door. There is no opening except the one pane," said our learned guide.

43   "Dear me!" said Holmes, and he smiled in a singular way as he glanced at our companion. "Well, if there is nothing to be learned here we had best go inside."

44   The lecturer unlocked the outer door and ushered us into his room. We stood at the entrance while Holmes made an examination of the carpet.

45   "I am afraid there are no signs here," said he. "One could hardly hope for any upon so dry a day. Your servant seems to have quite recovered. You left him in a chair, you say; which chair?"

46   "By the window there."

47   "I see. Near this little table. You can come in now. I have finished with the carpet. Let us take the little table first. Of course, what has happened is very clear. The man entered and took the papers, sheet by sheet, from the central table. He carried them over to the window table, because from there he could see if you came across the courtyard, and so could effect an escape."

48   As a matter of fact he could not," said Soames, "for I entered by the side door."

49   "Ah, that's good! Well, anyhow, that was in his mind. Let me see the three strips. No finger impressions—no! Well, he carried over this one first and he copied it. How long would it take him to do that, using every possible contraction? A quarter of an hour, not less. Then he tossed it down and seized the next. He was in the midst of that when your return caused him to make a very hurried retreat—very hurried, since he had not time to replace the papers which would tell you that he had been there. You were not aware of any hurrying feet on the stair as you entered the outer door?"

50   "No, I can't say I was."

51   "Well, he wrote so furiously that he broke his pencil, and had, as you observe, to sharpen it again. This is of interest, Watson. The pencil was not an ordinary one. It was above the usual size, with a soft lead; the outer colour was dark blue, the maker's name was printed in silver lettering, and the piece remaining is only about an inch and a half long. Look for such a pencil, Mr. Soames, and you have got your man. When I add that he possesses a large and very blunt knife, you have an additional aid."

52   Mr. Soames was somewhat overwhelmed by this flood of information. "I can follow the other points," said he, "but really in this matter of the length—"

53   Holmes held out a small chip with the letters NN and a space of clear wood after them.

54   "You see?"

55   "No, I fear that even now—"

56   "Watson, I have always done you an injustice. There are others. What could this NN be? It is at the end of a word. You are aware that Johann Faber is the most common maker's name. Is it not clear that there is just as much of the pencil left as usually follows the Johann?" He held the small table sideways to the electric light. "I was hoping that if the paper on which he wrote was thin some trace of it might come through upon this polished surface. No, I see nothing. I don't think there is anything more to be learned here. Now for the central table. This small pellet is, I presume, the black, doughy mass you spoke of. Roughly pyramidal in shape and hollowed out, I perceive. As you say, there appear to be grains of sawdust in it. Dear me, this is very interesting. And the cut—a positive tear, I see. It began with a thin scratch and ended in a jagged hole. I am much indebted to you for directing my attention to this case, Mr. Soames. Where does that door lead to?"

57   "To my bedroom."

58   "Have you been in it since your adventure?"

59   "No; I came straight away for you."

60   "I should like to have a glance round. What a charming, old-fashioned room! Perhaps you will kindly wait a minute until I have examined the floor. No, I see nothing. What about this curtain? You hang your clothes behind it. If anyone were forced to conceal himself in this room he must do it there, since the bed is too low and the wardrobe too shallow. No one there, I suppose?"

61   As Holmes drew the curtain I was aware, from some little rigidity and alertness of his attitude, that he was prepared for an emergency. As a matter of fact the drawn curtain disclosed nothing but three or four suits of clothes hanging from a line of pegs. Holmes turned away and stooped suddenly to the floor.

62   "Halloa! What's this?" said he.

63   It was a small pyramid of black, putty-like stuff, exactly like the one upon the table of the study. Holmes held it out on his open palm in the glare of the electric light.

64   "Your visitor seems to have left traces in your bedroom as well as in your sitting-room, Mr. Soames."

65   "What could he have wanted there?"

66   "I think it is clear enough. You came back by an unexpected way, and so he had no warning until you were at the very door. What could he do? He caught up everything which would betray him and he rushed into your bedroom to conceal himself."

67   "Good gracious, Mr. Holmes, do you mean to tell me that all the time I was talking to Bannister in this room we had the man prisoner if we had only known it?"

68   "So I read it."

69   "Surely there is another alternative, Mr. Holmes. I don't know whether you observed my bedroom window?"

70   "Lattice-paned, lead framework, three separate windows, one swinging on hinge and large enough to admit a man."

71   "Exactly. And it looks out on an angle of the courtyard so as to be partly invisible. The man might have effected his entrance there, left traces as he passed through the bedroom, and, finally, finding the door open have escaped that way."

The Complete Original Illustrated Sherlock Holmes, pp. 566–570

Questions

1. What is the problem that confronts Holmes and Watson?

2. What are the clues?

3. At this point in the mystery, are there any suspects? If so, who are they, and why do you consider them suspects?

PART TWO
DEALING WITH COMPLEXITY

173

4 Critical Thinking and Contemporary Issues

CHAPTER OUTLINE

CHAPTER OUTCOMES

After completing Chapter 4, you should be able to:

- Distinguish between critical thinking and random thinking.
- Discuss the benefits and uses of critical thinking.
- List, explain, and demonstrate the characteristics of critical thinking.
- Define contemporary issue.
- Find topics and central messages in contemporary issue passages in order to determine what is at issue, distinguish among opposing viewpoints, and express personal viewpoints.

Think About It!

These two headline front pages report about New Orleans after the Katrina hurricane. They use the same picture but different headlines. What is the central message of each of these front pages? Do the messages differ because of the headlines? What about the choice of a second photo in each case? Share your thoughts with other students in your class.

■ Critical Thinking Versus Random Thinking

Take a few moments just to let some thoughts pass through your mind. What are you thinking about? Are you reflecting on what you did last night or what you intend to do this weekend? Are you worried about an assignment that is due or a test that is coming up? Maybe you are focusing on an important person in your life. Perhaps you are just thinking about how hungry or tired you are. The possibilities are endless.

What you just did was an example of **random thinking**, which is *thinking without a clear purpose or objective in mind.* We all do this kind of thinking countless times each day, often without even realizing it. Sometimes we are simply daydreaming, thinking about past experiences, or wondering or worrying about some future activity. Thoughts pop into mind and just as quickly out; they come and go without much effort on our part. Nothing is really accomplished as a result, except perhaps a rest or escape from whatever we may be doing at that particular time.

Random thinking is not critical thinking. How do they differ? Let's look at an example.

Suppose that you and a friend are considering whether to take a particular course next semester. The two of you approach another student who enrolled for that course last year, and she informs you that she dropped it after two weeks because it was so boring. On the basis of that conversation, your friend decides not to take the course. Although you are tempted to do the same thing, you decide instead to give the matter more thought because you do not think it wise to base your decision solely on the opinion of one student, who might have had a personal reason for not appreciating the course. For example, she could have had a problem at the time that interfered with her ability to fulfill the course requirements, or she could have been uncomfortable with the instructor's personality and teaching style. These may have been good reasons at the time for her not to stay in the course, but that does not mean that they should have an effect on your decision. Consequently, rather than automatically accepting one person's opinion, you decide to spend more time and effort getting additional information before coming to a final decision.

You organize your efforts by first getting a class schedule for next semester in order to find out the days and times that the course is offered and which faculty teach it. You want to determine if you can fit the course into your schedule and whether you have a choice of instructor. Second, you check the college catalog so that you can read the course description to see what it is about in a general sense and whether it can be used as part of your program of study. Third, you obtain a copy of a recent course syllabus from the department, a counselor, the instructor, or a student so that you can get additional information on assignments and grading. Fourth, you ask around so that you can find and talk to more students who have taken the course. Fifth, you discuss the course with a faculty member and your counselor or academic adviser.

After considering carefully all the information you gathered, you now feel confident about coming to a conclusion regarding whether to enroll in the course. You know that it fits into your program of study and your schedule, and you have a better understanding of its content. Furthermore, you are aware of who teaches the course and can determine whether you are comfortable with his or her teaching style, grading policies, and personality. No matter what you ultimately decide to do, you have placed yourself in a much stronger position to make the right decision *for you*. However, you do continue to reconsider that decision right up until the time of registration, just in case you find out some additional information that changes your mind.

The process that you used in the example above involved **critical thinking**, which is best described as *a very careful and thoughtful way of dealing with events, issues, problems, decisions, or situations*. As you can see, critical thinking can be very helpful to you. Let's take a brief look at its many benefits and uses.

■ Benefits and Uses of Critical Thinking

Critical thinking is important because it makes you a much more careful decision maker who has the best chance of assessing situations accurately, making sense of issues and events, and coming up with solutions to problems. Because critical thinkers do not accept blindly everything they see, hear, or read, they place themselves in better positions to understand what is going on around them, to avoid costly mistakes, and to accomplish whatever they set out to do.

There are no limits to the uses of critical thinking. It can help you evaluate textbook material and other types of reading; uncover motivations and assess arguments; consider options, products, advertisements, and commercials; and judge policies and programs such as those offered by the various levels of government. The benefits of critical thinking for you are very real and substantial no matter what roles you play in life now and in the future, including those of student, professional, parent, and citizen. Make it a habit to think critically about everything!

■ Characteristics of Critical Thinking

How do you know for sure when you are thinking critically? The answer to that question involves a discussion of its characteristics. Critical thinking requires:

- flexibility
- a clear purpose
- organization
- time and effort
- asking questions and finding answers
- research
- coming to logical conclusions

Let's consider each of these characteristics in more detail.

Flexibility

Critical thinking is **flexible thinking** because it involves a willingness to consider various possibilities before coming to a conclusion. Critical thinkers do not jump to conclusions or automatically accept what they first see, hear, or read. They are willing to gather and consider additional information, even if it does not support what they initially think or want to do. In the course selection example, it would have been easy for you simply to accept the first student's opinion and your friend's decision regarding the course. Even though you may have been tempted to take the quick and easy way out, you delayed your decision until you had a chance to gather more information. Realizing that your first reaction to the course was negative, you still managed to keep an open mind and were willing to consider carefully other viewpoints.

Critical thinkers, then, are aware of their initial feelings about decisions, issues, problems, or situations yet willing to look at other possibilities before taking action. *They are also willing to allow others the opportunity to voice their opinions, and they give careful consideration to those opinions before coming to their own conclusions.* In the end, critical thinkers may stick with their initial feelings, but only after much investigation and thought.

ACTIVITY 1   *DIRECTIONS: Think about an example from your life in which you showed flexibility and an example from your life in which you did not. Be prepared to discuss your two examples.*

Directions: Read and think carefully about the following passage. Decide which side of the argument you disagree with and why. Show flexibility by writing a paragraph in support of that position. In other words, you are being asked to ignore your personal viewpoint and support the opposite one. You may consult the Web sites listed to get more ideas. You will be asked to provide the reasons why you disagree with the argument and also discuss the paragraph you wrote in support of it.

Should the Voting Age Be Lowered to Sixteen?

1   In California, some legislators have proposed giving partial voting rights to teens. Fourteen-year-olds would receive a one-quarter vote and sixteen-year-olds would receive a half vote. Internationally, Germany and Austria have already lowered their voting ages to sixteen. Students and elected officials in Tanzania have made demands to lower the voting age from eighteen. This is because Tanzanians finish their education at fourteen and because of falling life expectancy rates due to the African AIDS epidemic.

2   Throughout its history, the United States has expanded voting rights. It started with removing restrictions based on property ownership. Later, the Fifteenth and Nineteenth Amendments granted suffrage respectively to African American men and all women. Passage of the Twenty-sixth Amendment lowered the voting age to eighteen. Should we continue to expand voting rights by lowering the voting age still further?

Pro

3   The government must represent the interests of all Americans, but we cannot guarantee that it will if we do not lower the age limit. There are issues that uniquely affect young voters. The government can overlook these unless teens hold it accountable by voting.

4   There is no magical transformation one undergoes when one turns eighteen. By sixteen, a person has more or less developed intellectually. Some sixteen-year-olds have more maturity than some adults.

5   The earlier young people are exposed to politics, the more likely they will participate when they're older. We should socialize American youth to become better citizens by introducing them to democracy through the election process. We may get a better voter turnout in the long run.

Con

6   In most states, the age when one acquires the legal rights and responsibilities of an adult is currently eighteen years. In a legal sense, young people are not recognized as independent members of society until they turn eighteen, after which they automatically have the right to vote.

7   High school students often do not complete their civics and American government education until their junior and senior years in high school. Individuals should have a proper foundation in the privileges and responsibilities of citizenship before they vote.

8   Lowering the voting age will not make any difference in the outcomes of elections. Most sixteen-year-olds are not interested in politics and likely would not vote. It might be worse if they did, since they would not have a very good idea of what they were doing.

9   Selected Web Sites:

http://www.youthrights.org/votingage.php

http://votesforadults.typepad.com/votes_for_adults/2004/04/

"Should the Voting Age Be Lowered to Sixteen?" from Karen O'Connor and Larry J. Sabato,
American Government: Continuity and Change, 2006, pp. 492–493

Clear Purpose

Critical thinking is deliberate thinking because it always involves a **clear purpose**, a specific goal. When you think critically, you are looking for reasons or explanations for events, considering various sides of an issue, attempting to solve a problem, coming to a decision, or making sense of a situation. For example, you may be trying to figure out how an event such as an automobile accident occurred, distinguish among the arguments on both sides of an issue such as abortion, come up with a solution to a problem such as a low grade in a course, decide where to go on vacation, or understand the reasons behind a political event such as a war or revolution. In the course example, the decision whether to register for the course was the purpose you, as a critical thinker, had in mind.

ACTIVITY 3

DIRECTIONS: Think about an experience from your past in which you demonstrated critical thinking by having a clear purpose—in other words, an example of an instance when you tried to reach a specific goal. The experience could involve you looking for reasons or explanations for events, considering various sides of an issue, attempting to solve a problem, coming to a decision, or making sense of a situation. Be prepared to discuss your example in class.

ACTIVITY 4

DIRECTIONS: Read the following article; then discuss it with a classmate. Together, try to come up with possible reasons or explanations for the actions of Joseph Chavis. Your purpose here is to try to make sense of the situation.

As a Lawyer, He's Exemplary; as a Robber, an Enigma

CHRISTINE BIEDERMAN

1   DALLAS, Jan. 19—Sitting beside his lawyer in Federal District Court today, a diminutive man in a conservative gray suit, starched, striped cotton shirt and conservative tie massaged his temples as if trying to banish a migraine.

2   When his case was called, he stepped before the bench and, in response to the judge's request to state his name and age, he cleared his throat and answered nearly inaudibly. Then, when the judge asked how much education he had, his wavering voice failed him; looking down at the podium, he began to cry.

3   Moments later, Joseph E. Chavis Jr., a 30-year-old lawyer known by colleagues and opponents alike as a quiet, studious and sincere man, would plead guilty to charges of bank robbery in a case that left many in disbelief.

4   A holder of a business degree from Texas A&M University and a law degree from Southern Methodist University, Mr. Chavis is recalled by his law professors as a model student and a caring mentor for other young black men and women making their way through the mostly white world of Dallas law firms.

5   After his arrest, just before Christmas, partners at Clark, West, Keller & Butler—the 100-year-old Dallas labor firm that has employed Mr. Chavis since he graduated from law school in 1990—stood by him and described him as a "terrific advocate and a first-rate lawyer." Friends say both Mr. Chavis and his wife, Debra Ann Lockhart, a fellow lawyer and law school classmate, devoted their spare time to Roman Catholic Church activities.

6   At first the charges against Mr. Chavis seemed a Kafkaesque nightmare of mistaken identity. After his arrest, members of his law firm, as well friends, relatives, former professors and even the dean of S.M.U.'s law school, said that the police had the wrong man, that the Joseph Chavis they knew could not have done this.

7   "So, on his way to work, he robs a bank," said Prof. William Bridge of the S.M.U. Law School. "It's just inconsistent with everything in his background and character, and therefore it's easier for me to believe that it's a mistake."

8   But the authorities continued to insist that there had been no mistake, and on Jan. 5, a Federal grand jury indicted Mr. Chavis.

9   In the course of robbing Bank United, a small bank in the exclusive University Park neighborhood, the authorities say, Mr. Chavis did everything but hold up a sign with his name and Social Security number.

10   The police and the Federal Bureau of Investigation say that about 9 A.M. on Dec. 18, Mr. Chavis left his condominium on the edge of the University Park area and drove two miles to the bank, which is within sight of S.M.U.'s law school in

University Park. Once there, they say, Mr. Chavis walked in without a disguise and asked for two rolls of quarters in exchange for $20.

11   Mr. Chavis then left, only to return a few minutes later. This time, prosecutors say, he walked up to a teller and said: "Good morning. I have a gun in my pocket. Please give me your money." He received exactly $1,340 and fled on foot, the authorities said.

12   An F.B.I. spokeswoman, Marge Poche, said that the bank's camera had yielded "a great picture of the suspect" and that within minutes, the "police spotted someone they believed could fit the description of the bank robber in the vicinity of Renaissance Tower," the downtown high-rise where Mr. Chavis worked.

13   "They searched the area, and some units found some discarded money in a bathroom of the parking garage that had a lock," Ms. Poche said.

14   The Federal prosecutors said security cameras showed Mr. Chavis putting something in a trash can. A search of the trash can, they said, turned up white quarter wrappers as well as the dark-brimmed baseball cap that the robber had been seen wearing. The baseball cap, which bore the logo of one of Mr. Chavis's clients, had been a gift for a legal job well done, his lawyer said.

15   About the same time, the police received a call saying banded bundles of money had been found under a water fountain in the hallway near a back entrance to the Clark, West law firm. An officer went to the firm and noticed that Mr. Chavis looked like the robber on the bank video; he was arrested that afternoon.

16   "All but about $10" of the bank's money was recovered, Ms. Poche said.

17   No one involved in the case has a satisfactory answer for the vexing questions it raises.

New York Times, January 20, 1996, p. 7

Organization

Students often complain that lack of time makes it difficult for them to accomplish everything that they have to do. There is no doubt that their lives are very busy, with classes to attend, assignments to be completed, studying to be done, and tests to be taken. As a typical college student, there are occasions when you must feel under a great deal of time pressure. For that reason, you probably schedule your daily activities very carefully so that you are able to get everything done. You have certain hours that you devote to going to and preparing for classes, and you work your other personal responsibilities around them. In other words, you use **organization,** or careful planning, to make the most productive use of your limited time.

Critical thinkers also depend on organization to help them deal effectively with events, issues, problems, decisions, and situations. In the example, you certainly used an organized approach to help you to make a decision regarding whether you should take the course. You went through a series of specific steps in order to gather more information, which placed you in a much stronger position when deciding what to do. Critical thinking always involves that kind of organization.

Time and Effort

At this point, it is probably obvious to you that critical thinking requires much **time and effort.** Furthermore, critical thinkers are willing to take time away from other activities so that they can concentrate on a specific event, issue, problem, decision, or situation. The examples you have read about and the activities that you have been asked to complete all involve not only setting aside time but also putting in extra effort. In the example, the easy road would have been for you to follow your first reaction, which was not to register for the course. You opted instead to take some additional time to gather information, because you felt that it would help you make the right decision. In short, you were taking the time and making the effort that critical thinking requires.

Asking Questions and Finding Answers

Critical thinkers are aware of what is going on around them. They observe their surroundings carefully and put substantial effort into looking for causes, explanations, or reasons. In other words, critical thinkers **ask questions** continuously and are very patient and persistent when trying to **find answers.** They often use words that are found in questions, such as *who, when, what, where, how,* and *why.* For example, critical thinkers would wonder: Who is responsible for determining the price of an automobile? Where can I find information about a fair price for a particular automobile? Where can I find information about a fair loan rate for an automobile? When is the best time to study for a test? How do I decide what career to pursue? What are the requirements for the career that I want to pursue? What provides the pressure that forces water through a faucet? Where does electricity originate from? How is sewage carried through underground pipes without clogging them? Why do leaves turn different colors in many areas of the United States? Have you thought about answers to these questions and others like them? If you have, you have experience at being a critical thinker.

When considering whether to take the course in our example, you asked questions like "Will the course fit into my program of study?" "How will it affect my schedule?" "Do I have a choice of instructor?"

"What is the course about?" and "How hard is it?" Furthermore, you were very persistent in trying to find answers *before* making a decision. In other words, you were being a critical thinker.

ACTIVITY 5

DIRECTIONS: During the next few days, take some time away from your usual routine to observe and think about your surroundings. Instead of rushing from one place to another, spend a few moments looking carefully at your neighborhood, school, or workplace, listening to what is going on, questioning what you see and hear, and finding answers by being patient and persistent. Then write an essay describing everything that you saw and heard, including possible answers to your questions. You will be asked to share your essay with your classmates.

ACTIVITY 6

DIRECTIONS: Look carefully at the following photographs and try to notice little things that seem interesting or unusual. Ask questions about what you see; then think about possible explanations. Discuss your explanations of each of these photos with your classmates.

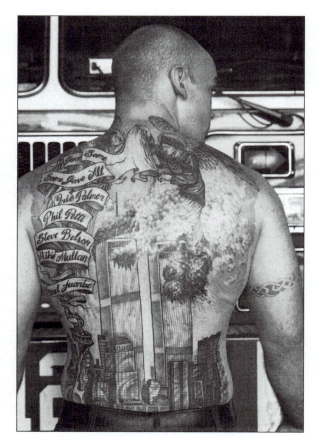

DIRECTIONS: Read the following article and develop questions that will help you make sense of the author's message. Think about possible answers to your questions, and discuss both your questions and answers with your classmates. Also, be prepared to discuss your own informed opinion about this issue.

Video Games Tied to Aggression

SHARON JAYSON

1   USA Today, March 1: A new review of 130 studies "strongly suggests" playing violent video games increases aggressive thoughts and behavior and decreases empathy.

2   The results hold "regardless of research design, gender, age or culture," says lead researcher Craig Anderson, who directs the Center for the Study of Violence at Iowa State University in Ames.

3   His team did a statistical analysis of studies on more than 130,000 gamers from elementary school age to college in the USA, Europe and Japan. It is published today in *Psychological Bulletin*, a journal of the American Psychological Association.

4   But Christopher Ferguson, an associate professor at Texas A&M International University in Laredo, says in a critique accompanying the study that the effects found "are generally very low." He adds that the analysis "contains numerous flaws," which he says result in "overestimating the influence" of violent games on aggression.

5   Ferguson says his own study of 603 predominantly Hispanic young people, published last year in *The Journal of Pediatrics*, found "delinquent peer influences,

antisocial personality traits, depression, and parents/guardians who use psycho-logical abuse" were consistent risk factors for youth violence and aggression. But he also found that neighborhood quality, parents' domestic violence and exposure to violent TV or video games "were not predictive of youth violence and aggres-sion." Anderson says his team "never said it's a huge effect. But if you look at known risk factors for the development of aggression and violence, some are bigger than media violence and some are smaller.

6   "If you have a child with no other risk factors for aggression and violence and if you allow them to suddenly start playing video games five hours to ten hours a week, they're not going to become a school shooter. One risk factor doesn't do it by itself." But he notes that video game violence is "the only causal risk factor that is relatively easy for parents to do something about." Both of his college-age kids grew up playing video games, Anderson says, but many games rated "E" (for "everyone") contain violence.

7   "The rating itself does not tell you whether it is a healthy or unhealthy game," he adds. "Any game that involves killing or harming another character in order to advance is likely to be teaching inappropriate lessons to whoever is playing it."

Sharon Jayson, "Video Games Tied to Aggression," *USA Today*,
March 1, 2010, p. 1A. Reprinted with permission.

Research

Critical thinking is a way of dealing with events, issues, problems, deci-sions, or situations in a very thoughtful, careful manner. For that reason, critical thinking often requires **research**, *the process of looking for and gather-ing information to increase your knowledge and understanding of a given topic.* In the example that we have been using, you did research to place yourself in a stronger position in deciding whether to take the course. You studied the class schedule, the catalog, and a syllabus and talked with students, faculty, and your counselor to gather as much information as possible concerning the course. In other words, all of the research that you did provided you with more information to help you make a decision.

The kind of research that critical thinkers do and the sources of information that they use vary with the matter at hand. In other words, research can involve using the Internet, going to libraries, reading official reports or documents, interviewing people, visiting various agencies and organizations, or some combination of these. For example, if a young man wants to find out more about the issue of gun control, he might go to the library or use the Internet to read about the topic in newspapers, maga-zines, books, or reports. In addition, he might talk with individuals who know something about the issue—perhaps police officials, gun owners, and members of various organizations that support and oppose gun control. By contrast, if he wants to investigate a traffic accident, he might study the police report, read newspaper accounts, talk with persons actually involved, and interview any witnesses who were present.

As these examples illustrate, critical thinkers are careful about using the sources that are most relevant, applicable, or appropriate and therefore most likely to provide useful, reliable information—information that is not only specific to the topic, but also accurate and trustworthy. Thus, our young researcher would probably not seek information about gun control from a mechanic, a physician, or an accountant unless the individual was somehow involved with the issue, nor would he read general magazines or books to find out about a particular traffic accident. You certainly used appropriate sources when doing research for the course decision. Each of the individuals you talked with was in a good position to provide useful information, and the written sources were all relevant to the matter under consideration.

Critical thinkers are not only aware of their own feelings and opinions; they also try to be aware of any **prejudice** or **bias** on the part of a given source. In other words, our researcher would determine if the source is providing information that supports a particular point of view instead of being impartial or evenhanded. For example, if he is discussing gun control with a representative of an organization that does not support it, such as the National Rifle Association, he would keep in mind that the information he is getting is probably slanted in one direction. Similarly, if our researcher is reading literature put out by that same organization, he realizes that it is likely to include only information supporting its viewpoint regarding the issue. This is not to say that he should necessarily ignore the information. However, at the very least, he would need to search for information from other sources that might offer opposing viewpoints. You were using critical thinking when you realized that the student who had dropped the course was only giving her personal point of view, which was not unbiased. That is precisely why you turned to additional sources of information before making a decision.

A Word of Caution When Using the Internet for Research   As you know, the Internet consists of an enormous number of computers that are linked through a worldwide network. It is a very rapid means of sharing information, *some* of which is excellent and *some* of which is not very worthwhile. This results from the fact that, unlike books and articles in periodicals and newspapers, there is no review by others before publication on the Internet. Thus, anyone can publish personal views on a variety of topics without having the information evaluated first by editors, experts, or others who are knowledgeable about the subject matter. Therefore, in those instances, you as the researcher must be extra careful about determining not only the relevance and impartiality of the information presented but its reliability as well. How should you go about doing that?

First, as with all sources, use common sense to make sure that the information offered is useful or appropriate for your research needs. Ask yourself whether a particular source focuses on the subject matter that is of interest to you and whether it does so in a fair and thorough manner. For instance, if you are investigating the issue of capital punishment, a source that devotes several pages to a discussion of the opposing viewpoints would probably be more useful than one that devotes a few paragraphs to life on death row.

Second, try to use material published by educational institutions, such as Harvard (with Web addresses that end in *.edu*), or posted on governmental (*.gov*) and military (*.mil*) sites. The information these sites provide is quite likely to be reliable. Sites maintained by professional organizations (*.org*), such as the American Medical Association, can usually be relied on for accurate information, but keep in mind that some organizations simply want to persuade you to accept their points of view. The National Rifle Association is a good example of such an organization. Commercial sources (sites that end in *.com*), such as Philip Morris USA, are more questionable because they are often trying to sell you their products or influence your thinking so that they can continue to make profits. Thus, if you were looking into the effects of cigarette advertising on young people, Philip Morris would probably not be a good source of information to use because of its obvious bias, whereas a report put out by the U.S. Office of the Surgeon General would be much more reliable.

Third, when possible, try to find the professional affiliation of the author in the credits or e-mail address so that you can determine his or her expertise on a given topic. For example, if you were investigating an issue involving medical ethics, a medical doctor who is also on the faculty of the University of Pennsylvania Medical School would probably be a more reliable source than an individual complaining about the high cost of medical treatment on a personal home page.

Fourth, check whether the author lists a bibliography of the sources used so that you can gauge whether the sources are reputable and scholarly. Publications such as the *New York Times, Newsweek, New England Journal of Medicine,* and textbooks in general are usually recognized by most people as providers of accurate, well-researched, and well-documented information.

Thus, if sources like those are listed, you can feel a bit more secure about using the author's material.

Finally, there are online databases on the Internet, such as EBSCO, ProQuest, and LEXIS-NEXIS, that provide access to full-text articles from scholarly and popular periodicals such as the *New England Journal of Medicine, Columbia Journalism Review, New York Times,* and *Newsweek.* Libraries have databases for references in their own collection and other tools, such as Research Quickstart, to acquire further Web site links by subject area. Furthermore, there are online encyclopedias, such as *World Book, Britannica,* and *Encarta,* that are good starting points for research. All of these sources can generally be relied upon for relevance, reliability, and impartiality. On the other hand, search engines, such as Yahoo and Google, use keywords to find complete or condensed information from a variety of sources that should be evaluated carefully by the researcher.

As you recall, the first textbook passage in Mastery Test 3-2 provides some additional hints on evaluating sources, including electronic ones. If necessary, refer to it to refresh your memory. Remember that the Internet can be a very helpful source of information, but you must exercise great care when using it for research purposes.

ACTIVITY 8	*Directions: Assume that you want to do research to answer the question "Does violence on television contribute to real violence in the United States?" How and where would you get information? Discuss this question with two of your classmates, and together come up with a list of possible sources that are appropriate to use. Be sure to include a variety of specific sources, and be ready to provide the reasons why you feel they are relevant to the issue. Also, try to determine if you think the sources are likely to be reliable and impartial.*

ACTIVITY 9	*Directions: With two other classmates, look carefully at the following three sources, taken from the Internet, on television violence and its effect on children and crime. Are the sources relevant, reliable, and impartial? Answer the following three questions about each site:*

1. Does the source focus on the subject matter and provide enough specific information to help me answer the question? (relevance)

2. Based upon my evaluation of the author and the source, is the information provided accurate and trustworthy? (reliability)

3. Is the information provided biased toward one particular point of view, or does it present opposing viewpoints? (impartiality)

Media violence good for kids

By Lacy Cordell

Published: Thursday, October 14, 2004
Updated: Saturday, December 5, 2009 18:12

 Tweet   0   email   share    print

Saying that violence in the media is having a negative effect on children is just an excuse for being a bad parent. I have a good reason for a child being terrible: the parent. I grant that a 2-year-old should not watch an R-rated movie, but sheltering kids too much will cause them shock when they reach the real world, and they will not know how to handle anything.

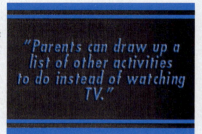

"Parents can draw up a list of other activities to do instead of watching TV."

Good parents raise their kids with the morals they want them to have and teach them how to handle life. My sister, brother and I were raised on horror movies, and we are not violent, and we didn't have nightmares. We were never expelled from school, and we don't have psychological problems. Plus, I definitely know the difference between Michael Myers slashing a victim's throat and a real-life serial killer.

Children need to see a little violence to realize what life is really like. Otherwise, they will grow up being sissies. Television doesn't desensitize children; it toughens them up. It doesn't blend reality and fiction, either. Nobody said in the 1950s, don't let your children watch the Coyote and the Roadrunner because they might think they could really fall off a cliff and survive.

A study was done on preschoolers in Kansas to see how these violent cartoons affected them.

"Children who watch the violent shows, even 'just funny' cartoons, were more likely to hit out at their playmates, argue, disobey class rules, leave tasks unfinished and were less willing to wait for things than those who watched the nonviolent programs," said Dr. Aletha Huston of the University of Kansas.

So basically, the children weren't robots who did exactly what they were told to do exactly when they were told to do it after watching those nasty cartoons. That doesn't sound like aggressive behavior; it sounds like a kid being a kid.

"Parents can limit the amount of time children spend watching television and encourage children to spend their time on sports, hobbies or with friends," according to the American Psychological Association. "Parents and kids can even draw up a list of other enjoyable activities to do instead of watching TV."

Parents who actually care whether television is having an effect on their child will take the advice of the APA and get their kids out of the house into fresh air. I promise the air won't kill them.

Just because your kids are playing sports or hanging out with friends doesn't mean that parents can remain selfish and lazy. They still have to monitor who their kids are hanging out with. Being a parent doesn't mean being a friend to your child. It means getting up and driving over to your child's friend's house to make sure they're really there.

If parents quit being self-absorbed, then they would be able to raise their kids into good human beings.

Nobody ever said parenting was easy, so why don't the parents quit whining about their children being influenced by this bad, bad world and take a little responsibility?

http://www.ac-ranger.com/2.6711/media-violence-good-for-kids-1.978351

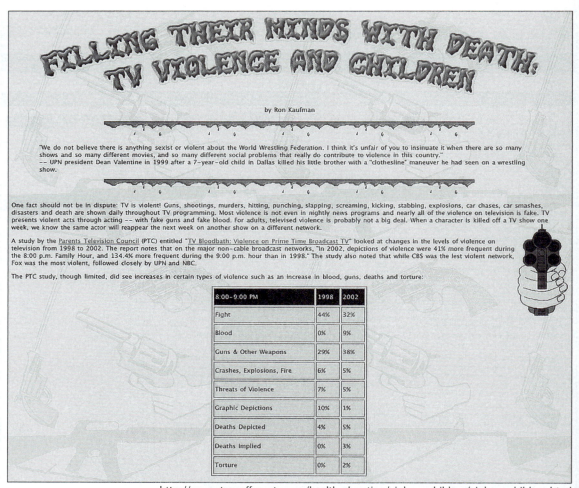

FILLING THEIR MINDS WITH DEATH: TV VIOLENCE AND CHILDREN

by Ron Kaufman

"We do not believe there is anything sexist or violent about the World Wrestling Federation. I think it's unfair of you to insinuate it when there are so many shows and so many different movies, and so many different social problems that really do contribute to violence in this country."
-- UPN president Dean Valentine in 1999 after a 7-year-old child in Dallas killed his little brother with a "clothesline" maneuver he had seen on a wrestling show.

One fact should not be in dispute: TV is violent! Guns, shootings, murders, hitting, punching, slapping, screaming, kicking, stabbing, explosions, car chases, car smashes, disasters and death are shown daily throughout TV programming. Most violence is not even in nightly news programs and nearly all of the violence on television is fake. TV presents violent acts through acting -- with fake guns and fake blood. For adults, televised violence is probably not a big deal. When a character is killed off a TV show one week, we know the same actor will reappear the next week on another show on a different network.

A study by the Parents Television Council (PTC) entitled "TV Bloodbath: Violence on Prime Time Broadcast TV" looked at changes in the levels of violence on television from 1998 to 2002. The report notes that on the major non-cable broadcast networks, "In 2002, depictions of violence were 41% more frequent during the 8:00 p.m. Family Hour, and 134.4% more frequent during the 9:00 p.m. hour than in 1998." The study also noted that while CBS was the lest violent network, Fox was the most violent, followed closely by UPN and NBC.

The PTC study, though limited, did see increases in certain types of violence such as an increase in blood, guns, deaths and torture:

8:00–9:00 PM	1998	2002
Fight	44%	32%
Blood	0%	9%
Guns & Other Weapons	29%	38%
Crashes, Explosions, Fire	6%	5%
Threats of Violence	7%	5%
Graphic Depictions	10%	1%
Deaths Depicted	4%	5%
Deaths Implied	0%	3%
Torture	0%	2%

http://vvww.turnoffyourtv.com/healtheducation/violencechildren/violencechildren.html

ACTIVITY 10

DIRECTIONS: Now that you and your two classmates have considered and evaluated various sources, write an essay in which you answer the question "Does violence on television contribute to real violence in the United States?" Your instructor will ask you to discuss your viewpoint in class.

Coming to Logical Conclusions

After completing research, critical thinkers try to come to **logical conclusions** about the events, issues, problems, decisions, or situations they are considering. *Conclusions are logical or reasonable if they are based solidly on the information or evidence gathered.*

Let us look one last time at the example we have been using about whether you should enroll for a particular course. Suppose, while doing the research, you found that the course fits both your schedule and program of study, that you are interested in at least some of its content, that you are comfortable with the instructor, assignments, and grading, and that most of the people you talk with like the course. Under those circumstances, it would be logical to conclude that it is good for you to take the course because most of the information supports that conclusion.

On the other hand, if you found that the course does not seem very interesting, that it is taught by only one instructor whom you are not too crazy about, and that only half the students you talked with liked it, a logical conclusion is that the course is not for you because most of the information points in that direction. Of course, the evidence could be approximately evenly divided, making it logical to conclude that it may or may not be the right course for you. In that instance, you would have to determine which factors—perhaps the content of the course, the instructor, or the requirements—are the most important to you and then decide accordingly. It is also important to emphasize that the information gathered could change in the future, thereby altering any one of those three possible conclusions. For instance, there could be a change of instructor, which could in turn affect course content, assignments, grading, and opinions regarding the course. That is why *critical thinkers always reconsider their conclusions to make sure that the evidence on which they are based has not changed or that no new information has been uncovered.*

To return to another example mentioned earlier, suppose that, in your investigation of a traffic accident, the police report, newspaper accounts, and several witnesses all state that one person went through a red light. A logical conclusion would be that this driver was responsible for the accident—certainly, most of the information points in that direction. But if none of the evidence is clear as to who actually caused the collision, then the only reasonable conclusion is that no one person can be held responsible, at least at this particular time. However, that conclusion could change if additional evidence comes to light that points to one person as the culprit. Again, it is always necessary for critical thinkers to reconsider their conclusions from time to time.

ACTIVITY 11

Directions: Pretend that there is an imaginary country with the following characteristics:

Rich and corrupt leaders

Crime on the increase

Extreme poverty among the masses

Many natural resources

What logical conclusions could you draw concerning the conditions in the country and what caused them, and what prediction can you make regarding its future? Discuss your conclusions with your classmates.

ACTIVITY 12

DIRECTIONS: With two of your classmates, look carefully at the six graphic aids that follow, paying particular attention to the captions and organization. For each, remember to answer the two questions we used in Chapter 3: "What is this graphic aid about?" and "What are the major points stressed?" Based on the information presented, draw as many logical conclusions as possible for each of the graphic aids.

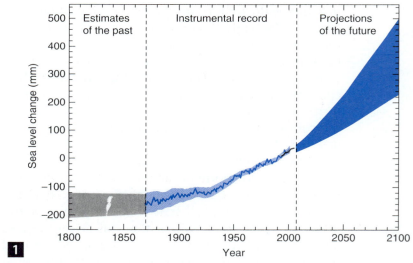

1

Sea Level Rise Projections to 2100

http://www.epa.gov/climatechange/science/futureslc_fig1.html
Last updated on Tuesday, September 08, 2009

30%
Smoking and alcohol use
(172,000 deaths due to smoking
and 19,000 deaths due to alcohol use)

30-35%
Unbalanced diet
(One-third of all cancer
deaths due to too many high
glycemic carbohydrates,
too many calories leading
to obesity, a lack of
physical activity)

16-20% Infections
(Deaths occur mostly in poor
countries due to hepatitis B
virus, human papillomavirus,
HIV, human T-cell leukemia/
lymphoma, and others.)

18-20%
Hormones

1%
Pollution
(Deaths occur mostly where
pollution is heavy)

2%
Occupation

2

Factors Believed to Contribute to Global Causes of Cancer

S. Heacht et al., Public Session/Panel Discussion (Linus Pauling Institute International Conference on Diet and Optimum Health, Portland, OR, May 2001); American Cancer Society, *Cancer Facts and Figures 2005* (Atlanta: American Cancer Society, 2005).

Rebecca J. Donatelle, *Health: The Basics,* 7th ed., p. 357, © 2007. Reprinted by permission of Pearson Education, Inc., Upper Saddle River, New Jersey.

Race or Ethnicity	Estimated # of AIDS Diagnoses, 2008	Cumulative Estimated # of AIDS Diagnoses, Through 2008*
American Indian/Alaska Native	199	3,741
Asian[a]	525	8,253
Black/African American	18,328	452,916
Hispanic/Latino[b]	7,043	180,061
Native Hawaiian/Other Pacific Islander	51	830
White	10,570	119,905
Multiple Races	435	7,054

* From the beginning of the epidemic through 2008.

[a] Includes Asian/Pacific Islander legacy cases.

3 [b] Hispanics/Latinos can be of any race.

Estimated Numbers of AIDS Cases in the 50 States and the District of Columbia, by Race or Ethnicity

http://www.cdc.gov/hiv/topics/surveillance/basic.htm

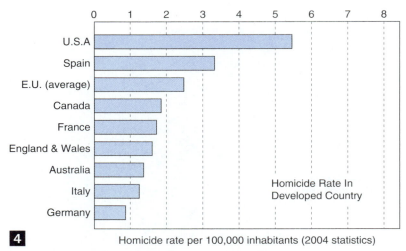

4

Homicide Rate 2004

Homicide rate per 100,000 inhabitants (2004 statistics)

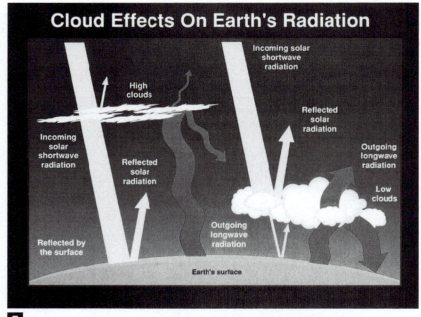

5

Cloud Effects on Earth's Radiation

CERES Instrument Team, NASA Langley Research Center. http://www.visibleearth.nasa.gov

COMPARISON OF PRICES OF THIS REPORT VERSUS LAST REPORT

Table 11 below summarizes the average prices collected for this report by region, and compares them to prices collected in the Price Report from October 2009. It should be noted that a portion of the price changes could be attributed to differing sample sizes and composition between the two reports.

Table 11. Comparison of Prices, Last Price Report versus Current Price Report

		Price for January 2010 Period	Price for October 2009 Period	Price Differential January vs. October
Gasoline ($ per gallon)	National Average	$2.65	$2.64	$0.01 / 0%
	New England	$2.76	$2.65	$0.11 / 4%
	Central Atlantic	$2.79	$2.69	$0.10 / 4%
	Lower Atlantic	$2.63	$2.48	$0.15 / 6%
	Midwest	$2.60	$2.61	($0.01) / 0%
	Gulf Coast	$2.56	$2.50	$0.06 / 2%
	Rocky Mountain	$2.49	$2.51	($0.02) / (1%)
	West Coast	$2.84	$2.90	($0.06) / (2%)
Diesel ($ per gallon)	National Average	$2.87	$2.79	$0.07 / 3%
	New England	$3.01	$2.88	$0.13 / 4%
	Central Atlantic	$2.98	$2.87	$0.10 / 4%
	Lower Atlantic	$2.81	$2.64	$0.17 / 7%
	Midwest	$2.78	$2.78	$0 / 0%
	Gulf Coast	$2.77	$2.65	$0.12 / 5%
	Rocky Mountain	$2.80	$2.71	$0.09 / 3%
	West Coast	$2.98	$2.94	$0.04 / 1%
Compressed Natural Gas ($ per GGE)	National Average	$1.85	$1.86	($0.01) / 0%
	New England	$2.30	$2.19	$0.11 / 5%
	Central Atlantic	$2.10	$2.17	($0.07) / (3%)
	Lower Atlantic	$1.74	$1.71	$0.03 / 2%
	Midwest	$1.73	$1.76	($0.02) / (1%)
	Gulf Coast	$1.98	$1.95	$0.03 / 1%
	Rocky Mountain	$1.26	$1.23	$0.03 / 2%
	West Coast	$2.24	$2.18	$0.06 / 3%
Ethanol (E85) ($ per gallon)	National Average	$2.38	$2.27	$0.11 / 5%
	New England	$3.16	$3.01	$0.15 / 5%
	Central Atlantic	$2.49	$2.40	$0.09 / 4%
	Lower Atlantic	$2.47	$2.29	$0.19 / 8%
	Midwest	$2.34	$2.21	$0.13 / 6%
	Gulf Coast	$2.38	$2.17	$0.21 / 10%
	Rocky Mountain	$2.25	$2.10	$0.15 / 7%
	West Coast	$2.42	$2.41	$0.01 / 0%

6

Comparison of Fuel Prices

U.S. Department of Energy, *Clean Cities Alternative Fuel Price Report*, January 2010. http://www.afdc.energy.gov/afdc/pdfs/afpr_jan_10.pdf

■ What Is a Contemporary Issue?

To review, *critical thinking is a careful, thoughtful way of dealing with events, issues, problems, decisions, or situations. It requires flexibility, a clear purpose, organization, time and effort, asking questions and finding answers, research, and coming to logical conclusions.* At this point, you have a good idea of what all of these characteristics mean and how they can be applied to the ordinary circumstances of everyday life. They can also be used in a broader sense as a way of dealing with and making better sense of topics of concern in the world around you, which are commonly called **contemporary issues.**

In this context, it is probably easiest to think of *contemporary* as a fancy word for "current." And an *issue* can be defined as a point, matter, or question to be disputed, decided, or debated—in other words, subject to very different and often conflicting interpretations, which we can call **opposing viewpoints.** A contemporary issue, then, is *a current point, matter, or question that is debatable and therefore subject to opposing viewpoints.*

Of course, we do not have to look very far to find a host of contemporary issues. Race relations, abortion, capital punishment, gay rights, violence in music, sexual harassment, teenage pregnancy, welfare, and gun control are obvious examples. It is precisely because they are debatable and often arouse our emotions when we read and talk about them that contemporary issues are appropriate topics for the careful, thoughtful treatment involved in critical thinking.

At the end of each chapter in this textbook, you will be asked to read about, think about, write about, and discuss some of the controversies surrounding many contemporary issues. Our approach will involve all of the characteristics of critical thinking that we have been discussing. In each case, you will:

1. Determine what is at issue
2. Distinguish among opposing viewpoints
3. Express a personal viewpoint

This three-step approach should enable you to understand the various viewpoints on the issues while at the same time giving you the opportunity to think carefully about your own point of view.

In many of the courses that you will be taking in your college career, you will be asked by instructors to read, write, or think about contemporary issues. For example, you may be required to read about racism for sociology, discuss the spread of AIDS in health, or write a paper on capital punishment for a criminal justice course. In addition, as an educated person, you will want to be able to speak knowledgeably with others about the major issues of the day, including the reasons behind the various points of view and your own personal viewpoints. For instance, you may find yourself in a position to discuss these matters with children and other family members or with colleagues on the job. As you can see, thinking critically about contemporary issues is useful to you not only as a college student but in the other roles that you play in life as well, both now and in the future. It is a skill that will serve you well throughout your life.

Before turning to a more detailed discussion of the three-step approach we will be using, read the following excerpt, which was taken from a typical college health textbook. Pay particular attention to the labels in the margins. Refer to this passage often as you read the explanation that follows it.

Topic (title)

Euthanasia

1   Medical science is now capable of prolonging the functioning of bodily systems long after the systems would normally have failed. It is not unusual to see patients in institutions living as near-vegetables for months and even years. Such individuals create a definite problem for family members and physicians: Would it not be better to put these patients out of their misery?

Context definition

2   On the question of this sort of "mercy killing," or *euthanasia,* Americans are divided into three groups. One group consists of the people who insist that all possible efforts be made to prolong the life of seriously ill patients. Those who take this stance maintain that any tampering with human life is a form of playing God and that the result is either murder or, if the patient concurs, murder combined with suicide.

**Central message
First viewpoint**

Rationale

Context definition

3   A majority of Americans, on the other hand, admit to a belief in *indirect euthanasia,* sometimes referred to as negative euthanasia. In forms of indirect euthanasia, death is not directly caused or induced; rather, it is allowed to take place through the withdrawal of specific treatments. Such indirect euthanasia is not uncommon in medical practice, though it is rarely acknowledged by doctors for fear of legal complications. This position has considerable authoritative backing, including that of the late Pope Pius XII, who declared that no extraordinary means need be taken to prolong human life.

Second viewpoint

Rationale

4   The third—and smallest—group consists of those who believe in *direct euthanasia.* The number of people who actually practice direct euthanasia is difficult to ascertain. Some physicians admit in private to having done so—either directly, by administering a lethal drug, or indirectly, by allowing the patient, the family, or the support staff to cause the death.

Third viewpoint

5   Such life-and-death decisions are far easier to make in the classroom than in the reality of a traumatic situation with a loved one. The primary difficulty does not involve logic so much as the poignancy of the environment in which decisions are made. Decision makers, plagued by long-standing illness, weary and bleary-eyed, emotionally drained, with daily life disrupted for many weeks or months (and perhaps feeling guilty, financially pressured, and involved with unfinished business), do not easily resort to the usual logic. Many a theoretically strong pro-life stance melts into a belief in euthanasia as soon as one is confronted with a loved one

Rationale

who is screaming in agony or lying in a comatose state amid life-sustaining machinery. On the other hand, one who has firmly believed in euthanasia may balk when the patient is one's own parent or child.

Essentials of Life and Health, pp. 331–333

Determining What Is at Issue

Whenever you read about a contemporary issue, you must determine first what specifically is at issue, keeping in mind that occasionally there may be more than one issue at hand. Furthermore, some issues may not be as obvious as others because they are not discussed in great detail. For example, you may be reading a magazine article that deals with the debate surrounding the possible benefits resulting from the medical use of marijuana. However, in discussing the issue, the writer may talk about the U.S. government's threat to prosecute doctors who prescribe marijuana and go on to say that if the government took that action, it could be a violation of both freedom of speech and privileged communication between doctor and patient. Consequently, you would want to address those two issues as well, even though they are not the dominant ones. As you deal with each of the passages in this chapter—and contemporary issues in general—remember to look for secondary issues.

It is also important that you be as specific as possible when identifying issues. In the example just given, for instance, identifying "marijuana" as the dominant issue would be too general. There are several issues surrounding marijuana, including legalization, mandatory prison terms for its possession, and possible benefits resulting from its medical uses. Instead, you would be correct if you focused on this last topic because that is precisely what the article discusses. As you consider each of the passages presented here, remember to be very specific when identifying issues, and be on the lookout for secondary ones.

How, then, do you determine what is at issue? First, it is a good idea to identify the **topic** of the passage by answering the question "What is this about?" As you know from our discussion in Chapter 2, the topic can usually be stated in one word or a phrase, and often it is the title or part of the title. It is the subject matter of most, if not all, of the sentences in a given passage, and most of the time it is indeed the issue, but only in a very general sense. In the excerpt from the health textbook, the topic is "euthanasia" or "mercy killing." It is easy to identify because of the title and the fact that the entire passage deals with that subject. Notice how the surrounding words define the term for you. Remember from Chapter 1 that the context often provides a quick, useful way of uncovering word meanings.

After determining the topic, you should identify the **central message** of the passage by answering the question "What is the central message that the writer is communicating about the topic?" The central message, as you should remember from Chapter 2, represents the specific aspect of the topic that the writer wishes to discuss, and often it can be found in one or more sentences. If it is not explicitly stated, it can be determined by a careful reading of the sentences in the passage, many of which generally provide direct support for the central message. In the textbook passage that we are using, the central message is provided in the sentence "On the question of this sort of 'mercy killing,' or *euthanasia*, Americans are divided into three groups." Most of the rest of the sentences in the passage lend direct support to it by providing details that develop or explain it further. The central message always tips you off to the major issue discussed in the passage, and it does it in a much more specific fashion. Hence, in our example, an accurate statement of the issue would read something like "Americans have three different viewpoints regarding euthanasia." In this particular passage, there are no secondary issues.

Keep in mind that the central message often reveals the writer's point of view, which will help you identify at least one opposing viewpoint and perhaps the reasons for it.

Distinguishing Among Opposing Viewpoints

In addition to determining what is at issue in each passage, you will be asked to state the differences among the opposing viewpoints. This will involve not only identifying the viewpoints but also providing the **rationale**, or specific reasons, that support each of them. For instance, if the issue has to do with whether capital punishment deters or prevents murder, you would provide the reasons offered in support of the viewpoint that says "yes" and the reasons offered in support of the viewpoint that says "no." However, sometimes a complete explanation for each of the opposing viewpoints is not provided. In those instances, you may have to use your knowledge or perhaps do some research to help you come up with the missing information. For example, in a class discussing whether capital punishment deters murder, one student mentioned the viewpoint that the death penalty does serve that purpose. She went on to provide one reason in support of that point of view: If a convicted murderer were put to death, indeed he would not be able to kill again. In that specific case, capital punishment would deter murder. Although the reason she gave for the viewpoint was not mentioned in the passage read by the class, she was able to offer it from her knowledge of the issue. As you deal with contemporary issues, there may be occasions when you too can provide missing reasons for a particular viewpoint.

Also remember that, as a critical thinker, you should be aware of not only the writer's bias but your own feelings toward the issues and the various viewpoints that you will be dealing with in the coming pages. You need to show flexibility by considering carefully *all* opposing viewpoints and the reasons behind them, no matter what your personal feelings are. With regard to the example of capital punishment, even if you are in strong support of one of the two viewpoints mentioned, you would be just as thorough and objective in presenting the viewpoint you do not support. In fact, as a result of doing so, you might change your initial point of view. As you know, that is a characteristic of the critical thinker.

How, then, do you determine the opposing viewpoints and the reasons for them? You can do this by focusing on the information that lends direct support to the central message. As you recall, the central message of the textbook passage that we are using is "On the question of this sort of 'mercy killing,' or *euthanasia,* Americans are divided into three groups." The passage then proceeds to define and explain the three viewpoints, including the rationale for each. Did you notice how some of the details are organized in a simple-listing-of-facts pattern of organization? Good!

The first viewpoint is held by individuals who oppose euthanasia. They "insist that all possible efforts be made to prolong the life of seriously ill patients." Their rationale is "that any tampering with human life is a form of playing God and that the result is either murder or, if the patient concurs, murder combined with suicide." We can use our knowledge of this issue to add here that miracles do occur, particularly with modern medicine, and therefore patients should be given every opportunity to survive.

The second viewpoint is favored by people who believe in indirect or negative euthanasia, in which "death is not directly caused or induced; rather, it is allowed to take place through the withdrawal of specific treatments." This point of view, according to the passage, has "considerable authoritative backing, including that of the late Pope Pius XII." Apparently, this "backing" is an important reason for the Americans who favor this particular position. If we have some background knowledge of this issue, we might add here that this viewpoint has the general support of the medical community and the courts, which is not the case with regard to direct euthanasia. This in turn could explain further why some people favor indirect over direct euthanasia.

The third viewpoint is supported by people who believe in direct euthanasia, which involves a doctor's "administering a lethal drug" or "allowing the patient, the family, or the support staff to cause the death." Although the passage gives no specific rationale for those who favor direct euthanasia, it does provide some additional reasons for people who favor both kinds of euthanasia: guilt, disruption of daily life, or the emotional, physical, and financial burden that go along with prolonged illness of a loved one. Thus we could guess that a possible rationale on the part of those favoring direct euthanasia would involve a quicker end to a terrible situation.

The details that support the central message of the passage have provided us with the opposing viewpoints and at least some of the rationale for each. We also have added some possible reasons of our own. As a critical thinker, you should always be prepared to do the same thing when dealing with contemporary issues.

Expressing a Personal Viewpoint

After determining what is at issue and distinguishing among opposing viewpoints, you can then express your personal viewpoint regarding the issue. Undoubtedly, you have your own opinions regarding many of the contemporary issues of the day, including those covered in this textbook. In fact, you will be asked to express your initial feelings toward each issue covered in this book *before* completing the three-step approach. Thus you can determine if your personal viewpoint changes after you have thoroughly considered the opposing viewpoints surrounding a given issue.

As already mentioned, it is important as a critical thinker that you be aware of your initial opinions and not permit them to interfere with a careful consideration of all viewpoints. For instance, you may have strong feelings of support or opposition regarding one or more of the viewpoints discussed in our textbook example dealing with euthanasia. That is fine, provided that you keep an open mind when distinguishing among the viewpoints, give careful thought to each of them, and at least consider the possibility that you might change your initial feelings after reading and thinking about the rationale for all points of view.

Having done that, you are in a better position to express your personal viewpoint even if it has not changed, because you have opened yourself up to other possibilities. When discussing your viewpoint, be sure to provide the reasons why you favor it over the others. For example, suppose that you support indirect euthanasia because you do not believe that extraordinary measures, such as a feeding tube or ventilator, should be taken to keep a person alive. Furthermore, in answer to those who do not favor any form of euthanasia, you believe that by using extraordinary measures, they are indeed playing God by preventing nature from taking its course. In addition, by doing so, they are perhaps prolonging a hopeless situation indefinitely, thereby placing loved ones under a tremendous physical, emotional, and financial burden. To those who support direct euthanasia, you respond that you do not favor that course of action because you believe it is playing God by deliberately bringing about certain death, to say nothing of the fact that it is both illegal and morally wrong.

Thus, you have given your personal viewpoint regarding euthanasia and the reasons why you support it over the other two. Some of those reasons were mentioned in the passage you read, and others were not. It is always permissible to use your knowledge of an issue to supply additional rationale for your point of view.

Furthermore, you could have just as easily come out in favor of one of the other viewpoints or even some combination of them as long as you provide your reasons for doing so. For instance, in discussing this issue, one student supported indirect euthanasia only after three different doctors certify that the situation is hopeless; otherwise, she did not favor it at all. She wanted to be reasonably sure that there was little chance of improvement. Another student agreed with the use of a feeding tube to keep someone alive but was opposed to the attachment of a ventilator. Although he agreed with preventing a patient from starving, he did not support the use of a machine to do all of the patient's breathing. In other words, he considered only the second option to be extraordinary. Thus under one set of circumstances he was not in favor of indirect euthanasia, while under another set of circumstances he was.

Turning to the issue of capital punishment, there are people who oppose it under all circumstances no matter what the crime. On the other hand, some people support it for certain crimes, such as premeditated murder, but oppose it for others, such as causing death in the course of a robbery. The possibilities for combinations of viewpoints are considerable when dealing with contemporary issues. As you focus on contemporary issues both in this textbook and in your daily life, do not stick automatically to just one point of view before considering others or some combination of them.

The diagram below illustrates the three-step approach to contemporary issues that we will be using:

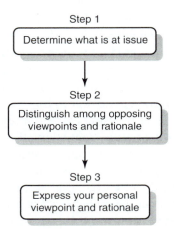

Step 1

Determine what is at issue

Step 2

Distinguish among opposing viewpoints and rationale

Step 3

Express your personal viewpoint and rationale

ACTIVITY 13

DIRECTIONS: Read the following five passages, and answer the questions that follow each of them. You will use the three-step approach to contemporary issues. The com-prehension questions will ask you to state the topic and central message of each passage before proceeding to determine what is at issue, distinguish among opposing viewpoints, and express a personal viewpoint. In addition, you will be asked to com-pare your personal viewpoint before and after you have thoroughly considered the opposing viewpoints brought out in the passages. Finally, to show flexibility, you will write a few paragraphs in support of the viewpoint that you do not favor. Keep in mind that some of the selections may deal with more than one issue.

The thought and discussion questions will often place you into hypothetical or imaginary situations involving the issues brought out in the passages. After think-ing about them, feel free to discuss the questions with your classmates and together come up with possible answers. Finally, you will be asked to contribute any questions of your own that come to mind when reading the passages. You should be prepared to discuss possible answers to both your questions and those of your classmates.

Eye on Vocabulary

You are aware of the importance of vocabulary development, particularly in college. With that goal in mind, when reading each passage, take note of any unfamiliar words you come across. As suggested in Chapter 1, list them and their definitions in your notebook or on note cards. Use the context, word parts, or the dictionary to determine their meanings. After the completion of each passage, your instructor may ask to see your notebook or note cards and may discuss keywords in class.

1

Facebook Is My Friend for Now

Its connections ability is impressive, but will it be more than a fad?

KAREN CYSON

1   It's ironic that as a nonbeliever in horoscopes I exhibit classic Gemini (the twins) behavior. I vacillate between being an early adopter of technology and a complete Luddite.

2   Answering machine? I had one of the first. Cell phone? For more than a decade. Twitter, text, MySpace, Facebook? No, thank you; can't see the point.

3   This was all true until last week when my son created a Facebook page for me and dragged me kicking and screaming (actually more like heel-dragging) into the 21st century:

4   I wasn't sure that being a part of an online group such as Facebook was important or even relevant to my life. After all, I was in phone and e-mail con-tact with my family and friends. My job and volunteer work keep me plenty busy.

It never occurred to me that I might need a new way to communicate and I certainly didn't need another "time-suck" to distract me. It would be an understatement to say my enthusiasm was tepid at best.

5   After doing a little research, I found that total membership is about 400 million and 175 million people log on to Facebook daily. Something significant must be going on here, even if it doesn't have the headline-grabbing importance of events such as the recent TEA Party Convention with its 600 attendees (about the size of the annual Tech vs. Apollo football game).

6   Only 48 hours after my first foray, I had been contacted by and connected with more than 40 friends, friends in real life, too. I was astonished by, and at the same time a tad apprehensive about, Facebook's ability to link up people through connections.

7   Was this good or scary?

8   On the positive side, Facebook is the "postcard" to e-mail's "letter." Friends can send out short bursts of information and everyone knows instantly rather than having to try to remember to tell everyone everything.

9   Yesterday I learned that one very happy friend, now 50, had finally been able to buy a French horn after not having one since high school. Another friend lost her job in the afternoon and had to only send one message, rather than going through pain with each telling, and instantly supportive replies began pouring in to her page.

10   On the negative side, those Facebook postcards are very similar to real postcards: they aren't in an envelope and anyone, unless you carefully conceal them, can read them. A Minneapolis prosecutor is in danger of having a hard-won murder conviction thrown out after her Facebook posts concerning race and the case were circulated. Divorce lawyers are mining old posts for nuggets of information.

11   A humorous Facebook problem was posted by a farmer husband of a friend who muses that his wife will spend so much time tending her Facebook Farmville (a game) critters that she'll neglect the six real calves he recently purchased. Knowing her as well as I do, he may have cause to worry.

12   Of greater concern should be the data mining occurring on Facebook. A social graph analysis program has indexed more than 215 million Facebook pages to date, and the programmer, former Apple engineer Pete Warden, has uploaded this data to the Web for academic research. The purpose is to analyze and cross-reference the data.

13   So far the stats coming out of the program are merely entertaining: In the southern United States, the top favorite page is "God." In the Pacific Northwest, it's Starbucks.

14   I question the relevance of such programming and doubt its ability to determine purpose based on frequency. Could Warden's program possibly know if I commented on Facebook about nightshade, whether I was writing about potatoes, peppers, petunias, posion or window coverings? And I doubt such a program can detect sarcasm and irony.

15   Whether Facebook is a fad or here to stay, it's a quick, useful and free tool for connecting with friends and family. I can also see pitfalls: privacy issues, addictive games, spam-causing surveys and quizzes.

16   The important idea to keep in mind is that it's public. Anything you say or do can be used against you. Writing on a Facebook page may be quick and concise, but it is as visible as a bumper sticker and nearly impossible to remove. I maintain my resolve not to tweet or text.

This is the opinion of Karen Cyson, a child care provider in Stearns County and vice president of Minnesota Mensa. Her column is published the third Friday of the month.

St.Cloud Times, Friday, Feb. 19, 2010 6B.

COMPREHENSION QUESTIONS

1. What is the topic of the passage?
2. What is the central message of the passage?
3. Determine what is at issue. What is your initial personal viewpoint?
4. Distinguish among opposing viewpoints, and provide the rationale for each.
5. Think carefully about the viewpoints. Express a personal viewpoint, and give the reasons why you favor it. Does it differ from your initial personal viewpoint? Why or why not?
6. Write a few paragraphs *in support of the viewpoint that you do* not *favor*.

THOUGHT AND DISCUSSION QUESTIONS

1. Use the context to figure out what the author means when she states, "Of greater concern should be the data mining occurring on Facebook." (Paragraph 12)
2. Why do you think the author refuses to twitter or text?
3. What questions or experiences came to mind when you were reading this selection? Be prepared to share them.

2

Media Bias: Is the News Affected by an Ideological Bias?

1   Is there a media bias? Conservative critics charge that up to 90% of journalists vote Democratic. They say that many of the political reporters and analysts are hired not because of their political experience but because of their

Democratic experience. For example, ABC News hired former Clinton White House adviser George Stephanopoulos to host the Sunday morning political talk show *This Week*. Liberals argue that conservatives have no right to talk, since Fox News reports news for conservatives. Also, the companies that own the media are regarded as conservative. They are hesitant to criticize possible sponsors. They, therefore, have stronger biases than do the personal beliefs of journalists.

Yes

2   Since journalists have their own personal bias, claims of professional objectivity are absurd. Journalistic professionalism is a myth. Even if journalists feel bound to be objective, it is hard to believe that all of them are all of the time. Plus, audiences have no other information with which to corroborate stories that the media report. Since they are unaccountable, journalists can impose their beliefs on unsuspecting American audiences.

3   Media companies expect the news media to make profits. Huge corporations demand that papers, television programs, and Web sites report only the stories that attract viewers rather than educating them, and that attract sponsors rather than holding them accountable. The result is that tabloid journalists report on minor scandals and not on Iraqi human rights abuse or threats from corporate mergers. This leads to further audience ignorance of important issues.

4   The American media insufficiently report news from other regions of the world. Americans lack sufficient knowledge about global events. This is dangerous, since these events directly affect American interests. On television, reports on world news usually come packaged as "Around the World in 80 Seconds." Newspapers typically put world news not immediately pertaining to American interests to the back pages.

No

5   Bias is a problem only with particular journalists. Even if a certain journalist is unprofessional, it does not follow that all journalists are. The vast majority of journalists have done nothing to lead us to believe that they are somehow politically biased. The practice of uncovering media bias is nothing more than a witch hunt.

6   Recently, all news media have begun tailoring their content to specific audiences because audiences for news have fractured into smaller pieces. Some media direct content toward specific beliefs. Calling certain newspapers or cable stations biased is wrong because these stations, rather openly, have begun presenting information about matters important to liberals or to conservatives. That's how the free market works.

7   There are simply too many sources of news for an audience to suffer the influence of media bias. Perhaps there was once a media bias when there were only a few television stations and national newspapers. Now, however, there are dozens of magazines, news Web sites, and smaller circulation newspapers that allow audiences different views of subjects. Audiences merely must learn about opposing positions on an issue and decide for themselves where they stand.

"Media Bias: Is the News Affected by an Ideological Bias?" from Karen O'Connor and Larry J. Sabato, *American Government: Continuity and Change*, 2006, pp. 566–567

COMPREHENSION QUESTIONS

1. What is the topic of the passage?
2. What is the central message of the passage?
3. Determine what is at issue. What is your initial personal viewpoint?
4. Distinguish among opposing viewpoints, and provide the rationale for each.
5. Think carefully about the viewpoints. Express a personal viewpoint, and give the reasons why you favor it. Does it differ from your initial personal viewpoint? Why or why not?
6. Write a few paragraphs *in support of the viewpoint that you do* not *favor*. You may want to check out the Web sites of your local newspaper or television station to get examples.

THOUGHT AND DISCUSSION QUESTIONS

1. News people naturally want to add spice and drama to their stories to increase their audience. Discuss an example of this.
2. News people are always trying to get the negative "scoop" on political candidates running for office. Think of an example and discuss this.
3. What questions came to your mind while you were reading this selection? Be prepared to share them for discussion.

3

Facts About Alcohol Poisoning

1   Excessive drinking can be hazardous to everyone's health! It can be particularly stressful if you are the sober one taking care of your drunken roommate, who is vomiting while you are trying to study for an exam.

2   Some people laugh at the behavior of others who are drunk. Some think it's even funnier when they pass out. But there is nothing funny about the aspiration of vomit leading to asphyxiation or the poisoning of the respiratory center in the brain, both of which can result in death.

3   Do you know about the dangers of alcohol poisoning? When should you seek professional help for a friend? Sadly enough, too many college students say they wish they had sought medical treatment for a friend. Many end up feeling responsible for alcohol-related tragedies that could have easily been prevented.

4   Common myths about sobering up include drinking black coffee, taking a cold bath or shower, sleeping it off, or walking it off. But these are just myths, and they don't work. The only thing that reverses the effects of alcohol is time—something you may not have if you are suffering from alcohol poisoning. And many different factors affect the level of intoxication of an individual, so it's difficult to gauge exactly how much is too much.

5   Alcohol depresses nerves that control involuntary actions such as breathing and the gag reflex (which prevents choking). A fatal dose of alcohol will eventually stop these functions.

6   It is common for someone who drank excessive alcohol to vomit since alcohol is an irritant to the stomach. There is then the danger of choking on vomit, which could cause death by asphyxiation in a person who is not conscious because of intoxication.

7   You should also know that a person's blood alcohol concentration could continue to rise even while he or she is passed out. Even after a person stops drinking, alcohol in the stomach and intestine continues to enter the bloodstream and circulate throughout the body. It is dangerous to assume the person will be fine by sleeping it off.

8   Even if the victim lives, an alcohol overdose can lead to irreversible brain damage. Rapid binge drinking (which often happens on a bet or a dare) is especially dangerous because the victim can ingest a fatal dose before becoming unconscious.

9   Don't be afraid to seek medical help for a friend who has had too much to drink. Don't worry that your friend may become angry or embarrassed. Remember, you cared enough to help. Always be safe, not sorry.

http://www.collegedrinkingprevention.gov/OtherAlcoholInformation/factsAboutAlcoholPoisoning.aspx

COMPREHENSION QUESTIONS

1. What is the topic of the passage?
2. What is the central message of the passage?
3. Determine what is at issue. What is your initial personal viewpoint?
4. Distinguish among opposing viewpoints, and provide the rationale for each.

5. Think carefully about the viewpoints. Express a personal viewpoint, and give the reasons why you favor it. Does it differ from your initial personal viewpoint? Why or why not?

6. Write a few paragraphs *in support of the viewpoint that you do* not *favor.* You may want to check out current Web sites on college drinking to find some examples.

THOUGHT AND DISCUSSION QUESTIONS

1. Fraternities have been known to have hazing sessions for new recruits in which they make the recruits drink large amounts of alcohol. What is your opinion on this practice? Should this practice be changed? How?

2. Do you see alcohol poisoning as a problem on your campus? Why or why not? Give examples.

3. List any questions that came to mind while you were reading this selection. Be prepared to discuss your questions with your classmates.

4

Shot in the Arm

JOHNNY TOWNSEND

1   I cried yesterday upon leaving the doctor's office.

2   I know, it sounds melodramatic. Men in our society aren't supposed to cry. It's just that the news was so devastating.

3   My bill was $120.

4   I had received "two" injections of cortisone in my left shoulder for tendonitis. (Technically, it was one injection but included a dose of anesthetic.) Each dose cost $6. That seemed reasonable to me.

5   But the office visit cost $45—a bit steep considering the doctor wasn't there for more than three minutes, and a minute of *that* consisted of his leaving the room to get the hypodermic and medicine. I understand there is a flat fee for office visits; shouldn't there then be a designated minimum amount of time that the doctor spends with each patient? This doctor ignored my questions, handed me the bill, and left while I was still putting on my shirt. Is it right to make me pay for his running behind schedule, when I've paid a fair fee?

6   As it was, I had waited an hour past my scheduled appointment to see him. Even if I'm just a peon, my time is still worth a good $5.50 an hour. Can't I deduct that?

7   But the really painful part of the bill was the $63 for actually performing the injection, which lasted all of eight seconds. If I'm paying $63 for his skill, what was the $45 for—his ability to tell me to remove my shirt? (Don't tell me it was for his diagnosis, because he'd made that a month earlier when he gave me my first injection at a cost of $81.)

8   Basically, since the doctor was only in the room with me for two minutes, at $120 I paid him a dollar a second to see me. At those rates, maybe I should be glad he didn't stay longer.

9   My shoulder had been hurting for three months before I finally went to the doctor. I'd been hoping it would get better on its own, but when I tried to reach for something and realized I could no longer stretch my left arm as far as my right, I became frightened. I suppose this is the way most poor people let problems develop too far.

10   I have a couple of friends I take down to Charity Hospital every few weeks—one for arthritis and another for a shattered bone that won't heal. I took a third friend there when he got the flu. Their waits of four, five, and six hours were demeaning and dehumanizing. Usually (except for the flu), they wouldn't even get to see a doctor but only set up an appointment to see one a month or two down the line. And when they showed up for *these* appointments, they had another four- to five-hour wait. Then they were diagnosed but often had to return in another few weeks to receive any treatment, with yet another four- to five-hour wait ahead of them.

11   I grew up in a middle-class home and just couldn't bear to go through all that myself. I am spoiled. I have three college degrees in English and work professionally as a college English instructor, where I earn $6,500 a year, with no benefits. I can't afford insurance. I don't know how I even saved enough for these two office visits, but they are the last.

12   After I had paid the $120, I walked in a daze to my car. I have finally become a complete nothing, I realized. People with money are everything, and people without it are nothing. It's certainly been said before, but I finally realized what it meant.

13   I don't expect anyone to feel sorry for me. As someone who frittered away his life on something so frivolous as English, I know exactly what society thinks of me. But as someone who grew up middle class, despite my miserable income of the past several years, I still managed to see myself as part of *us,* not *them.*

14   I, too, looked down on the poor somewhat, as ignorant or lazy or whatever. Oh, it's true that because of my liberal-arts background I was very nice and sensitive to *them,* but I hung on as long as I could to being part of *us,* believing I was only an honorary *them.* I was only clinging to respectability by my fingernails, but that doctor bill ripped my fingernails right off.

15   I was raised conservative but became much more liberal as an adult. Still, I am an odd mixture and maintain some strong views on both sides. I do think that entitlement programs and welfare too often promote dependence and lack of ambition, as well as punish those who try to escape poverty.

16   But honestly, how many people are going to say, "You know, the government is paying for my health care, so I think I'll go out and get appendicitis today"? Do people really say, "I hate rich people. I want them to pay more taxes for me. I was going to let that lump in my breast just sit there, but I think I'll go get it checked just to be spiteful"? Has anyone really been heard to remark, "Since I don't have to pay for it, I think I'll go develop some intestinal polyps. A colonoscopy sounds like a lot of fun. It'll liven up my boring, lazy week"?

17   The fact is that many people will never earn more than minimum wage and will be forever stuck in jobs with no benefits. And most people, even if they do work hard, will never be able to afford health care. If I'd had a torn rotator cuff, my doctor said it could cost a couple of thousand dollars to repair. We dregs of society may deserve to live in cruddy apartments and shop for clothes at thrift stores, but do we really deserve to wait half a year to be treated for something others are cured of in a week? Do only those who are smart enough or talented enough or lucky enough (or brutal enough or avaricious enough) to become wealthy deserve health care?

18   I've been back at school for a year now, taking my pre-med prerequisites with a grade-point average of 4.0. With or without health-care reform, I'm going to get the health care I deserve. It would be nice to think, though, that maybe the millions of other Americans without health care might get some, too. No matter where we stand as individuals on the issue of reform, it is clear that the health-care system on some substantial level needs a shot in the arm.

The Humanist, November 1995, p. 4

COMPREHENSION QUESTIONS

1. What is the topic of the passage?
2. What is the central message of the passage?
3. Determine what is at issue. What is your initial personal viewpoint?
4. Distinguish among opposing viewpoints, and provide the rationale for each.
5. Think carefully about the viewpoints. Express a personal viewpoint, and give the reasons why you favor it. Does it differ from your initial personal viewpoint? Why or why not?
6. Write a few paragraphs *in support of the viewpoint that you do* not *favor.*

THOUGHT AND DISCUSSION QUESTIONS

1. If you were a doctor, how would you react to a patient who could not afford to pay your fees? Why? Would you agree to provide medical care to a homeless person? Why or why not?
2. If you were a doctor, what possible rationale would you give if you were accused of charging high fees?
3. List any questions that came to mind while you were reading this selection, and be prepared to discuss possible answers to them.

5

The Debate Over Stem Cells

1   Stem cells are unique—and controversial. Stem cells are body cells with two important characteristics: (1) they are unspecialized (meaning their specific function is yet to be determined) and capable of renewing themselves by dividing repeatedly, and (2) they can be induced to become specialized cells that perform specific functions, such as muscle cells that make the heart beat or nerve cells that enable the brain to function.

2   These qualities have led many scientists to believe that stem cells have the potential to cure debilitating health problems such as Alzheimer's, heart disease, diabetes, Parkinson's, and glaucoma. These conditions all involve the destruction of certain crucial cells—in the case of type 1 diabetes, for example, the pancreatic cells that secrete insulin. In the laboratory, researchers are working to coax stem cells to develop into these pancreatic cells. The plan is to transplant the new cells into diabetic patients, where they could replace the patients' damaged cells and produce insulin. If successful, this approach could prevent the destructive complications of the disease and free diabetics from the painful burden of injecting insulin for the rest of their lives. Other therapies under investigation involve growing new cells to replace those ravaged by spinal injuries, heart attacks, muscular dystrophy, and vision and hearing loss.

3   The controversy over stem cells arises from their origins. Generally stem cells are derived from eggs that were fertilized in vitro. Typically these are "extra" embryos created during fertility treatments at clinics but not used for implantation. Only four to five days old, embryonic stem cells are *pluripotent* (capable of developing into many different cell types).

4   Embryonic stem cell research has provoked fierce debate. Opponents believe that an embryo is a human being and we have no right to create life and then destroy it, even for humanitarian purposes. Advocates counter that the eggs from which these embryos developed were given freely by donors and would otherwise be discarded.

5   Are adult stem cells a solution to this ethical dilemma? An adult stem cell is an undifferentiated cell found in body tissues and which can specialize to replace certain types of cells. For example, human bone marrow contains at least two kinds of adult stem cells. One kind gives rise to the various types of blood cells, while the other can differentiate into bone, cartilage, fat, or fibrous connective tissue. Other tissues that may contain adult stem cells include the brain, liver, skeletal muscles, and blood vessels. While research indicates that adult stem cells may be more versatile than previously thought, many scientists believe that embryonic stem cells, with their unlimited potential, are far more promising medically.

6   In the United States, embryonic stem cell research is limited by law. Federal funding—a major source of support for universities and labs—is restricted to experiments on only 71 stem cell lines (a stem cell line refers to a set of pluripotent, embryonic stem cells that have grown in the laboratory for at least six months). Some scientists worry that this pool is too small to develop valid medical therapies. Opponents believe that even this compromise allows unethical practices to continue. California has established a research initiative that would ban human reproductive cloning but permit embryonic stem cell research for therapeutic purposes.

7   As debate rages in the United States, embryonic stem cell research is moving forward in other countries. For example, the United Kingdom has licensed a British university to clone stem cells for diabetes research, and South Korean scientists have developed better laboratory techniques for deriving new stem cell lines.

Rebecca J. Donatelle, *Health: The Basics*, 7th ed., p. 421, © 2007. Reprinted by permission of Pearson Education, Inc., Upper Saddle River, New Jersey.

COMPREHENSION QUESTIONS

1. What is the topic of the passage?
2. What is the central message of the passage?
3. Determine what is at issue. What is your initial personal viewpoint?
4. Distinguish among opposing viewpoints, and provide the rationale for each.
5. Think carefully about the viewpoints. Express a personal viewpoint, and give the reasons why you favor it. Does it differ from your initial personal viewpoint? Why or why not?
6. Write a few paragraphs *in support of the viewpoint that you do* not *favor.* You may want to check out one of the Web sites below or a couple of current Web sites on stem cell research to get some examples.

   www.allaboutpopularissues.org/pros-and-cons-of-stem-cell-research.htm
   www.time.com/time/magazine/printout/0,8816,1220538,00.html

THOUGHT AND DISCUSSION QUESTIONS

1. Do you feel that embryonic stem cell research is ethical? Explain your answer.
2. Would you feel different about stem cell research if you or a loved one suffered from a disease that might respond to stem cell therapy? Why or why not?
3. Find a Web site that does not support your view of stem cell research. List the arguments from the web site. Be prepared to share your opinions for discussion.

ACTIVITY 14

DIRECTIONS: Your instructor is going to divide the class into groups, each of which will choose a contemporary issue to investigate. Each group will then be divided into two debate teams for the purpose of representing the major opposing viewpoints regarding the issue. Toward the end of the semester, the two teams will debate the issue in class, with your instructor serving as the moderator.

LOOKING BACK ... LOOKING FORWARD

To check your progress in meeting this chapter's learning objectives, complete the Mastery Tests in this chapter.

THINK AGAIN!

Suppose that you are alone in the forest with a friend, and you are both riding horses. An argument starts over whose horse is slower. After several minutes of bickering, you make a $100 bet and decide to have a race immediately. However, the race does not work because you each make your horse go as slowly as possible on purpose so that you can win the money. Assuming that you want to settle the matter right there on the spot, can you figure out a fair way to determine whose horse is slower?

CRITICAL READING

Do you have a strong opinion about a contemporary issue? Investigate the Web for opposing viewpoints on an issue of your choice. Write an essay in which you give the arguments for both sides of the issue and indicate which viewpoint you think is stronger. If you need some help in identifying issues, go to the University of Washington Libraries site, http://uwashington.worldcat.org/search?q=issues+opposing+views&fq=&start=1&dblist=638 for some suggestions on links to single-issue pro and con arguments.

LISTENING SPRINGBOARD INQUIRY

Carnegie Mellon University has a lecture series called "Journeys." The series was originally called "The Last Lecture," which was to focus on this idea: If the lecturer had one last lecture to give, what would it be? Computer science professor Randy Pausch gave his last lecture, "Achieving Childhood Dreams," on September 18, 2007. He died of terminal cancer on July 25, 2008.

1. Go to http://www.youtube.com and type in the search bar: *Randy Pausch.* Listen to/watch the report with Diane Sawyer: *Randy Pausch, The Last Lecture April 2008, Interview parts 1–5.* For each part, write down the advice given and important lessons discussed.
   - What inspired you the most?
   - If you had six months to live, how would you live your life?

• What are the special things you would do or say to your family and friends?

_____

_____

_____

Randy Pausch's book, co-authored with Jeffery Zaslow, *The Last Lecture*, is probably available through your library. For more information on the Internet, go to http://www.thelastlecture.com/ or http://www.youtube.com (search bar: *Randy Pausch*).

2. Go online and find the lyrics to "Time in a Bottle," a song by Jim Croce. What message does the songwriter/singer want to impart? What do you think the circumstances could be for the situation?

_____

_____

_____

PLAY ON, OH LOVELY MUSIC

Remember to follow these steps:

- first, read the narrative and all the questions
- second, examine the picture carefully
- third, answer the questions in the order they appear and come up with the solution

Have fun!

Gaston Quirkenbocker was a superb violinist. He had organized the Quirkenbocker Quartet and made it famous. He was the glue that held it together and gave it balance and fervor and coherence. Nevertheless, his colleagues feared and hated him.

This was so because he had a violent temper and had once reportedly broken the hand of a talented pianist who'd had the nerve to criticize him. But the musicians suppressed their feelings and never dared to say or do anything overt.

Some say Ulric von Tramm, the violist, hated him most, but Ignatz Smith, the cellist, disagreed. "I think Evelina (Evelina Forceps, the pianist) hated him more. Women have deeper feelings." But their personal animosity was of no concern to Quirkenbocker himself.

"People hate me," he said, "because they envy me. Even little Paige Turner, who turns the pages for Evelina, would like to kill me, so let them snivel." And with that, he twirled his mustache, which he redesigned every two months.

One recent Sunday evening during a particularly sumptuous concert, at the moment depicted in the sketch, Quirkenbocker suddenly went livid and stopped the performance cold. He turned to the audience and accused his colleagues of a plot to sabotage him; he gave each of them in turn a vicious slap, and walked off the platform.

In the ensuing argument backstage, Quirkenbocker was shot and killed. His three colleagues were charged with murder and conspiracy to commit a murder. They were subsequently convicted and sentenced to ten years each in prison.

By examining the picture, can you decide who was responsible for the trick that was the underlying cause of the crime?

Questions

1. Who had an opportunity to tamper with Gaston's score? _____.

2. Whose picture did Quirkenbocker find when he turned the page of his score? _____.

3. Did the other members of the Quirkenbocker Quartet find anything unusual when they turned their pages?   ☐ Yes   ☐ No

4. Why did Gaston stop the performance? _____.

5. Who do you think tampered with Gaston's score? _____.

Text and illustration from Lawrence Treat, *Crime and Puzzlement—My Cousin Phoebe: 24 Solve-Them-Yourself Picture Mysteries* (Henry Holt and Co., 1991), pp. 15–16

Play On, Oh Lovely Music

Name _____   Date _____

MASTERY TEST 4–1

DIRECTIONS: Fill in the blanks and answer the questions.

1. _____ thinking has no clear purpose or objective.

2. Critical thinkers are in a better position to _____ what is going on around them, avoid costly _____, and _____ whatever they set out to do.

3. What is critical thinking? _____

   _____

   _____

4. What are the benefits and uses of critical thinking? _____

   _____

   _____

   _____

   _____

   _____

   _____

   _____

   _____

   _____

   _____

   _____

   _____

   _____

5. Name the characteristics of critical thinking, and describe each of them in a sentence or two. _____

   _____

   _____

   _____

   _____

_____

_____

_____

_____

_____

_____

_____

_____

_____

_____

_____

_____

_____

_____

_____

6. When using the Internet for research, the critical thinker
   a. should first make sure that a particular source is both appropriate and relevant.
   b. should try to use material from *.edu, .gov,* and *.mil* sites because they are most likely to be reliable.
   c. should look for the professional affiliation and bibliography of the author.
   d. should always be aware of possible bias.
   e. all of the above
   f. none of the above

7. _____, _____, and _____ are online databases that provide access to full-text articles from scholarly and popular periodicals.

8. _____ and _____ are examples of search engines that use key words to find information.

9. What is a contemporary issue? _____

   _____

   _____

10. As a critical thinker, it is important that you be aware of the _____, or specific reasons, for a given viewpoint.

Name _____   Date _____

DIRECTIONS: *For each of the following passages, determine what is at issue and distinguish among the opposing viewpoints, including the rationale for each.*

1

The No Child Left Behind Act

1   Many educators and politicians agree on the goals set by the No Child Left Behind Act (NCLB): higher educational standards, greater school accountability, qualified teachers, and closing the gap in student achievement. However, the two major political parties criticize NCLB, even though both parties voted for the act. Republicans complain that NCLB allows federal intrusion into the educational rights of states. Democrats worry that the federal government is not providing enough funding to meet NCLB's guidelines. American education achievement lags behind education in other democratic countries. The question is whether NCLB adequately addresses this problem.

Pro NCLB

2   NCLB gives state and local school districts the flexibility to meet its requirements. States can define standards and the means to meet and measure them. As long as NCLB guidelines are met, the states are generally free to innovate, educate, and test according to their needs.

3   NCLB is not an unfounded mandate. State school systems have the option of accepting or rejecting NCLB funding. Federal spending accounts for only 8% of all educational expenditures in the United States.

4   NCLB addresses the needs of parents with children in public schools. States have failed to meet the guidelines set forth by various federal policy initiatives. They have thus failed the expectations of parents as well. For example, Goals 2000 (1994) mandated a 90% high school graduation rate by 2000 and a number one rank in math and science for American students internationally. By 2000, the graduation rate was only 75%. American students ranked not first but nineteenth in math and eighteenth in science.

Con NCLB

5   NCLB requirements force school districts to teach to the test. Rather than teaching analytical and creative thinking, the testing requirements force school districts to have students cram for the exam. This undermines the primary goal of a true education.

6   NCLB does not distinguish between disabled and non-English-speaking students and able students proficient in English. A primary problem with NCLB is that it combines all students. This is an unfair burden on educators in school systems

with a disproportionate number of disabled or non-English-speaking students. NCLB's punitive sections assume an able, English-speaking student body.

7   NCLB should be considered an intrusion on the rights of state educational institutions. NCLB erodes the line separating federal and state authority. If school systems are not addressing the concerns of parents and educational problems, it is the proper duty of the state to address these issues.

"The No Child Left Behind Act" from Karen O'Connor and Larry J. Sabato,
American Government: Continuity and Change, 2006, pp. 116–117

Issue: _____

Opposing viewpoints and rationales: _____

_____

_____

_____

_____

_____

2

Do You Trust the Media?

1   These days, more and more news is *about* the news, thanks to a wave of media malfeasance that has Americans wondering whether they can trust anything they read, watch or hear. Among the biggest scandals: CNN and *Time*'s admission that their joint report about the United States' use of nerve gas in Vietnam had little basis in fact; the firing of a *Boston Globe* columnist and a *New Republic* writer for making up quotes and events; and prestigious news outlets caught spreading unfounded rumors during the early days of the Clinton-Lewinsky brouhaha.

2   These exposés arrive amid a growing credibility crisis. The percentage of Americans who think that news outlets usually get the facts straight has plummeted from 55 to 34 over the past 13 years, according to The Pew Research Center for The People & The Press.

3   Some say news quality is compromised by the intense, often minute-to-minute competition among a growing number of outlets, including cable shows, Internet sites and some dozen TV newsmagazines. As *Nightline*'s executive producer recently said, "Everybody is ratcheting up the speed and that's totally wrong.... You can work too fast and make mistakes."

4   Others say the battle for ratings and advertising dollars also affects the news. "We're moving from journalism as a profession toward news as marketing," says Jim Naureckas of Fairness & Accuracy In Reporting, a watchdog group. Big-business

media, he argues, would rather run "sensationalist stories that can be played for tears, fears or outrage" than cover serious political and economic issues.

5   Journalists' own biases are part of the problem too, adds Deborah Lambert of Accuracy in Media, a watchdog group that monitors the media for liberal bias. To "make a splash," she charges, some reporters give vent to personal passions instead of presenting information fairly. "To these journalists, truth has become a quaint relic."

6   Yet many believe news gathering is better than ever. "We never had a 'good old days' when no one made mistakes on deadline," says Dick Schwarzlose, a professor at Northwestern University's Medill School of Journalism. Nor are competition, sensationalism or bias anything new (the term *yellow journalism* was coined in the late nineteenth century); it's just that today, reporters as well as their audience are far more aware when the media falls short. Says Schwarzlose, "The vast majority of people in the news business are doing their best to provide good information."

7   Robert Lichter, Ph.D., who heads the Center for Media and Public Affairs, questions whether bias-free news is ideal. The founding fathers' vision of a free press wasn't a few respected sources spooning out "objective" facts, he notes, but a welter of conflicting sources and viewpoints—precisely what today's consumer faces.

8   Journalism's defenders point out that most people know which sources are usually trustworthy and which play the news for thrills. The Pew survey, for example, found that 93 percent of Americans have little or no faith in the accuracy of supermarket tabloids. Meanwhile, believability of serious news outlets is becoming more of a concern—especially now that members of the media are watchdogging each other, says Bill Kovach, curator of Harvard's Nieman Foundation journalism fellowships. "When you make ratings your number-one priority and credibility number two, eventually you get slammed," he says. "I hope CNN and the others have learned that lesson by now."

9   Is the media less trustworthy than ever?

Issue: _____

Opposing viewpoints and rationales: _____

_____

_____

_____

_____

_____

_____

_____

3

Artificial Tans: Sacrificing Health for Beauty?

1   Men and women of all ages, shapes, and sizes are searching for an easy way to get that glamorous tan before or instead of spending time in the sun. Are any of the sun substitutes a safe alternative?

Tanning Booths and Beds

2   On an average day, more than 1.3 million Americans visit a tanning salon including many teenagers and young adults. Researchers using data from the *National Longitudinal Study of Adolescent Health* report that more than 25 percent of white female adolescents and 11 percent of males used tanning booths at least three times in the last year. Adolescents who tanned easily were more likely to visit tanning booths, while women who reported higher levels of physical activity were less likely to use them.

3   Most tanning salon patrons incorrectly believe that tanning booths are safer than sitting in the sun. However, the truth is that there is no such thing as a safe tan from *any* source! Essentially, a tan is the skin's response to an injury; and every time you tan, you accumulate injury and increase your risk for disfiguring forms of skin cancer, premature aging, eye problems, unsightly skin spots, wrinkles and leathery skin, and possible death from melanoma. To make matters worse, the industry is difficult to monitor and regulate because of the many salons that are springing up across the country. Dermatologists cite additional factors that make tanning in a salon as bad or worse than getting a tan the old fashioned way of sitting in the sun:

• Tanning facilities sometimes fail to enforce regulations, such as insuring that customers wear eye protection and that overexposure does not occur.

• Some tanning facilities do not calibrate the ultraviolet (UV) output of their tanning bulbs or ensure sufficient rotation of newer and older bulbs, which can lead to more or less exposure than you paid for. Tanning facility patrons often try for a total body tan. The buttocks and genitalia are particularly sensitive to UV radiation and are prone to develop skin cancer.

• Another concern is hygiene. Don't assume that those little colored water sprayers used to "clean" the inside of the beds are sufficient to kill organisms. Any time you come in contact with body secretions from others, you run the risk of an infectious disease.

Spray-On Tans

4   Some companies offer a sunless option that involves spraying customers in a tanning booth with the color additive dihydroxyacetone (DHA), which interacts with the dead surface cells in the outermost layer of the skin to darken skin color. Dihydroxyacetone has been approved by the FDA for use in coloring the skin since 1977 and has typically

been used in lotions and creams. Its use is restricted to external application, which means that it shouldn't be sprayed in or on the mouth, eyes, or nose because the risks, if any, are unknown. If you choose to use DHA spray at home or in tanning booths, be sure to cover these areas. Remember that the spray is a dye and does not increase your protection from the damaging rays of the sun.

Tanning Pills

5   Although there are no tanning pills approved by the FDA, some companies market pills that contain the color additive canthaxanthin. When large amounts of canthaxanthin are ingested, the substance can turn the skin a range of colors, from orange to brown. However, canthaxanthin is only approved for use as a color additive in foods and oral medications—and only in small amounts. Tanning pills have been associated with health problems, including an eye disorder called canthaxanthin retinopathy, which is the formation of yellow deposits on the eye's retina. Canthaxanthin has also been reported to cause liver injury and a severe itching condition called urticaria, according to the American Academy of Dermatology.

Rebecca J. Donatelle, *Health: The Basics*, 7th ed., p. 367, © 2007. Reprinted by permission of Pearson Education, Inc., Upper Saddle River, New Jersey.

Issue: _____

Opposing viewpoints and rationales: _____

_____

_____

_____

_____

_____

_____

_____

_____

4

Is Homework a Valuable Use of Time?

1   Like so many methods in education, homework has moved in and out of favor. In the early 1900s, homework was seen as an important path to mental discipline, but by the 1940s, homework was criticized as too much drill and low-level learning.

Then in the 1950s, homework was rediscovered as a way to catch up with the Soviet Union in science and mathematics, only to be seen as too much pressure on students during the more laid-back 1960s. By the 1980s, homework was in again as a way to improve the standing of American children compared to students around the world (Cooper & Valentine, 2001a). Everyone has done homework–were those hours well spent?

POINT: Homework does not help students learn

2   No matter how interesting an activity is, students will eventually get bored with it–so why give them work both in and out of school? They will simply grow weary of learning. And important opportunities are lost for community involvement or leisure activities that would create well-rounded citizens. When parents help with homework, they can do more harm than good–sometimes confusing their children or teaching them incorrectly. And students from poorer families often must work, so they miss doing the homework; then the learning discrepancy between the rich and poor grows even greater. Besides, the research is inconsistent about the effects of homework. For example, one study found that in-class work was better than homework in helping elementary students learn (Cooper & Valentine, 2001a).

COUNTERPOINT: Well-planned homework can work for many students

3   Harris Cooper and Jeffrey Valentine reviewed many studies of homework and concluded that there is little relationship between homework and learning for young students, but the relationship between homework and achievement grows progressively stronger for older students. There is recent evidence that students in high school who do more homework (and watch less television after school) have higher grades, even when other factors such as gender, grade level, ethnicity, SES, and amount of adult supervision are taken into consideration (Cooper & Valentine, 2001a; Cooper, Valentine, Nye, & Kindsay, 1999). Consistent with these findings, the National PTA makes these recommendations:

4   [F]or children in grades K–2, homework is most effective when it does not exceed 10–20 minutes each day; older students, in grades 3–6, can handle 30–60 minutes a day; in junior and senior high school, the amount of homework will vary by subject. (Henderson, 1996, p. 1)

Anita Woolfolk, *Educational Psychology Active Learning Edition*, p. 542, © 2008 by Pearson Education, Inc. Reproduced by permission of Pearson Education, Inc.

Issue: _____

Opposing viewpoints and rationales: _____

_____

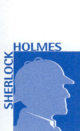

SHERLOCK HOLMES AND DR. WATSON

Rob Rector

Directions: As a critical thinker, read the following review of the movie Sherlock Holmes, *which was taken from the Internet, and then answer the Thought and Discussion questions.*

1   Playing like a big-budget episode of *CSI: Victorian London*, Guy Ritchie's latest imagining of *Sherlock Holmes* had a curious effect on me.

2   It made me interested to see a sequel.

3   The film itself ditches the normal "background story" tropes in favors of focusing on Holmes' relationship with Watson (curious), his pugilistic tendencies (curiouser), and his ability to deduce crimes from the slightest strands of evidence (curious*iest*?). And while it is far from a definitive take on Doyle's enduring literary creation, there is more under its deerstalker than recreating Holmes as an action hero and it lays groundwork for what could be a rather interesting franchise in the right hands.

4   First, can we all just take a step back and be somewhat happy that younger audience members may want to delve into literature as a result of the film, seeking mysteries beyond what the gang of the Mystery Machine can solve? Granted, their short attention spans might sputter out by the fourth paragraph of *The Strand*. But it's a start, right?

5   Of Holmes' many passions, his love of bare-knuckle brawling and forensics take the lead in this adaptation. And while Ritchie's version (Holmes is the most filmed literary character) may play fast and loose with some of the detective's history, it is more accurate than not.

6   Robert Downey Jr. is the perfect left-field fit for the eccentric detective, for he approaches his roles in much the same way Holmes approaches his cases, which is far from the well-traveled path. It's also refreshing to see Jude Law in a subdued, nuanced performance that cashes in on the praise he first received earlier in his career.

7   The mystery itself is not as engaging. Involving black magic, remote-controlled bombs, and cliffhanger conclusions, *Sherlock Holmes* works far better in its more intimate moments than when it tries to muscle into summer escapist mode. Watching Holmes deduce entire backstories by mere cursory glances is all the rush needed. There is also little effort devoted to periphery relationships, such as those between Holmes, Watson, and Inspector Lestrade (played by accomplished British actor Eddie Marsan), Holmes and his duplicitous muse Irene Adler (Rachel McAdams), and Watson with fiancée Mary Morstan (Kelly Reilly).

8   Ritchie, though visually entertaining at times, is perhaps the wrong choice to helm this hero. Too often he falls back on dizzying edits and over-stylized bombast (though the boatyard bomb scene is quite effective). But its door is left wide open for a franchise, and with a bit more restraint (and perhaps a different director) and

more insight into the unraveling mystery itself, viewers can rest comfortably in the Baker Street address of this cinematic home sweet *Holmes.*

http://blogcritics.org/video/article/movie-review-sherlock-holmes-20091/

Thought and Discussion Questions

1. Do you agree with the statement "Movies based on novels are not as good as the novels themselves"? Why or why not?

2. Do you agree that this adaption of *Sherlock Holmes* should depict him as a brawling action hero where there are "remote-controlled" bombs and black magic? Why or why not?

3. Pretend that you are a movie critic. See Ritchie's movie *Sherlock Holmes* if possible. Which points made by the reviewer do you agree with? Which points do you disagree with? Why?

4. (Optional) Call up a review of this movie on YouTube [www.youtube.com] *or* see what other viewers have said about it on http://www.rottentomatoes.com/m/sherlock_holmes_2009/ Add your opinion to the YouTube site or to the Web site.

CHAPTER OUTLINE

CHAPTER OUTCOMES

After completing Chapter 5, you should be able to:

- Define *problem* and *solution.*
- List and describe the five steps involved in the basic method for personal problem solving.
- Apply the method to a typical problem situation.
- Continue to find topics and central messages in contemporary issue passages to determine what is at issue, distinguish among opposing viewpoints, and express personal viewpoints.

Think About It!

Look carefully at each of the symbols presented below. What does each symbol mean to you? Discuss your answers with your classmates.

1

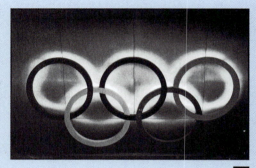

2

3

PROBLEM-SOLVING EXERCISE

For purposes of giving you the opportunity to practice both your thinking and problem-solving skills together, an exercise like this will be presented at the beginning of each of the remaining chapters in this textbook. The exercises will deal with a variety of hypothetical situations.

Hypothetical Situation

Suppose that you would really like to date a fellow student who is in one of your classes, but that person shows absolutely no interest in you. Every attempt that you have made to start a conversation has failed. In fact, your glances and smiles are ignored with little or no eye contact in return. Nevertheless, you continue to be very attracted to your classmate and interested in starting a relationship because you think that this could be the "love of your life."

Think about this situation for a few moments, and then write a short essay in which you discuss how you would resolve it. Feel free to discuss your thoughts with your classmates.

■ What Is a Problem?

"I have a problem!" "We have a problem!" "You have a problem!" "She has a problem!" "There is a problem!" How often have you heard statements like these? Probably quite often. Problems or personal challenges are a big part of life. As one student aptly put it, "To have problems is to be alive." In that we cannot avoid them, what exactly do we mean when we talk about problems?

The dictionary defines a **problem** as "a question, matter, situation, or person that is perplexing or difficult" or "any question or matter involving doubt, uncertainty, or difficulty." These definitions are fine, but they really do not describe what it feels like to have a problem. We all have a wide variety of problems as we go through life yet really never think about an accurate definition of what it is we are experiencing.

To put it in simple terms, *there is a problem when we feel uncertain, dissatisfied, or upset with things, persons, or circumstances because they are either not doing what we think they should be doing or not going the way that we want or expected.* Thus, we experience such problems as an automobile that will not start, a good friend who has been ignoring us lately, a boss who does not value our work, and an inability to stop smoking even though we want to quit. We can try to ignore problems like these and hope that they disappear, but usually they will not go away by themselves. Furthermore, they remain *our* problems and do not necessarily become anyone else's. Hence we are often forced to search on our own for possible solutions.

ACTIVITY 1   DIRECTIONS: *Make a confidential list of personal challenges or issues that you have experienced recently.*

■ What Is a Solution?

The dictionary defines a **solution** as "the act, method, or process of solving a problem" or "the act or process of explaining, settling, or disposing of a difficulty, problem, or doubt." In other words, *solutions are the means by which we rid ourselves of problems.* As a result, we no longer feel uncertain, dissatisfied, or upset with the things, persons, or circumstances that were either not doing what we thought they should be doing or not going the way that we wanted or expected.

The means, or how we choose to get ourselves out of difficult situations, will vary greatly. For instance, returning to the examples of the problems mentioned earlier:

> The automobile that will not start can be fixed, junked, or traded in for another.
> The good friend can be approached to talk about reasons for the change in behavior in order to come up with possible remedies, or the friendship can be ended if that is what is decided.
> A discussion can be held with the boss to determine why our work is not appreciated, a higher-up can be consulted, or another job can be found.
> Attempts can be made to stop smoking by wearing a nicotine patch, through the use of hypnosis, or by joining a support group.

There are always at least a few possible solutions to consider before deciding which one offers the best chance of success for eliminating a given problem.

ACTIVITY 2   DIRECTIONS: *List the solutions that you came up with to solve the personal challenges or issues you noted in Activity 1.*

■ How Do You Solve Problems?

In Activities 1 and 2, you listed problems or challenges that you experienced recently and their solutions. Is there a specific approach that you follow consistently when trying to solve problems? For example, do you run down all the possible solutions before choosing one, or do you go from one solution to the next by using trial and error? What approach did your classmates and you use to resolve the hypothetical situation presented in the problem-solving exercise at the start of the chapter?

Your approach to problem solving may not be clear to you or easy to describe. In fact, it is possible that you do not turn consistently to a definite method at all. Perhaps you use past experiences to help you sort things out. Maybe there are instances in which you do nothing, hoping that problems will go away by themselves. In short, there are different ways of dealing with problems, and we all have our individual preferences. However, we do agree on one thing: We want our problems to disappear quickly.

■ Problem Solving and Critical Thinking

In Chapter 4, we noted that critical thinkers are careful and thoughtful in their approach to the world and that this enables them to make the most of limited time and helps them handle the complexities of life. Carefulness and thoughtfulness is particularly important when dealing with problems, because as a result of thinking critically, you place yourself in a stronger position to come up with the best solutions. In fact, all of the seven characteristics of critical thinking described in Chapter 4 are necessary ingredients for effective problem solving: *flexibility, a clear purpose, organization, time and effort, asking questions and finding answers, research, and coming to logical conclusions.*

■ A Basic Method for Personal Problem Solving

The structured five-step approach to problem solving that follows may not eliminate all of your problems or guarantee perfect solutions, but it does provide a basic, simple, organized way of trying to deal with the things, persons, or circumstances that are challenging you. As we proceed with the discussion, you may in fact discover that you are already using at least some of the steps as part of your approach to problems.

Step 1: Identify the Problem

Before attempting to solve a problem, you have to make sure that you know what the problem is. This may seem obvious, but sometimes it is difficult to uncover what exactly is bothering you. For example, you may be angry at a friend who owes you money, not because of the money itself, but because she has ignored your constant reminders. Thus, the real problem involves the fact that she is apparently not paying attention to you or not living up to her part of the bargain. In short, you may feel that you are being treated with a lack of respect or that a trust has been broken.

When defining a problem, you must be careful to go beneath the surface, to be very specific, and not confuse means (ways of accomplishing goals) with the ends (the goals themselves). In the example just mentioned, the repayment of the money by your friend could simply be a means that really does not get at the overall problem of being ignored or treated with a lack of respect.

As part of this step, it is important to realize that the problem is yours and not necessarily anyone else's. *You* are the one who is uncertain, dissatisfied, or upset, and *you* have to take action to make things better. If other persons are involved, they may be perfectly happy to keep things exactly as they are. In fact, others may not even be aware that you are feeling unhappy about something. To take our example, your friend may not realize that you are angry about the money situation, or if she is aware of it, she may be quite willing to let things continue as they are indefinitely. With regard to the situation described in the problem-solving exercise at the beginning of the chapter, the problem of the fellow student not showing any interest in you may be very clear from your vantage point, but your classmate probably sees no problem at all and thus feels no need to take any kind of action.

Even if other people are not involved in what is bothering you, you must still come to terms with the fact that the solution to the problem requires action on your part. You may seek the advice of others, but ultimately you are the one who must do something to eliminate a given problem. Problems usually do not disappear by themselves, so you must take ownership of them.

Step 2: Gather Information and Determine If the Problem Can Be Broken Down

After identifying the problem, defining it very specifically, and taking ownership of it, you need to gather as much information about it as possible. Depending on the nature of the problem, this could involve doing research and include discussions with various people who are knowledgeable about it, particularly those who have actually caused the problem or perhaps been involved in it in some other way. They can be very helpful in providing clarification.

As mentioned in Chapter 4, you must take into account whether the information gathered is relevant, reliable, and impartial. This may involve determining the motivations or purposes of the sources that you are using. Once you have evaluated and given careful thought to the information that you have gathered, you are in a much better position to proceed toward a solution.

As part of this step, you should determine if the problem can be broken down into smaller problems that can be worked on one at a time. Frequently, the solving of those smaller problems can lead to the solution of the overall one. For instance, you may be dissatisfied because you have a C average in your psychology course, and you really want to get a higher grade. Perhaps this problem can be broken down by subdividing it into smaller ones that are more specific and perhaps more manageable, such as ineffective note taking, poor test taking, lack of comprehension of the textbook, or not enough time spent on preparation for the class. By subdividing your problem, you can then focus on the problem areas that need improving and come up with strategies or solutions for them, thereby, ideally, resolving the overall problem. For example, you can take a note-taking or test-taking workshop to learn new techniques, improve on your reading skills by getting tutorial help and practicing, or simply spend more hours on course preparation. Over time, any of these could lead to a better grade in the course, thereby solving the major overriding problem of an average that is below what you want.

Looking back at the problem-solving exercise at the beginning of the chapter, after doing some research and gathering information from friends or other students, perhaps you find that your classmate is ignoring you because of involvement in another relationship or simply as a result of shyness. These facts help you break down the problem so that you can then decide whether to continue your pursuit and, if that is the case, arrive at a strategy such as getting involved in the same outside activities as your classmate. That might allow you to get acquainted in a more casual, less threatening atmosphere. As a result of breaking down the problem, you are in a better position to resolve it.

Step 3: Think About Possible Solutions and Weigh the Advantages and Disadvantages of Each

After you have identified the problem, defined it very specifically, taken ownership of it, gathered the facts, and determined if it can be broken down, you need to come up with a list of possible solutions. If the problem involves another person, as it often does, it is often advisable, if possible, to get that person involved at this stage even if he or she was already approached for information in Step 2. This is important for at least two reasons: First, the other party would likely supply additional information that is helpful when trying to devise a solution; and second, it is unrealistic to expect someone to cooperate with a given solution if the person had little or no part in the process through which it was decided on. In fact, as a result of not consulting with that other person, the proposed solution is likely to become no solution at all!

Obviously, to get another person involved, you have to communicate *your* specific definition of the problem—why *you* are uncertain, dissatisfied, or upset—and any of the information that you may have gathered concerning it. A *mutually* agreeable time has to be set up for that purpose. It is useless to try to discuss a problem if the other person is preoccupied with something else. In short, for this method to work, all concerned parties must be ready and willing to talk.

Whether you are working alone or with others, it is at this stage that a list of possible solutions is drawn up, indicating the advantages and disadvantages of each. It may help to *write these out* so that they can be properly analyzed and revised as you think them over. This is not something that can be rushed, so enough time should be set aside to review the options thoroughly. Remember, critical thinking is by definition a lengthy process, especially when trying to deal with problems.

Looking again at the problem-solving exercise at the beginning of this chapter, you might decide to take the direct approach and get your classmate involved at this stage by being totally honest about your interest in going out on a date. The big advantage of doing this is that it gets the matter out in the open and brings it to a head quickly. However, if the lack of interest has been a result of another relationship or shyness on the part of that student, then at this early stage, this possible solution could make matters even worse for you by scaring off your classmate. For that reason, it might be better in this particular situation for you to consider other possible solutions on your own.

Another possibility is to forget about the whole thing. This has the advantage of saving time and energy, but the disadvantage of depriving yourself of the opportunity to date someone who is very appealing to you. Also, you may not want to accept defeat at this early stage without giving it your best shot.

One final possible solution was mentioned in Step 2, and it involves your finding out your classmate's interests so that you can participate in the same activities outside of class. The advantage of this possible solution is that you may get to know each other better, and your classmate may become friendlier after recognizing that you have similar interests. The major disadvantage involves your expenditure of much time and energy participating in activities that may not really excite you.

Step 4: Choose a Possible Solution

After enumerating the advantages and disadvantages of as many potential solutions as you can think of, you select the one with the greatest chance of succeeding. This is likely to be the solution with advantages that outweigh the disadvantages. If the problem involves other people, the solution must of course be arrived at after discussion with them. Everyone concerned must agree that this is the very strongest possible solution at the time, the one that has the best chance of solving the problem. Once a decision has been made—whether you make it alone or with others—it is crucial that the solution chosen be supported completely and that the reasons for its selection be kept in mind always.

Turning once again to the problem-solving exercise, at this point you would choose the possible solution that you think has the best chance of resolving the problem to your satisfaction—in other words, the one that will result in a date with your classmate. Of the three possible solutions discussed in Step 3, the one that seems to be the strongest without having any important disadvantages involves your participation in some of the same outside activities as your classmate. As a result of this apparent interest in similar activities, the hope is that you would get to know each other, which in turn could lead ultimately to a date. The only real disadvantage is the time and energy you would use to participate in additional activities that you would not normally choose to do. Under the circumstances, that seems like a small price to pay, considering your strong desire to go out with your classmate.

Step 5: Check Back on the Problem and the Possible Solution

You never know for sure if the possible solution chosen is going to work until you try it. For that reason, both the problem and the proposed solution must be reconsidered after enough time has gone by to allow the latter a chance to succeed. Once again, when others are using this approach with you, it is necessary to discuss together the extent of the progress made. If the proposed solution is not correcting the problem, either the solution has to be revised or another one has to be selected. This will necessitate that at least one or perhaps all of the previous steps be revisited.

Considering the problem-solving exercise one last time, if your involvement in those activities does seem to be changing your classmate's reaction to you, you will want to continue with your chosen solution, at least for a while longer. On the other hand, if there is no change after a reasonable period of time, you may want to turn to either of the remaining possible solutions that we discussed. For example, you could attempt the direct approach, thinking that at this point you have nothing to lose by being blunt, or decide instead to simply give up and go on with your life. Giving up the fight would not result in a date, but at least the problem has been eliminated to the extent that you can turn your attention perhaps in a more promising direction.

Although you will not be able to use Step 5 for the hypothetical problems used in this text, it is very important that you apply it to the real problems in your life. You want to be sure that you have arrived at the best possible solutions.

■ Applying the Method to a Typical Problem Situation

Let us look at one more example of how the basic five-step problem-solving approach was used in a personal situation. Richard and Susan have been married for 30 years and have experienced all the ups and downs that go along with a marriage of that duration. In recent years, Richard has been getting up at 4 A.M to run five miles for health reasons. After finishing the run and taking a shower, he would take clean clothes from the dresser drawers in the bedroom. Unfortunately, Richard got into the bad habit of leaving the drawers half open, which was starting to upset Susan. Although she mentioned it to him on several occasions, Richard did not attach much importance to the matter and continued to leave the drawers open.

Step 1: Identify the Problem

Things went on like that for a while until Susan realized that this was her problem, because Richard was perfectly willing to continue what he was doing indefinitely. When she thought about it more thoroughly, it was not the half-open drawers per se that bothered her but the fact that Richard was apparently ignoring her. Furthermore, she saw no reason why she had to be the one to close them when Richard was perfectly capable of doing that for himself. After all, she was his wife, not his servant! The situation clearly required action on her part, or it would never be resolved to her satisfaction.

Step 2: Gather Information and Determine If the Problem Can Be Broken Down

Because of the nature of this problem, Susan did not have to do research or consult other people about it, but she thought it appropriate to ask Richard why he was leaving his dresser drawers half open. As it turned out, it was a good thing that she bothered to ask him, because he explained that the drawers stick, and he was afraid that by forcing them closed, he would make too much noise, thereby disturbing her sleep at that early hour. By making Susan aware of his thoughtful motivations, Richard clarified the situation for her. Although she appreciated his consideration, Susan continued to feel dissatisfied about the drawers' being left open and

Richard's apparent assumption that it is her responsibility to close them. At this stage, she could not think of any way to break down the problem, so Susan proceeded to the next step.

Step 3: Think About Possible Solutions and Weigh the Advantages and Disadvantages of Each

Susan approached Richard on the matter, and they agreed to sit down and discuss it at length. She explained that even though she appreciated his consideration about not making too much noise in the morning, the fact that he continued to leave the dresser drawers half open was upsetting to her. Susan was careful to emphasize that the real issues surrounding the problem involved his ignoring her constant complaints and his apparent belief that she was responsible for closing the drawers.

They agreed to consider the advantages and disadvantages of some possible solutions to the problem. One possible solution was for Richard not to run so early in the morning, but he explained that he could not fit a run in at any other time. Besides, he liked exercising at that early hour. For those two reasons, that proposed solution was unacceptable. Another possible solution was for Richard to force the drawers closed even if that made noise. Susan rejected that possibility because she was sure that it would disturb her sleep. A final possible solution involved Richard's taking out his clean clothing the night before so that he would not even have to go into the drawers in the early morning hours. Although this had the minor disadvantage of adding some clutter, it had the advantage of enabling Richard to adhere to his exercise schedule without disturbing Susan while at the same time eliminating her dissatisfaction with dresser drawers left half open.

Step 4: Choose a Possible Solution

After much discussion, they agreed that the third possible solution was the most acceptable because its advantages far outweighed its disadvantages. Apparently, it would solve the problem without creating any serious new problems for either Susan or Richard. They decided to give it a try.

Step 5: Check Back on the Problem and the Possible Solution

Richard and Susan discussed both the problem and the agreed-on solution two weeks later after it became obvious that Richard was still leaving the drawers half open at least some of the time. He explained that it was not intentional, but he was having a difficult time remembering to put his clothes out the night before. Because they had both thoroughly explored the other possible solutions and found them wanting, they decided to try to revise the one that they were currently using rather than going back through all the steps to find another solution. Susan certainly did not want to start nagging Richard about taking his clothes out the night before, so they came up with the idea that he would write a reminder to himself on the large message board in the kitchen until he got into the habit of gathering his clothes at night. With this slight adjustment, the problem was finally solved. Richard could have clean clothes while Susan slept in peace in a bedroom with closed dresser drawers.

Not all personal problems get resolved this easily, and of course there are much more serious ones that people face every day. Nevertheless, this example serves as a demonstration of how this basic method can be used to solve problems. The five-step approach is only one way of trying to deal with the complexities and difficulties of life that confront us all. When using this approach for the first several times, try to be very structured by following all of the steps in order. After a while, you will see that the steps can often be combined because the lines between them are not exact. In short, some flexibility is not only possible but desirable in most circumstances.

The diagram below illustrates the five-step approach to basic problem solving that you should apply to the problems encountered in your life.

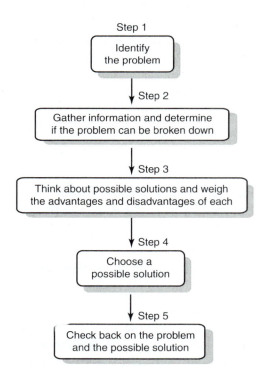

ACTIVITY 3

Directions: With two of your classmates, decide on a hypothetical problem, and apply the basic method for personal problem solving to it. Because it is a hypothetical problem, use only the first four steps of the approach.

ACTIVITY 4

Directions: Using the first four steps of the approach, try to come up with possible solutions in the following problem situations. In each case, write an essay explaining step by step how you went about arriving at the solution. As you go through the steps with Problem 1, make sure that you identify specifically what you think the problem is after considering the various possibilities. Because the problem is not explicitly stated in this particular situation, you will have to come to a logical conclusion about what is wrong.

Problem 1

James is a good friend of yours, but lately he has been acting strange. His behavior is erratic, and his mood swings from silliness to depression to anger. He does not seem to care about college anymore, which has led to low grades and the strong possibility of his failing out. Furthermore, James has lost his part-time job because of continual tardiness and absenteeism. Consequently, he is often broke and seems desperate for money. He no longer talks with you much and is hanging around with a different group of friends. You are very concerned about his well-being.

Problem 2

In this situation, as in the first one, identify the problem by considering carefully the information presented and drawing a logical conclusion. Put yourself in Anita's place as you proceed through the first four steps of the approach. After you have completed your essay, your instructor will pair you off with a classmate *of the opposite sex* so that you can exchange essays and discuss your work.

1   Andy passed Anita's locker every morning on his way to first period class. He began by just staring at her when he walked by. Then she noticed that when he passed her in the hallways or stairwells, he kept on looking.

2   At first, the 14-year-old thought Andy was flirting, but as she paid more attention to his gaze, she realized something didn't feel right. Anita felt uncomfortable with Andy's looks. It felt dirty, as if Andy had some kind of X-ray vision and was trying to see through her clothes to what was underneath.

3   One morning, Anita was standing by her locker. Suddenly, from behind she felt a guy's body pressed full front up against her. As she turned to see who it was, she felt Andy Porter's hand grabbing tightly on her behind and squeezing it. Anita spun around with anger to look Andy in the eye. He glared at her with that ugly intensity she had experienced in the past. A sly smile emerged on Andy's lips, and Anita could feel her insides buckling.

4   Thoughts of Andy and his behavior distracted Anita in school for the next two weeks. She had difficulty concentrating. She found herself drifting off in class, thinking of ways she could avoid Andy. Her Spanish teacher remarked about the decline in her class participation and the impact that would have on her "B" average. Mr. Marks, her history teacher, talked with Anita about her lateness to class and the negative consequences should she continue this behavior.

5   When Monday morning arrived, Anita once again experienced the gnawing knot of fear in her stomach as she approached the high school. Anita had shared her upset feelings with her close friends, but they just didn't understand. They thought she was lucky to have Andy Porter interested in her. He was one of the "hot" senior guys and having him "flirt" with her could only improve Anita's social status.

6   Anita could not relate to their opinion at all. She felt horrible. She lingered in the parking lot waiting for the first bell to ring. Although Anita realized she would be late again for Mr. Marks' class, she also knew that her tardiness would assure her of missing Andy in the hallway.

7   Anita finally entered the building and walked rapidly to her locker, head down, books held tightly against her chest. Suddenly overtaken by anger, she slammed her locker closed. Anita's eyes began to well up with tears, and the knot in her stomach began throbbing.

NJEA Review, March 1995, pp. 28–29

Problem 3

Last academic year, you took a science course in which a term paper was required. You spent much of the semester doing research and writing what turned out to be a 20-page paper. All of your effort and hard work paid off, because the instructor was very pleased with the result and gave you an "A." During the summer, your best friend informed you that she will be taking the same course during the spring semester and expects to fulfill the term paper requirement by submitting your paper with her name on it. She believes strongly that favors like this one are what friends are for.

Problem 4

Your mother is suffering from malignant cancer and is in pain much of the time. Day after day, she remains in a near-comatose state but occasionally does awaken for short periods. During those times, she is fairly lucid when you have conversations with her. Although her doctors refuse to predict when she will die, they do not offer much hope for her survival. Because she is having difficulty breathing and is steadily losing weight from her inability to eat, the hospital has asked for your permission to attach a ventilator and feeding tube. These measures could keep her alive indefinitely, although they probably would not improve her deteriorating condition. You have no brothers or sisters, and your father, who has Alzheimer's disease, is in a nursing home. Furthermore, your mother does not have a living will, nor has she ever made her wishes known.

Problem 5

As you proceed through the four steps with the problem stated here, read the article that follows it as a way of gathering information for Step 2.

You are a single parent with a full-time job and an 8-year-old son. Thomas is a hyperactive child who is consistently disruptive in school. The teacher has called you several times about his behavior, and you have met with the principal regarding the matter. You have warned Thomas several times, but he just seems to be ignoring you. In fact, he has started to question your authority in other areas as well and constantly talks back to you. He refuses to follow your instructions, such as your request that he put his dirty clothes in the hamper. You have become angry and impatient with him, and you are starting to lose your temper. In fact, you have threatened to spank him on more than one occasion unless he changes his behavior.

Spanking Is Becoming the New Don't

CLARE COLLINS

1   Have you ever spanked your child? Perhaps a better question is, would you admit to it?

2   "We spank as a last resort, when the children are either very rebellious or very rude," said Kellie Nienajadly, a Syracuse mother of a 2-year-old and a 3-year-old. "There's only so much reasoning you can do with children this young."

3   On the other hand, Rose Zagaja, who lives outside Hartford and has two children, ages 7 and 8, adamantly opposes spanking. "I think it's degrading and infuriating" to the child, she said.

4   Ms. Nienajadly's and Ms. Zagaja's differing views point to an emotional debate over a form of discipline that few of today's adults escaped as children. Is spanking merely a quick and decisive form of discipline, or is it to be shunned as ineffective, even cruel?

5   A recent Harris poll found that spanking is far from an uncommon parental act: 80 percent of the 1,250 adults surveyed said they had spanked their children. And 87 percent of those polled said that spanking is sometimes appropriate.

6   The telephone poll, conducted between Feb. 6 and 9, had a margin of error of plus or minus three percentage points. It did not ask respondents how frequently they spanked, nor did it define spanking.

7   The poll's findings run counter to the advice handed out by a growing number of child development experts who say spanking not only is ineffective but also breeds aggression.

8   "Spanking teaches kids that when someone is doing something you don't like and they won't stop doing it, you hit them," said Murray A. Straus, a professor of sociology at the University of New Hampshire in Durham and the author of *Beating the Devil Out of Them: Corporal Punishment in American Families* (Lexington Books, 1994), which argues against spanking.

9   Dr. Straus said that studies he had conducted found that children who are frequently spanked are more likely to act aggressively toward their peers and may then go on to be aggressive teenagers and depressed, abusive adults.

10   According to Dr. Straus's definition, spanking refers to any kind of swatting or slapping "intended to cause a child physical pain but not injury, for purposes of correction or control."

11   "Spanking is very subjective," Dr. Straus said. "Some people think you have to hit hard enough to leave a mark that doesn't last very long. Others would define that as abuse." He would like to see corporal punishment outlawed in this country. Spanking is illegal in many European countries.

12   "Parents spank young children because they don't know what else to do," said Alvin Rosenfeld, a child psychiatrist in Manhattan and co-author of *The Art of the Obvious* with the late Bruno Bettelheim. "Spanking does work. It puts a stop on certain behaviors. But the question is, does it achieve what you're trying to achieve?"

13   Even the strongest of statements against physical punishment usually stop short of condemning parents who have spanked. "We're all human," said Linda S. Budd, a St. Paul psychologist and the author of *Living with the Active Alert Child* (Parenting Press, 1993). "The fact that you lost it once and smacked your child doesn't mean you've ruined him for life. It does indicate a need to slow down and stop before you act."

14   Some experts condone spanking, usually on an extremely limited basis when the issue is safety or willful disobedience. One of the most widely quoted is James C. Dobson, the author of *The New Dare to Discipline* (Tyndale House Publishers, 1992).

15   Dr. Dobson, who writes that his theories are firmly rooted in Judeo-Christian beliefs, advocates spanking for children between the ages of 18 months and 10 years who directly challenge a parent's authority. He states in his book that spanking—which should be done in a calm, "I'm doing this for your own good" fashion—"is the shortest route to an attitude adjustment."

16   John Rosemond, a psychologist, supports spanking but suggests it be followed by consequences appropriate to the misbehavior. For instance, if a child leaves the house when told not to and is spanked, the parent should then take away television or other privileges. Mr. Rosemond says spanking can be far less detrimental than extreme verbal abuse or overly severe punishment.

17   More and more, though, spanking is emerging as the don't of the 1990s.

18   Dr. Budd said that she and most of her colleagues had given up on forms of therapy that change behaviors out of fear. She favors alternative methods of disciplining like time-outs and the taking away of privileges.

19   Although still a majority, the number of parents who spank is on the decline, said Dr. Straus, whose first study, in 1968, showed that "94 percent of the adult U.S. population believed it was sometimes necessary to give a child a spanking."

20   In a survey he conducted in 1994, Dr. Straus found that only 68 percent of the adult population—even fewer than in the Harris poll—believed in spanking. "In my line of work, that's actually an astronomical speed of social change," he said.

21   The Harris poll seems to support his contention that spanking is on the decline. It found that among the newest generation of parents—ages 18 to 24—31 percent said they had never spanked, compared with 19 percent among all parents. That trend is likely to continue, since the survey also found that most parents who were not spanked have not spanked their children.

22   Parents who do spank often feel they can't admit to it without risking harsh criticism. In a recent forum on Compuserve, the online service, only a handful of parents who responded to a query about spanking would speak for attribution. "It used to be parents who *didn't* spank were the ones who wouldn't be quoted," Dr. Straus said. "They were seen as the crackpots."

23   Spanking, Dr. Rosenfeld said, does nothing to further the long-term goal of successful parenting: raising happy, well-socialized adults. "Spanking deprives you of an opportunity to show your child that you have superior reasoning skills," he added.

24   "I came to the realization that spanking isn't all that effective," said Jebbie Crowe of Mystic, Conn., who is the mother of six children ages 14 to 28. She spanked her oldest children but changed her theory with her youngest. "My kids actually preferred it to other punishments because it was over quickly," she said. "It was an easy way out for both of us."

25   Dr. Budd says she believes that many parents spank because they have unrealistic expectations. "Often, parents just don't understand child development," she said. "They spank a child for being developmentally appropriate."

26   Dr. Budd said she had seen parents slap a toddler's hand because she kept pushing her plate off the highchair tray. "It would be better to just take the plate away," she said.

27   But what about matters of safety? "If a child is running in the street, it would be better to make her go inside for a while every time she does that, until she understands the limit," Dr. Budd said.

28   And rather than spanking a child who is rude or otherwise out of control, Dr. Rosenfeld recommended saying: "You must go to your room. I'm so disappointed in the way you're behaving. You are a good boy, a smart boy, but you are annoying me."

29   "In the long run," he added, "removing your approval works much better than spanking."

30   What if despite your best intentions, you do lose it? "Apologize," Dr. Budd said. "Own up to your mistake. That's parenting at its best."

ACTIVITY 5

DIRECTIONS: Your instructor will divide the class so that half will respond to Problem 1 and half to Problem 2. After reading the following passage, use the first four steps of the problem-solving approach to make a decision. Discuss your answers in class.

1. You are applying for a new job and worry about somewhat inappropriate language and photos you have on a social-networking site. All of your friends use the site to communicate and share comments and photos. Some of your best friends have settings that allow anyone to see what is posted and you are concerned about this. How do you handle this?

2. Assume that you are an employer about to hire an intern for a position in your company. Your boss asks you to check the background of the top candidates. In checking references, you discover that some of the candidates are on social-networking sites. Should you check these sites for inappropriate content, to assist in determining the best candidate?

Students Shield Facebook Pages from Potential Employers

PRIVACY SCREEN: Job seekers change names on social network site to hide questionable content

ANDREW KATZ

1   WASHINGTON—Some students worried about how their online presence will be perceived by a potential employer are taking the extraordinary security step of changing their names on the social network Facebook.

2   In this down economy, with heavy competition for jobs, college students and new graduates are among those joining an emerging national trend of modifying account names to elude snooping recruiters.

3   "I had an internship that required me to do it because I worked for a politician and I couldn't be associated with any kind of organization," said Emily Winchatz, a Capitol Hill intern and senior government and philosophy major at the University of Maryland, College Park.

4   "(Fellow interns) said my best bet would be to just get off Facebook altogether or change my name so I couldn't be searched," said Winchatz, who replaced her last name with her middle name on the network.

5   Andrew Noyes, public policy communications manager in Facebook's Washington, D.C., office, couldn't comment on this specific trend, but said information security is a "top priority" and the company constantly works to improve its systems for users.

6   Launched from a Harvard dorm room in February 2004, Facebook began as a way of linking students at the country's most elite universities, but quickly expanded by connecting workplaces, high schools and, now the public, through by-the-second status updates, multimedia and "wall" posts.

7   Lauren Berger, who earned the nickname "Intern Queen" after completing 15 internships during her four-year college career, is familiar with the trend and discusses it often on her college speaking tour.

8   "It is too easy for them to type in your name and look you up on Facebook when you apply for a job," she said. "If they see inappropriate content they might not interview you—they might not hire you."

9   Berger, who graduated from the University of Central Florida in 2006, said a handful of employers fired interns last year because of questionable content on their Facebook pages. She urged students to keep in mind that, if hired, they become a representation of that company and an "extension of the brand."

10   A January 2010 report commissioned by Microsoft that examined the impact of an online reputation on hiring practices supports Berger's assertions.

11   The "Online Reputation in a Connected World" report conducted by Cross-Tab Marketing Services noted that 75 percent of recruiters said their companies had formal policies that required human resources teams to research applicants online and 63 percent had visited candidates' social networking sites before making any hiring decisions.

12   On the contrary, only 7 percent of Americans surveyed believed information about them online had affected previous job searches, the report states, while 70 percent of U.S. hiring managers said they had eliminated candidates based on what they found.

13   Andrea Donohue, who graduated from Maryland last May with a degree in French, was aware of companies that screened social networks for prospective applicants and ditched her Facebook surname to cloak her online identity.

14   "I was looking for jobs and I just didn't really want employers to be able to find me," she said, adding that she was also cautious about potential bosses having access to her page through mutual friends.

15   "I cleaned out my friend list because a lot of people on there were people I had one class with freshman year that I haven't talked to since," said Donohue. "I don't know if they're going to get a job with someone interviewing and they say, 'Oh, you know this person? Let me look at their profile.'"

16   Carol Vellucci, career center director at the University of Baltimore, understands students' unease, saying that most recruiters will check social networking sites when there's time to do so.

17   "Concerns about social media are definitely legit," said Velucci in a state-ment. "We always tell (students) to be careful about what they post and where they post it."

18   Jackie Sauter, web content manager at American University's Kogod School of Business, wasn't aware of the name-changing trend but said students should be apprehensive.

19   "In this day and age, almost every employer is checking people out on social networks," she said, but "if you pay attention to your privacy settings and you're vigilant about it, you can absolutely protect your privacy and still put forth a good image to a potential employer."

20   Sarah Barton, a senior at Stevenson University outside Baltimore, hadn't thought about changing her account name until a law professor recently acknowl-edged performing client background checks on Facebook.

21   Although she opted to merely adjust the viewer settings for her photos—partly because her middle name is so uncommon it could actually draw more attention to her page—the 21-year-old paralegal studies major said she knew of friends who had altered their names during job searches.

22   Also an adjunct online journalism professor at UMCP, her alma mater, Sauter had a few extra tips to stay under the radar: adjust your privacy settings to remove profiles from searches, create a second page for professional contacts and restrict access to photos, as they can be "some of the most damning evidence on Facebook to a potential employer."

23   "There's a way that you can use your presence on a social network to help yourself," she said, "because at the end of the day, you control what information you're putting out there, so you don't really have anyone to blame but yourself if something goes awry."

Andrew Katz, "Students shield Facebook pages from potential employers,"
Watertown Daily Times, March 18, 2010, pp. C1, C6.

ACTIVITY 6

DIRECTIONS: During the course of the semester, try to solve two of your personal chal-lenges by using the five-step approach. Toward the end of the semester, your instructor will ask each student to discuss how well the approach worked. You will not be asked to reveal the details of your personal problems.

ACTIVITY 7

DIRECTIONS: For the following passages on contemporary issues, use the same proce-dure as in Chapter 4. First, answer the comprehension questions, *which ask you to state the topic and central message of each passage, before proceeding to determine what is at issue, distinguish among opposing viewpoints, and express a personal viewpoint. In addition, you will be asked to compare your personal viewpoint before and after you have thoroughly considered the opposing viewpoints brought out in the passages. Finally, to show flexibility, you will write a few paragraphs* in support of the viewpoint that you do *not* favor. *Keep in mind that some of the selections may deal with more than one issue.*

You will then proceed to answer the thought and discussion questions *before contributing any questions of your own that may come to mind while reading the passages. Feel free to discuss all of the questions with your classmates and together come up with possible answers.*

Eye on Vocabulary

When reading each of the following passages in Activity 7, take note of any unfamiliar words you come across. List them and their definitions in your notebook or on note cards. Use the context, word parts, or the dictionary to determine their meanings. After the completion of each passage, your instructor will ask to see your notebook or note cards and may discuss key words in class.

1

Body Snatchers

1   A dead man, his skin peeled away, frolics with his own skeleton, which has been removed from his body. The two hold hands like children whirling in the middle of a playground. Nearby, a similarly exposed body tosses a football, while another poses as if conducting an orchestra. Scores of viewers stream by, gawking at stringy white tendons, rosy muscles, and alert-looking eyes.

2   These cavorting cadavers are part of Bodies…the Exhibition, a traveling show of 22 whole humans and more than 260 real organs and body parts preserved using a gruesomely effective technique made famous by German artist Gunther von Hagens (see "Gross Anatomy" by Alan Burdick, *Discover*, March 2004). Premier Exhibitions, the organizer of this spectacle—which has attracted more than 375,000 visitors in Tampa and New York—insists that it displays the bodies for edification, just as medical schools have done for centuries. Critics counter that the exhibition may more accurately recall a darker side of that history, when medical students bought dug-up corpses from the body snatchers of Victorian London.

3   "I don't care if they're presenting it as medical education," says Harry Wu, executive director of the Laogai Research Foundation, a group concerned with atrocities in Chinese prisons and detention camps. "The question that must be answered is: How and where did they get these bodies?"

4   Premier Exhibitions says that Sui Hongjin, the Chinese doctor who oversaw the preservation process, has assured the company that he used unclaimed corpses of people who died of natural causes. But according to Wu, Sui has been implicated in using executed prisoners for commercial ventures. In 2004, news reports confirmed that bullet holes were found in the heads of two specimens showcased by Sui's former partner, von Hagens, who returned seven displayed bodies when word leaked of their ambiguous origins. Commercial use of executed prisoners might seem scandalous, but in China it is not illegal. A 1984 law allows the use of their bodies

for medical purposes without consent, Wu notes, and thousands of prisoners in that country are put to death each year, according to human-rights groups.

5   When the exhibit opened in Tampa in August 2005, the Anatomical Board of Florida protested the opening of the exhibition but ultimately failed to find suitable grounds to shut it down. The heart of Wu's argument is that the exhibition may be unethical even if it is perfectly legal. The show is now in Houston, where, for $24.50, viewers can see forgotten souls purchased, preserved, and posed for our entertainment. If we really want to understand who we are, Wu suggests, maybe we should look away.

Yasmine Mohseni, *Discover*, April 2006, p. 10

COMPREHENSION QUESTIONS

1. What is the topic of the passage?
2. What is the central message of the passage?
3. Determine what is at issue. What is your initial personal viewpoint?
4. Distinguish among opposing viewpoints, and provide the rationale for each.
5. Think carefully about the viewpoints. Express a personal viewpoint, and give the reasons why you favor it. Does it differ from your initial personal viewpoint? Why or why not?
6. Write a few paragraphs *in support of the viewpoint that you do* not *favor.*

THOUGHT AND DISCUSSION QUESTIONS

1. The Bodies Exhibition has attracted many visitors. Why do you think so many people are interested in this exhibit? Would this type of exhibit interest you? Why or why not?
2. List the positive aspects of viewing an exhibit such as this.
3. What issues concern critics of this exhibit?

Go to http://www.bodiestheexhibition.com/ or Google *Bodies…the Exhibition* if you need more information.

2

The Invisible Rich

Knight Kiplinger

1   A while back I was leading a personal-finance seminar at a high school, and I posed this question to the teens: "When you see a man cruise by in his $65,000 BMW 550i, what do you assume about him?" The answer: "He's rich." And a man who drives by in a ten-year-old Chevy? "He's struggling."

2   **Elusive realities.** Just the answers I was looking for, and they provided a launching pad for a lively discussion of deceptive appearances and realities. By

the end of it, these teens had a clearer sense of how little you can determine about wealth from a person's visible consumption.

3   The BMW, I noted, is probably leased (perhaps for three years, no money down), so we can infer only that the driver earns enough to handle a $1,131 monthly lease payment. We know nothing about his net worth, which may be great...or may be almost nonexistent.

4   And the man in the old Impala? Maybe he is struggling financially, but there's another possibility: His income is just as great as that of the dude in the Bimmer, but he's not saddled with a lease payment—and he's investing the money in mutual funds that are growing at 10% a year.

5   The message in all this: The biggest barrier to becoming rich is living like you're rich before you are. Why? Because all that discretionary spending—the chic apartment, frequent travel and restaurant meals, consumer electronics, fancy clothes and cars—crowds out the saving that will enable you to be rich someday.

6   I often hear complaints from young adults, twentysomethings to those in their early thirties, that they'll never be able to buy a home because they can't afford the down payment. But when I probe them about their budgets, I find that they earn enough to make a down payment in just three or four years—if they cut back on their spending, and if their starter-home expectations are reasonable.

7   Know who grasps this best in American society today? Recent immigrants, whether they're from Latin America, Africa, Asia, or Eastern Europe. Many of them come to the U.S. almost penniless. They work long hours at modest wages and send some of those earnings to relatives back home. But, miraculously, they still have money left over each month because they live simply. Often they double up with friends and family in crowded housing.

8   What do they do with their savings? They buy a home, often in a less desirable neighborhood that other strivers are leaving behind. They fix it up, rent rooms to friends and relatives, and then trade up to a nicer home. They may keep their first and second homes as rental properties, becoming hands-on landlords.

9   A niece of mine sells new homes in the outer Virginia suburbs of Washington, D.C. The houses cost $500,000—a "middle market" price in this affluent area. Many of her buyers are Latinos. They don't look or act rich, and they often need translation help. Many of them arrived in the U.S. with nothing but ambition. They worked hard, started small businesses and saved 30% of their incomes.

10   Someday, when they finally feel as financially secure as they will actually be, they might start living it up. They might buy—not lease—a BMW, most likely a used model. High school kids will assume them to be rich and cast admiring glances at them and their fancy cars.

11   **Proudly invisible.** But just like overspending, the habit of frugality is hard to break. Maybe these folks will just keep the old Chevy. They will remain proud members of the Invisible Rich—a growing army of super savers whose net worth is

more impressive than their income. They'd rather live within their means, sleep well, and forgo the covetous attention of their fellow citizens. Not a bad way to live at all.

COMPREHENSION QUESTIONS

1. What is the topic of the passage?
2. What is the central message of the passage?
3. Determine what is at issue. What is your initial personal viewpoint?

THOUGHT AND DISCUSSION QUESTIONS

1. Thinking about first appearances, what are some things that go through your mind when you see an individual driving an old car? What are some things that go through your mind when you see someone driving a very expensive car?
2. What can actually be some reasons why a person would be driving an old car or an expensive new car?
3. What are some things that you might reconsider to help you plan your finances better?
4. What are other deceptive appearances that may affect the way we treat others?

3

A True Crime Story

A Tragic Moment in New Mexico: Reflections on a Nation Gripped by Violence

Ken Englade and Tony Hillerman

1   Five Points, in a seedy South Valley section of Albuquerque, New Mexico, is a convergence of five streets, littered parking lots, and shopping centers half boarded up. A still, deserted place at 5:40 A.M. on a dark, 20-degree Sunday morning, January 9, 1994.

2   A man in his 60s enters one of the lots on his morning exercise walk, heading south. A Buick Riviera recently stolen by its two teen occupants cruises slowly along Five Points Road, also heading south. The car circles the lone figure.

3   On its fourth drive-by one of the youths jumps from the car, holding a police baton, demands money and clubs the man several times. The flat crack of a pistol

shot pierces the air and Eddie Torres, 16, falls back and runs to the car, which screeches away. Dean Kern, 63, blood running down his cheek, gun in hand, staggers off looking for assistance.

4   Kern is hailed as a hero. Torres—after he has been arrested in the hospital and later sent to prison for aggravated battery—is dubbed a thug. But the phenomenon—civilians arming themselves and teens doing hard time—appears less a solution than a desperate, even dangerous, stopgap.

5   That a 63-year-old would resort to such drastic action is supported by a recent *USA Today*/CNN/Gallup poll: Americans have finally had it with youthful offenders. Sixty percent of respondents said a teen convicted of murder should get the death penalty, and more than 20 states (among them New Mexico) have or are planning tough new juvenile laws.

6   Meanwhile, because of crime's prevalence many older people are avoiding activities they felt safe taking part in a few years ago. That may be why those 65 and over are, according to 1992 Bureau of Justice statistics, the least likely victims of violent crimes or theft. But at what cost to their quality of life?

7   To many, like Dean Kern, locking themselves indoors is not an option, yet continuing their activities as before is risky at best.... Some believe their only recourse is to arm themselves when going out. Is this, truly, the final and only option?

8   Today Kern is cautious and fearful—he wouldn't allow his face to be photographed. Torres is bitter and vengeful—and could be released from prison as early as next year. Exactly what did happen between the two of them may unfortunately raise more questions than it can answer.

9   What *is* clear is that we generally perceive crime from one point of view, and from that perspective solutions may appear straightforward, even simple.

10   But if we examine this crime from all vantage points—and face its tempestuous issues of violence, an armed populace, and justice itself—it becomes evident that finding a viable solution is as complex as the moment of crime itself.

11   For 17 years Dean Kern has risen habitually at 4:30 and begun his day with a rigid physical regimen. In 1976 he suffered a severe heart attack. As part of his recovery program he took up jogging five miles a day around the perimeter of Kirtland Air Force Base where he used to work as manager of the telephone exchange.

12   After he retired in 1986, his knees could no longer take the hard pounding so he gave up jogging for swimming and walking. Three days a week he swam laps at a neighborhood pool; the other four days he walked a five-mile circle around his home, a tiny but comfortable bungalow he built in 1955 with a GI loan.

13   Shortly after 5:00 A.M. on Sunday, January 9, the tall, slim, sandy-haired man whose sartorial preferences run to jeans and Western-style snapfront shirts zipped up his padded down jacket, put on his hand-knit wool stocking cap (a gift from a neighbor grateful for a favor), and grabbed his .25 caliber Colt automatic from the top shelf of the hall closet.

14   Years earlier Kern had developed the habit of carrying the fist-sized pistol he originally bought for his wife but later appropriated for his own use because it was small and light—just the right size to fit in his jogging-suit pocket. He took it then to protect himself in case he encountered any of the stray or wild dogs that inhabited the desert around the Air Force base.

15   He continued to pack the weapon after he retired because part of the South Valley neighborhood where he walked in the mornings had become a campsite for the homeless, some of whom Kern feared might be strung out on drugs one day and come looking for a handy source of revenue.

16   About ten minutes into his route he came upon Five Points. "I was just walking, thinking, lining out my day." As he turned south on Sunset Road and was cutting through one of the parking lots, he suddenly became aware of a car.

17   "It came to the traffic signal but didn't want to wait for the light, so it cut across the lot I was in. Passed right in front of me, maybe 20 feet away." The windows were tinted and rolled up, but a street light showed two heads silhouetted in the front seat. The car exited the lot onto Sunset a block away. Then hesitated. Then turned around.

18   "When I saw it do that, I picked up my pace and crossed Sunset to get to the other side. It passed by again on the street."

19   The car backed up, turned around, and went by him a third time. "I knew then I was in big trouble." Kern was in front of a furniture store. Parked nearby was a truck with a for sale sign on it. "They made a U-turn and came back toward me again. I walked behind the truck to keep it between me and them."

20   When he came around the truck, a figure had already jumped out of the car and was slapping a sidehandled police baton in his hand.

21   Kern took off running. But workmen had been repaving the parking lot and planting trees there, and sand and gravel covered the pavement. Kern slipped and almost tumbled to the ground. Before he could regain his balance the attacker was all over him.

22   He felt one sharp blow bounce off his skull, two thud against his arm. He tried to outrun his assailant but couldn't. The baton cracked him two more times on the head. Despite Kern's thick cap and heavy jacket, the blows "took the hide off my arm and broke the skin on my head. I told myself, 'If I go down, I'm in bad shape.' "

23   Not able to get away, still being pummeled and honestly fearing for his life, Kern finally yanked the pistol from his pocket. "I put it against him and pulled the trigger. "

24   The effect was instantaneous. The attacker cried out and threw up his arms, staggered backward, then ran back to the car. Tires screaming, the car spun around and sped away.

25   Kern stood there, dazed, and said a silent prayer. If it hadn't been for the wool cap's cushioning effect, he probably would have been knocked unconscious

or his brains might have been leaking onto the sidewalk. Staggering to a pay phone, he dialed 911.

. . .

26   A lot of people think ironing is women's work, but it always gave Eddie Torres considerable pleasure. While his friends may have laughed if they had seen him hunched over the ironing board on the night of January 8 in the small trailer he shared with his mother, Torres wasn't worried about his macho image. Holding up his party shirt to inspect, he smiled in self-congratulation. A *cholo* (street-wise young Latino male) had to be respected. Looking sharp definitely earned him respect.

27   Torres was really pumped up for the party he was going to that night. Throwing it was an "older" woman (she was 25, he 16) he had met shortly after arriving in New Mexico two months before.

28   The party was everything he'd hoped for—good music, good booze, good dope. Then something happened that would change Eddie Torres's already grim life for the worse. "I was talking with the girl when somebody told me to chill out with her and swung me around," he said. Torres was more surprised than hurt. That would've never happened in the Los Angeles suburb where he'd grown up. Known by his fellow cholos there as "Crook," he had a reputation as someone to be reckoned with. His gang, East Side Paramount, was one of the largest and most violent in all of Los Angeles County, and its name was tattooed across the back of his neck and shoulders in inch-tall letters.

29   "I hit him, and they took him to the bathroom. A few minutes later the girl told me to leave." Drunk and upset, he stormed outside with two homeboys: one called "Gino," and Kevin Baca, 17, whom he'd met a month before.

30   Torres wandered into a nearby parking lot—and his eyes locked onto a solitary Buick Riviera. Quicker than most people can adjust the rear-view mirror, Torres broke in, hot-wired it, and had the Riviera quietly rolling down the street.

31   Baca dropped Gino off at his home and Torres followed Baca's car to Baca's house. Then Baca jumped behind the wheel of the Buick and the pair went looking for some action, which meant a fight. "I was still hyper about what happened at the party. Then I see this *vato* (guy)."

32   There, in the middle of Five Points, a lone figure was crossing the parking lot. "The guy was acting crazy. He had his hand in his jacket like he had a gun, like he was tough or somethin'. I said, 'Go back towards him, I'll show him who's tough.'"

33   They drove back and passed real close, and the stranger stared at Torres. *"Me vió."* ("He looked at me.") Torres thought the man had challenged, or "mad-dogged," him. "I wanted to beat him up," Torres said.

34   They circled the man twice more ("I was scoping it out for cops") before Torres felt safe. Spotting a police baton under the seat of the Riviera, he grabbed it and lunged out of the Buick. "I don't know why I didn't just let him go," he

said. "But I was drunk, I just wanted to get him." Blocking the man's path and smacking the polished wooden club, Torres barked, "Give me your money!"

35   "He tried to run away," Torres recalled later, "but I hit him [with the night-stick] on the head and shoulder."

36   All of a sudden the man straightened up and swung toward *him.* "I heard something real loud," Torres said. "There wasn't much pain, but I got dizzy. I felt something inside me."

37   He lurched back to the car and screamed at Baca to take him home. "I couldn't breathe. I said to myself, 'I'm going to die.'"

38   They picked up his mother at home and minutes later found a pay phone. As Torres waited, bleeding and shivering, his mother dialed 911.

39   The youngest of four gang-member brothers, Torres's indoctrination into their world started early on. He had his first serious brush with authorities—for breaking into a car—at eight. He went on to pile up arrests for burglary, auto theft, narcotics violations, and assault and battery ("I used to look for innocent-looking kids coming out of school and just beat 'em up. I knew it wasn't right, but it was what I liked to do").

40   There was a time, Torres says, when things might have turned out differently. For a while his father, Eddie Sr., a butcher, was able to keep his brothers clean and straight. "He was real strict, man, the way he grew my brothers up. He kept them in the right direction. Couldn't cuss, couldn't go out, nothin'."

41   And then, as in so many families, the arguments between their parents began, escalated, then eventually forced their mother, Dorie, to leave and take the boys. "After that, Mom would say the same things to us, but we wouldn't listen. That's when I started kicking back with my brothers and homeboys. I saw the things they were doing and thought it was all right."

42   Hoping to get her youngest son away from his brothers' and gang's influence and into a more stable environment, Dorie took Eddie Jr. to Albuquerque, where her sister lived.

43   Nine days after the shooting, while Torres was recuperating in the hospital, police arrested him on charges of aggravated battery with a deadly weapon, armed robbery, and conspiracy to commit armed robbery. Nancy Neary, the assistant district attorney, saw Torres as a classic sociopath. "Empathy is not a concept this kid has within himself," she said. "He was totally without remorse. He would kill Mr. Kern or anyone else the same way I'd swat a fly."

44   Feeling the county judges were lenient with juveniles and would never give him the maximum on all three counts, Neary made the boy an offer: Plead guilty to aggravated battery and she'd drop the other charges. Torres agreed. In New Mexico, victims have the right to be heard. So Kern drafted a letter that read, in part: "I feel I need to take this opportunity . . . to plead with you to keep this man away from us for as long as the law permits. . . . There is no way [law-enforcement

officials] can prevent these types of crimes or protect us from these kinds of pred-itors [*sic*]. Only you can do that, Judge. Please put this young man away for as long as you can. Please keep him off us."

45   The Children's Court Judge Tommy E. Jewell has a reputation as a "liberal" jurist, always willing to give an offender a break if he believes the person can be rehabili-tated. When Torres's case showed up on his calendar, however, the youth's record painted a grim picture. Jewell later stated that Torres was "a threat to society" and he was "pessimistic" that the young man would be changed by the experience.

46   The judge sentenced Torres to three years in prison. In a very few specified cases, courts can also add time to a sentence when there are "aggravating circumstances" for such things as the age of the victim. Because Kern was 63, Jewell tacked an extra year on to Torres's sentence. It was remarkably stiff con-sidering the judge's reputation. When asked if such incarceration may only teach Torres to be a better criminal, Jewell replied, "A new and improved Eddie Torres in the crime-producing world is really a frightening thought." (As for Kevin Baca, he pleaded guilty to conspiracy to commit armed robbery and was eventually sentenced to two years' probation.)

47   According to Janet Velazquez, Torres's attorney, incarceration may actually be the young man's best—and last—chance to turn his life around. She noted that Torres tended to do well in structured environments, such as juvenile camps, where he got A's and B's. To date he's finished 10th grade, an anomaly in the gang world. "In school he's bright," she said. "But take him out of that structure…"

48   The Southern New Mexico Correctional Facility is a medium-security prison built to house 480 men (and holding 570 at the time of this interview). It is sur-rounded not by walls but by two tall chain-link fences, one topped, the other covered, with razor wire. It sits low and half-hidden amid the pale desert scrub just off Interstate 10, a few miles west of Las Cruces.

49   On the day of his interview for this article, Eddie Torres strolls into the visi-tor's room in a lazy, liquid cholo gait. His eyes, sparkling in the bright overhead lights, reflect a detached, but shrewd, awareness. At 5-foot-8 and 140 pounds, he isn't physically threatening, but he certainly looks bigger and older than the average 16-year-old. He speaks quietly, with control—uncommonly mature for a youth his age—as he recalls the incident that had brought him there. "I was drunk," he says. "I knew I shouldn't have gone out there. I didn't want to rob him."

50   *Did you know at the time you were beating a 63-year-old?*

51   "I saw him, but I didn't know he was an older man. I regretted that *big time* afterwards. I knew how I'd feel if it had been my uncle or somebody."

52   *Are you bitter about being sent to prison?*

53   Torres slowly pulls his shirttail out and lifts it, exposing a long, ugly scar running from his navel to his sternum. "That *vato* didn't have to shoot me. He

could've just pointed the gun at me or fired it in the air—I would've run away. I only wanted to beat him up. I wasn't trying to kill him."

54   *Do you understand why he felt he had to shoot you?*

55   "He wasn't wrong to shoot me, but he didn't have to tell the police. I wouldn't have said nothing. I told 'em it was a drive-by."

56   *Mr. Kern has become a local hero for how he defended himself. Do you think he's a hero?*

57   "F— no, he's no hero! Shooting someone doesn't make anyone a hero. A lot of old people think if they go out and [shoot criminals], they're protecting society. *That pissed me off.* My brothers got real mad after they heard about that; they wanted to come out here and get the old guy. "

58   *If you stay out of trouble when you get out, what do you want to do with the rest of your life?*

59   "Get a good job, a house, a lady and kids. Maybe my own business. Construction business. I'd like to build houses.

60   "But I'll probably be back [in prison] for something else."

61   *What would you do if you ran into Mr. Kern again?*

62   [*Softly*] "I'll probably kill him if I ever see him again."

63   Today, nearly a year after the crime, Dean Kern still worries about Torres's street philosophy of revenge, called *venganza* in the barrios. But what disturbs him more is the specter of the next "Torres" lurking in the early morning mist where he walks. "Suppose it happens again?" he asks. "Are people going to say, 'Ol' Dean must be out there trolling for these guys'?"

64   Kern poses the question but never answers it. Although carrying a concealed weapon in Albuquerque can be punishable by 90 days in jail and a fine, little was said about it during the proceedings. Defense attorney Velazquez, although asserting that carrying a concealed weapon "is a crime in my book," opted not to pursue the issue. "That was up to the prosecutor and D.A. By ignoring it, though, [they put] a stamp of approval on vigilante behavior. My concern is that *that* will be the message."

65   Prosecutor Neary shrugs off the violation. "Although Mr. Kern technically did something illegal, as far as I'm concerned he did nothing wrong. He didn't shoot immediately—he fired only after he'd been hit several times and couldn't get away. If it had been my mother-in-law, those blows would have destroyed her."

66   For his part, Kern admits he has changed his pre-dawn route—"I don't walk where cars go anymore"—but not his means of self-protection: He still carries his pistol.

67   To some experts and sociologists, youths like Eddie Torres seem destined to follow the criminal path on which—to whatever extent—family, culture or society has pushed them. They seem to have refused, or been unable, to resist their fate.

68   The fate of victims like Dean Kern, however, seems changed forever. After the incident he received more than 50 telephone calls and numerous letters applauding his action. "I didn't get one negative comment," he says.

69   One woman wrote saying that he was her hero. "But," he adds with a chuckle, "she also offered some advice: 'Practice, man, practice!'"

70   It's easy to be so sure, so brazen, from a comfortable distance. But ask Kern today how he feels about his entrance into the world of *venganza:* "I have no remorse; I was defending myself. But I'm worried about his friends. He knows what I look like—and that's enough."

Modern Maturity, January/February 1995, pp. 22–31

COMPREHENSION QUESTIONS

1. What is the topic of the passage?
2. What is the central message of the passage?
3. Determine what is at issue. What is your initial personal viewpoint?
4. Distinguish among opposing viewpoints, and provide the rationale for each.
5. Think carefully about the viewpoints. Express a personal viewpoint, and give the reasons why you favor it. Does it differ from your initial personal viewpoint? Why or why not?
6. Write a few paragraphs *in support of the viewpoint that you do* not *favor.*

VOCABULARY QUESTION

Use the context to define the following words: *cholo, vato, me vió,* mad-dogged, *venganza.*

THOUGHT AND DISCUSSION QUESTIONS

1. In your view, why did Eddie Torres behave the way he did? Do you know anyone who behaves like him? How should you deal with a person like Eddie Torres? Why?
2. Is there any hope now for Eddie Torres? Why or why not?
3. How would you have reacted had the woman asked you to leave the party? Why?
4. If you were Dean Kern, what would you have done in a similar situation? Why? Should he be applauded for his action? Why or why not?
5. What can we do as a society to prevent conflicts like the one in this article from occurring?
6. List any questions that came to mind while you were reading this selection, and be prepared to discuss possible answers to them.

4

Arranged Marriages Still Common, Still Succeeding

SAMIEH SHALASH

1   LEXINGTON, Ky.—When Yogesh Shukla's parents called him from India in May 2003, he wasn't prepared for their news: "We've selected a wife for you."

2   But a few months later, the former University of Kentucky student, who was 24 at the time, was packing a suitcase to attend his wedding. The first time he saw his bride, Sarita Tiwari, was when they exchanged engagement rings.

3   "It was really all very odd-feeling," Yogesh said. "You see the person in front of you, you're going to spend your entire life with them, but you don't really know her."

4   Yogesh and Sarita grew up expecting an arranged marriage. Researchers say about 96 percent of marriages are arranged in India; worldwide, the proportion is 60 percent.

5   The Western concept of dating is often taboo in other cultures because of traditions and religious beliefs. At the University of Kentucky, 465 of the 1,457 international students are from India. Many return home when they're ready to find mates.

6   Their decision to stay out of the dating game in spite of America's dating culture often piques the curiosity of their peers.

7   "Some ask me, 'How can you go for this?'" Yogesh said. "Some find it interesting and others think it's absurd." People often laugh in disbelief when he tells them he talked to his wife just twice before their wedding.

8   He smiles sheepishly when he tells of asking Sarita whether she wanted to play computer games on their wedding night.

9   Now he simply considers himself lucky to be with a woman he describes as "always brightening up my day."

10   "I can't imagine being with anyone else," he said as Sarita laughed beside him on the love seat in their Lexington apartment. "Not anyone with a single different characteristic."

11   The practice of arranging marriages spans cultures and religions, said Robert Epstein, a researcher and former editor of *Psychology Today*.

12   It's most popular in South Asia and with Muslims and Orthodox Jews, whose religious beliefs prohibit them from dating.

13   Most Westerners think "arranged" means parents determine who their child will be with, Epstein said. But the matchmaking process is reminiscent of courtship—although parental involvement is key, ultimate decisions are left to both potential mates.

14   Single people are often introduced through relatives and friends, and a suitor usually visits a woman at her family's home for a chaperoned meeting.

15   First discussions include everything from the number of children they want to dietary preferences to gauge compatibility.

16   "They get a chance to check each other out and can go to a parent or matchmaker and say 'No, bring me someone else.'" Epstein said.

17   Sarita tells of Yogesh's family visiting to size her up while her parents inquired about their son.

18   "It was a long process," Sarita said. Her parents talked to Yogesh's family for almost four months, and about 10 suitors before him, before deciding he was the one.

19   "They didn't want to arrange a marriage, then think, 'Oh, it was the wrong choice'," she said.

20   Epstein said Americans can learn from arranged marriages.

21   He deems the American culture of dating and "love marriages" based on physical attraction and romance "really, really horrible."

22   "People in different cultures think we're crazy," Epstein said. "What probably 99 percent of Americans believe is that love is something that we obtain in life by chance, something we stumble onto."

23   But true love comes from adjusting to each other in a marital relationship, said Lexington Theological Seminary President Robert Cueni.

24   As a pastor, he conducted weddings for 40 years in Kansas City, Mo., where he used to live. Statistically, half of those marriages will end in divorce.

25   "If you're not totally happy in a relationship, you're looking around American society and saying, 'Who else? Is there someone with whom I could be perfectly happy?'" he said. "The answer is no."

26   He said arranged marriages might work better because expectations of adjustment are more realistic than those of people in dating cultures.

27   "I don't think people are matched in heaven," Cueni said. "Somehow or the other, marriages are hammered out on the anvil of daily experience of give and take.

28   "Couples must figure out what it takes to supply emotional needs to one another. That can happen whether you're Hindu, Muslim, Christian or anything else."

29   Arranged marriages might seem successful, but the Indian divorce rate of 5 percent can be misleading, said Bhagirath Majmudar, an Emory University professor who has conducted 160 Indian weddings in Atlanta.

30   "There's multiple factors behind that statistic," he said. "There's always a family demand or family pressure or certain expectations."

31   Priyanka Jain knows what Majmudar's talking about. The University of Kentucky graduate student has never dated. At 25, she's the eldest of three daughters in her family, all of whom are in New Delhi, India.

32   "They think it's high time for me to get married," she said. "My younger sister is just one year younger and ready for marriage, but they want me to be first."

33   Majmudar said that most Indians would never offend their parents, so they agree to marriages they're not enthusiastic about.

34   He's seen many male international students begin dating American women, then break it off for fear of upsetting traditional parents.

35   Jain thinks casual dating is a good way to get hurt and a bad way to find someone to spend your life with.

36   "It's not considered right in this society, but it's my decision to not go out and date," she said. "And I'm free. My parents wouldn't mind if I found someone on my own."

37   Jain will consult with her parents before marrying anyone but said she hasn't done well meeting suitable men and will probably end up with someone they choose.

38   Regardless of how she gets married, Jain hopes to stay that way. Divorce, which was almost unheard of in India 50 years ago and only recently became legal there, is still a social taboo.

39   Majmudar said he's seen many examples of people who married the wrong person.

40   "A little dark chapter of our society is that there are literally tortured women," he said, referring to mental and physical abuse in arranged relationships. "Many times I've been there in India, women commit suicide. It's a frightening thing."

41   Strong-minded, educated women who don't want to divorce sometimes just say "I'm quitting" and leave their husbands, Majmudar said.

42   "The previous philosophy that even when you are miserable you should stay with your husband is rapidly vanishing," he said. "Both in India and here."

Watertown Daily Times, Sunday, May 22, 2005, Sunday Weekly, p. 5

COMPREHENSION QUESTIONS

1. What is the topic of the passage?
2. What is the central message of the passage?
3. Determine what is at issue. What is your initial personal viewpoint?
4. Distinguish among opposing viewpoints, and provide the rationale for each.
5. Think carefully about the viewpoints. Express a personal viewpoint, and give the reasons why you favor it. Does it differ from your initial personal viewpoint? Why or why not?
6. Write a few paragraphs *in support of the viewpoint that you do not favor.*

THOUGHT AND DISCUSSION QUESTIONS

1. Why do you think that arranged marriages exist in some cultures? Why do you think arranged marriages are successful in these cultures?
2. How is information gathered about individuals when arranged marriages are considered? How is this similar or different from how you would determine whether an individual is a match for a permanent relationship?

3. How is meeting someone on an Internet dating site similar to how other cultures determine a match? How is it different?
4. How is the relationship after the marriage similar or different from what Westerners might experience?

5

Why Women Make Better Cops

Tessa DeCarlo

1   It's Friday night in Madison, Wisconsin, and officers from the police department's Blue Blanket team—a special drug, gang and gun squad—are cruising past an East Side low-income neighborhood, a site they've often had occasion to visit. Tonight the mood in the neighborhood, whose residents are mostly African American, is tense; a rumored party hasn't materialized and about 50 young people are now hanging around waiting for something to happen.

2   Just then an emergency call comes in, reporting that a young man has beaten up his girlfriend. As the officers, led by Sergeant Tony Peterson and Detective Marion Morgan, approach the crowd to see if they can find him, several kids cry out, "Marion! Marion!" She is the only black officer in the group, and the young people's voices are somewhere between affectionate and mocking.

3   The police approach a teenager who partly fits the reported batterer's description: young, black male; tall; denim jacket. But the man, who's apparently been drinking, isn't in any mood to cooperate. "I want to talk to my lawyer," he yells. "You're just doing this because I'm black!"

4   "We can do this the easy way, but now we're going to have to do it this way," says Peterson, as he and another officer deftly snap the man into handcuffs and lead him over to a police car to pat him down, check for outstanding warrants and ask a few questions. It turns out he isn't the man they're looking for, and after a few minutes he's released.

5   But in the meantime, one of his friends, another teenager in a black-and-red University of Wisconsin team jacket, has begun complaining loudly about the police, and a group of younger kids gathers around. Morgan puts her hand on the arm of the older boy, who towers over her. She's arrested him before on various charges, none of them very serious.

6   "You know we're here so everyone can live peacefully and safely," she tells him in a firm but not angry voice. "If *you* called in a complaint, you'd want us to come and deal with it. It doesn't help when someone like you, with standing in the neighborhood, cops an attitude and gets all these shorties going"—she nods

toward the kids standing around. "I'm just telling you how it felt to me, and it felt like you were disrespecting me."

7   "I wouldn't disrespect you, you know that," the young man says, abashed.

8   She pats him on the arm, and he shrugs, looking a little embarrassed.

9   "We're not the enemy," she says.

10   "I know that," he answers.

A Better Kind of Cop?

11   According to many law enforcement officials, stories like this one show why women in police work aren't just as good as men—they're sometimes better.

12   "There's such an obvious need for more women in this business," says Nick Pastore, chief of police in New Haven, Connecticut. In his view, when it comes to the skills that really count, "women are much more effective."

13   America celebrates strong-arm police officers in movies and TV shows, but in real life, too much macho causes more problems than it solves. When police departments are permeated by "good old boy" attitudes and filled with what Pastore calls "young, male, suburban adventure-seekers eager to bash heads," they tend to confuse the war on crime with a war on minorities, women, gays and the rest of the community they're supposed to be serving.

14   Until two decades ago, a woman's only entrée into the hypermasculine world of policing was to become a clerk, or a "policewoman" restricted to working with juveniles. The passage of the Equal Employment Opportunity Act of 1972 prompted a flood of discrimination lawsuits and court orders that forced the stationhouse doors open—but not very far. Women still make up less than ten percent of the nation's police officers and about three percent of police supervisors.

15   That's a loss not only for women who want to be police officers but for everyone who wants safer communities and better policing. Because women—precisely because they don't conform to the locker-room mores of traditional law enforcement—often make better cops.

16   "Women officers are less authoritarian and use force less often than their male counterparts. They're better at defusing potentially violent confrontations, possess better communication skills and respond more effectively to incidents of violence against women," said Katherine Spillar, national coordinator for the Feminist Majority Foundation, in testimony before a commission investigating police brutality in Los Angeles.

17   Many police veterans agree. "Women officers are no less tough or strong or capable of dealing with the world of the streets," says Hubert Williams, president of the Police Foundation and former chief of police in Newark, New Jersey. "But on the whole they're better listeners, with a special knowledge of families and children, able to engage effectively and develop working relationships. That's why they're so valuable to law enforcement."

Women Fighting Crimes Against Women

18   The woman had called police in the Louisiana town several times before. Her marriage had fallen apart but her husband refused to leave. He hit her and threatened her and sabotaged her car so that she needed him to drive her to and from her job.

19   "This man beats me up, and the officers won't do anything," the woman sobbed when the police arrived yet again.

20   But this time the two officers who answered the call were women. "We told him, 'Look, whatever it was you did to her car, you get out there now and undo it,'" one of the officers recalls. "He was angry. If we'd been men, he would have fought. But I told him, 'I'm just a little-bitty person, so if you come at me, I'm not going to fight—I'll just shoot.' " The man decided to cooperate.

21   The officers wouldn't leave until he replaced the distributor cap on his wife's car. "Then we told him that if she ever called us again, we'd come back and kick his butt," the officer says.

22   The woman didn't call again, but a few months later one of the women officers ran into her on the street. Her husband had agreed to a divorce and moved out of state.

23   Why hadn't any of the other police who'd visited this woman helped her out? "This is an old-fashioned, good-old-boy place," says the Louisiana cop, who doesn't want her name used. "When the male officers go on a domestic, I hear them saying things like, 'The bitch don't keep the house clean—you *ought* to be whuppin' her ass.'"

24   Domestic violence is one of the most pressing issues in police work. A 1993 federal inquiry estimated that more than 21,000 domestic assaults, rapes and murders are reported to police each week. By some estimates, "family disturbances" account for more calls received by police each year than any other kind of crime.

25   But traditional male-dominated police departments take these calls less seriously than robberies and other crimes involving strangers. A study conducted by the Police Foundation cited police failure to make arrests in family violence cases as one of the most serious aspects of the nation's domestic violence problem.

26   One reason for poor police performance in this area may be that male officers are particularly prone to domestic violence themselves, and therefore resist treating it as a serious crime. "There's a lot of domestic violence being committed by officers," says a female cop from a large Southeastern city. "It's that macho image, saying, 'I'm the authority and I'm above the law.'"

27   Research bears her out. One 1991 study found that while violence—ranging from slapping to punching to stabbing—is an element in 16 percent of U.S. marriages, the rate among a sample of 425 police officers, 90 percent of them male, was as high as 41 percent.

28   A third study—concerning 72 male officers in the Midwest—bolstered a suspicion long held by observers of law enforcement: that the more violent an officer is at home, the more prejudiced he is against victims of domestic violence and the less likely he is to make arrests in such cases.

29   Arrest rates are influenced by many factors, including local laws and whether prosecutors are willing to bring cases to trial. But officers' attitudes do play a role. "Studies in the past 20 years show that women officers take domestic violence calls more seriously and treat it more seriously as a crime," says Katherine Spillar, who's now on the advisory board of the National Center for Women and Policing.

30   New Haven's Pastore noticed a difference in this area after he fast-tracked eight women into detective positions in his department. "These women have really concentrated on abuse against women and sexual assault," he says—crimes Pastore believes were given less focus when the system was all male. "Twice in the past year the same thing has happened: Friends of the accused have come to me and said, 'Since when do you have women doing these cases? They're so tenacious.... Chief, can you take some heat off?' Their performance in this area alone is worth the presence of women on the force."

Are Women Cops Tough Enough?

31   The belief that women are less violent—and therefore less able to stand up to force or dish it out when necessary—used to be a prime argument for a male-only police force. But once affirmative action opened policing to women, extensive research confirmed that although women are, in general, smaller and less powerful than men, especially in terms of upper-body strength, they are just as capable of policing as men.

32   For example, a 1987 study of 3,701 violent conflicts between police and citizens in New York City, including both assaults and gunplay, confirmed that female cops were just as brave as males. "Female officers, whether with a partner or alone, are more than willing to get involved in violent confrontations apparently without any fear of injury or death," the study concluded.

33   Take the case of San Francisco inspector Holly Pera, who before joining the force was a member of the San Francisco Ballet and then a teacher. A specialist in cases involving children, Pera teamed up with Inspector Kelly Carroll, a six-foot-one-inch male, to arrest a recently released ex-con who had reportedly robbed and sodomized several boys. High on crack cocaine, the man resisted arrest, attacking both officers. During the struggle, the suspect managed to get hold of Carroll's gun and was about to shoot him from a few feet away when Pera stepped between them. She and the ex-con both fired: His shots missed and hers hit him in the chest. He died of his wounds at the hospital. "I have never witnessed a single more courageous act," says Carroll. "There's no doubt she saved my life."

34   But the same research that showed women cops are as tough as their male colleagues discovered something equally important: Women officers *misuse* violence far less. In another study of New York City cops, for example, this one in 1989, researchers found that although female officers were involved in just as many violent confrontations as male officers, they received fewer civilian complaints, were involved in fewer shootings and used deadly force less often.

35   Women officers are frequently more effective in volatile situations because they focus on cooling everyone down, rather than asserting their own authority.

36   "I'm not going to get fired up because they call me a whore or a dyke," says a female trooper from Connecticut. "I just say, 'Forgive me, I have to be here. Now give me your side of the story'. Whereas a lot of male officers are going to say, 'What did you call me?' and—whoomp!—you've got another fight going."

37   "We tell officers that when you lose your temper, *you* are in danger," says Sheriff Jackie Barrett of Fulton County, Georgia. Staying cool and sidestepping unnecessary physical confrontations, she says, are "a function of maturity and of strength—*inner* strength."

38   Often courage can mean *not* using force and still getting results. In the Midwest two officers, a woman and a man, were called to a bar late at night by two frightened female bartenders. A nearby club had just let out, and although it was closing time at the bar, too, suddenly the bartenders were faced with a crowd of more than 200 people. With most of them drunk and refusing to leave, the scene was turning ugly.

39   The woman officer went into the bar and didn't notice until too late that the male officer had stayed outside. But there was no turning back. Using what she calls her mom voice ("You may not even like your mom, but you obey her"), she told the barful of rowdies, "It's time for you to go home now." Anyone who didn't leave would immediately be arrested, she told the crowd. "There are five police cars outside"—as far as she knew, there were only two, including hers—"and the doors will be locked and you'll all be processed right here."

40   "I got some lip," she recalls, "but everybody left. There were no fights and I didn't have to arrest a single person."

41   When she went outside she found four male officers standing around in the street. "They were waiting to see if I could handle the call," she says. "I'm considered not aggressive enough because I don't rush in and arrest the first person I see. But I don't get into fights, either, and I don't need 15 other officers for backup."

Los Angeles: Boys in Blue

42   Of course the absence of a Y chromosome doesn't automatically make someone a good cop, any more than it makes her a good mother or a bad driver. Some female officers are hot tempered and high-handed, and plenty of male cops are caring, compassionate people with excellent interpersonal skills.

43   However, traditional policing still tends to devalue those skills—in men as well as women—in favor of bullyboy aggressiveness and an "us against them" attitude toward not only crooks but the public at large. The result can be that police become part of the crime problem themselves.

44   This has been vividly demonstrated in Los Angeles, where cops were notorious for manhandling citizens long before the videotaped beating of Rodney King by four police officers in 1991. The gigantic cost of community ill will toward the L.A. Police Department was clear during the riots a year later, when police couldn't even enter riot-torn areas and citizens trying to defend their lives and property had to fend for themselves.

45   The independent commission formed to investigate the LAPD in the wake of the beating condemned the department's authoritarian, often confrontational policing style and found a direct connection between its proclivity for violence and its attitude toward women.

46   "Traditional views concerning the nature of police work in general—that is, that police work is a male-oriented profession with a major emphasis on physical strength—foster a climate in which female officers are discouraged," said the commission's final report. "A corollary of that culture is an emphasis on use of force to control a situation and a disdain for a more patient, less aggressive approach."

47   Transcripts of computerized transmissions between police cars show just how brutal the LAPD's internal culture had become. "I hope there is enough units to set up a powwow around the suspect so he can get a good spanking and nobody c it…" was one typical computer transmission. Said another, "U wont believe this…that female call again said susp returned…I'll check it out then I'm going to stick my baton in her."

48   But one group of cops in L.A. did not succumb to run-amok machismo. The independent commission reported that female LAPD officers were much less likely to resort to use of excessive force. In 1991 women made up about 13 percent of the LAPD, but the commission found that of the 808 officers involved in frequent use of force, women accounted for only 30, or 3.7 percent. Among the 120 officers with the most use-of-force reports, not a single one was a woman.

49   As Katherine Spillar notes, one officer tried to stop the beating of Rodney King, "but the men told her to stay out of it."

50   The commission's findings aren't unique to Los Angeles. "In every department there's a small number of cops who get a huge number of civilian complaints," says Samuel Walker, a criminologist at the University of Nebraska at Omaha. "In all the cases where we've gotten information on who the bad boys are, female officers never show up on the list."

51   The Los Angeles City Council, which is currently paying out $28 million a year to settle civilian complaints against police, got the message. In 1992 it called on the LAPD to bring its percentage of female officers up to 43 percent—the percentage of

women in the city's overall workforce, and far higher than that of any police department in the nation. Last year the council took the additional step, making 43 percent the LAPD's annual hiring goal.

Madison: Human Beings, Not Robocops

52   Right now, the city with one of the highest percentages of women cops is Madison, Wisconsin. Twenty-seven percent of its force is female; in addition, a third of its detectives and 25 percent of all those ranked above officer status are women.

53   Chief Richard Williams says women officers are essential to the department's community-oriented style of policing. "We want to reflect the community, and 50 percent of the people out there are women," he explains. "We want people to see us as human beings, rather than Robocops with dark glasses and no feelings." Williams says his department is doing that, not just by adding women to police ranks but by redefining what a police officer is.

54   Instead of recruiting eager young warriors with high-school educations and a couple of years in the military, Madison is voting for maturity and independent thinking by favoring candidates ages 25 to 29 with college degrees and well-developed communication skills.

55   Although women officers in Madison say the department isn't free of sexism, they describe many of the male officers as what Officer Carren Corcoran calls '90s guys: "They have good relationships with their wives, good communication with citizens, they don't try to take over our calls and they talk to suspects instead of just smashing the guy against the car."

56   The respect Madison officers feel for each other is paralleled by the force's relations with the community. In Los Angeles, officers often demand that suspects lie prone on the pavement. In Madison, officers address everyone as Sir or Ma'am and ask politely for identification and permission to pat a suspect down. Most of the time permission is given, and what is elsewhere a ritual of dominance and submission becomes a surprisingly good-natured interaction.

57   Madison officers say being respectful of citizens makes their job easier. "If you rip someone's self-respect and self-esteem away from them, that doesn't get you anywhere," says Sergeant Patricia Rickman.

58   Officers from Milwaukee and Chicago, whose departments are run on more traditional lines, "think we're all pansies here because we talk too much," she adds, laughing. "That's fine—we talk and we don't get hurt."

59   In other cities, social worker is the worst thing you can call a cop, but officers in the Madison Police Department see much of what they do in exactly those terms. Officer Sue Armagost has a master's degree in social work and worked with battered women for three years before becoming a cop. She says, "This is social work with a gun and a little more authority and a whole lot more job security."

60   Forget the gunfights and car chases in the movies and cop shows. Here are the crime-fighting highlights of one three-day weekend in Madison last fall:

- A six-year-old boy is accused of stealing a $1.99 toy gun from a supermarket.
- A man has beaten up his girlfriend. He leaves the house when she calls the police and has to be pursued for several blocks before he is arrested. The officers explain to the girlfriend her legal options for seeking protection from him in the future.
- A worried mother files a missing-person report on her pregnant 15-year-old, who has disappeared with a boyfriend. (She turns up six hours later.)
- A 17-year-old boy from a nearby farm town is hanging around a neighborhood at one o'clock in the morning with two small children in the back of his truck. He says they are from a nearby homeless shelter and that he gave their father a lift here, supposedly so he could cash a money order. The officers convince the boy to hand the children over to them and go home. They also call his parents.
- The children's parents are found a half hour later. The father has crack cocaine hidden in his mouth and is arrested. The mother and children are given some phone numbers for social services and taken back to the homeless shelter.
- A man reports he's been robbed, then admits he made up the story because he has spent his mother's bus money on drugs. He threatens suicide and must be taken to a crisis center.
- A confused 65-year-old woman turns up on a residential street several miles from where she lives. The officer finds her caregiver and returns the woman to her home.

61   This scenario is not unique to Madison. Even in the nation's largest, toughest cities, an officer on patrol spends 80 to 95 percent of work time answering service calls, talking to citizens and writing reports. Cops who don't like "social work" aren't well-suited to their jobs.

Toughing It Out

62   Despite their advantages, women police officers are still relatively rare. Although a 1990 Police Foundation survey of about 200 large municipal departments found that some 20 percent of police-academy applicants and graduates are now women, most major police department's female ranks remain stuck around the ten to 12 percent mark. *The Police Chief* magazine reports that women still make up only 8.6 percent of new hires nationally.

63   The biggest reason is that hostility to women officers is still rampant. A survey of 280 male officers in Washington, Oregon, Idaho and Montana, published in *The Police Chief* last year, found that 68 percent object to the idea of having a woman partner.

64   Often hostility takes the form of harassment. The LAPD is currently the target of a class-action lawsuit charging deliberate and systemic discrimination against

women and minorities, ranging from rudeness and name-calling to sexual assault. Male resistance can sometimes take even harsher forms. In a story published last year about alleged harassment within the Maryland State Police, *The Baltimore Sun* reported one female trooper's charges about what happened when she refused a superior officer's requests for a date: He sent her into a riot situation with No backup. Baltimore attorney Kathleen Cahill, who is representing two female officers in sexual harassment suits against the agency, says one of her clients has received death threats that appear to have come from fellow officers. "If a woman speaks out in an office setting and her superiors retaliate, that's very serious," she says. "But women who blow the whistle on law enforcement are afraid they're going to die. When the police threaten your life, who do you call for help?"

65   Yet police departments are changing, whether the old guard likes it or not. And those changes will almost certainly mean an ever bigger role for women.

66   First, rising educational standards for police officers mean departments must recruit from the widest possible pool. "Agencies in major cities reject, on average, more than 90 percent of candidates," says the Police Foundation's Williams. "We would not be able to keep the police cars rolling without women."

67   Second, the future of policing is brain power, not muscle, which helps level the playing field for women. "In the future the really good cops are going to be preventing crime and disorder by understanding those things in an analytic way," predicts Karin Schmerler, a former researcher with the Police Executive Research Forum, a nonprofit law enforcement think tank. "Policing is becoming proactive rather than reactive, and therefore more of a thinking, creative kind of job."

68   One example of that is offered by Austin, Texas, chief of police Elizabeth Watson, one of only two women chiefs in major American cities. Old-style, control-oriented policing, she points out, has failed to stop drug dealing in residential neighborhoods. Unless police devote long hours to surveillance (unlikely in this budget-slashing era), they can't make arrests that hold up in court because they can't catch dealers in the act. As a result, says Watson, more and more police departments are helping local residents to organize and take action, for example, by slapping nuisance suits on crack-house landlords, agitating for better street lighting and creating citizen surveillance teams that can provide police with photos of drug deals, license-plate numbers and other evidence.

69   "We need to work in partnership with communities and other agencies, using problem-solving, communication and other interpersonal skills," says Watson. "Those are characteristics that were not considered as critical for officers in the past but that women are generally very good at."

70   Finally, *women cops love their work with a fervor that can't help but attract more* women to the ranks. Interviews with more than 30 women officers from around the country yielded many stories of harassment and discrimination, of on-the-job injuries and brushes with death. But not one of these women wishes she were doing anything else.

71   One lieutenant, the only woman supervisor in her Midwestern agency, has suffered intense harassment, including being stalked by a former fellow officer,

but has never considered changing careers. "When you're on patrol you have a lot of autonomy; you're pretty much your own boss," she says. "You're taking care of people, helping them when they're hurt, protecting them. It's different each day. It's the best job in the world."

72   As a girl, Marianne Scholer noticed that women in TV crime shows were always the victims. "I didn't want to have to be helped—I wanted to do the helping," she says. "I knew that being feminine didn't have to mean being helpless." A lieutenant in the Orange County, Florida, sheriff's office, she recently won a medal of valor for rescuing three people, including a child, from a burning building. "This is what I want to do," she says. "Every day, every hour brings an opportunity for you to be there for somebody."

Glamour, September 1995, pp. 260–273

COMPREHENSION QUESTIONS

1. What is the topic of the passage?
2. What is the central message of the passage?
3. Determine what is at issue. What is your initial personal viewpoint?
4. Distinguish among opposing viewpoints, and provide the rationale for each.
5. Think carefully about the viewpoints. Express a personal viewpoint, and give the reasons why you favor it. Does it differ from your initial personal viewpoint? Why or why not?
6. Write a few paragraphs *in support of the viewpoint that you do* not *favor.*

THOUGHT AND DISCUSSION QUESTIONS

1. Should the police have put handcuffs on the teenager who partly fit the reported batterer's description? Why or why not? What would you have done if you had been one of the police officers present? Why?
2. In your view, are women cops tough enough? Why or why not?
3. Would you rather have a male or a female cop patrolling your neighborhood? Why?
4. In your view, does the author deal with the subject matter of the article in an unbiased way? Why or why not?
5. List any questions that came to mind while you were reading this selection, and be prepared to discuss possible answers to them.

PROBLEM SOLVING

Go to the Huffington Post, an Internet news site (http://www.huffingtonpost.com). Find an article about an issue or topic that could affect you or someone you know, in a challenging way. Print the article. After reading the article, write the five steps of solving this issue should this actually become a challenge in your life.

LISTENING SPRINGBOARD INQUIRY

Go to the Web site for Dr. Mehmet Oz, host of the very popular TV show Dr. Oz (http://www.doctoroz.com/), and click on "Videos and More" in the menu bar. Select a video from this site or listen to a message from "Oz Radio" that interests you. Listen to and take notes on the topic.

Video or Oz Radio topic:

_____

If there is another individual in the video or radio message, who is it? What is his or her title or position? What relationship does that person have to the topic?

_____

_____

_____

_____

Does this message or discussion address a problem? Do the speakers suggest solutions? What is the problem, and what solutions are suggested?

_____

_____

_____

_____

_____

_____

LOOKING BACK...LOOKING FORWARD

To check your progress in meeting this chapter's learning objectives, complete the Mastery Tests in this chapter.

THINK AGAIN!

The following problem was presented by one of my critical-thinking students:

Suppose you bought a house with two floors, plus a basement and an attic. There are three separate lights in the attic that are controlled by three separate switches in the basement.

One night you are all alone and decide to match each of the three switches in the basement with the specific light in the attic that it controls. Assume that you want to accomplish this task immediately and that you can only make one trip to the basement and one trip to the attic. Can you figure out how you would go about doing it?

SPIT FIRE

Remember to follow these steps:

- first, read the narrative
- second, examine the picture carefully
- third, answer the questions and come up with a solution

Have fun!

Because Jesse Varlet was a spitfire and everybody knew it, Police Chief Felicity Keene stopped by occasionally to see Jesse to find out what she was up to. But one Wednesday afternoon Felicity found her strangled and lying next to her kitchen counter, as shown.

Felicity realized at once that there were three suspects. The first was Jesse's estranged husband, Nicholas, whom she was divorcing. The second was her neighbor, Angel Blackhead, the only honest-to-goodness gangster in all of West Copernicus, and with whom she was feuding over her right to use a shortcut which traversed a corner of his property. The third was Sweet William, a neighborhood handyman, big in muscle and small in brain power, who mowed lawns and had made passes at Jesse in the past. She had sworn to a friend that she'd never go near "that big dumb oaf."

None of the three had a credible alibi. Sweet William claimed he'd gone into the house for a drink of water, seen the body, and then panicked and ran away lest he be accused. Both Nick and Angel said they'd never been near the house, but refused to elaborate.

Felicity did all the right things, such as calling in the medical examiner and the state Bureau of Investigation, after which she sat down and examined the evidence and reached her own conclusion.

What was it, and what was her reasoning?

Questions

1. Do the wine and glasses indicate a friendly meeting?   ☐ Yes   ☐ No

2. Did Sweet William leave the lawn without finishing his job?   ☐ Yes   ☐ No

3. Is it likely that Jesse sat down with Sweet William for a friendly drink?   ☐ Yes   ☐ No

4. Is it likely that she had a friendly drink with Nick?   ☐ Yes   ☐ No

5. Which of the three suspects would have jimmied open the cabinet door in order to have a drink with Jesse?

_____.

6. Do you think that Nick had an 11 A.M. appointment with Jesse?   ☐ Yes   ☐ No

7. Do you think that Jesse had a drink with either Sweet William or Angel?   ☐ Yes   ☐ No

8. Who killed Jesse?

_____.

Text and illustration from Lawrence Treat, *Crime and Puzzlement—My Cousin Phoebe: 24 Solve-Them-Yourself Picture Mysteries* (Henry Holt and Co., 1991), pp. 21–22

Spit Fire

Name _____   Date _____

MASTERY TEST 5-1

DIRECTIONS: Answer the questions and fill in the blanks.

1. Define the word *problem.*

_____

_____

_____

2. Define the word *solution.*

_____

_____

_____

3. Name and describe briefly the steps involved in the basic method for personal problem solving.

_____

_____

_____

_____

_____

_____

_____

_____

_____

4. When identifying a problem, it is important not to confuse

_____ (ways of accomplishing goals) with the

_____ (goals themselves).

5. If your problem concerns another person, is it necessary to get that person
involved in all steps? Explain your answer.

_____

_____

_____

6. Name two specific problems discussed in the following story.

_____

_____

_____

Whose Job Is It?

This is a story about four people named Everybody, Somebody, Anybody, and Nobody.
There was an important job to be done, and Everybody was asked to do it. Everybody
was sure Somebody would do it. Anybody could have done it, but Nobody did it.
Somebody got angry about that, because it was Everybody's job. Everybody thought
Anybody could do it, but Nobody realized that Everybody wouldn't do it. It ended up
that Everybody blamed Somebody when Nobody did what Anybody could have done.

Problems: _____

_____

_____

_____

Name _____ Date _____

DIRECTIONS: *Using the first four steps of the basic method for personal problem solving, try to come up with possible solutions for the following problem situations.*

1

You have been dating the "love of your life" for the past year, and the two of you have decided to get married. One evening, while talking over wedding plans, you express your overwhelming desire to have children. During the course of the conversation, you are shocked to find out that your prospective spouse does not want kids. Even though the subject has never been discussed before, you always assumed that there would be no disagreement. You are madly in love but at a loss as to what to do because having children has been a lifelong dream.

_____

_____

_____

_____

_____

_____

_____

_____

_____

_____

2

A 9,000-Year-Old Secret

JERRY ADLER

1   When last heard from, 9,000-year-old Kennewick Man was in federal court, his battered bones the subject of a tug of war between scientists who wanted to study them and Indian tribes who sought to bury them. Almost from the moment he came tumbling out of the muddy bank of the Columbia River during a speedboat race in 1996, the proto-American with the "Caucasoid-like" skull has been arousing passions on all sides. Was he a messenger from the past, bearing evidence that the New World was populated not just once, by way of the now vanished land bridge from Siberia, but at different times, by unrelated groups, from diverse parts of the world? If so, who were his people—and who were the ones who embedded a stone spearpoint in his right hip? Or was he merely an uncommonly remote ancestor of the Northwest Indian tribes who live along the river today, and who are thereby entitled to bury him

according to *their* rites? Last week he was in the news again as scientists began studying the 300-odd pieces in which he was found, hoping to answer the first questions raised by any human remains: how did he die, and how was he buried?

2   The examination, ordered by a federal magistrate in 2002 and affirmed by an appeals court last year, came as a disappointment to the Indian coalition which had claimed the skeleton under the Native American Graves Protection and Repatriation Act. This 1990 law, which gives tribes custody of human remains to which they can plausibly assert a cultural kinship, was meant to remedy the wholesale 19th-century plundering of Indian corpses for museums and private collections. But it had never been tested in a case involving a hypothesized ancestor separated by hundreds of generations. And the proportions of Kennewick Man's skull were different—not as long or broad, but bigger front to back—from modern Indian skulls (and from any other present-day population). One early description used the word "Caucasoid," giving rise to a boomlet in speculation about Europeans' settling North America from the east. Anthropologists now say the closest match appears to be with the Ainu, an ethnic minority in Japan.

3   The Indian position is that it doesn't matter when Kennewick Man lived, or what size his head was. "[Indian] remains are sacred to the native peoples because we are a part of this earth and we were put here to take care of the land," says Rex Buck Jr., a religious leader among the Wanapum. They were supported by the Department of the Interior, which was eager to show its good will by turning the skeleton over for burial. Nor did the tribes feel the need to research how their ancestors got to America, because they already know the answer. "From our oral histories, we know that our people have been part of this land since the beginning of time," Armand Minthorn of the Umatillas contended.

4   To the scientists, the chance to examine the remains was self-evidently a triumph for reason. "It comes down," says Douglas Owsley of the Smithsonian, "to the right to ask questions of the past." He and 10 colleagues spent a week poring over the bones, studying faint chemical stains and microscopic patterns of breakage and the tiny beads of calcium carbonate that accumulate on the downside, indicating how the corpse was positioned. To minimize handling of the skeleton, which the Indians still hope to rebury, the scientists scanned the bones and made three-dimensional models that could be measured and pieced together to give a better idea of what Kennewick Man might have looked like under the skin. As to his world, and who else lived in it, that information must await new discoveries elsewhere. In 1998, apparently in response to the Indians' fears that more skeletons might be unearthed, the government buried the discovery site under 2 million pounds of dirt.

_____

_____

_____

_____

_____

DIRECTIONS: *Along with your partner, read the second part of "The Adventure of the Three Students," and add to your notes from Part One. Answer the questions that follow it.*

The Return of Sherlock Holmes

The Adventure of the Three Students: Part Two

A. CONAN DOYLE

1   Holmes shook his head impatiently.

2   "Let us be practical," said he. "I understand you to say that there are three students who use this stair and are in the habit of passing your door?"

3   "Yes, there are."

4   "And they are all in for this examination?"

5   "Yes."

6   "Have you any reason to suspect any one of them more than the others?"

7   Soames hesitated.

8   "It is a very delicate question," said he. "One hardly likes to throw suspicion where there are no proofs."

9   "Let us hear the suspicions. I will look after the proofs."

10   "I will tell you, then, in a few words the character of the three men who inhabit these rooms. The lower of the three is Gilchrist, a fine scholar and athlete; plays in the Rugby team and the cricket team for the college, and got his Blue for the hurdles and the long jump. He is a fine, manly fellow. His father was the notorious Sir Jabez Gilchrist, who ruined himself on the turf. My scholar has been left very poor, but he is hard-working and industrious. He will do well.

11   "The second floor is inhabited by Daulat Ras, the Indian. He is a quiet, inscrutable fellow, as most of those Indians are. He is well up in his work, though his Greek is his weak subject. He is steady and methodical.

12   "The top floor belongs to Miles McLaren. He is a brilliant fellow when he chooses to work—one of the brightest intellects of the University, but he is wayward, dissipated, and unprincipled. He was nearly expelled over a card scandal in his first year. He has been idling all this term, and he must look forward with dread to the examination."

13   "Then it is he whom you suspect?"

14   "I dare not go so far as that. But of the three he is perhaps the least unlikely."

15   "Exactly. Now, Mr. Soames, let us have a look at your servant, Bannister."

16   He was a little, white-faced, clean-shaven, grizzly-haired fellow of fifty. He was still suffering from this sudden disturbance of the quiet routine of his life. His plump face was twitching with his nervousness, and his fingers could not keep still.

17 "We are investigating this unhappy business, Bannister," said his master.

18 "Yes, sir."

19 "I understand," said Holmes, "that you left your key in the door?"

20 "Yes, sir."

21 "Was it not very extraordinary that you should do this on the very day when there were these papers inside?"

22 "It was most unfortunate, sir. But I have occasionally done the same thing at other times."

23 "When did you enter the room?"

24 "It was about half-past four. That is Mr. Soames's tea time."

25 "How long did you stay?"

26 "When I saw that he was absent I withdrew at once."

27 "Did you look at these papers on the table?"

28 "No, sir; certainly not."

29 "How came you to leave the key in the door?"

30 "I had the tea-tray in my hand. I thought I would come back for the key. Then I forgot."

31 "Has the outer door a spring lock?"

32 "No, sir."

33 "Then it was open all the time?"

34 "Yes, sir."

35 "Anyone in the room could get out?"

36 "Yes, sir."

37 "When Mr. Soames returned and called for you, you were very much disturbed?"

38 "Yes, sir. Such a thing has never happened during the many years that I have been here. I nearly fainted, sir."

39 "So I understand. Where were you when you began to feel bad?"

40 "Where was I, sir? Why, here, near the door."

41 "That is singular, because you sat down in that chair over yonder near the corner. Why did you pass these other chairs?"

42 "I don't know, sir. It didn't matter to me where I sat."

43 "I really don't think he knew much about it, Mr. Holmes. He was looking very bad—quite ghastly."

44 "You stayed here when your master left?"

45 "Only for a minute or so. Then I locked the door and went to my room."

46 "Whom do you suspect?"

47 "Oh, I would not venture to say, sir. I don't believe there is any gentleman in this University who is capable of profiting by such an action. No, sir, I'll not believe it."

48 "Thank you; that will do," said Holmes. "Oh, one more word. You have not mentioned to any of the three gentlemen whom you attend that anything is amiss?"

49 "No, sir; not a word."

50 "You haven't seen any of them?"

51 "No, sir."

52 "Very good. Now, Mr. Soames, we will take a walk in the quadrangle, if you please."

53 Three yellow squares of light shone above us in the gathering gloom.

54   "Your three birds are all in their nests," said Holmes, looking up. "Halloa! What's that? One of them seems restless enough."

55   It was the Indian, whose dark silhouette appeared suddenly upon his blind. He was pacing swiftly up and down his room.

56   "I should like to have a peep at each of them," said Holmes. "Is it possible?"

57   "No difficulty in the world," Soames answered. "This set of rooms is quite the oldest in the college, and it is not unusual for visitors to go over them. Come along, and I will personally conduct you."

58   "No names, please!" said Holmes, as we knocked at Gilchrist's door. A tall, flaxen-haired, slim young fellow opened it, and made us welcome when he understood our errand. There were some really curious pieces of mediæval domestic architecture within. Holmes was so charmed with one of them that he insisted on drawing it on his note book, broke his pencil, had to borrow one from our host, and finally borrowed a knife to sharpen his own. The same curious accident happened to him in the rooms of the Indian—a silent, little, hook-nosed fellow, who eyed us askance and was obviously glad when Holmes's architectural studies had come to an end. I could not see that in either case Holmes had come upon the clue for which he was searching. Only at the third did our visit prove abortive. The outer door would not open to our knock, and nothing more substantial than a torrent of bad language came from behind it. "I don't care who you are. You can go to blazes!" roared the angry voice. "To-morrow's the exam, and I won't be drawn by anyone."

59   "A rude fellow," said our guide, flushing with anger as we withdrew down the stair. "Of course, he did not realize that it was I who was knocking, but none the less his conduct was very uncourteous, and, indeed, under the circumstances rather suspicious."

60   Holmes's response was a curious one.

61   "Can you tell me his exact height?" he asked.

62   "Really, Mr. Holmes, I cannot undertake to say. He is taller than the Indian, not so tall as Gilchrist. I suppose five foot six would be about it."

63   "That is very important," said Holmes. "And now, Mr. Soames, I wish you good-night."

64   Our guide cried aloud in his astonishment and dismay. "Good gracious, Mr. Holmes, you are surely not going to leave me in this abrupt fashion! You don't seem to realize the position. To-morrow is the examination. I must take some definite action tonight. I cannot allow the examination to be held if one of the papers has been tampered with. The situation must be faced."

65   "You must leave it as it is. I shall drop round early to-morrow morning and chat the matter over. It is possible that I may be in a position then to indicate some course of action. Meanwhile you change nothing—nothing at all."

66   "Very good, Mr. Holmes."

67   "You can be perfectly easy in your mind. We shall certainly find some way out of your difficulties. I will take the black clay with me, also the pencil cuttings. Good-bye."

68   When we were out in the darkness of the quadrangle we again looked up at the windows. The Indian still paced his room. The others were invisible.

69   "Well, Watson, what do you think of it?" Holmes asked, as we came out into the main street. "Quite a little parlour game—sort of three-card trick, is it not? There are your three men. It must be one of them. You take your choice. Which is yours?"

70   "The foul-mouthed fellow at the top. He is the one with the worst record. And yet that Indian was a sly fellow also. Why should he be pacing his room all the time?"

71   "There is nothing in that. Many men do it when they are trying to learn anything by heart."

72   "He looked at us in a queer way."

73   "So would you if a flock of strangers came in on you when you were preparing for an examination next day, and every moment was of value. No, I see nothing in that. Pencils, too, and knives—all was satisfactory. But that fellow *does* puzzle me."

74   "Who?"

75   "Why, Bannister, the servant. What's his game in the matter?"

76   "He impressed me as being a perfectly honest man."

77   "So he did me. That's the puzzling part. Why should a perfectly honest man—well, well, here's a large stationer's. We shall begin our researches here."

78   There were only four stationers of any consequence in the town, and at each Holmes produced his pencil chips and bid high for a duplicate. All were agreed that one could be ordered, but that it was not a usual size of pencil and that it was seldom kept in stock. My friend did not appear to be depressed by his failure, but shrugged his shoulders in half-humorous resignation.

79   "No good, my dear Watson. This, the best and only final clue, has run to nothing. But, indeed, I have little doubt that we can build up a sufficient case without it. By Jove! my dear fellow, it is nearly nine, and the landlady babbled of green peas at seven-thirty. What with your eternal tobacco, Watson, and your irregularity at meals, I expect that you will get notice to quit and that I shall share your downfall—not, however, before we have solved the problem of the nervous tutor, the careless servant, and the three enterprising students."

80   Holmes made no further allusion to the matter that day, though he sat lost in thought for a long time after our belated dinner. At eight in the morning he came into my room just as I finished my toilet.

81   "Well, Watson," said he, "it is time we went down to St. Luke's. Can you do without breakfast?"

82   "Certainly."

83   "Soames will be in a dreadful fidget until we are able to tell him something positive."

84   "Have you anything positive to tell him?"

85   "I think so."

86   "You have formed a conclusion?"

87   "Yes, my dear Watson; I have solved the mystery."

88   "But what fresh evidence could you have got?"

89   "Aha! It is not for nothing that I have turned myself out of bed at the untimely hour of six. I have put in two hours' hard work and covered at least five miles, with something to show for it. Look at that!"

90   He held out his hand. On the palm were three little pyramids of black, doughy clay.

91   "Why, Holmes, you had only two yesterday!"

92   "And one more this morning. It is a fair argument that wherever No. 3 came from is also the source of Nos. 1 and 2. Eh, Watson? Well, come along and put friend Soames out of his pain."

93   The unfortunate tutor was certainly in a state of pitiable agitation when we found him in his chambers. In a few hours the examinations would commence, and he was still in the dilemma between making the facts public and allowing the culprit to compete for the valuable scholarship. He could hardly stand still, so great was his mental agitation, and he ran towards Holmes with two eager hands outstretched.

94   "Thank Heaven that you have come! I feared that you had given it up in despair. What am I to do? Shall the examination proceed?"

95   "Yes; let it proceed by all means."

96   "But this rascal—?"

97   "He shall not compete."

98   "You know him?"

99   "I think so. If this matter is not to become public we must give ourselves certain powers, and resolve ourselves into a small private court-martial. You there, if you please, Soames! Watson, you here! I'll take the arm chair in the middle. I think that we are now sufficiently imposing to strike terror into a guilty breast. Kindly ring the bell!"

The Complete Original Illustrated Sherlock Holmes, pp. 570–574

Questions

1. Who are the suspects? Name and describe each of them.

2. What additional clues have you discovered?

3. At this point, do you suspect any one of them more than the others? Why or why not?

PART THREE

CRITICAL READING: EVALUATING WHAT YOU READ

6 Using Inference

CHAPTER OUTLINE

CHAPTER OUTCOMES

After completing Chapter 6, you should be able to:

- Continue to apply the basic method for personal problem solving.
- Define critical reading.
- Define inference.
- Use knowledge, experience, and clues to draw inferences in problem situations and when reading passages concerning contemporary issues.
- Use the Internet to infer.
- Use figurative language to infer.
- Continue to find topics and central messages in contemporary-issue passages to determine what is at issue, distinguish among opposing viewpoints, and express personal viewpoints.

Think About It!

Take a close look at the message in Photograph 1. Given what you know about smoking and the clues on the message, make an "educated guess" regarding what the message is urging you to do. Discuss your ideas with your classmates.

Look at the message on the sign in Photograph 2. Use your background knowledge and the clues on the sign to make an "educated guess" regarding what the message is saying about satellite radio. Do you know the name of any radio announcer who uses satellite radio? This may be a clue to the message. Discuss your ideas with your classmates.

PROBLEM-SOLVING EXERCISE

Using your notebook, apply the first four steps of the basic method for personal problem solving to the following hypothetical situation. Make sure to label each step clearly as you discuss what you would do.

Hypothetical Situation

You are very close friends with a married couple whom you have known for many years. While driving through town, you spot one of them entering a restaurant with a person of the opposite sex. The following afternoon, you see them once again going into the same restaurant together. They seem to be very comfortable with each other and in a rather jovial mood.

■ What Is Critical Reading?

As a college student, you are expected to derive meaning from whatever information you encounter in textbooks and other sources. In Chapters 1, 2, and 3, we reviewed a number of reading skills:

- Using context, word parts, a glossary, and the dictionary to determine word meanings
- Distinguishing main ideas, major details, and minor details
- Recognizing patterns of organization
- Uncovering the central message of a selection
- Summarizing and paraphrasing
- Overviewing a textbook
- Previewing a textbook chapter
- Developing questions from chapter headings and answering them
- Underlining or highlighting
- Reading a textbook chapter using specific strategies (SQ4R, concept mapping, KWL).

All of these skills help you better, comprehend reading material particularly material found in textbooks.

Critical reading can be defined as *very high-level comprehension of written material requiring interpretation and evaluation skills that enable the reader to separate important from unimportant information, distinguish between facts and opinions, and determine a writer's purpose and tone.* Critical reading also entails *using inference to go beyond what is stated explicitly, filling in informational gaps, and coming to logical conclusions.* These various skills require much thought, and that is why critical reading is dependent on critical thinking. Indeed, all of the characteristics of critical thinking discussed in Chapter 4 can be applied to critical reading. The diagram on the next page illustrates the relationship between critical thinking and critical reading skills.

You have already had some practice in separating important from unimportant information, particularly when answering questions developed from textbook chapter headings and when dealing with contemporary issues. In the remaining chapters, you will continue to practice that skill. The other critical reading skills—using inference, distinguishing between facts and opinions, and uncovering purpose and determining tone—are covered here in Part Three. Let's begin with a discussion of inference.

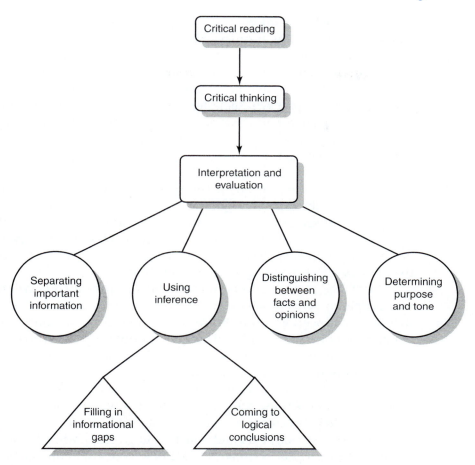

■ Drawing Inferences

Inferences are a part of communication in everyday life—in listening, speaking, reading, and writing. The receiver of information gains a better understanding of a topic or idea through this interactive process that involves what is known and what is learned.

Applied to reading, an inference is a reasonable or educated guess about what the author does not say based on what he or she does say. Inferences must be made when an author suggests an idea but does not directly state it. These ideas are implied, or inferred.

Inferring, or drawing conclusions, makes you think in depth about stated and unstated information. You often use your personal experience to comprehend what is inferred. Inferring requires background information and **abstract thinking** in order to think as the writer wishes you to think. The clues the writer gives you steer your thinking. A valid inference is one that has a sufficient amount of supportable and verifiable information.

Pretend that you have had Professor Arlene Brown as a mathematics instructor for the past two semesters. She is a friendly person who always greets her classes in a warm manner. This past Tuesday, Professor Brown gave a difficult midterm examination in your algebra course. It covered rather complex material, and many of your classmates were concerned about their grades.

When the class met again on Thursday morning, Professor Brown arrived late, and when she came through the door she was not smiling at all. In fact, she walked briskly to the front of the room, slammed her briefcase on the desk, gruffly told the students to take out their notebooks, and began to cover new material immediately. Consequently, most of your classmates concluded that Professor Brown was upset about something.

They based that conclusion on three factors: first, their *knowledge* of the way people in general behave when they are upset; second, the *experience* they have had with Professor Brown in previous sessions; third, their using her behavior or actions as *clues*. That she was upset was a reasonable conclusion because it rested solidly on their knowledge and experience and flowed logically from the clues or facts at hand.

Some students went one step further by concluding that Professor Brown was upset because the class had done poorly on the midterm exam. Therefore, they became even more concerned about their test scores. However, you were skeptical and reluctant to go along with that line of reasoning. Although your classmates based their conclusion on knowledge and experience, you felt that it was not as solid as the previous one because there was a lack of specific clues pointing in that direction. They may ultimately end up being correct, but without additional information, their hunch was by no means certain. So it was probably wise for you to be cautious.

Now let's add some information to the story. Suppose Professor Brown, after slamming her briefcase on the desk, blurted out, "Men!" Could you then conclude reasonably that she had had an argument with her husband? Maybe, but you certainly might end up being wrong, because once again there are not enough clues. She could just as easily have had an argument that morning with some other male, such as a driver who cut her off on the way to school, her automobile mechanic, the dean, or another faculty member.

What if, instead, she had shouted, "Men! They are impossible to live with!" Would you then feel safe concluding that she had had an argument with her husband? Although that conclusion would be more likely in that it does rest on an additional clue, it might also turn out to be incorrect because she could be living with a boyfriend, son, brother, father, or room-mate. It would become a much stronger conclusion if she had exclaimed, "Men! They are impossible to live with! Don't ever get married!" There would finally be enough clues to support the original conclusion that she had had a disagreement with her husband.

What we have been discussing here are **inferences**—"educated guesses" by which we go beyond what is explicit in order to fill in informational gaps, come to logical conclusions, and make sense of the world around us. They are "educated" because they are not wild guesses but are instead based *on knowledge*, *experience*, and the *clues or facts* of the situation. In short, the more knowledge, experience, and clues we have, the better our chances of coming up with sound inferences and hence logical and reasonable conclusions.

Using Knowledge to Infer

Knowledge of different subjects or topics varies from person to person: It comes down to what we have learned and experienced through the years. In that sense, knowledge really cannot be separated from experience because the latter adds to our knowledge base. On the other hand, our knowledge helps shape the way we interpret our experiences.

It follows, then, that the more we know and the more we have experienced, the easier it will be to draw inferences, depending of course on the circumstances. There will be occasions when we are in a much better position to make educated guesses and other occasions when we will not be able to do so with any degree of confidence. For example, look at the photograph on the following page.

Certainly, most of us have enough knowledge to realize that this is a picture of a bus that is used for sightseeing purposes. However, what if I asked you to infer where the photograph was taken? There is one clue, and that is the name "Beantown." If you know the name of the city that is called "Beantown," you would feel very secure answering that the photograph was probably taken in the city of Boston. Thus your knowledge helped you use the clue to answer the question. People without that knowledge would be forced either to do some research or to take a wild guess. If they took a wild guess, the chances are fairly high that they would be wrong. Following are examples of how knowledge can play a significant part when it comes to drawing inferences.

Examples:

1. FACT: All of the people with a certain disease know one another and are not necessarily related.

   In order to make an inference, you would need to know something about diseases and how they are spread. You could then infer that the disease is probably not diabetes or heart failure but something that is passed on such as a cold or the flu.

   INFERENCE: The disease is contagious.

2. FACT: Certain states have a significantly higher death rate than others. Which states are they?

   In order to make this inference, you would need to know that a large number of older people live in these states, possibly because they tend to retire there. Therefore, the death rate is higher in these states than other states.

   INFERENCE: The states are Arizona and Florida.

3. FACT: The flowers we planted come up and bloom every year. What type of flowers are they?

   In order to make this inference, you would need to know that some flowers—annuals—need to be planted every year and that others—perennials—grow back every growing season.

   INFERENCE: The flowers are perennials.

We all need to accept the fact that we do not know everything, and no two people will possess the same degree of knowledge on every matter. In other words, we should not be embarrassed if we do not have enough knowledge in certain situations to draw inferences, and in those instances, it is probably better not to draw inferences because there is a greater chance of being wrong. Keep in mind that there will be other situations in which we will find ourselves in better positions to come to logical conclusions. Furthermore, knowledge is not a constant but increases as we go through life.

ACTIVITY 1

DIRECTIONS: *Read the following, and use your background knowledge to make an inference. Be prepared to share your answers with your classmates.*

a. The man was worried. His car came to a halt and he was alone. It was extremely dark and cold. The man took off his overcoat, rolled down the window, and got out of the car as quickly as possible. He used all of his strength to move as fast as he could. He was relieved when he saw he was not far from shore because it was cold and snowy.

What can you infer happened?

_____

_____

www.Cartoonbank.com

"On the Internet, nobody knows you're a dog."

b. What do you think the dog is planning?

_____

_____

THE FAMILY CIRCUS   By Bil Keane

7-14
© 2005 Bil Keane, Inc.
Dist. by King Features Synd.
www.familycircus.com

**"You just click on it and they put it
in your shopping cart."**

c. Why is the father concerned?

_____

_____

_____

Using Experience to Infer

We have already discussed the relationship between knowledge and experience. Our experiences add to our knowledge base and place us in a better position to come to logical conclusions about our surroundings. Once again, our experiences vary from person to person and therefore with regard to how much they help us draw inferences in different situations.

For instance, look at the cartoon on the next page and see if you can determine what it is implying. What background knowledge do you have to figure out the inference? What is the image trying to portray to the viewer?

Examples from Personal Experience:

- **Listening:** The phone rings, you pick it up and there is a hesitation before a person speaks. What can you infer?
  - You could infer that it is a telemarketing call. You might think this because you know that a computer randomly selects the phone

STAHLER.
THE COLUMBUS DISPATCH.
2009.

UNIVERSAL
OPEN
ENROLLMENT CARE
MEDICAID HMOs SCHIP
BLUE CROSS PAY OR PLAY
MEDICARE COST SHIFTING CO-OP PUBLIC OPTION
CATASTROPHIC COSTS DIRECT-TO-CONSUMER ADVERTISING
GUARANTEED ELIGIBILITY NANNY GOVERNMENT GUARANTEED ISSUE
NATIONAL HEALTH INSURANCE EXCHANGE PAY-FOR-PERFORMANCE
BOARD CERTIFIED CAFETERIA PLAN DEDUCTIBLE FLEX PLAN
EMPLOYER CONTRIBUTION NETWORK PRE-EXISTING CONDITION
PROVIDER
EMPLOYER-BASED
COBRA HEALTH INSURANCE
WAITING PERIOD FEE FOR SERVICE
SELF-INSURED HEALTH INSURANCE

© Columbus Dispatch/Dist. by United Feature Syndicate, Inc.

numbers for these types of calls and there is a gap of about two seconds before the telemarketer begins the message.

- You might also infer that the caller does not recognize your voice and/or the person has the wrong number.

- **Listening:** The fire siren in town goes off. What can you infer?
  - You may infer that there is a fire or an emergency somewhere.
  - If it goes off around lunchtime, you may infer that it is the 12:00 noon siren instead of a fire or emergency.

- **Speaking:** You tell someone that an umbrella is needed today.
  - The listener may infer that it is raining.
  - The listener may infer that you need protection from the sun.

- **Reading:** You see the headline in the newspaper, "Ethiopia on the Brink of Famine Again: World Must Act."
  - You may infer that Ethiopia is a poor country that has encountered vast and extreme famine before.
  - You may infer that this article is encouraging the world to help Ethiopia in some way to solve a crisis.

- **Reading:** Daily, it seems, junk mail with advertisements, brochures, or contests arrives to try to persuade you to buy a product or participate in some way. You receive a flyer that says, "to win a 19" flat-screen television just return this card."
  - You may infer that you have won the television, when you actually just have a chance to win it.

- **Writing:** You just received a present. Before you unwrap the gift, you are asked to write down your guesses as to its contents.
  - You write what you think it might be based on the size of the box.
  - You write what you think it might be based on the occasion for the present such as a specific holiday or birthday.
  - You write what you suspect it might be after shaking the box.

ACTIVITY 2	DIRECTIONS: *Read the following, and use your personal experience to make an inference. Be prepared to share your answers with your classmates.*

1. "Whenever Stanley plays quarterback on the football team, the team loses."

   _____

   _____

2. As you are driving, you see a police car with flashing lights directly behind you.

   _____

   _____

3. In the mirror, John Bell noticed that his hair was graying at the temples. As he picked up the morning paper, he realized that he could no longer see it clearly. Looking at his hands holding the paper, he saw that they were wrinkled.

   _____

   _____

4. Juan goes to his car one morning and discovers an interior light on. He turns the ignition and nothing happens.

   _____

   _____

Using Clues to Infer

As you have seen, in addition to knowledge and experience, we all depend on clues to help us draw inferences. The clues or facts presented in a given situation interact with our knowledge and experiences, thus enabling us to make sense of our surroundings. For example, look at the following photograph, and list at least three characteristics of the person who uses this space as an office. When you are done, proceed to the explanation.

Although you do not know for sure, you can conclude reasonably that this person is disorganized or just has lots of tasks going on at the same time.

It would appear that this person might work through lunch break or late at night because of the banana peel, coffee cups, and snacks strewn around. He or she has to meet deadlines. There is a "To Do List" on the computer and a journal or calendar propped open on the desk. There are files labeled "images or pictures." This might mean that this person works for a newspaper or television station or in another job in which writing, photographs, and deadlines are important. Look at other clues and come up with your own explanation.

As you can see, by using the clues in the photograph in combination with your knowledge and experiences, you were able to infer some things about the person who uses this office. Much like a detective, you pieced together some important information that gave meaning to what you were observing. We all do this kind of exercise very often without even realizing it, and much of the time, our inferences are correct. Obviously, the more clues or facts available in a given situation, the better the chances of our inferences being accurate.

ACTIVITY 3

DIRECTIONS: After reading the excerpt, write down what may be inferred from the discussion statements. Be prepared to discuss your answers in class.

The last hour of Eddie's life was spent, like most of the others, at Ruby Pier, an amusement park by a great gray ocean. The park had the usual attractions, a boardwalk, a Ferris wheel, roller coasters, bumper cars, a taffy stand, and an arcade where you could shoot streams of water into a clown's mouth. It also had a big new ride called Freddy's Free Fall, and this would be where Eddie would be killed, in an accident that would make newspapers around the state.

> At the time of his death, Eddie was a squat, white-haired old man, with a short neck, a barrel chest, thick forearms, and a faded army tattoo on his right shoulder. His legs were thin and veined now, and his left knee, wounded in the war, was ruined by arthritis. He used a cane to get around. His face was broad and craggy from the sun, with salty whiskers and a lower jaw that protruded slightly, making him look prouder than he felt. He kept a cigarette behind his left ear and a ring of keys hooked to his belt. He wore rubber-soled shoes. He wore an old linen cap. His pale brown uniform suggested a workingman, and a workingman he was.
>
> Excerpted from *The Five People You Meet in Heaven* by Mitch Albom,
> Random House (2003), pp. 1–2

Discussion: What do the following phrases suggest to you?

- The title "The Five People You Meet in Heaven"
- "It also had a big new ride called Freddy's Free Fall, and this would be where Eddie would be killed, in an accident"
- "an amusement park by a great gray ocean"
- "Eddie would be killed, in an accident that would make newspapers around the state"
- "a barrel chest, thick forearms"
- "a faded army tattoo on his right shoulder"
- "a lower jaw that protruded slightly, making him look prouder than he felt"
- "kept a cigarette behind his left ear"
- "ring of keys hooked to his belt. He wore rubber-soled shoes. He wore an old linen cap. His pale brown uniform"
- "and a workingman he was"

ACTIVITY 4

DIRECTIONS: *Read and think critically about the words to the Lee Ann Womack song "I Hope You Dance," which were found on the Internet (http://lyrics.astraweb.com). Use your inference skills to answer the questions that follow.*

I Hope You Dance

LEE ANN WOMACK

WORDS AND MUSIC BY TIA SILLERS AND MARK SANDERS

I hope you never lose your sense of wonder,
You get your fill to eat but always keep that hunger,
May you never take one single breath for granted,
God forbid love ever leave you empty handed,
I hope you still feel small when you stand beside the ocean,
Whenever one door closes I hope one more opens,

Promise me that you'll give faith a fighting chance,
And when you get the choice to sit it out or dance

I hope you dance. I hope you dance.
I hope you never fear those mountains in the distance,
Never settle for the path of least resistance,
Livin' might mean takin' chances but they're worth takin',
Lovin' might be a mistake but it's worth makin',
Don't let some hell bent heart leave you bitter,
When you come close to sellin' out reconsider,
Give the heavens above more than just a passing glance,
And when you get the choice to sit it out or dance

I hope you dance. I hope you dance.
I hope you dance. I hope you dance.
(Time is a wheel in constant motion always rolling us along,
Tell me who wants to look back on their years and wonder where
those years have gone.)

I hope you still feel small when you stand beside the ocean,
Whenever one door closes I hope one more opens,
Promise me that you'll give faith a fighting chance,
And when you get the choice to sit it out or dance

Dance. I hope you dance.
I hope you dance. I hope you dance.
I hope you dance. I hope you dance.
(Time is a wheel in constant motion always rolling us along,
Tell me who wants to look back on their years and wonder where
those years have gone.)

QUESTIONS

1. In your view, to whom is the song being sung? Why?
2. Write your interpretation of the lines listed below:
   a. "I hope you never lose your sense of wonder"
   b. "You get your fill to eat but always keep that hunger"
   c. "I hope you still feel small when you stand beside the ocean"
   d. "Whenever one door closes I hope one more opens"
   e. "I hope you never fear those mountains in the distance"
   f. "Never settle for the path of least resistance"

g. "When you come close to sellin' out reconsider"
h. "Give the heavens above more than just a passing glance"
i. "And when you get the choice to sit it out or dance I hope you dance. I hope you dance."

Using Critical Thinking Skills to Infer: The Internet

Much of what we read comes via the Internet in e-mails and Web sites. It is important to take time and think critically about these sources of information. It is important to learn to read between the lines and be critical of Internet sources. E-mails can contain scams or take advantage of the reader. Web sites can contain inaccurate and unreliable information. Advertisements on the Internet can be misleading. The following examples illustrate some of the danger areas when using Internet materials.

- **E-mail:** The e-mail below is an example of those sent to numerous e-mail accounts to solicit assistance. What can you infer from the facts of this e-mail?

From: Thomas Fike
Sent: Saturday, October 07, 2010 9:29 AM
To: gsbruce@aol.com
Subject: Work at home via Internet and make from $500.00 a week.

Hello,

A large European wholesale company is looking for representatives in USA. This job will let you make from $500.00 a week.

Your duties will include receiving payments from our customers and sending the money to our company via Western Union or Money Gram. You will need to establish a banking account with one of the USA banks or to use your personal bank account.

If you are interested in our job offer please send us the following information to inowest_com@yahoo.co.uk.

- your full name
- your email
- contact phone number
- references (if available)
- your account number

Thank you.

If you have any job related questions please email us at lidoberg@yahoo.uk.

Yours sincerely,
Thomas Fike
lidoberg@yahoo.uk

This e-mail implies that if the reader provides an account number, the reader will get lots of money deposited into the account each week. These types of e-mails are misleading and can lead to identity theft.

- **Web site:** The following Web article was created for an online newspaper called *The Onion*. What is the article on video games implying? Are the facts accurate, and how can you determine this?

Video-Game Violence Blamed In Giant-Robot Shooting Spree

1   Old Murakumo Dome, Mars—A concerned parents' group is blaming a tragic shooting in the Martian Colonies on "excessive and reprehensible video-game violence."

2   Parents Against Robot-On-Robot Violence (PARORV) is calling for a ban on the giant-robot-themed PlayStation 2 game "Armored Core 2," which the group claims inspired a 17-year-old giant robot's Feb. 22 slaying of 13 giant robots and himself.

3   According to Martian authorities, the young assailant was obsessed with the violent game.

4   "From what we've seen, this appears to be a case of a giant robot who, through excessive exposure to giant-robot-battle video-game scenarios, lost the ability to distinguish fantasy from reality," PARORV spokeswoman Marianna Cutchek said.

5   The giant robot, a heavily armored high-end Zio Matrix AC, became addicted to the video game over the past year. Described by neighbors as "quiet" and "sullen," he played "Armored Core 2" for upwards of nine Martian hours a day, avoiding contact with other giant robots his own age and becoming progressively more withdrawn.

6   Despite the presence of warning signs, no one could have anticipated what happened at 3:12 P.M. Martian Standard Time, when the robot, armed to the teeth with the latest in giant-robot assault-weapons technology, entered the Old Murakumo Dome, a remnant of the first terraforming. Upon entering, the troubled young robot opened fire on a random crowd of giant robots before turning his continuous-fire high-energy weapon on himself.

7   "There's no way this robot could have learned that much about the effective attack patterns for dual shoulder-mounted plasma cannons on his own," said XJC-46398B, bereaved mother of one of the victims. "He had practice, either in the split-screen versus mode or in one of more than 30 separate solo mission levels."

8   Sony, maker of the PlayStation 2, denied culpability.

9   "You can't blame something like this on a game," Sony spokesman Mitsuko Yamaguchi said. "Sure, it's easy to point the finger at a convenient scapegoat, but what about the real questions: Where did this robot acquire enough credits to outfit his AC

with such heavy hardware in the first place? Why didn't the AC's high-AP head unit's onboard computer facilities receive counseling before it was too late? And, of course, any time a robot goes berserk, it has to be asked: Where were the manufacturers?"

10   The tragedy has prompted many within the giant-robot community to call for increased regulation of fighting-robot-themed video games. It is the latest in a string of controversies for the embattled entertainment industry, which is reeling from charges that the popular TV show *BattleBots*, in which remote-controlled robot fighters battle "to the death" in an arena-like setting, glamorizes robot-on-robot violence.

From *The Onion*, February 28, 2001. Reprintd with permission of THE ONION, Copyright © 2001, by ONION, INC. www.the onion.com

This Web site article is claiming that a PlayStation game was responsible for violence among robots in a colony on Mars. The setting, characters, and plot are entirely fictitious and very entertaining.

ACTIVITY 5

Directions: Read and think critically about the following examples. What do they imply, and why must you be careful of the message? Discuss your thoughts with your classmates.

- **Internet advertisement:** Advertisements are often part of a legitimate Web site, such as a site for *The New York Times, USA Today, The Washington Post, Time Magazine,* and *Newsweek.* What inferences do you make from the advertisements on the screen? Why must you be careful of the messages?

usatoday.com, September 11, 2010. Reprinted with permission.

- **E-mail solicitation:** This e-mail was sent before the Christmas holidays. What can you infer from the message?

From: Les Coriyn@aol.ru
Sent: Tuesday, December 26, 2010 10:22 AM
To: undisclosed-recipients
Subject: I wish you a Merry Christmas

Dear Friends,

Please excuse me for this letter.

My name is Les. I'm student and I live with my mother in a small town Bayres, Russia. My mother cannot see and she receive pension very rare which is not enough even for medications.

I work very hard every day to be able to buy necessities for my mother, but my salary is very small, because my studies still not finished.

Due to problems stoped gas in our district and now we cannot heat our home. The winter is coming and the temperature becomes colder each day. I am very afraid that the temperature inside our home will become very cold and we will not be able to survive.

Therefore I finded several e-mail addresses and thank to the free internet access in our local library I decided to appeal to you with prayer in my heart for small help.

If you have any old sleping bag, warm blanket, electric heater, warm clothes and shoes, canned and dried food, vitamins, medicines from cold, I will be very grateful to you if you could send it to our postal address which is:

Les Coriyn
B-216 M Street
Bayres 2085
Russia

From all my heart I wish you a Merry Christmas and a Happy New Year. I wish that the New Year will bring hapiness in your family and all your dreams come true.

Les and my mother Elena.
E-mail: Les.Coriyn@aol.ru

- **Internet example:** Find an example from the Internet that implies something in a way so as to mislead the reader. Be prepared to share the example with your classmates and explain the inference and its implications for the reader.

Using Figurative Language Clues to Infer

In many types of writing, the author uses **figurative language** such as similes and metaphors to suggest meaning. The following table defines figures

Simile	A direct comparison using the word "like"	The river is like glass.
Metaphor	An indirect comparison	The river is glass.
Hyperbole (Overstatement)	Use of words to make a stronger point	The basset hound dug a hole to China.
Idiom	Words that do not translate literally, but their meanings have generally become part of American conversation	It is raining cats and dogs.

of speech and gives examples. Do you see how such language is used to paint a vivid picture so that the reader can infer meaning?

What do the example sentences mean?

- Simile: The river is like glass. (The river is calm.)
- Metaphor: The river is glass. (The river is calm.)
- Hyperbole: The basset hound dug a hole to China. (The dog dug a very deep hole.)
- Idiom: It is raining cats and dogs. (It is raining very hard.)

ACTIVITY 6

DIRECTIONS: *Write what you think these figurative-language statements imply, and identify the type of figure of speech used.*

1. The course was a bear.

_____

2. My brother sleeps like a log.

_____

3. I've told you a million times to clean your room!

_____

4. The noisy roommate was getting on my nerves.

_____

ACTIVITY 7

DIRECTIONS: *Read the following descriptions from the book Memoirs of a Geisha, and identify what figurative language is used.*

In our little fishing village of Yoroido, I lived in what I called a "tipsy house." It stood near a cliff where the wind off the ocean was always blowing. As a child it seemed to me as if the ocean had caught a terrible cold, because it was always wheezing and there would be spells when it let out a huge sneeze—which is to say there was a burst of wind with a tremendous spray. I decided our tiny house must have been offended by the ocean sneezing in its face from time to time, and took to leaning back because it wanted out to get of the way. Probably it would have collapsed if my father hadn't cut a timber from a wretched fishing boat to prop up the eaves, which made the house look like a tipsy old man leaning on his crutch (8).

[Hint: What are the metaphor and simile?]

_____

_____

_____

The first time I saw his pinned sleeve, I couldn't help averting my eyes in alarm. I'd never before seen anyone who'd lost a limb—though when I was a little girl, an assistant of Mr. Tanaka's had lost the tip of his finger one morning while cleaning a fish. In Nobu's case, many people felt his arm to be the least of his problems, because his skin was like an enormous wound. It's hard to describe the way he looked, and probably it would be cruel for me to try. I'll just repeat what I overheard another geisha say about him once: "Every time I look at his face, I think of a sweet potato that has blistered in the fire (233)."

[Hint: What are the metaphor and simile?]

_____

_____

_____

From Golden Arthur, _Memoirs of a Geisha_, Vintage Books, (1997), pp. 8 and 233

■ Looking at the World with a Questioning Mind

In Chapter 4, we noted that critical thinking involves asking questions, persistence in trying to find answers, and coming to logical conclusions that are based on sound reasoning and the information or evidence that has been gathered. In other words, to be a critical thinker, you must always be inquisitive about what is going on around you and constantly seeking answers. This in turn sometimes involves filling in the gaps by using your knowledge, experience, and the clues that are present to come to logical conclusions.

Now you see the connection between inferences and critical thinking, because in most instances in order to infer you must first question and then think carefully about what you see, hear, or read. Most of the time, no one is going to supply you with questions, so it is up to you to look at the world with a questioning mind. Then you must evaluate the information gathered to determine if you can answer your questions. It is at this point that you decide whether it is necessary to use inferences to help you.

■ Using Inferences with Contemporary Issues and Problem Solving

When we read critically, it is often necessary to "read between the lines" by using inferences to fill in the gaps. We have already reviewed the importance of understanding a writer's stated and unstated messages in Chapter 2 when we talked about main ideas and central messages. As already mentioned, you will be introduced to facts/opinions, purpose, and tone later on in this textbook.

In Chapter 4, when dealing with contemporary issues, you used inferences at times to help uncover unstated secondary issues, opposing viewpoints, and the rationale for those viewpoints. For example, for Selection 4, "Shot in the Arm," you not only had to infer the secondary issue involving how patients are treated by doctors but also had to supply reasons for one of the opposing viewpoints regarding why doctors often charge high fees.

Inferences can also be useful in basic problem solving. For instance, in Problem 1 in Activity 4 in Chapter 5, you were advised that because the problem was not stated explicitly, you would have to draw a logical conclusion about what was wrong. In other words, you were asked to use your knowledge, experience, and the facts that were given to infer what was bothering James. After thinking about the situation and discussing it in class, it was decided that one of the most likely possibilities was that James had some kind of substance abuse problem. Problem 2 in the same activity also required that you come to a logical conclusion by inferring from the information given that sexual harassment was the problem that Anita was experiencing.

Finally, in the hypothetical situation for the problem-solving exercise at the beginning of this chapter, you had to be very careful to gather additional information as part of Step 2, *before* trying to infer the nature of your friend's relationship. You could not possibly address the situation with any degree of certainty until completing that important step. Thus you saw the importance of questioning what you observe and the necessity for caution when using inferences.

As you make your way through college, remember to read and think with a questioning mind. This is a very important part of being both a critical reader and a critical thinker! Go beneath the surface, and do not accept information at face value. Use your knowledge, experience, and the clues or facts available to help you draw inferences so that you can fill in some of the gaps and come to logical conclusions. However, remember not to go too far beyond the information presented, because your conclusions may not have a solid foundation, and therefore they could be wrong.

ACTIVITY 8

Directions: Your instructor is going to divide the class into small groups in order to apply the basic method for personal problem solving to the following situation. When discussing the situation in your group, try to figure out what logical conclusion the author came to and what solution he or she decided upon. Your instructor will tell you how the entire episode turned out.

You are in the surgeon's office with your daughter three weeks after he operated successfully on her for a thyroid tumor, and you ask him to recommend an internist because you have a lump on the side of your neck. Dr. Rosin informs you that the neck area is one of his specialties and starts immediately to examine you. After about two minutes, he advises you that one of your salivary glands is swollen. He proceeds to prescribe two antibiotics, schedules an X-ray for you at the hospital to determine if there is a stone in the gland, and sets up another appointment with him in three weeks.

On your return visit, you tell Dr. Rosin that you think the lump changes in size and is smaller at least some of the time. After reexamining you for about three minutes, he declares that the X-ray showed no evidence of a stone, the antibiotics have been ineffectual, and in his opinion the lump has gotten bigger. You ask him if the X-ray showed anything else, and he advises you that he was only testing for a stone. Furthermore, Dr. Rosin warns that either the gland is inflamed or it has a tumor that has a 50-50 chance of being malignant. Even if it is just inflamed, he continues, you will probably wake up one morning in excruciating pain with the lump three times bigger. He adds that he would not wish that kind of pain on his worst enemy.

Dr. Rosin explains further that he could do a needle biopsy in his office to determine if the lump is malignant, but he does not advise doing that because in his opinion those kinds of biopsies usually do not give accurate readings. He urges you to have surgery and explains how the operation will be performed, adding cautiously that he will not know for three days after surgery whether or not the lump is malignant. Finally, Dr. Rosin explains that the chances are high that during surgery, a nerve in your neck will get severed, affecting your lower lip when you smile. However, he assures you that the functioning of your mouth will not be affected. After listening, you tell him that you will have to think about what to do, and he agrees with that course of action. As you are leaving, he concludes by saying that if you decide on the operation, you should schedule it through his office. Otherwise, he would like to see you in about a month.

ACTIVITY 9

Directions: First, read and think critically about the following short story written by Kate Chopin. Then, without looking back at it, summarize and/or paraphrase your ideas. Finally, use your inference skills to determine why the author titled the story "The Storm." Be prepared to discuss your summary and conclusions with your classmates.

The Storm

A Sequel to "The 'Cadian Ball"

KATE CHOPIN

1

1   The leaves were so still that even Bibi thought it was going to rain. Bobinôt, who was accustomed to converse on terms of perfect equality with his little son, called the child's attention to certain sombre clouds that were rolling with sinister intention from the west, accompanied by a sullen, threatening roar. They were at Friedheimer's store and decided to remain there till the storm had passed. They sat within the door on two empty kegs. Bibi was four years old and looked very wise.

2   "Mama'll be 'fraid, yes," he suggested with blinking eyes.

3   "She'll shut the house. Maybe she got Sylvie helpin' her this evenin'," Bobinôt responded reassuringly.

4   "No, she ent got Sylvie. Sylvie was helpin' her yistiday," piped Bibi.

5   Bobinôt arose and going across to the counter purchased a can of shrimps, of which Calixta was very fond. Then he returned to his perch on the keg and sat stolidly holding the can of shrimps while the storm burst. It shook the wooden store and seemed to be ripping great furrows in the distant field. Bibi laid his little hand on his father's knee and was not afraid.

2

6   Calixta, at home, felt no uneasiness for their safety. She sat at a side window sewing furiously on a sewing machine. She was greatly occupied and did not notice the approaching storm. But she felt very warm and often stopped to mop her face on which the perspiration gathered in beads. She unfastened her white sacque at the throat. It began to grow dark, and suddenly realizing the situation, she got up hurriedly and went about closing windows and doors.

7   Out on the small front gallery she had hung Bobinôt's Sunday clothes to air and she hastened out to gather them before the rain fell. As she stepped outside, Alcée Laballière rode in at the gate. She had not seen him very often since her marriage, and never alone. She stood there with Bobinôt's coat in her hands, and the big rain drops began to fall. Alcée rode his horse under the shelter of a side projection where the chickens had huddled and there were plows and a harrow piled up in the corner.

8   "May I come and wait on your gallery till the storm is over, Calixta?" he asked.

9   "Come 'long in, M'sieur Alcée."

10   His voice and her own startled her as if from a trance, and she seized Bobinôt's vest. Alcée, mounting to the porch, grabbed the trousers and snatched Bibi's braided jacket that was about to be carried away by a sudden gust of wind. He expressed an intention to remain outside, but it was soon apparent that he might as well have been out in the open; the water beat in upon the boards in driving sheets, and he went inside, closing the door after him. It was even necessary to put something beneath the door to keep the water out.

11   "My! what a rain! It's good two years sence it rain' like that," exclaimed Calixta as she rolled up a piece of bagging and Alcée helped her to thrust it beneath the crack.

12   She was a little fuller of figure than five years before when she married; but she had lost nothing of her vivacity. Her blue eyes still retained their melting quality; and her yellow hair, dishevelled by the wind and rain, kinked more stubbornly than ever about her ears and temples.

13   The rain beat upon the low, shingled roof with a force and clatter that threatened to break an entrance and deluge them there. They were in the dining room—the sitting room—the general utility room. Adjoining was her bedroom, with Bibi's couch alongside her own. The door stood open, and the room with its white, monumental bed, its closed shutters, looked dim and mysterious.

14   Alcée flung himself into a rocker and Calixta nervously began to gather up from the floor the lengths of a cotton sheet which she had been sewing.

15   "If this keeps up, *Dieu sait* if the levees goin' to stan' it!" she exclaimed.

16   "What have you got to do with the levees?"

17   "I got enough to do! An' there's Bobinôt with Bibi out in that storm—if he only didn't left Friedheimer's!"

18   "Let us hope, Calixta, that Bobinôt's got sense enough to come in out of a cyclone."

19   She went and stood at the window with a greatly disturbed look on her face. She wiped the frame that was clouded with moisture. It was stiflingly hot. Alcée got up and joined her at the window, looking over her shoulder. The rain was coming down in sheets obscuring the view of far-off cabins and enveloping the distant wood in a gray mist. The playing of the lightning was incessant. A bolt struck a tall chinaberry tree at the edge of the field. It filled all visible space with a blinding glare and the crash seemed to invade the very boards they stood upon.

20   Calixta put her hands to her eyes, and with a cry, staggered backward. Alcée's arm encircled her, and for an instant he drew her close and spasmodically to him.

21   "*Bonté!*" she cried, releasing herself from his encircling arm and retreating from the window, "the house'll go next! If I only knew w'ere Bibi was!" She would not compose herself; she would not be seated. Alcée clasped her shoulders and looked into her face. The contact of her warm, palpitating body when he had

unthinkingly drawn her into his arms, had aroused all the old-time infatuation and desire for her flesh.

22   "Calixta," he said, "don't be frightened. Nothing can happen. The house is too low to be stuck, with so many tall trees standing about. There! aren't you going to be quiet? say, aren't you?" He pushed her hair back from her face that was warm and steaming. Her lips were as red and moist as pomegranate seed. Her white neck and a glimpse of her full, firm bosom disturbed him powerfully. As she glanced up at him the fear in her liquid blue eyes had given place to a drowsy gleam that unconsciously betrayed a sensuous desire. He looked down into her eyes and there was nothing for him to do but to gather her lips in a kiss. It reminded him of Assumption.

23   "Do you remember—in Assumption. Calixta?" he asked in a low voice broken by passion. Oh! she remembered; for in Assumption he had kissed her and kissed and kissed her; until his senses would well nigh fail, and to save her he would resort to a desperate flight. If she was not an immaculate dove in those days, she was still inviolate; a passionate creature whose very defenselessness had made her defense, against which his honor forbade him to prevail. Now—well, now—her lips seemed in a manner free to be tasted, as well as her round, white throat and her whiter breasts.

24   They did not heed the crashing torrents, and the roar of the elements made her laugh as she lay in his arms. She was a revelation in that dim, mysterious chamber; as white as the couch she lay upon. Her firm, elastic flesh that was knowing for the first time its birthright, was like a creamy lily that the sun invites to contribute its breath and perfume to the undying life of the world.

25   The generous abundance of her passion, without guile or trickery, was like a white flame which penetrated and found response in depths of his own sensuous nature that had never yet been reached.

26   When he touched her breasts they gave themselves up in quivering ecstasy, inviting his lips. Her mouth was a fountain of delight. And when he possessed her, they seemed to swoon together at the very borderland of life's mystery.

27   He stayed cushioned upon her, breathless, dazed, enervated, with his heart beating like a hammer upon her. With one hand she clasped his head, her lips lightly touching his forehead. The other hand stroked with a soothing rhythm his muscular shoulders.

28   The growl of the thunder was distant and passing away. The rain beat softly upon the shingles, inviting them to drowsiness and sleep. But they dared not yield.

29   The rain was over; and the sun was turning the glistening green world into a palace of gems. Calixta, on the gallery, watched Alcée ride away. He turned and smiled at her with a beaming face; and she lifted her pretty chin in the air and laughed aloud.

3

30   Bobinôt and Bibi, trudging home, stopped at the cistern to make themselves presentable.

31   "My! Bibi, w'at will yo' mama say! You ought to be ashame'. You oughtn' put on those good pants. Look at 'em! An' that mud on yo' collar! How you got that mud on yo' collar, Bibi? I never saw such a boy!" Bibi was the picture of pathetic resignation. Bobinôt was the embodiment of serious solicitude as he strove to remove from his own person and his son's the signs of their tramp over heavy roads and through wet fields. He scraped the mud off Bibi's bare legs and feet with a stick and carefully removed all traces from his heavy brogans. Then, prepared for the worst—the meeting with an over-scrupulous housewife, they entered cautiously at the back door.

32   Calixta was preparing supper. She had set the table and was dripping coffee at the hearth. She sprang up as they came in.

33   "Oh, Bobinôt! You back! My! but I was uneasy. W'ere you been during the rain? An' Bibi? he ain't wet? he ain't hurt?" She had clasped Bibi and was kissing him effusively. Bobinôt's explanations and apologies which he had been composing all along the way, died on his lips as Calixta felt him to see if he were dry, and seemed to express nothing but satisfaction at their safe return.

34   "I brought you some shrimps, Calixta," offered Bobinôt, hauling the can from his ample side pocket and laying it on the table.

35   "Shrimps! Oh, Bobinôt! you too good fo' anything!" and she gave him a smacking kiss on the check that resounded. "*J'vous réponds*, we'll have a feas' tonight! umph-umph!"

36   Bobinôt and Bibi began to relax and enjoy themselves, and when the three seated themselves at table they laughed much and so loud that anyone might have heard them as far away as Laballière's.

4

37   Alcée Laballière wrote to his wife, Clarisse, that night. It was a loving letter, full of tender solicitude. He told her not to hurry back, but if she and the babies liked it at Biloxi, to stay a month longer. He was getting on nicely; and though he missed them, he was willing to bear the separation a while longer—realizing that their health and pleasure were the first things to be considered.

5

38   As for Clarisse, she was charmed upon receiving her husband's letter. She and the babies were doing well. The society was agreeable; many of her old friends and acquaintances were at the bay. And the first free breath since her

marriage seemed to restore the pleasant liberty of her maiden days. Devoted as she was to her husband, their intimate conjugal life was something which she was more than willing to forego for a while.

39   So the storm passed and everyone was happy.

The Complete Works of Kate Chopin. Ed. Per Seyersted. Baton Rouge: Louisiana State UP, 1969.

ACTIVITY 10

DIRECTIONS: Read the following passages, and answer the questions that follow. Continue to use inferences, when needed, to draw logical conclusions.

Eye on Vocabulary

When reading each of the following passages, take note of any unfamiliar words you come across. List them and their definitions in your notebook or on note cards. Use the context, word parts, or the dictionary to determine their meanings.

1

For New-Sport Athletes, High School Finishes 2nd

MATT HIGGINS

1   In a sport skewing younger every year, Ryan Sheckler was one of the youngest professional skateboarders ever. By eighth grade, he had defeated competitors twice his age and won several contests, including the 2003 X Games skateboard park event on national television.

2   Immortalized as a character in a best-selling video game franchise and in movies, Sheckler wanted a role that many teenage skateboarding stars repudiate: that of a regular student, in his case, at San Clemente (Calif.) High School.

3   "I wanted to see what high school was all about," Sheckler said in an e-mail message. "I wanted to be with my friends and go to the dances and football games."

4   Two years ago this month, he began his freshman year. He wrestled in the 103-pound weight class, and hung out with friends in the cafeteria. But after returning from a skateboarding trip to Australia in February 2005, he realized that as he sat in history class, his future was inexorably rolling away.

5   "It was a good experience, but it was a disaster," his mother said of high school. "He was out of circulation for six months, out of the magazines. It hurt his career."

6   As salaries soar and sponsors stoop to sign younger talent, Sheckler's situation has become increasingly common across action sports like skateboarding,

snowboarding, surfing and motocross. For those who do not drop out of school altogether, the approach to education has been somewhat similar to what young athletes in sports like tennis and figure skating have established: home schooling, independent study and sports academies.

7   "As athletes get younger and these sports get more competitive, you have to stay in the game," said Circe Wallace, a retired snowboarder turned action sports agent. "I've been in this business 15 years, and it's always been those with parents that understand the freedom and flexibility of home schooling that go the furthest."

8   On the East Coast, some surfers have turned to home schooling. Young surfers must travel to California, Hawaii, and Australia to prove themselves on better waves. Because mounting absences threaten to wipe out the academic year, home schooling becomes an attractive option.

9   In motocross, where a 13-year old can earn more than $100,000 annually, 90% of minors are either home schooled or drop out of school, according to Jimmy Button, a professional racer who is now an agent.

10   Button said the prevailing mentality in motocross, like skateboarding, did not place a priority on school. "A lot of parents aren't worried about missing education," he said. "They just want their kid to ride as fast as possible."

11   Sheckler skateboards daily. He travels frequently for contests and appearances, such as a trip to New York recently to be the host of a party coinciding with MTV's Video Music Awards. All of this leaves little time for six-hour school days and homework.

12   Although the Shecklers would not discuss his earnings, Ryan's sponsors include the apparel maker Volcom, Red Bull, the cell phone service Amp'd Mobile and Etnies, with whom he has a signature sneaker. And last year prize money from contests alone exceeded six figures. Still, Gretchen Sheckler, who has a bachelor's degree in finance, was determined that her son would finish high school.

13   So in 2005 Ryan Sheckler enrolled in another school near his home, the private Futures-Halstrom High in Mission Viejo, where he began his junior year last week.

14   "I quit my career to start managing his," Gretchen Sheckler said. "I said, 'I'll do this for you if you get your high school diploma.'"

15   Each week, Sheckler works with teachers for 45 minutes per subject. He completes assignments on his own time, and earns school credit for work experience. Skateboarding serves as a surrogate for gym. Philanthropic and media engagements count. And so does travel to Spain, the Czech Republic and the United Arab Emirates.

16   Since leaving traditional school, Sheckler's grades have improved, he said. He is featured again in skateboarding magazines. And he won the Dew Action Sports Tour's skateboard park championship in 2005.

17   Gretchen Sheckler said academics have kept her son grounded. "Their lives are so jaded," she said of professional skateboarders. "They don't have normal real world experience. He has to have those real world experiences and persever-ance for eight months of class to make it through geometry or algebra."

18   Yet, according to his mother, Ryan is a normal high school student in at least one respect. When it comes to homework, she said, "He waits till the last minute."

COMPREHENSION QUESTIONS

1. What is the topic of the passage?
2. What is the central message of the passage?
3. Determine what is at issue. What is your initial personal viewpoint?
4. Distinguish among opposing viewpoints, and provide the rationale for each.
5. Think carefully about the viewpoints. Express a personal viewpoint, and give the reasons why you favor it. Does it differ from your initial personal viewpoint? Why or why not?
6. Write a few paragraphs *in support of the viewpoint that you do* not *favor.*

THOUGHT AND DISCUSSION QUESTIONS

1. Would you ever consider home schooling for your children? Why or why not?
2. What can you infer about the author's viewpoint of home schooling for athletes? Show where you found evidence in this piece to support your answer.
3. How do you interpret Gretchen Sheckler's comment, "Their lives are so jaded" in the next to the last paragraph.
4. What is your opinion of college sports athletes who leave college because they are drafted into professional sports? Support your viewpoint with an example.
5. List any questions that came to mind while you were reading this selection, and be prepared to discuss possible answers to them.

2

Using E-Mail

1   E-mail is an important and growing online marketing tool. A recent study of ad, brand, and marketing managers found that nearly half of all the companies surveyed use e-mail marketing to reach customers. U.S. companies currently spend

about $1.5 billion a year on e-mail marketing, up from just $164 million in 1999. And this spending will grow by an estimated 20 percent annually through 2011.

2   But there's a dark side to the growing use of e-mail marketing. The explosion of **spam**—unsolicited, unwanted commercial e-mail messages that clog up our e-mailboxes—has produced consumer irritation and frustration. According to one research company, spam now accounts for 88 percent of all e-mail sent. A recent study found that the average consumer received 3,253 spam messages last year. E-mail marketers walk a fine line between adding value for consumers and being intrusive.

3   To address these concerns, most legitimate marketers now practice *permission-based e-mail marketing*, sending e-mail pitches only to customers who "opt in." Financial services firms such as Charles Schwab use configurable e-mail systems that let customers choose what they want to get. Others, such as Yahoo! or Amazon.com, include long lists of opt-in boxes for different categories of marketing material. Amazon.com targets opt-in customers with a limited number of helpful "we thought you'd like to know" messages based on their expressed preferences and previous purchases. Few customers object and many actually welcome such promotional messages.

4   When used properly, e-mail can be the ultimate direct marketing medium. Blue-chip marketers such as Amazon.com, Dell, L.L.Bean, Office Depot, Schwab, and others use it regularly, and with great success. E-mail lets these marketers send highly targeted, tightly personalized, relationship-building messages to consumers who actually *want* to receive them.

Gary Armstrong and Philip Kotler, Marketing: An Introduction, 9th ed., p. 348, © 2009.
Reprinted by permission of Pearson Education, Inc., Upper Saddle River, New Jersey.

COMPREHENSION QUESTIONS

1. What is the topic of the passage?
2. What is the central message of Paragraph 1? Paragraph 2? Paragraph 3?
3. Determine what is at issue. What is your initial personal viewpoint?
4. What is the problem, and what is the solution in this passage?
5. Think carefully about the viewpoints in this passage. Express a personal viewpoint, and give the reasons why you favor it. Does it differ from your initial personal viewpoint? Why or why not?
6. Write a few paragraphs about your recent experiences with "spam." What kind of things convince you that the e-mails are not legitimate?

THOUGHT AND DISCUSSION QUESTIONS

1. Is it safe to conclude that the passage is credible and can be verified with other resources? Why or why not?
2. In your view, does the author present a neutral approach to e-mail marketing? Why or why not?

3. Give an example of a problem e-mail that you received. Be specific about why this e-mail was problematic.
4. Can you infer from this article that the author believes that e-mail marketing is a good marketing strategy? Why or why not?
5. List all the ways you personally use e-mail in your life.

3

The Hold-'Em Holdup

MATTATHIAS SCHWARTZ

1   Greg Hogan Jr. was on tilt. For months now, Hogan, a 19-year-old Lehigh University sophomore, had been on tilt, and he would remain on tilt for weeks to come. Alone at the computer, usually near the end of one of his long online gambling sessions, the thought "I'm on tilt" would occur to him. Dude, he'd tell himself, you gotta stop. These thoughts sounded the way a distant fire alarm sounds in the middle of a warm bath. He would ignore them and go back to playing poker. "The side of me that said, 'Just one more hand,' was the side that always won," he told me months later. "I couldn't get away from it, not until all my money was gone." In a little more than a year, he had lost $7,500 playing poker online.

2   "Tilt" is the poker term for a spell of insanity that often follows a run of bad luck. The tilter goes berserk, blindly betting away whatever capital he has left in an attempt to recoup his losses. Severe tilt can spill over past the poker table, resulting in reputations, careers and marriages being tossed away like so many chips. This is the kind of tilt Hogan had, tilt so indiscriminate that one Friday afternoon this past December, while on his way to see "The Chronicles of Narnia" with two of his closest friends, he cast aside the Greg Hogan everyone knew—class president, chaplain's assistant, son of a Baptist minister—and became Greg Hogan, the bank robber.

3   On Dec. 9, 2005, Hogan went to see "Narnia" with Kip Wallen, Lehigh's student-senate president, and Matt Montgomery, Hogan's best friend, in Wallen's black Ford Explorer. Hogan, who was sitting in front, asked Wallen to find a bank so he could cash a check, and Wallen pulled over at a small, oatmeal-colored Wachovia. Inside, Hogan paused at the counter for a moment and then joined the line. He handed the teller a note that said he had a gun, which was a bluff. "Are you kidding?" her face seemed to say. He did his best to look as if he weren't. With agonizing slowness, she began assembling the money. Moments later, a thin sheaf of bills appeared in the tray: $2,871. Hogan stuffed it into his backpack, turned around and walked back out to the car.

4   Wallen drove on to the theater, unaware of what had just happened. The three friends were soon settling into 135 minutes of "Narnia." Hogan found he

couldn't concentrate on the movie. He was certain that he'd seen someone writing down the license of Wallen's Explorer outside the bank. He wondered what his father's congregation back in Barberton, Ohio, would say when they heard what had become of their pastor's eldest son.

5   The movie ended, and the trio returned to campus. Hogan went immediately to Sigma Phi Epsilon, his fraternity, and used some of the stolen money to pay back brothers who had lent him hundreds of dollars. He then joined a few friends at an off-campus pizzeria for dinner. Someone's cell phone rang, with the news that police had stormed the Sig Ep house. No one knew why. Hogan stayed silent. After dinner, his friends dropped him off at orchestra practice. Allentown police officers were waiting for him. They handcuffed him and took him to headquarters, where he confessed almost immediately.

6   Hogan's first call was to his parents back home in Ohio. They had just finished eating dinner at T.G.I. Friday's. "He was at the end of himself," Greg Hogan, Sr. told me. "He couldn't believe he had done it. Not that he was denying anything, but he felt like he was watching another person's life."

7   To wired college students today, Internet gambling is as familiar as beer, late-night pizza and the Saturday night hook-up. Poker—particularly Texas hold 'em—is the game of choice. Freshmen arrive already schooled by ESPN in the legend of Chris Moneymaker, the dough-faced 27-year-old accountant who deposited $40 into his PokerStars.com account and parlayed it into a $2.5 million win at the World Series of Poker in Las Vegas. Throughout the dorms and computer labs and the back rows of 100-level lecture halls you can hear the crisp *wsshhp, wsshhp, wsshhp* of electronic hands being dealt as more than $2 billion in untaxed revenue is sucked into overseas accounts each year.

8   Researchers say that Internet poker is addictive. Players say that it's addictive. The federal government says that it's illegal. But colleges have done little to stop its spread on campus. Administrators who would never consider letting Budweiser install taps in dorm rooms have made high-speed Internet access a standard amenity, putting every student with a credit card minutes away from 24-hour high-stakes gambling. Online casinos advertise heavily on sites directed at college students like CollegeHumor.com, where students post pictures of themselves playing online poker during lectures with captions like: "Gambling while in class. Who doesn't think that wireless Internet is the greatest invention ever?" Some schools have allowed sites to establish a physical on-campus presence by sponsoring live cash tournaments; the sites partner with fraternities and sports teams, even give away a semester's tuition, all as inducements to convert the casual dorm-lounge poker player to a steady online customer. An unregulated network of offshore businesses has been given unfettered access to students, and the students have been given every possible accommodation to bet and lose to their heart's content. Never before have the means to lose so much been so available to so many at such a young age.

9   An estimated 1.6 million of 17 million U.S. college students gambled online last year, mostly on poker. According to a study by the Annenberg Public Policy Center, the number of college males who reported gambling online once a week or more quadrupled in the last year alone. "The kids really think they can log on and become the next world champion," says Jeffrey Derevensky, who studies youth problem gambling at McGill University in Montreal. "This is an enormous social experiment. We don't really know what's going to happen."

10   Greg Hogan is far from the only college student to see the game's role in his life grow from a hobby to a destructive obsession. Researchers from the University of Connecticut Health Center interviewed a random sample of 880 college students and found that 1 out of every 4 of the 160 or so online gamblers in the study fit the clinical definition of a pathological gambler, suggesting that college online-poker addicts may number in the hundreds of thousands. Many, like Lauren Patrizi, a 21-year-old senior at Loyola University in Chicago, have had weeks when they're playing poker during most of their waking hours. Rarely leaving their rooms, they take their laptops with them to bed, fall asleep each night in the middle of a hand and think, talk and dream nothing but poker. By the time Patrizi finally quit, the game seemed to be both the cause of all her problems and her only means of escaping them. "I kept on playing so I wouldn't have to look at what poker had done to my bank account, my relationships, my life," she told me.

11   In its outline, Hogan's story closely resembles that of the stereotypical compulsive gambler. Before the rise of online poker, however, such a story typically involved a man in his 30's or 40's and took a decade or more to run its course. Greg Hogan, on the other hand, went from class president to bank robber in 16 months. His fall took place not at the blackjack table or the track but within the familiar privacy of his computer screen, where he was seldom more than a minute away from his next hand of poker. He'd been brought up too well to waste himself in some smoky gambling den and knew too much to play a mere game of chance. He wanted to compete against his peers, to see his superior abilities yield dollars for the first time, a transaction he equated with adulthood. His stubborn faith in his own ability—a trait that had served him so well through his first 19 years—proved to be his undoing.

Excerpted from: http://www.nytimes.com/2006/06/11/magazine/
11poker.html?ex=1176091200&en=f249285799039283&ei=5070,
Mattathias Schwartz, The Hold-'Em Holdup, *The New York Times Magazine*, June 11, 2006

COMPREHENSION QUESTIONS

1. What is the topic of the passage?
2. What is the central message of the passage?
3. Determine what is at issue. What is your initial personal viewpoint?
4. What would be the opposing viewpoint and its rationale?

5. Express a personal viewpoint, and give the reasons why you favor it. Does it differ from your initial personal viewpoint? Why or why not?

6. Write a few paragraphs *in support of the viewpoint that you do* not *favor.*

THOUGHT AND DISCUSSION QUESTIONS

1. What is your experience as a college student with online gambling? What is your viewpoint on this issue?

2. How do you interpret the statement, "The kids really think they can log on and become the next world champion"?

3. In your opinion, what can colleges do to discourage online gambling?

4. What can you infer from the statement, "This is an enormous social experiment"?

5. List any questions that came to mind while you were reading this selection, and be prepared to discuss possible answers to them.

4

Body Piercing and Tattooing: Risks to Health

1   One look around college campuses and other enclaves for young people reveals a trend that, while not necessarily new, has been growing in recent years. We're talking, of course, about body piercing and tattooing, also referred to as forms of "body art." For decades, tattoos appeared to be the sole propriety of bikers, military guys, and general roughnecks; and in many people's eyes, they represented the rougher, seedier part of society. Body piercing, on the other hand, was virtually nonexistent in our culture except for pierced ears, which didn't really appear until the latter part of the twentieth century. Even then, pierced ears were limited, for the most part, to women. Various forms of body embellishment, or body art, however, can be traced throughout human history when people "dressed themselves up" to attract attention or be viewed as acceptable by their peers. Examinations of cultures throughout the world, both historic and contemporary, provide evidence of the use of body art as a medium of self- and cultural expression. Ancient cultures often used body piercing as a mark of royalty or elitism. Egyptian pharaohs underwent rites of passage by piercing their navels. Roman soldiers demonstrated manhood by piercing their nipples.

2   But why the surge in popularity in current society, particularly among young people? Today, young and old alike are getting their ears and bodies pierced in record numbers, in such places as the eyebrows, tongues, lips, noses, navels, nipples, genitals, and just about any place possible. Many people view the trend as

a fulfillment of a desire for self-expression, as this University of Wisconsin-Madison student points out:

"... The nipple [ring] was one of those things that I did as a kind of empowerment, claiming my body as my own and refuting the stereotypes that people have about me.... The tattoo was kind of a lark and came along the same lines and I like it too.... [they] both give me a secret smile."

3   Whatever the reason, tattoo artists are doing a booming business in both their traditional artistry of tattooing as well as in the "art" of body piercing. Amidst the "oohing" and "aahing" over the latest artistic additions, however, the concerns over health risks from these procedures have been largely ignored. Despite the warnings from local health officials and federal agencies, the popularity of piercings and tattoos has grown.

4   The most common health-related problems associated with tattoos and body piercing include skin reactions, infections, and scarring. The average healing times for piercings depend on the size of the insert, location, and the person's overall health. Facial and tongue piercings tend to heal more quickly than piercings of areas not commonly exposed to open air or light and which are often teeming with bacteria, such as the genitals. Because the hands are great germ transmitters, "fingering" of pierced areas poses a significant risk for infection.

5   Of greater concern, however, is the potential transmission of dangerous pathogens that any puncture of the human body exacerbates. The use of unsterile needles—which can cause serious infections and can transmit HIV, hepatitis B and C, tetanus, and a host of other diseases—poses a very real risk. Body piercing and tattooing are performed by body artists, unlicensed "professionals" who generally have learned their trade from other body artists. Laws and policies regulating body piercing and tattooing vary greatly by state. While some states don't allow tattoo and body-piercing parlors, others may regulate them carefully, and still others provide few regulations and standards by which parlors have to abide. Standards for safety usually include minimum age of use, standards of sanitation, use of aseptic techniques, sterilization of equipment, informed risks, instructions for skin care, record keeping, and recommendations for dealing with adverse reactions. Because of the varying degree of standards regulating this business and the potential for transmission of dangerous pathogens, anyone who receives a tattoo, body piercing, or permanent make-up tattoo cannot donate blood for one year.

6   Anyone who does opt for tattooing or body piercing should remember the following:

- Look for clean, well-lit work areas, and ask about sterilization procedures.
- Before having the work done, watch the artist at work. Tattoo removal is expensive and often undoable. Make sure the tattoo is one you can live with.

- Right before piercing or tattooing, the body area should be carefully sterilized and the artist should wear new latex gloves and touch nothing else while working.
- Packaged, sterilized needles should be used only once and then discarded. A piercing gun should not be used because it cannot be sterilized properly.
- Only jewelry made of noncorrosive metal, such as surgical stainless steel, niobium, or solid 14-karat gold, is safe for new piercing.
- Leftover tattoo ink should be discarded after each procedure.
- If any signs of pus, swelling, redness, or discoloration persist, remove the piercing object and contact a physician.

Rebecca J. Donatelle, *Health: The Basics*, 4th ed., pp. 322–323, © 2001. Reprinted by permission of Pearson Education, Inc., Upper Saddle River, New Jersey.

COMPREHENSION QUESTIONS

1. What is the topic of the passage?
2. What is the central message of the passage?
3. Determine what is at issue. What is your initial personal viewpoint?
4. Distinguish among opposing viewpoints, and provide the rationale for each.
5. Think carefully about the viewpoints. Express a personal viewpoint, and give the reasons why you favor it. Does it differ from your initial personal viewpoint? Why or why not?
6. Write a few paragraphs *in support of the viewpoint that you do* not *favor.*

THOUGHT AND DISCUSSION QUESTIONS

1. What does the author mean by "'oohing' and 'aahing' over the latest artistic additions"?
2. In your view, why have tattoos and body piercings become popular among young people? Do you agree with those who assert that it is done only for purposes of showing off? Why or why not?
3. If you had a 13-year-old son, would you permit him to be pierced or tattooed? Why or why not? If you had a 13-year-old daughter, would you permit her to be pierced or tattooed? Why or why not? If your answers to the two questions above are different, explain why.
4. Is it safe to conclude that the author is opposed to tattoos and body piercing? Why or why not?
5. List any questions that came to mind while you were reading this selection, and be prepared to discuss possible answers to them.

5

Quick, What's a Good Price?

1   It's Saturday morning and you stop by your local supermarket to pick up a few items for tonight's backyard barbeque. Cruising the aisles, you're bombarded with price signs, all suggesting that you just can't beat this store's deals. A 10-pound bag of Kingsford Charcoal Briquettes goes for only $3.99 with your frequent shopper card ($4.39 without the card). Cans of Van Camps Pork & Beans are 4 for $1.00 (4 for $2.16 without the card). An aisle display hawks big bags of UTX potato chips at an "everyday low price" of just $1.99. And a sign atop a huge mass of Coke 12-packs advertises 2 for $7.

2   These sure look like good prices, but *are* they? If you're like most shoppers, you don't really know. In a recent *Harvard Business Review* article, two pricing researchers conclude, "for most of the items they buy, consumers don't have an accurate sense of what the price should be." In fact, customers often don't even know what prices they're actually paying. In one recent study, researchers asked supermarket shoppers the price of an item just as they were putting it into their shopping carts. Less than half the shoppers gave the right answer.

3   To know for sure if you're paying the best price, you'd have to compare the marked price with past prices, prices of competing brands, and prices in other stores. For most purchases, consumers just don't bother. Instead, they rely on a most unlikely source. "Remarkable...they rely on the retailer to tell them if they're getting a good price," say the researchers. "In subtle and not-so-subtle ways, retailers send signals to customers, telling them whether a given price is relatively high or low." In their article, the researchers outline the following common retailer pricing cues.

4   • **Sale Signs.** The most straightforward retail pricing cue is a sale sign. It might take any of several familiar forms: "Sale!" "Reduced!" "New low price!" "Price after rebate!" or "Now 2 for only...!" Such signs can be very effective in signaling low prices to consumers and increasing sales for the retailer.

5   While sales signs can be effective, overuse or misuse can damage both the seller's credibility and its sales. Unfortunately, some retailers do not always use such signs truthfully. Still, consumers trust sale signs. Why? "Because they are accurate most of the time," say the researchers. "And besides, customers are not that easily fooled." They quickly become suspicious when the sale signs are used improperly.

6   • **Prices Ending in 9.** Just like a sale sign, a 9 at the end of a price often signals a bargain. You see such prices everywhere. For example, browse the Web sites of discounters such as Target, Best Buy, or PetsMart: it's almost impossible to find even one price that doesn't end in 9! "In fact, this pricing tactic is so common," say the researchers, "you'd think customers would

ignore it. Think again. Response to this pricing cue is remarkable." Normally you'd expect that demand for an item would fall as the price goes up. Yet in one study involving women's clothing, raising the price of a dress from $34 to $39 increased demand by a third. By comparison, raising the price from $34 to $44 yielded no difference in demand.

7   But are prices ending in 9 accurate as pricing cues? "The answer varies," report the researchers. "Some retailers do reserve prices that end in 9 for their discounted items. For instance, J. Crew and Ralph Lauren generally use 00-cent endings on regularly priced merchandise and 99-cent endings on discounted items. Comparisons of prices at major department stores reveal that this is common, particularly for apparel. But at some stores, prices that end in 9 are a miscue—they are used on all products regardless of whether the items are discounted."

8   • **Signpost Pricing (or Loss-Leader Pricing).** Signpost pricing is used on fre-quently purchased products about which consumers tend to have accurate price knowledge. For example, you probably know a good price on a 12-pack of Coke when you see one. New parents usually know how much they should expect to pay for disposable diapers.

9   Retailers offer selected signpost items at or below cost to pull customers into the store, hoping to make money on the shopper's other purchases. For instance, Best Buy often sells recently released DVDs at several dollars below wholesale price. Customers get a really good deal. And although Best Buy loses money on every DVD sold, the low DVD prices increase store traffic and purchases of higher-margin complementary products, such as DVD players.

10   • **Pricing-Matching Guarantees.** In price matching, stores promise to meet or beat any competitor's price. Best Buy, for example, says "we'll meet or beat any local competitor's price, guaranteed!" If you find a better price within 30 days on something you bought at Best Buy, the retailer will refund the difference plus 10 percent.

11   Evidence suggests that customers perceive that stores offering price-matching guarantees have overall lower prices than competing stores. But are such perceptions accurate? "The evidence is mixed," say the researchers. Consumers can usually be confident that they'll pay the lowest price on eligi-ble items. However, some manufacturers make it hard to take advantage of price-matching policies by introducing "branded variants"—slightly different versions of products with different model numbers for different retailers. Some pricing experts argue that price-matching policies are not really tar-geted at customers. Rather, they may serve as a warning to competitors: "If you cut your prices, we will, too." If this is true, price-matching policies might actually reduce price competition, leading to higher overall prices.

Watch Your Pricing Cues!

12   Used properly, pricing cues can help consumers. Used improperly, however, these pricing cues can mislead consumers, tarnishing a brand and damaging customer relationships.

13   The researchers conclude: "Customers need price information just as they need products. They look to retailers to provide both. Retailers must manage pricing cues in the same way that they manage quality. No retailer who values customers would deceive them with inaccurate pricing cues. By reliably signaling which prices are low, companies can retain customers' trust—and build more solid relationships."

Philip Kotler and Gary Armstrong, *Principles of Marketing*, 11th Edition, © 2006, pp. 340–341. Reprinted by permission of Pearson Education, Inc., Upper Saddle River, New Jersey.

COMPREHENSION QUESTIONS

1. What is the topic of the passage?
2. What is the central message of the passage?
3. Determine what is at issue. What is your initial personal viewpoint?
4. Distinguish among opposing viewpoints, and provide the rationale for each.
5. Think carefully about the viewpoints. Express a personal viewpoint, and give the reasons why you favor it. Does it differ from your initial personal viewpoint? Why or why not?
6. Write a few paragraphs *in support of the viewpoint that you do* not *favor.*

THOUGHT AND DISCUSSION QUESTIONS

1. Is it safe to conclude that the passage above was well researched? Why or why not?
2. In your view, does the author present a neutral approach to retail pricing? Why or why not?
3. Give an example of something you purchased that used one of these pricing techniques. Do you think you got a deal? Why or why not?
4. Can you infer from this article that the author believes that most retailers are honest? Why or why not?
5. List any questions that came to mind while you were reading this selection, and be prepared to discuss possible answers to them.

LOOKING BACK...LOOKING FORWARD

To check your progress in meeting this chapter's learning objectives, log in to www.myreadinglab.com, go to your Study Plan, and click on the Reading Skills tab. Choose Inference from the list of subtopics. Read and view the assets in the Review Materials section, then complete the Practices and Tests in the Activities section. You can check your scores by clicking on the Gradebook tab.

THINK AGAIN!

The following passage came from a psychology textbook. After reading the passage carefully, use your inference skills to figure out what suggestion the colleague made to remedy the backward curtain problem without having to replace the motor.

The Case of the Backward Curtain

A colleague of mine was in the hospital suffering from a bad back. He was confined to his bed and was dependent upon others to do many things for him. One of the few tasks he could do for himself was to open and close the curtains in his room by pressing buttons on a console beside his bed. But when he pressed the button labeled "Open," the curtains closed; pressing "Close" opened the curtains. A hospital maintenance man was called to fix the mechanism. He defined the problem as a defective motor that controlled the curtain and began to disconnect the motor when my colleague suggested, "Couldn't we look at this problem differently?"

Anthony F. Grasha, *Practical Applications of Psychology* 4th ed., p. 93

CRITICAL READING

Do you have or know someone who has video addiction? What are the pros and cons of video games for college students? Investigate the Web, and write a paragraph in which you support your viewpoint on this issue. Some Web sites to explore are:

http://serendip.brynmawr.edu/exchange/node/1719

http://www.video-game-addiction.org/

http://news.bbc.co.uk/2/hi/uk_news/1036088.stm

LISTENING SPRINGBOARD INQUIRY

Watch the video "How Great I Am" "Powerful Beyond Measure!" by Tony Robbins, the very famous "*Entrepreneur, Author & Peak Performance Strategist.*"

You can find the video at www.youtube.com. Search for Tony Robbins "How Great I Am" "Powerful beyond Measure!"

What is the message of this video? What can you infer about Tony Robbins from watching this video? Would his message be useful to someone in your life? Is it useful to you? Why and how?

FOOTSTEPS IN THE DARK

Remember to follow these steps:

- first, read the narrative and all the questions
- second, examine the picture carefully
- third, answer the questions in the order they appear, and come up with the solution

Have fun!

Detective Mercymee's sketch of C. T. Jenny's bungalow is here reproduced. Jenny, a coin collector, had a valuable collection, which is now missing. He was killed by a savage blow from a poker.

The footsteps, made by traversing the grease spot, matched the shoes of a cat burglar known as Meeow. Meeow admitted having been in Jenny's house, but when interrogated he denied killing Jenny and made the statements copied down here. By examining the sketch, can you decide whether Meeow told the truth and was innocent of the Jenny homicide?

Questions

Do you think that the following statements are true, false, or that there is insufficient evidence to support any conclusions?

1. "I busted the kitchen window to get in." ☐ True ☐ False ☐ Insufficient evidence

2. "I stop at the kitchen door to give the joint the once-over, but I don't see nothing." ☐ True ☐ False ☐ Insufficient evidence

3. "I walk over to the cabinet and yank open a drawer." ☐ True ☐ False ☐ Insufficient evidence

4. "I circle the room to kind of see what's what." ☐ True ☐ False ☐ Insufficient evidence

5. "In front of the fireplace I stop cold." ☐ True ☐ False ☐ Insufficient evidence

6. "Because I see a dead body lying there in the next room." ☐ True ☐ False ☐ Insufficient evidence

7. "I want nothing to do with what I see, so I beat it straight out." ☐ True ☐ False ☐ Insufficient evidence

8. Do you think that Meeow killed Jenny? ☐ Yes ☐ No

Text and illustration from Lawrence Treat, *Crime and Puzzlement: 24 Solve-Them-Yourself Picture Mysteries* (David R. Godine, Publisher, 1981), pp. 26–27

Footsteps in the Dark

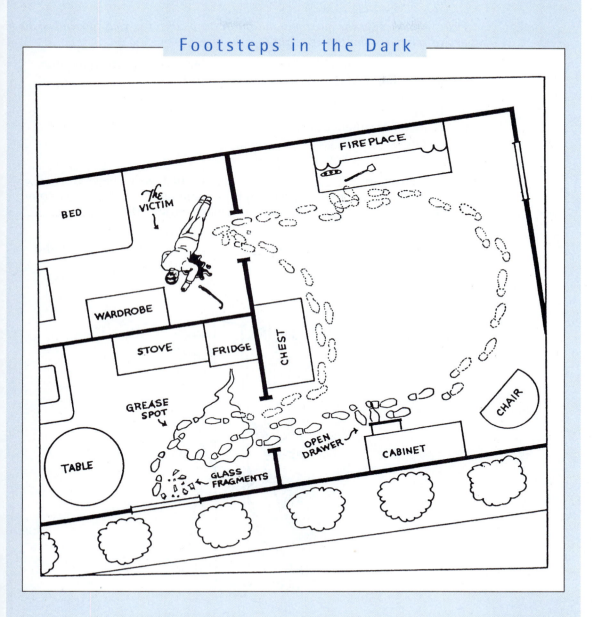

Name _____   Date _____

MASTERY TEST 6-1

DIRECTIONS: *Answer the questions and fill in the blanks. Use your inference skills to answer questions four through eight.*

1. A very high-level comprehension of written material, which requires interpretation and evaluation skills, is called
   a. critical thinking.
   b. inference.
   c. literal comprehension.
   d. critical reading.
   e. none of the above

2. Inferences are _____ guesses by which we go beyond what is _____ in order to fill in informational _____, come to _____ conclusions, and make sense of the _____ around us.

3. Inferences should be based on _____, _____, and _____.

New York Times, September 17, 2006, wk 13

4. What can you infer from the cartoon concerning airport security?

_____

_____

_____

5. Can you figure out what is being carried by the truck in the photograph?

_____

_____

_____

_____

_____

6. What war is being discussed in the following passage?

1   The war affected black Americans in many ways. Several factors operated
to improve their lot. One was their own growing tendency to demand fair
treatment. Another was the reaction of Americans to Hitler's barbaric treatment of millions of Jews, which compelled millions of white citizens to reexamine their views about race. If the nation expected blacks to risk their lives for
the common good, how could it continue to treat them as second-class citizens? Black leaders pointed out the inconsistency between fighting for democracy abroad and ignoring it at home. "We want democracy in Alabama," the
NAACP announced, and this argument too had some effect on white thinking.

2   Blacks in the armed forces were treated more fairly than they had been in
World War I. They were enlisted for the first time in the air force and the
marines, and they were given more responsible positions in the army and navy.
The army commissioned its first black general. Some 600 black pilots won their
wings. Altogether about a million served, about half of them overseas.

John A. Garraty, *A Short History of the American Nation*, p. 473

7. Read the passage; then answer the questions that follow.
[Hint: What happens in November each year?]

As a group, they are a very special breed apart from the rest of us. They have
one goal on their minds from the moment they wake up in the morning until the
moment they go to sleep at night. Although promises make up a big part of their
speeches, those promises are seldom kept. Their remarks are often couched in
glowing terms that are difficult to understand but always focused on the things
they think we want to hear. We can't trust them! It has been that way for centuries,
and it is not going to change any time soon.

a. What group is the writer discussing?
b. What goal is the writer referring to?
c. Is the writer optimistic or pessimistic about the future?
d. Is the passage mostly fact or mostly opinion?

8. Read the passage; then answer the questions that follow.
[Hint: This person is in prison.]

I have been here for so many years that I can barely remember what it is like
on the outside. The fight has been long and hard, but it all comes to an end at midnight. Although there is one last chance, that chance now seems slim at best. How
I wish I could turn back the clock to that warm day in July when everything went
up in smoke. If only I had ignored what he did, it might have turned out differently.
Will God forgive me?

a. What is going to happen to the person in the passage?
b. What is her "one last chance"?
c. How did she get into this situation?
d. To whom is she speaking?

Name _____   Date _____

DIRECTIONS: *First, read and think critically about the words to the following poem. Then, use your inference skills to identify the central message of the poem and interpret the meaning of each stanza.*

Come with Me

MARK HILLRINGHOUSE

1   Don't go off shopping at the mall.
    You'll only curse yourself for getting stuck in so much traffic.
    You'll walk a mile just to find your car.
    No one will be around to help you.
    And you'll have to hold your stomach in
    just to fit into those new pants.
    When you get home all your purchases will look tawdry,
    and you'll only have to drive back to return everything.
    Come with me and instead we will spread a blanket
    over the long grass and lie on our backs
    and watch the orange leaves tumble under a blue sky.

2   Don't go running for high office.
    Politics are a poor nourishment for the tired soul.
    Come election you'll realize you'll be stumping every night
    shaking hands for a few meager votes.
    After losing, no one will remember your name.
    Let the city run itself, let others fight for a seat on the council.
    Come with me and together we will find a bar
    in a crowded city and spend the evenings there
    drinking and talking to strangers.

3   Don't go off and become a teacher,
    you'll only make yourself miserable.
    Come June you'll realize you'll be out working all summer
    just to make ends meet.
    When it's time for bed, you'll be up grading papers.
    The IRS will hit you over and over for new taxes
    and you'll never be able to save more than a week's pay.
    Come with me and together
    we will launch a boat and watch the ripples
    our oars make in the water as we row
    far, very far, away from shore.

4   Don't go off and become a poet,
you'll only learn to regret it.
Poetry is too solitary a craft for a lonely traveler.
After years of trying you'll never attain greatness.
Everything you write will pass into obscurity.
Even your own family will suffer from your own lack of meaning.
Let others climb over each other for a place at the podium,
each one thinking his work better than the next.
Up there the light is pale and the air is thin.
Throw away your notebooks and pen
and forget about the immortals.
Come with me and together
we will tilt our heads into the night air
and laugh at the thousand brilliant stars.

Name _____   Date _____

DIRECTIONS: *First, read and think critically about the following short story. Then, without looking back at it, summarize and/or paraphrase the story in your notebook. Finally, use your inference skills first to identify the central message and then to determine the reasons why the boy said, "Thank you, m'am."*

Thank You, Ma'm

LANGSTON HUGHES

1   She was a large woman with a large purse that had everything in it but hammer and nails. It had a long strap and she carried it slung across her shoulder. It was about eleven o'clock at night, and she was walking alone, when a boy ran up behind her and tried to snatch her purse. The strap broke with the single tug the boy gave it from behind. But the boy's weight, and the weight of the purse combined caused him to lose his balance so, instead of taking off full blast as he had hoped, the boy fell on his back on the sidewalk, and his legs flew up. The large woman simply turned around and kicked him right square in his blue jeaned sitter. Then she reached down, picked the boy up by his shirt front, and shook him until his teeth rattled.

2   After that the woman said, "Pick up my pocketbook, boy, and give it here."

3   She still held him. But she bent down enough to permit him to stoop and pick up her purse. Then she said, "Now ain't you ashamed of yourself?"

4   Firmly gripped by his shirt front, the boy said, "Yes'm."

5   The woman said, "What did you want to do it for?"

6   The boy said, "I didn't aim to."

7   She said, "You a lie!"

8   By that time two or three people passed, stopped, turned to look, and some stood watching.

9   "If I turn you loose, will you run?" asked the woman.

10   "Yes'm," said the boy.

11   "Then I won't turn you loose," said the woman. She did not release him.

12   "I'm very sorry, lady, I'm sorry," whispered the boy.

13   "Um-hum! And your face is dirty. I got a great mind to wash your face for you. Ain't you got nobody home to tell you to wash your face?"

14   "No'm," said the boy.

15   "Then it will get washed this evening," said the large woman starting up the street, dragging the frightened boy behind her.

16   He looked as if he were fourteen or fifteen, frail and willow-wild, in tennis shoes and blue jeans.

17   The woman said, "You ought to be my son. I would teach you right from wrong. Least I can do right now is to wash your face. Are you hungry?"

18   "No'm," said the being-dragged boy. "I just want you to turn me loose."

19   "Was I bothering *you* when I turned that corner?" asked the woman.

20   "No'm."

21   "But you put yourself in contact with *me*," said the woman. "If you think that that contact is not going to last awhile, you got another thought coming. When I get through with you, sir, you are going to remember Mrs. Luella Bates Washington Jones."

22   Sweat popped out on the boy's face and he began to struggle. Mrs. Jones stopped, jerked him around in front of her, put a half nelson about his neck, and continued to drag him up the street. When she got to her door, she dragged the boy inside, down a hall, and into a large kitchenette-furnished room at the rear of the house. She switched on the light and left the door open. The boy could hear other roomers laughing and talking in the large house. Some of their doors were open, too, so he knew he and the woman were not alone. The woman still had him by the neck in the middle of her room.

23   She said, "What is your name?"

24   "Roger," answered the boy.

25   "Then, Roger, you go to that sink and wash your face," said the woman, whereupon she turned him loose—at last. Roger looked at the door—looked at the woman—looked at the door—*and went to the sink.*

26   "Let the water run until it gets warm," she said. "Here's a clean towel."

27   "You gonna take me to jail?" asked the boy, bending over the sink.

28   "Not with that face, I would not take you nowhere," said the woman. "Here I am trying to get home to cook me a bite to eat and you snatch my pocketbook! Maybe you ain't been to your supper either, late as it be. Have you?"

29   "There's nobody home at my house," said the boy.

30   "Then we'll eat," said the woman. "I believe you're hungry—or been hungry—to try to snatch my pocketbook."

31   "I wanted a pair of blue suede shoes," said the boy.

32   "Well, you didn't have to snatch *my* pocketbook to get some suede shoes," said Mrs. Luella Bates Washington Jones. "You could of asked me."

33   "M'am?"

34   The water dripping from his face, the boy looked at her. There was a long pause. A very long pause. After he had dried his face and not knowing what else to do dried it again, the boy turned around, wondering what was next. The door was open. He could make a dash for it down the hall. He could run, run, run, run, *run!*

35   The woman was sitting on the day-bed. After awhile she said, "I were young once and I wanted things I could not get."

36   There was another long pause. The boy's mouth opened. Then he frowned, but not knowing he frowned.

37   The woman said, "Uh-hum!" You thought I was going to say *but* didn't you? You thought I was going to say, *but I didn't snatch people's pocketbooks.* Well, I wasn't going to say that." Pause. Silence. "I have done things, too which I would not tell you, son—neither tell God, if he didn't already know. So you set down while I fix us something to eat. You might run that comb through your hair so you will look presentable."

38   In another corner of the room behind a screen was a gas plate and an icebox. Mrs. Jones got up and went behind the screen. The woman did not watch the boy to see if he was going to run now, nor did she watch her purse which she left behind her on the day-bed. But the boy took care to sit on the far side of the room where he thought she could easily see him out of the corner of her eye, if she wanted to. He did not trust the woman *not* to trust him. And he did not want to be mistrusted now.

39   "Do you need somebody to go to the store," asked the boy, "maybe to get some milk or something?"

40   "Don't believe I do," said the woman, "unless you just want sweet milk yourself. I was going to make cocoa out of this canned milk I got here."

41   "That will be fine," said the boy.

42   She heated some lima beans and ham she had in the icebox, made the cocoa, and set the table. The woman did not ask the boy anything about where he lived, or his folks, or anything else that would embarrass him. Instead, as they ate, she told him about her job in a hotel beauty-shop that stayed open late, what the work was like, and how all kinds of women came in and out, blondes, red-heads, and Spanish. Then she cut him a half of her ten-cent cake.

43   "Eat some more, son," she said.

44   When they were finished eating she got up and said, "Now, here, take this ten dollars and buy yourself some blue suede shoes. And next time, do not make the mistake of latching onto *my* pocketbook *nor nobody else's*—because shoes come by devilish like that will burn your feet. I got to get my rest now. But I wish you would behave yourself, son, from here on in."

45   She led him down the hall to the front door and opened it. "Good-night! Behave yourself, boy!" she said, looking out into the street.

46   The boy wanted to say something else other than "Thank you, m'am" to Mrs. Luella Bates Washington Jones, but he couldn't do so as he turned at the barren stoop and looked back at the large woman in the door. He barely managed to say "Thank you" before she shut the door. And he never saw her again.

Langston Hughes, "Thank You, Ma'am" from *The Short Stories of Langston Hughes.*

CHAPTER OUTLINE

What Is a Fact?

What Is an Opinion?

Distinguishing Between Facts
and Opinions

Facts and Opinions in Combination

Relating Facts and Opinions to Problem
Solving and Contemporary Issues

CHAPTER OUTCOMES

After completing Chapter 7, you
should be able to:

- Continue to apply the basic
method for personal problem
solving.

- Define *fact* and *opinion.*

- Define *objective* and *subjective.*

- Identify clue or value words in an
opinion.

- Distinguish between facts and
opinions and understand why it is
important to do so, particularly
when dealing with problems and
contemporary issues.

- Continue to find topics and
central messages in
contemporary-issue passages to
determine what is at issue,
distinguish among opposing
viewpoints, and express personal
viewpoints.

Think About It!

Look carefully at the photographs below. Then for each, write a paragraph in your notebook in which you describe what you see in detail. What caption or title would you give each of the photographs?

After you have written your paragraphs and captions, read them carefully, and try to distinguish between the facts and your opinions. Discuss your conclusions with your classmates.

1

2

PROBLEM-SOLVING EXERCISE

Using your notebook, apply the first four steps of the basic method from Chapter 5 for personal problem solving to the following hypothetical situation. Make sure to label clearly each step as you discuss what you would do. This situation is similar to a real-life one experienced by a student.

Hypothetical Situation

You are a single parent living alone with a 2-year-old child. This past September you enrolled as a full-time college student with the hope of pursuing a career in social work so that you can make a better life for you and your son. So far, college has been a challenging but rewarding experience.

Because you have no immediate family living in this part of the country, you have to bring your son to a daycare center while you attend classes. Although financial aid covers your books and tuition, you are forced to work at home as a typist for an agency to support the two of you. However, there never seems to be enough money to make ends meet.

Furthermore, it is very difficult to get either typing or schoolwork done with your son running around the apartment. Thus, you are living under a great deal of stress, which is affecting your performance at school and your relationship with your son. You lose your temper often and yell at him constantly. Things have to change quickly.

ACTIVITY 1

DIRECTIONS: *Discuss the meaning of this quote. Why does Baruch say it is acceptable to be wrong with an opinion but not to be wrong with facts?*

Every man has a right to be wrong in his opinions.
But no man has a right to be wrong in his facts.

Bernard M. Baruch, 1870–1965, American Financier

■ What Is a Fact?

A *fact* is something that can be proved true through **objective** evidence. Facts are accurate, verified, or confirmed in an *unbiased* manner. As you know, *unbiased* means "evenhanded," "objective," "impartial," or "without prejudice." You can prove, verify, or confirm a fact by personal observation, by using the observations of others, or by checking with reliable sources—such as studies that have been conducted, reputable books that have been written, or noted experts in a given field.

Personal observation simply involves checking something for ourselves, such as going to a person's home to verify that the person lives there. However, for practical reasons, we sometimes have to rely on the observations of others who serve as witnesses when we are unable to be there ourselves. For information about an event that occurred in the past or one that is happening in a far-off place that we cannot get to—such as the taking down of the Berlin Wall in Germany—we must rely on the eyewitness accounts of others. Finally, sometimes we must rely on written materials or other people who have more expertise than we do in a particular subject to determine if something is indeed factual. For instance, most people would rely on what they have read in medical literature, including the results of studies conducted by prominent physicians, to conclude a statement dealing with heart disease is factually accurate.

One of the keys to uncovering facts, then, is our determination that they have been or can be proved in an unbiased way. In other words, we have to be reasonably certain that the observations, experts, and any additional sources that we use or that are presented to us by others are as evenhanded as possible and not clouded by personal opinion.

Also, keep in mind that facts can change over time as conditions change, resulting in the elimination of some facts and the addition of others. For example, it was once a fact that there were 48 states in the United States, but that was no longer a fact after the addition of the states of Alaska and Hawaii in 1959, thereby bringing the total to 50. Thus, one fact was replaced by another. In short, determining whether something is a fact is an ongoing process that involves careful evaluation and continuous reevaluation, both of which are important characteristics of critical thinking.

ACTIVITY 2   *DIRECTIONS: In your notebook, list ten facts, and be prepared to discuss them in class.*

■ What Is an Opinion?

An *opinion* is something that cannot be objectively proven and is **subjective** in nature. Opinions are beliefs, personal judgments, or viewpoints about something that has not been proved, verified, or confirmed in an unbiased manner. Many times opinions are easy to detect by certain **clue words** or value words that emphasize a value, judgment, or tone that the individual has about the subject. Emotive words such as *great, relaxing, or improving* express a feeling about a subject. The words *strict, liberal, or informational* express a value judgment. Words that express a certain tone about a subject could be *nostalgic, angry, or humorous.* In obvious cases, words such as *good, bad, right,* or *wrong* are often used with opinions. However, sometimes people are more subtle when offering their opinions, which makes their opinions more difficult to recognize. For example, the statements "Bill Clinton was a bad president" and "Bill Clinton, as president, left something to be desired" both express negative opinions, but the first is stronger and more obvious than the second. They are both opinions, or subjective statements.

Also, be on the lookout for opinions that are couched in factual terms, such as "The fact of the matter is that abortion is wrong!" Just because the word *fact* is used does not make the statement a fact.

Finally, opinions can sometimes turn into facts after they have been proved, verified, or confirmed in an unbiased manner. For instance, a week before your birthday, you can claim that it is going to rain on that day, which is your opinion. However, if it does rain on that day, your original claim has become a fact, which can now be proved. Thus, opinions like facts, can change over time and should therefore be reevaluated.

When dealing with opinions in general, you should not automatically disregard them. First of all, you need to take into consideration who is offering a given opinion. *An expert or some other person who has extensive education, training, or experience in a given area is in a strong position to offer an opinion in that area.* That kind of opinion, sometimes called an **informed opinion**, should be taken seriously. For example, the foreign policy views of the chair of the U.S. Senate Foreign Relations Committee are worth careful consideration, as are those of a cancer researcher if the subject involves the causes of that disease. Opinions in general are also worth looking at because they can give you new ideas and viewpoints that you may not have thought about before. In short, always make it a practice to evaluate the opinions you encounter and give special consideration to their sources.

ACTIVITY 3

DIRECTIONS: In your notebook, list ten opinions, and be prepared to discuss them in class.

■ Distinguishing Between Facts and Opinions

Read the list of ten statements below; place an *O* next to the statements that you think are opinions and an *F* next to those that you think are facts.

1. Washington, D.C., which is the capital of the United States, is a beautiful city.
2. World War II was the last major war to be fought in the twentieth century.
3. The winters in Canada are really horrible because they are usually very cold.
4. Ronald Reagan, who was the fortieth president of the United States, was a wonderful leader.
5. The Berlin Wall, which separated East from West Berlin, has been taken down.
6. There are 50 states in the United States, and it is a widely accepted fact that Puerto Rico will become the fifty-first.
7. Experts tell us that the Mercedes-Benz is the best automobile on the market today.
8. Carbon monoxide is a poisonous gas that can be extremely deadly.
9. The United States is the most powerful country in the world.
10. Heart disease, which strikes people of all ages, can be caused by high blood pressure, smoking, and lack of exercise.

Now let's examine the responses.

Statement 1 combines both *fact* and *opinion* because Washington *is* the capital of the United States, but whether it is a beautiful city is a matter of opinion. Certainly, some people would agree that it is beautiful while others may not. It could depend on both the definition of the word *beautiful* and the other cities to which Washington is being compared.

Statement 2 is an *opinion* because it could be argued convincingly that there have been other major wars fought since World War II, including the one in Vietnam, which caused the loss of many American and Vietnamese lives. Furthermore, it really depends on one's definition of the word *major*. For example, does it mean many casualties, number of countries involved, or something else?

Statement 3 is a combination of *fact* and *opinion* because, although it is true that the winters in Canada are usually very cold, some people would argue that cold does not necessarily make them horrible. For instance, many Canadians like cold weather because it enables them to earn a living or do things that they enjoy doing, such as skiing, skating, and playing hockey.

It is a fact that Ronald Reagan was the fortieth President of the United States, but not everyone is of the opinion that he was a wonderful leader. Thus, Statement 4 is also a combination of a *fact* and an *opinion*.

Statements 5, 8, and 10 are all *facts* that can be supported by checking various sources. They can be proved and are generally accepted by everyone.

Statement 6 is a combination of a *fact* and an *opinion*. Whereas the first part of the statement is obviously a fact, the second part is an opinion because it is a prediction and a matter of conjecture that Puerto Rico will become the fifty-first state. Also, the use of the word *fact* in the sentence does not necessarily prove that the information is indeed factual.

Statement 7 is an *opinion* for two reasons: First, the "experts" are not identified, so we do not know if they are reliable, and second, no data is presented that would indicate how the word *best* is being used in the sentence. For example, does it refer to economical gas mileage, reliability, extensive safety equipment, exceptional good looks, or all of those pluses taken together?

Finally, Statement 9 is also an *opinion* because the meaning of the word *powerful* as used in the sentence is not clear. If it refers to military power, a strong case can be made for the accuracy of the statement, although some people would argue that as long as other countries possess nuclear weapons, no single country, including the United States, is all-powerful. By contrast, if it refers to economic power, more people might argue that the United States is indeed *not* the most powerful country in the world.

As you can see, it is sometimes not simple to distinguish between opinions and facts, yet if you think and read critically, you will be able to separate fact from opinion as part of evaluating what you see, hear, and read. In other words, you should not automatically accept information without first considering its accuracy, its source, and the motivations of whoever is presenting it. Otherwise, you are in danger of accepting opinions as facts, and that could have a negative effect on the decisions you make in life. For example, you could end up taking the wrong course, choosing the wrong solution to a problem, accepting the wrong version of a story, buying the wrong product, dating the wrong person, or voting for the wrong candidate. Thus, the cost of confusing facts and opinions can be quite substantial.

■ Facts and Opinions in Combination

As you just saw, facts and opinions are often used in combination, which makes it more difficult to distinguish between them. Sometimes this is done inadvertently when we are trying to express ourselves orally or in writing, but it can also be an intentional device to influence or persuade others. Commercials that influence our decisions as to what to purchase or whom to vote for and propaganda that attempts to persuade people to think in a certain way or support a certain course of action come to mind as examples of how this technique can be used effectively.

For instance, a political commercial that states "Inflation is rising dramatically. But don't worry—our candidate has the answer! Remember that when you vote next Tuesday!" is probably a combination of fact and opinion. A rising inflation rate can be proved by published statistics, but whether or not the candidate has the answer to the problem is not so simple to prove, at least not at this time. Of course, the whole purpose of the commercial is to get you to vote for that candidate. If indeed the official does eventually solve the inflation problem after the election, the latter part of the original commercial has become a fact. Remember, if you can identify a clue or value word that emphasizes a judgment about a subject, it is probably an opinion or partially an opinion. Once again, you must carefully evaluate and continuously reevaluate what you see, hear, and read.

ACTIVITY 4   *DIRECTIONS: In your notebook, list ten statements that combine facts and opinions, and be prepared to discuss them in class.*

■ Relating Facts and Opinions to Problem Solving and Contemporary Issues

When engaged in problem solving, you are already aware of the importance of gathering information as part of Step 2 of the approach that we have been using. No matter where the information comes from, it is crucial that it be as factual as possible. Otherwise, you could base your possible solutions on opinions or biased information, in which case they may not turn out to be solutions at all.

For example, if you are trying to solve the problem of a car engine that is smoking and you accept the opinion of a person who knows little about car engines, you are likely to waste your time, effort, and money. But if you consult a reliable car repair manual or take the advice of a reputable mechanic, you will probably end up with a solution to the problem. In short, the more you base possible solutions on facts, the better your chances of resolving problems.

As you already know, the ability to distinguish between facts and opinions is an important part of critical reading in general, no matter what kind of material you have in front of you. When you read, you should know whether or not you are dealing with information that is reliable and factual. Textbook material, which is objective for the most part, fits into that category due to its educational focus and because it is usually reviewed and approved by publishers and scholars prior to publication. When doing other kinds of reading, you need to be more vigilant because facts and opinions are often interspersed.

That is certainly the case with contemporary issues, which tend to arouse emotions and bring out an array of opinions and opposing viewpoints. Furthermore, the ratio of facts to opinions will vary widely from passage to passage. Some will consist mostly of facts, some will consist mostly of opinions, and some will fall somewhere in between.

In addition, writers will not always make their purpose, tone, or mood, obvious or mention the sources from which they have gotten their information. In those instances, you will either have to do research yourself or make a decision on the spot regarding the credentials of the writer and the reliability of the publication in which the information appeared. As you know, you can spend a great deal of time doing research, and sometimes that will be necessary if your purpose, for example, is to write a term paper for one of your courses. However, on other occasions, when you may be reading for pleasure, you can use your inference skills to come to a logical conclusion as to the writer's purpose and the reliability of the publication so that you can ultimately determine if the information is unbiased.

We will deal thoroughly with purpose and tone in Chapter 8, but keep in mind at this point that recognizing purpose is an important part of determining what proportion of the material before you is factual and how much is opinion. As you can see, uncovering bias is not an exact science. It does require time and effort on your part, but that is what critical reading and critical thinking are all about.

ACTIVITY 5

DIRECTIONS: Write a three-paragraph essay on a contemporary issue of your choice. Make the first paragraph mostly fact, the second paragraph mostly opinion, and the third paragraph a combination of both. Be prepared to read your essay aloud in class.

ACTIVITY 6

DIRECTIONS: The following problem was taken from a psychology textbook. After reading and thinking about it carefully, get together with one of your classmates to discuss how to gather facts to solve it.

Suppose that you live in a town that has one famous company, Boopsie's Biscuits and Buns. Everyone in the town is grateful for the 3B company and goes to work there with high hopes. Soon, however, an odd thing starts happening to many employees. They complain of fatigue and irritability. They are taking lots of sick leave. Productivity declines. What's going on at Boopsie's? Is everybody suffering from sheer laziness?

Carol Tavris and Carole Wade, *Psychology in Perspective,* 2nd ed., p. 437

ACTIVITY 7

DIRECTIONS: Read the following passages and answer the questions that follow. When reading each passage, try to make a determination as to what is fact and what is opinion. As part of that process, it will be helpful for you to take note of the writer's credentials if they are included, any sources mentioned, and the publication from which the passage was taken. Also, remember to use inference skills when appropriate.

Eye on Vocabulary

When reading each passage, take note of any unfamiliar words you come across. List them and their definitions in your notebook or on note cards. Use the context, word parts, or the dictionary to determine their meanings. After the completion of each passage, your instructor will ask to see your notebook or note cards and may discuss keywords in class.

1

GPS Tracking Devices—Teens vs. Parents, Law Enforcement vs. Invasion of Privacy

KORBIN NEWLYN

1   GPS (Global Positioning System) tracking devices have many beneficial uses. However, controversy over the covert use of this relatively new technology has ethical scholars, right to privacy advocates, law enforcement, and teens and parents at odds with each other.

2   GPS tracking devices have a multitude of uses; the majority of them are mostly beneficial. However, GPS devices sometimes involve privacy issues that can, at times, lead to controversy.

Fleet Vehicles and GPS Tracking Devices

3   You'll find that there are many companies both large and small that use GPS tracking devices to follow the location of their vehicles. The majority of trucking companies have the capability to tell you where all of their vehicles are at any given point
in time. In a similar manner, taxi companies as well as repair companies have the
capability to monitor their trucks' location so that they can dispatch them in a more
efficient manner.

4   However, there are people that believe this gives the companies who choose
to use GPS tracking devices more information than is needed about their drivers.
For instance, trucking companies have the capability to know how much time a
trucker has spent on the road, when and for what period of time he stops for
sleep or meals and if he has taken any unscheduled side trips.

5   Dispatchers at these companies may be privy to personal information that is
none of their business, such as a driver having lunch each day at the same place,
and it is not his residence. Some individuals are of the opinion that this constitutes
an invasion of personal privacy.

Teens and GPS Tracking Devices

6   There are some parents who use GPS tracking devices to know the location of their
teens. They may download GPS tracking software technology to the mobile phones
of their teens, or they may place a GPS tracking device somewhere in their car. The
teenagers may or may not be aware that their parents are monitoring them.

7   There is likely quite a few teens who believe that this is an invasion of their privacy.

GPS Tracking Devices and Surveillance

8   Does the thought run through your mind if your spouse having an affair? Curious to
find out what your brother-in-law is up to? If you place a hidden GPS tracking device
on their vehicle, you will at least know where they are going in their car. You may
have to come to your own conclusions as to what they are actually doing there.

9   There are many people who would agree that this would be an invasion of privacy and quite a few would be offended if they either knew or suspected you were
tracking them. Things get a little more involved when police use GPS tracking devices.

10   GPS tracking devices have been used by police to successfully solve crimes.
An example of the conflict between serving justice and invasion of privacy; say
the police put a GPS tracking device on the car of a person they suspect of being
a murderer. They successfully track the murderer as he unknowingly leads them
to the victims grave. Is this an invasion of privacy? Should law enforcement
officials be allowed to use GPS tracking devices this way?

11   If, for instance, the police need to obtain a search warrant from a judge to
use a GPS tracking device, should a private citizen be able to use this technology
without a warrant? Should the average private citizen even be allowed to use
GPS tracking device technology at all? At times the right to privacy and the right
to information are in conflict, this is one of those time.

12   All technology has moral and ethical implications that we as individuals and society as a whole has to grapple with. The right to privacy is the ethical dilemma we are forced to deal with when we use GPS tracking device technology.

http://www.buzzle.com/articles/gps-tracking-devices-teens-
vs-parents-law-enforcement-vs-invasion-of-privacy.html

COMPREHENSION QUESTIONS

1. What is the topic of the passage?
2. What is the central message of the passage?
3. Determine what is at issue. What is your initial personal viewpoint?
4. Distinguish among opposing viewpoints, and provide the rationale for each.
5. Think carefully about the viewpoints. Express a personal viewpoint, and give the reasons why you favor it. Does it differ from your initial personal viewpoint? Why or why not?
6. Write a few paragraphs *in support of the viewpoint that you do* not *favor.*

THOUGHT AND DISCUSSION QUESTIONS

1. If you were to use GPS tracking, explain how you would use it.
2. What other uses of GPSs can you think of or find on the Internet? What are the pros and cons of these uses?
3. Do you think the information presented is mostly fact, mostly opinion, or a combination of both? Why? Provide specific examples.
4. Do you think the statements are unbiased? Why or why not?
5. List any questions that came to mind while you were reading this selection and be prepared to discuss possible answers to them.

2

Kisses and Misses

1   Remember the "Seinfeld" episode. "The Kiss Hello"? The hilarious 30-minute segment in which every woman in Jerry's apartment building was puckered up when they greeted him? The one in which Jerry slapped a moratorium on hello smooches?

2   "Uh, listen. I decided I can't kiss hello anymore. I'm sorry. It's nothing personal. It just makes me a little uncomfortable and I can't do it. I'm sorry," he said, after backing away from a neighbor poised to plant a quick one.

3   While it might be your nature to greet someone with a kiss, not everyone likes it. For certain, there's no place for tongue wrestling or pats on the behind at social events, but is a handshake too cold?

4   "Kissing on the cheek is always a warmer introduction than the standard handshake in a social setting if you know the person... you are greeting well," said etiquette expert Trinka Taylor.

5   "Kissing on the lips should be withheld for only those you are in a close relationship with.

6   "If faced with a bold kisser, turn your head so the offender will miss your lips as a target."

7   And if you're the overly affectionate one, Taylor suggests that you stick to the basic on-the-cheek version.

8   When it comes to kissing, some nationalities have their own customs. According to Blistex, the folks who make things like fruit smoothies lip balm, the French adopted a four-kiss greeting beginning with the left cheek.

9   In Belgium, a one-kiss greeting is the rule when addressing someone near your age. For those who are at least 10 years older, three smooches is a mark of respect. And in Germany, kissing is restricted to family and very close friends. Handshakes are preferred.

10   When it's the first smooch in a romantic relationship, it's hard telling where it might lead. Take former first lady Barbara Bush, for example, who has been quoted as saying, "I married the first man I ever kissed. When I tell my children that, they just about throw up."

11   Or perhaps, in the case of the late Italian conductor, Arturo Toscanini, a kiss can help ward off a bad habit: "I kissed my first woman and smoked my first cigarette on the same day. Believe me, never since have I wasted any more time on tobacco."

12   Guys seem to be publicly more affectionate toward each other than they were decades ago. Consider the kisses (and ignore the head-butting for a moment) exchanged by the tough soccer players during the final game of the World Cup or "man-hugs" shared by buddies.

13   For most practical purposes, the man-hug is a combination handshake and a one-armed hug. The right hand remains locked in the handshake while the left arm reaches around for a pat on the back.

14   Think back to the NBA play-offs and all of the man-hugs by the Cleveland Cavaliers.

15   But when it comes to hugging the opposite sex, college senior Ian Grissett has a theory.

16   "A girl who pats you on the back when hugging just wants to be friends. One who holds the embrace without the pat is looking for something more than friendship. And a woman who rubs your back during a hug is someone you've been dating a while," he said.

17   "Or, your mom," Taylor added.

18   Actress Drew Barrymore once said, "Oh, I love hugging. I wish I was an octopus, so I could hug 10 people at a time!"

19   Wonder if they would include back pats?

Kim Hone-McMahan, "Smooch Smarts: To Kiss or Not To Kiss When You Greet. Here's the Drill," *Akron Beacon Journal*, August 10, 2006, p. E1. Reprinted with permission of the Akron Beacon Journal and Ohio.com.

COMPREHENSION QUESTIONS

1. What is the topic of the passage?
2. What is the central message of the passage?
3. Determine what is at issue. What is your initial personal viewpoint?
4. Distinguish among opposing viewpoints, and provide the rationale for each.
5. Think carefully about the viewpoints. Express a personal viewpoint, and give the reasons why you favor it. Does it differ from your initial personal viewpoint? Why or why not?
6. Write a few paragraphs *in support of the viewpoint that you do* not *favor.*

THOUGHT AND DISCUSSION QUESTIONS

1. What are the different ways you might greet someone, and what are the circumstances by which you would use these different greeting styles?
2. Think about five different inappropriate greetings, and tell why these might be considered a faux pas.
3. Proper etiquette may be different in other nationalities. Do an Internet search, and compare greeting styles among other cultures. If you were traveling to these countries, why would you need to know these styles?
4. List a country and a custom that an individual should be aware of before traveling to that location.
5. What type of custom, greeting, or gesture is accepted as appropriate that may be inappropriate in another culture?

3

Cities Saving Trees, Fending Off Lawsuits by Using Rubber Walkways

By Rick Hampson

1   The streets of America were never paved with gold, but now some of its sidewalks are made of rubber.

2   Dozens of communities have installed rubber because it co-exists with tree roots more easily than concrete. The latter buckles as roots grow under it; rubber merely bends. As a result, trees are spared from root damage, municipalities from trip-and-fall lawsuits.

3   "A rubber sidewalk? It sounds preposterous," admits Richard Valeriano, senior sidewalk inspector for the city of Santa Monica, Calif., and father of the rubber sidewalk.

4   The idea came to him in a dream after a day of staring down at yard after yard of pavement cracked by ficus tree roots.

5   That night, in his sleep, he saw concrete pavement rippling, flowing, undulating. But he didn't know what it meant until he noticed his health club installing a rubber indoor sports floor. "That," he says, "is when the penny dropped."

6   The city worked with the sports floor manufacturer on a rubber sidewalk prototype made from recycled tires. After the modular, pre-molded panels passed test-exposure to hazards such as rollerblades, bike stands and high heels, the city began laying rubber in 2001.

7   Rubbersidewalks of Gardena, Calif., began commercial production in 2004. Lindsay Smith, the company's president, says more than 60 municipalities have ordered panels.

8   She says that unlike poured concrete, the rubber panels have spaces between them, so rainwater can trickle down more easily to the roots, making them less likely to press up in search of moisture. The panels are removable, so arborists can trim and redirect roots without tearing up the sidewalk. They also help recycle the nation's vast supply of old tires.

9   Rubber sidewalks are soft—not bouncy, really, but with more give than concrete. "You can drop a glass on it, and it won't break," Valeriano says. In sales demonstrations, Smith does just that.

10   The sidewalks on Sutton Manor Road in New Rochelle, N.Y., are so wracked by linden tree roots that pedestrians use the street, says Terry Gargan, a semi-retired maritime lawyer. "I look at the sidewalks on this street, and I see 20 potential lawsuits."

11   But not in front of his house, where the city installed a slate-colored rubber sidewalk. He says people notice the difference only when they step on it and feel a certain spring. "They come up and ring the bell: 'What's the story?'"

12   Earlier this year, Washington D.C., spent about $60,000 to install 4,000 square feet of rubber sidewalks on several leafy blocks in the city's Northeast section.

13   On Sept. 13, the Boston City Council voted to study installing such sidewalks there.

14   Council member Rob Consalvo says some constituents in his largely suburban district were demanding the removal of trees whose volcanic roots effectively closed sidewalks to baby strollers, wheelchairs and the elderly.

15   Unless the price of concrete explodes, however, rubber may remain little more than a niche surface for use around large trees. Even in Santa Monica, rubber sidewalks have been installed at only 80 addresses.

16   It's expensive—two to three times the cost of concrete, partly because of the cost of shipment from Southern California.

17   Smith says that will change in the East when her company opens a plant next year in Lockport, N.Y.

18   She also says that the value of a large shade tree should be considered in the price of a rubber sidewalk, along with the cost (and noise) of having to tear up and replace buckled concrete every two or three years.

19   For kids, there's a downside: You can't immortalize yourself by stick-drawing your initials in wet rubber. An upside: fewer skinned knees.

20   Valeriano predicts that rubber will spread gradually across the streetscape. "I could never have thought of that if I tried," he says. "It had to come in a dream."

Rick Hampson, "Tree Roots Can't Ravage This Sidewalk: Cities Saving Trees, Fending Off Lawsuits by Using Rubber Walkways," *USA Today*, September 20, 2006, p. A3.
Reprinted with permission.

COMPREHENSION QUESTIONS

1. What is the topic of the passage?
2. What is the central message of the passage?
3. Determine what is at issue. What is your initial personal viewpoint?
4. Distinguish among opposing viewpoints, and provide the rationale for each.
5. Think carefully about the viewpoints. Express a personal viewpoint, and give the reasons why you favor it. Does it differ from your initial personal viewpoint? Why or why not?
6. Write a few paragraphs *in support of the viewpoint that you do not favor.*

THOUGHT AND DISCUSSION QUESTIONS

1. If you wanted to replace the sidewalk in front of your home with rubber panels and could only afford concrete, what could you do?
2. List all the positive and negative aspects of replacing concrete with rubber sidewalk panels.
3. Do an Internet search for "rubber sidewalks," and find out where these sidewalks have been installed and what positive and negative reactions they have created among the residents of these locations.
4. Think of some other options that have become popular replacements for traditional methods or for the natural environment. Are these positive or negative options?
5. Do you think the article is unbiased? Why or why not?
6. List any questions that came to mind while you were reading this selection, and be prepared to discuss possible answers to them.

4

Do Competitive Sports Teach Valuable Life Lessons to Youth?

Yes

1   Several factors, such as one's attitude toward competition, the manner in which competition is organized, and the behavior of important adults—such as parents

and coaches—can contribute to making competition either worthwhile or hurtful. The current crisis in youth sports will be resolved only if we dedicate ourselves to ensuring that youth sports programs are indeed worthwhile, and by working together to eliminate destructive attitudes and behaviors.

2   There are four important reasons that I believe we should tackle the problems in youth sports by encouraging—not prohibiting—competitive sports for children. First, if children are taught emotional skills and psychological skills to help them be effective competitors, these skills will be helpful throughout life.

3   Examples of some of these coping skills include: knowing how to relax and calm down in pressure situations or when being evaluated, using one's imagination in support of reaching one's goals, being able to receive and utilize criticism, and learning how to focus attention.

4   Second, competitive sports expose children to losing. Learning how to deal with loss is a valuable experience for children. Third, competitive sports show children that there are standards of excellence in each sport. Such experience is an important part of developing a mastery approach.

5   Competition provides performers in any given area with a way to measure their progress. Those who would argue that competition should be abolished must propose an alternative means of measuring improvement. I think that simply looking at our own performance over time is not adequate. ... Expertise develops when the urge to improve, to become as good as other skilled performers, or even better, occurs. This urge is the ego side of the competitive instinct. But without competition, it is nearly impossible to imagine how excellence could develop.

6   Finally, competitive youth sports programs provide children with the opportunity to learn new skills and work on existing skills, to set goals and try to achieve them and to work with others in team situations. These experiences can be fundamental in providing children with a sense of self-esteem. Good physical self-esteem can help children develop fitness and health habits, which build a strong foundation for an active and healthy life.

Shane Murphy, The Cheers and the Tears: A Healthy Alternative to the
Dark Side of Youth Sports Today (Jossey-Bass, 1999)

No

7   Competing drags us down, devastates us psychologically, poisons our relationships, interferes with our performance. But acknowledging these things would be painful and might force us to make radical changes in our lives, so instead we create and accept rationalizations for competition: It's part of "human nature." It builds character.

8   The last of these beliefs is the most remarkable. The contention that competition is psychologically beneficial contradicts the intuitive knowledge that I believe most of us possess. Despite direct awareness of what competition does

to people ... some individuals persist in claiming that its effects are constructive. This is a powerful example of how it is possible to adjust our beliefs so as to escape the threatening realization that we have been subjecting ourselves to something terrible, that we have internalized a corrosive personality attribute.

9   Also, this may be why the traditional assumption that "competitive sport builds character" is still with us today in spite of overwhelming contrary evidence. Apart from the absence of data to support it, the adage itself is exceedingly slippery. One sports sociologist reports that of all the writers he has encountered who repeat this assertion, not one actually defined the word character, let alone provided evidence for the claim. Character was typically assumed to be understood as desirable and wholesome, or it was defined implicitly by association with such adjectives as "clean-cut," "red-blooded," "upstanding," "desirable" and so forth. For the late Gen. Douglas MacArthur, competition was a "vital character builder" in the sense that it "make[s] sons into men." This definition, besides being irrelevant to half the human race, tells us nothing about which features of being a man are considered desirable.

10   In what may be the only explicit research of this claim, [authors] Ogilvie and Tutko could find "no empirical support for the tradition that sport builds charac-ter. Indeed, there is evidence that athletic competition limits growth in some areas." Among the problematic results they discovered were depression, extreme stress, and relatively shallow relationships. [They] also found, as mentioned before, that many players "with immense character strengths" avoid competitive sports. Finally, they discovered that those who do participate are not improved by competition; whatever strengths they have were theirs to begin with.

Alfie Kohn, *No Contest: The Case Against Competition* (Houghton Mifflin, 1992)

COMPREHENSION QUESTIONS

1. What is the topic of the passage?
2. What is the central message of the passage?
3. Determine what is at issue. What is your initial personal viewpoint?
4. Distinguish among opposing viewpoints, and provide the rationale for each.
5. Think carefully about the viewpoints. Express a personal viewpoint, and give the reasons why you favor it. Does it differ from your initial personal viewpoint? Why or why not?
6. Write a few paragraphs *in support of the viewpoint that you do* not *favor.*

THOUGHT AND DISCUSSION QUESTIONS

1. Do you agree with Shane Murphy when he states, "Learning how to deal with loss is a valuable experience for children"? Why or why not?
2. How do you define "character"? Do you believe that "competitive sport builds character"? Why or why not?

3. Use your inference skills to determine what Alfie Kohn means when he states that General Douglas MacArthur's definition is "irrelevant to half the human race."

4. Do you think the information presented is mostly fact, mostly opinion, or a combination of both? Why? Provide specific examples.

5. Do you think the statements are unbiased? Why or why not?

6. List any questions that came to mind while you were reading this selection, and be prepared to discuss possible answers to them.

5

Living Together First Has Little Effect on Marriage Success

Chance of Divorce Not Much Greater, Large Survey Shows

SHARON JAYSON, *USA TODAY*

1   Couples who live together before marriage and those who don't both have about the same chances of a successful union, according to a federal report out Tuesday that turns earlier cohabitation research on its head.

2   The report, by the National Center for Health Statistics, is based on the National Survey of Family Growth, a sample of almost 13,000. It provides the most detailed data on cohabitation of men and women to date.

3   Past research—using decades-old data—found significantly higher divorce rates for cohabitors, defined as "not married but living together; with a partner of the opposite sex." But now, in an era when about two-thirds of couples who marry live together first, a different picture is emerging in which there are few differences between those who cohabit and those who don't.

4   Of those married 10 or more years, 60% of women and 62% of men had ever cohabited; 61% of women and 63% of men had cohabited only with the one they married. Meanwhile, 66% of women and 69% of men married 10 years had never cohabited.

5   Differences "are there, but they are not huge," says statistician Bill Mosher, the report's co-author.

6   Sociologist Pamela Smock of the University of Michigan in Ann Arbor considers the data definitive. "On the basis of these numbers, there is not a negative effect of cohabitation on marriages, plain and simple," she says.

7   Paul Amato, a sociologist at Pennsylvania State University, says the new data suggest that "maybe the effect of premarital cohabitation is becoming less of a problem than it was in the past. If it becomes normative now, maybe it's not such a big deal."

8   The report takes a closer look at those who live together before marriage, including race and ethnicity, education level, upbringing and whether couples were engaged when they moved in.

9   "There's a real difference in the types of cohabitations out there," Mosher says. "We can show that now with these national data."

10   The data show that those who live together after making plans to marry or getting engaged have about the same chances of divorcing as couples who never cohabited before marriage. But those who move in together before making any clear decision to marry appear to have an increased risk of divorce.

11   Men who were engaged when they moved in with their future spouse had about the same odds that their marriage would last at least 10 years as those who didn't live together before the wedding: 71% for engaged men and 69% for non-cohabiting men. Among engaged women, the probability the marriage would survive for 10 years was similar (65%) to the probability for women who didn't cohabit (66%).

12   That's finding Scott Stanley, co-director of the Center for Marital and Family Studies at the University of Denver, sees in smaller samples. For Stanley, the "nature of commitment at the time of co-habitation is what's important."

13   "There is a lot of interesting work being done on differences among different groups of cohabitors as to why, when and how they cohabit," he says.

14   But others who are firmly against cohabitation, such as Mike McManus, co-founder of Marriage Savers, a "ministry" that aims to reduce the divorce rate, calls the findings worrisome.

15   "I think it's going to lull some people into thinking there's no problem with living together," says McManus, co-author of *Living Together: Myths, Risks & Answers.* "It appears to say you can cohabit and it doesn't matter, but it doesn't look at all the couples who begin cohabiting and how many of them are able to make a marriage last. It doesn't say how many marriages broke up" before 10 years.

16   Although the new federal data were from a 2002 survey, it's the most recent nationally representative sample of 12,571 people ages 15 to 44, including 7,643 women and 4,928 men.

17   Andrew Cherlin, a sociologist at Johns Hopkins University, says the report may quell fears of cohabitation "as a long-term substitute for marriage," as in some European countries.

18   "American cohabitors either marry or break up in a few years," he says.

Sharon Jayson, "Living Together First Has Little Effect on Marriage Success,"
USA Today, March 3, 2010, p. 7D. Reprinted with permission.

COMPREHENSION QUESTIONS

1. What is the topic of the passage?
2. What is the central message of the passage?
3. Determine what is at issue. What is your initial personal viewpoint?
4. Distinguish among opposing viewpoints, and provide the rationale for each.
5. Think carefully about the viewpoints. Express a personal viewpoint, and give the reasons why you favor it. Does it differ from your initial personal viewpoint? Why or why not?
6. Write a few paragraphs *in support of the viewpoint that you do* not *favor.*

THOUGHT AND DISCUSSION QUESTIONS

1. What is *cohabitation,* and what are the types mentioned in the article? If there is a difference in what the data reports with regard to the different types of cohabitation, what is it?
2. What does Amato mean when he says "maybe the effect or premarital cohabitation is becoming less of a problem than it was in the past. If it becomes normative now, maybe it's not such a big deal"?
3. In the article, who has an opposing view with regard to the data and who has a neutral view and what are these views?
4. Do you think the information presented is mostly fact, mostly opinion, or a combination of both? Why? Provide specific examples.
5. Do you think the statements are unbiased? Why or why not?
6. List any questions that came to mind while you were reading this selection and be prepared to discuss possible answers to them.

LOOKING BACK ... LOOKING FORWARD

To check your progress in meeting this chapter's learning objectives, log in to www.myreadinglab.com, go to your Study Plan, and click on the Reading Skills tab. Choose Critical Thinking from the list of subtopics. Read and view the assets in the Review Materials section, then complete the Practices and Tests in the Activities section. You can check your scores by clicking on the Gradebook tab.

THINK AGAIN!

Assume that *you* are the person making the statement "Brothers and sisters, I have none. But that man's father is my father's son." What is the relationship of *that man* to you? Get together with a classmate, and discuss the possibilities.

INVESTIGATION

WEB SITE   WSI

FACT AND OPINION

In everyday life, it is important to identify what is objective (a fact) and what is subjective (an opinion). The Internet is a valuable tool for finding all kinds of information and many of us rely on reputable Web sites to help us find things. Go to the following sites and answer the following questions.

1. Go to the *New York Times* Web site, http://www.nytimes.com, and find sentences in one or two articles that are objective and subjective. Sometimes the different section titles will help you find an article that expresses an opinion.

    a. Newspaper section: _____

       Article title: _____

       Objective sentence: _____

       Subjective sentence: _____

    b. Newspaper section: _____

       Article title: _____

       Objective sentence: _____

       Subjective sentence: _____

       What are the newspaper sections that usually identify a collection of opinions?

       _____

2. Go to the *USA Today* Web site, http://www.usatoday.com, and write a headline that is matter-of-fact and one that uses a value word. Label each objective or subjective.

    a. Article title: _____

       Label: _____

    b. Article title: _____

       Label: _____

3. Go to the *Rotten Tomatoes* Web site, http://www.rottentomatoes.com/, which has previews and reviews of movies and games. Look up a movie that you are interested in going to see, and read the reviews. Write two objective sentences and two subjective sentences from the reviews that impress you enough to either go see the movie or not. Underline any value words that you find.

    a. Movie title: _____

       Objective sentence: _____

    b. Movie title: _____

       Objective sentence: _____

c. Movie title: _____

   Subjective sentence: _____

d. Movie title: _____

   Subjective sentence: _____

LISTENING SPRINGBOARD INQUIRY

Go to Public Radio International at http://www.pri.org/ and listen to a current topic featured on this Web site.

Title of the selection: _____

Who is the individual speaking and/or what is his or her title or position? What is the topic of this message?

_____

_____

_____

What are the keys points of the message?

_____

_____

Is the speaker making an argument, or trying to persuade you of a solution to a problem? If so, can you tell when he or she is supporting the argument with facts or with opinions? How can you tell?

_____

_____

_____

GANG OF FOUR

Remember to follow these steps:
- first, read the narrative and all the questions
- second, examine the picture carefully
- third, answer the questions in the order they appear and come up with the solution

Have fun!

Burglars broke a window and entered the home of Samuel F. Whippersnapper, a coin collector, and rifled his collection. He grappled with them and was shot and fatally wounded in the course of the struggle. He had time, however, to call the police, who stopped a car with these four suspects in it and brought them to the station house, together with the coat, which had some of the stolen coins in a pocket.

Whippersnapper died clutching the button which is shown. The police were satisfied that the other objects sketched, which were found at Whippersnapper's, belonged to the burglars. From the above facts and an examination of the evidence and the four suspects, can you decide who shot Whippersnapper?

Questions

1. Who do you think broke the window? ☐ Dan Jurous   ☐ "Bull" Dozer   ☐ Helen Wheels ☐ "Brains" B. Heind

2. At what time did the struggle occur? _____

3. Do you think that more than one person was involved in the burglary?   ☐ Yes   ☐ No

4. Does the button come from the coat found in the car?   ☐ Yes   ☐ No

5. Do you think that "Bull" Dozer was involved in the struggle?   ☐ Yes   ☐ No

6. Do you think that the wearer of the coat killed Whippersnapper?   ☐ Yes   ☐ No

7. Who do you think shot Whippersnapper?   ☐ Dan Jurous   ☐ "Bull" Dozer   ☐ Helen Wheels ☐ "Brains" B. Heind

Text and illustration from Lawrence Treat, *Crime and Puzzlement: 24 Solve-Them-Yourself Picture Mysteries* (David R. Godine, Publisher, 1981), pp. 44–45

Gang of Four

Name _____   Date _____

MASTERY TEST 7-1

Directions: Answer the questions and fill in the blanks. For Statements 7 through 10, indicate whether the statement is a fact, an opinion, or a combination of both.

1. Define the term *fact*. _____

   _____

   _____

2. Define the term *opinion*. _____

   _____

   _____

3. A statement is unbiased when it is
   a. evenhanded.
   b. objective.
   c. impartial.
   d. without prejudice.
   e. all of the above

4. You can prove or verify a fact by personal _____, by using the observations of _____, or by checking with reliable _____.

5. "As a critical thinker, you must disregard all opinions." Is this statement true or false?

6. An _____ opinion is one given by a person with extensive education, training, or experience in the particular area being discussed.

7. It is a fact that capital punishment serves as a deterrent to murder. _____

8. Although the Supreme Court has made a landmark decision regarding abortion, the issue is far from settled. _____

9. The Virginia Tech shooting was given extensive coverage by the media. _____

10. The Soviet Union no longer exists, but there still is much instability in Europe. _____

Name _____   Date _____

DIRECTIONS: For each of the longer selections that follow, indicate whether the information presented is mostly fact, mostly opinion, or a combination of both. Also, indicate which of the passages, if any, present information that is informed opinion.

1

Pluto Demotion Draws Protest

1   LAS CRUCES, New Mexico (AP)—Size doesn't matter.

2   That was the message as friends and colleagues of the late Clyde Tombaugh, the astronomer who discovered Pluto, gathered on the New Mexico State University campus to protest the International Astronomical Union's recent decision to strip Pluto of its status as a planet.

3   About 50 students and staff members turned out Friday for the good-natured challenge. Some were wearing T-shirts and carrying signs that read "Protest for Pluto" and "Size Doesn't Matter."

4   Tombaugh's widow, Patricia, and their son, Al Tombaugh, also participated.

5   NMSU astronomer Bernie McNamara told the crowd that textbooks shouldn't be rewritten.

6   "Why not? Because the debate is not over," McNamara said.

7   The IAU determined last week that a planet must orbit the sun and be large enough to assume a nearly round shape as well as "clear the neighborhood around its orbit." Pluto's oblong orbit overlaps Neptune's, which led the IAU to downsize the solar system to eight planets from the traditional nine.

8   McNamara argued that only about 400 of the union's thousands of members were present when the August 24 vote was taken.

9   "This was not a statement by the astronomical community at large," he said, adding that a petition opposing the IAU definition of a planet is circulating among the world's planetary scientists and astronomers.

10   Tombaugh was 24 when he discovered Pluto while working at Lowell Observatory in Flagstaff, Arizona, in 1930. He came to NMSU in 1955 and founded the school's research astronomy department.

11   His legacy is visible across the city, where an observatory, a campus street and an elementary school bear his name.

12   Some say Tombaugh's discovery was significant because it took 60 years for stronger telescopes to locate another object with an unusual orbit like Pluto's, and 73 years before scientists discovered a bigger object in the area.

13   "Clyde Tombaugh was an American hero," said Herb Beebe, a longtime colleague. "For that reason alone, Pluto's status as a full-fledged planet should be kept."

_____

_____

_____

2

Should Humans Be Cloned?

New methods can create a baby who is your genetic twin.

Yes

1   The cloning of human beings is now possible. Scientists can take an egg cell, remove its DNA, insert DNA from a cell of any person, and create an embryo who is that person's younger but identical twin. This technology offers a miracle option for families who cannot have children of their own by any other method. After 25 years as a fertility specialist, trying to help couples have babies, I have joined with scientists in Europe and elsewhere to develop that option. By doing so, I believe, we will be helping humanity.

2   It is true that the cloning of animals—such as Dolly the sheep, created in Scotland in 1997—has so far had a high failure rate and is fraught with risks. But those risks have been exaggerated, and many of them have resulted from improper cloning. Meanwhile, I can show you e-mails from thousands of families eager to accept those risks. They say in their messages that if they are able to have a child through cloning, they will love that son or daughter just as much as they would any other.

3   Believe it or not, the genie is out of the bottle. Human cloning will be done whether we like it or not. I think we should accept it, make it legal, regulate it, and make sure it is done in a responsible, scientifically correct way—not left to unscrupulous black-market exploiters.

Panos Zavos, Ph.D., Director, Andrology Institute of America Lexington, KY.

No

4   Don't think about human cloning from the point of view of the person being cloned. Think about it as if you were the younger, duplicated copy. If you do, you'll see at once why cloning a human being is deeply unethical.

5   First, the known grave risks of abnormality and deformity seen in animal cloning make attempts at human cloning an immoral experiment on the resulting child-to-be. Second, even if you were a healthy clone, would you want to be constantly compared with the adult original in whose image you have been made?

Wouldn't you want to have your own unique identity and an open-ended future, fully a surprise to yourself and the world?

6   If you were the clone of your "mother," would it help your adolescence to turn into the spitting image of the woman Daddy fell in love with? If you were the clone of your "father" but your parents later divorced, would you like to look just like the man your mother now detests?

7   Third, don't you think it is a form of child abuse for parents to try to determine in advance just exactly what kind of a child you are supposed to be? Do you want to live under the tyranny of their biologically determined expectations?

8   Finally, would you like to turn human procreation into manufacture, producing children as artifacts? Cloning is tyrannical and dehumanizing. We should have none of it.

Leon R. Kass, M.D., Professor, Committee on Social Thought, University of Chicago,
New York Times Upfront, April 30, 2001, p. 26

CHAPTER

8

Recognizing Purpose and Tone

CHAPTER OUTLINE

The Importance of Recognizing
Purpose

    To Inform

    To Persuade

    To Entertain

    Combination of Purposes

The Importance of Recognizing Tone

    Matter-of-Fact Tone

    Humorous Tone

    Angry Tone

    Sad Tone

    Ironic Tone

CHAPTER OUTCOMES

After completing Chapter 8,
you should be able to:

■ Continue to apply the basic
method for personal problem
solving.

■ Define *purpose* and *tone*.

■ Recognize the various kinds of
purpose.

■ Recognize the various kinds of tone.

■ Continue to find topics and
central messages in contemporary-
issue passages to determine what
is at issue, distinguish among
opposing viewpoints, and express
personal viewpoints.

Think About It!

Use your inference skills to determine the *purpose* of the message on each of the signs in the following photographs. In other words, what are readers being urged to do or not do? Discuss the purposes with your classmates.

If you want her to have a shot at reaching the stars, she needs to get her baby shots now.

Every child deserves the best opportunities life has to offer. Especially yours.

The odds of becoming an astronaut and reaching the stars are out of this world. But the chances are more than 1 in 4 that your baby isn't protected against childhood diseases like polio, measles, chicken pox, tetanus and others.

So, even if you're sure your child is up to date and on schedule with her baby shots, ask your doctor at every visit. It couldn't hurt.

In fact, it could give her the chance to grow up to be whatever she wants to be.

Even if it's something out of this world.

PROBLEM-SOLVING EXERCISE

Using your notebook, apply the first four steps of the basic method for personal problem solving to the following hypothetical situation. Be sure to label each step clearly as you discuss what you would do. This situation is similar to a real-life one experienced by several students.

Hypothetical Situation

> For several weeks, you have been enrolled in an introductory business course that is required in your program of study. From the beginning of the semester, you have not been comfortable with the instructor. His lectures are difficult to follow, and he is gruff and impatient when you ask questions, both in and out of class. Furthermore, you feel that he grades your test papers unfairly by taking off too many points for answers that are basically correct. In short, you get the impression that he simply does not like you.
>
> Although you have a C average, you need a much higher grade in your major courses in order to continue your education and eventually secure a better job. In fact, you have not received a grade lower than a B in all the other courses that you have taken to this point. You fear that this predicament is not going to get any better, and you are at a loss as to what to do about it.

■ The Importance of Recognizing Purpose

Throughout this textbook, we have emphasized the importance of evaluating what you see, hear, and read as a necessary part of critical thinking. You have been cautioned not to rush to judgment by accepting everything at face value but instead to take the time to consider what you have before you, regardless of your personal viewpoint. When reading, part of the evaluation process involves recognizing the writer's **purpose**, or *reasons for writing*. That, in turn, can help you distinguish between facts and opinions, uncover bias, and assess the overall reliability of information.

Although writers always have a purpose for writing, they usually do not come right out and say what it is. Consequently, it is up to the reader to make an inference or an educated guess regarding their motivations, based on:

- Author's background or affiliation
- Publication in which the writing appears
- The information itself
- How the information is presented

For example, a physician who is a member of the American Medical Association may write a piece in a popular magazine dealing with the high cost of malpractice insurance in order to persuade readers to be sympathetic to rising medical fees. In doing so, she may not state that purpose explicitly but instead present convincing information that supports that point of view without providing any contradictory information. Thus, the reader could infer her purpose by taking into consideration the fact that

she is a physician who is affiliated with a major medical association representing doctors, by keeping in mind that the article appears in a magazine
that is read widely by the general public, and by recognizing that the information provided appears to be one-sided.

Generally speaking, a writer's purpose for writing is usually to *inform*,
to *persuade*, to *entertain*, or some combination of the three. The ease with
which you will be able to recognize these purposes will often depend on
how obvious a particular writer chooses to present the material. As noted,
it will sometimes be necessary for you to use your inference skills. Let us
look more closely at each of the three purposes.

To Inform

When the purpose is to inform, *a writer simply provides facts, data, or information about a given subject so that you can learn more about it.* Textbook
writers generally have this as their overall purpose. For example, read the
following passage from a biology textbook.

Biology Is Connected to Our Lives in Many Ways

1   Endangered species, genetically modified crops, global warming, air and water pollution, the cloning of embryos, nutrition controversies, emerging diseases, medical
advances—is there ever a day that we don't see several of these issues featured in
the news? These topics and many more have biological underpinnings. Biology, the
science of life, has an enormous impact on our everyday life.

2   Most of these issues of science and society also involve technology. Science and
technology are interdependent, but their basic goals differ. The goal of science is to
understand natural phenomena. In contrast, the goal of technology is generally to
apply scientific knowledge for some specific purpose. Biologists and other scientists
often speak of "discoveries," while engineers and other technologists more often
speak of "inventions." The beneficiaries of those inventions also include scientists,
who put new technology to work in their research. And scientific discoveries often
lead to new technologies.

3   The potent combination of science and technology has dramatic effects on society. For example, discovery of the structure of DNA by James D. Watson and Francis
Crick some 50 years ago and subsequent achievements in DNA science have led
to the many technologies of DNA engineering that are transforming many fields,
including medicine, agriculture, and forensics (DNA fingerprinting, for example).
Perhaps Watson and Crick envisioned their discovery as someday leading to important

applications, but it is unlikely that they could have predicted exactly what those applications would be.

4   Technology has improved our standard of living in many ways, but not without consequences. Technology that keeps people healthier has enabled the Earth's population to grow more than tenfold in the past three centuries, to double to over 6 billion in just the past 40 years. The environmental effects of this growth can be devastating. Global warming, toxic wastes, acid rain, deforestation, nuclear accidents, and extinction of species are just some of the repercussions of more and more people wielding more and more technology. Science can help us identify such problems and provide insight into what course of action may prevent further damage. But solutions to these problems have as much to do with politics, economics, and cultural values as with science and technology. Now that science and technology have become such powerful aspects of society, every thoughtful citizen has a responsibility to develop a reasonable amount of scientific literacy. The crucial science-technology-society relationship is a theme that adds to the significance of any biology course.

5   Biology—from the molecular level to the level of the biosphere—is directly connected to our everyday lives. Biology offers us a deeper understanding of ourselves and our planet and a chance to more fully appreciate life in all its diversity.

Neil A. Campbell, Jane B. Reece, Martha R. Taylor, Eric J. Simon,
Biology: Concepts and Connections, 5/e, Pearson Education, Inc., 2006 p.12

The writer's purpose here is to inform the reader about the many important connections that the subject of biology has to our everyday lives, including its contributions to technology and medicine and its help in finding solutions to environmental problems. Several examples are provided for support and clarification.

ACTIVITY 1   *Directions: Write a short informational essay dealing with a contemporary issue in which you present only facts. Then, using the same essay, add some material that encourages the reader to do something.*

ACTIVITY 2   *Directions: Bring to class an example of a passage from your textbook or the Internet that was written to inform readers.*

To Persuade

When a writer's purpose is to persuade, *the writer is trying to get the reader to think in a certain way or take a particular action.* Although some facts may be presented, the writer's real intention is to get others to agree with the opinion being expressed or to engage in some activity in support of that point of view. For instance, as you read the following passage, think about the author's purpose.

The Littlest Killers

Lord of the Flies, Chicago Style

BRENT STAPLES

1   Imagine the terror of a 5-year-old child, dangling 14 stories above the pavement, as his brother tries fruitlessly to save him from two other boys, ages 10 and 11, who are determined to see him drop.

2   The image of Eric Morse, hurled to his death in Chicago in 1994, has been a recurrent one in both local and national politics. Newt Gingrich cited it in speeches. Henry Cisneros, the Secretary of Housing and Urban Development, called it a clinching fact in the Government's decision to take over the Chicago Housing Authority, deemed by federal authorities the most dangerous and ill managed in the country. The Illinois Legislature easily passed a bill permitting 10-year-old children to be charged with murder and—as "super predators"—sent to maximum-security jails. The rush to jail young children is catching on elsewhere as well. Nationwide last year, 700 pieces of legislation were introduced aimed at prosecuting minors as adults.

3   The judge who last week sent Eric Morse's killers to jails for juveniles came near to rending her robes as she described Eric's plunge and asked how the boys who caused his death had become so indifferent to human life. No one who has spent time in, or even near, Chicago public housing projects should need to ask such a question. Eric's fall—and the world he lived in—bears a disturbing resemblance to *Lord of the Flies,* William Golding's novel about a band of British schoolboys marooned on a jungle island. Without adults to keep them in check, the boys turn to blood lust and murder. A boy who tries to reason gets his skull split open when he is thrown from a cliff.

4   Eric was killed for refusing to steal candy for his tormentors. The public housing complex where he died qualifies as an "island" in Golding's sense—an island of poverty and pathology, cut off from the city proper. Of the 15 poorest census tracts in America, 11 are Chicago public housing communities. The city designed and treated them as pariah states, even while they were bright, shining steppingstones for the black middle class. Public housing was far too densely built, walled off with freeways and railroad lines used as ghetto walls. As the poverty deepened, there was simply no way to dilute it.

5   Chicago's Ida B. Wells housing development has few adult men. The women are disproportionately teenagers. At the time of Eric's death, a third of the complex's 2,800 apartments were abandoned, used primarily by drug dealers who hawked heroin from the windows. In a survey at a nearby high school, half the students said they had been shot at; 45 percent said they had seen someone killed. The boys who dropped Eric from the window did not originate the act. The gangs, which both boys knew well, occasionally used such punishment on members who tried to quit. Bear in mind that this environment is sustained with federal dollars.

6   The conduct of the two young killers was all the more understandable given that they have I.Q.'s of 60 and 76, with perhaps less emotional maturity than 5-year-old Eric. The judge in the case has ordered psychiatric treatment and follow-up care. But in light of what experts describe as Illinois's poor record with treatment—and its high failure rate with juveniles—the prospects for treatment seem poor. In Massachusetts or Missouri, the two would have been sent to facilities with fewer than two dozen beds and extensive psychiatric help. In Illinois, the boys could go to lockdowns with hundreds of others—many of them gangsters who will recreate the projects behind bars.

7   Few things are more horrifying than the murder of a child. But in view of the antecedents, Eric Morse's death was almost a naturally occurring event. The projects have become factories for crime and killers, with homicide taking younger and younger victims each year. The judge who sentenced Eric's killers called it "essential to find out how these two young boys turned out to be killers, to have no respect for human life and no empathy for their victim." We know quite well what made them killers. What we need is the political will to do something about it.

Brent Staples, "The Littlest Killers." From *The New York Times*, © February 6, 1996 The New York Times. All rights reserved. Used by permission and protected by the Copyright Laws of the United States. The printing, copying, redistribution, or retransmission of the Material without express written permission is prohibited.

The passage above does present facts regarding the murder of Eric Morse by two other boys and the very poor conditions in the Chicago public housing projects that have led to crimes like that. However, the writer concludes by stating: "We know quite well what made them killers. What we need is the political will to do something about it" (paragraph 7). We can infer from those statements that the writer is urging readers to support measures that will help correct the conditions in the housing projects or politicians who favor such measures. In short, he is trying to get us to agree with his point of view regarding the causes of crimes like the murder of Eric Morse and asking us to take action to eliminate them.

ACTIVITY 3   *DIRECTIONS: Write a short essay dealing with a contemporary issue in which you try to persuade the reader to think in a certain way or take a particular action.*

ACTIVITY 4   *DIRECTIONS: Bring to class an example of a passage from a magazine, newspaper, or the Internet that was written to persuade readers.*

To Entertain

A writer whose purpose is to entertain must try to *bring enjoyment to readers by treating a topic in a light, cheerful, funny, or laughable manner.* For example, as you read the passage that follows, think about its purpose.

However, *to entertain* does not always mean something is funny. An entertaining passage can captivate a reader with suspense rather than humor. It can engage the audience by stirring their emotions or imagination. The reaction can be one of fear, sympathy, and/or laughter.

Fork Manufacturer Introduces Fifth Tine to Accomodate Growing American Mouthfuls

February 18, 2010 ISSUE 46•07

EVANSVILLE, IN—In an effort to keep pace with the rapid growth of American mouthfuls, flatware manufacturer KitchenMaster announced yesterday the addition of a fifth tine to its line of dinner forks. "These days, a traditional four-tined fork is just not enough to handle the quantities of food people shove down their throats," said company spokesman Ken Krimstein, holding up a fork supporting six separate tortellini, two turkey sausages, and some mashed potatoes. "To stay relevant to our customer base and bring back some of those who have given up on using utensils entirely, this was an adjustment we just had to make." Krimstein added that the augmented forks would soon be followed by 25 percent deeper spoons and 3-gallon gravy boats.

From *The Onion*, February 18, 2010. Reprinted with permission of THE ONION. Copyright © 2010, by ONION, INC. www.theonion.com.

The passage above is from *The Onion,* a satirical newspaper that is read by many college students and can be found on most campuses. Notice that the humor is through irony or satire. The writer uses a contemporary issue in the news and makes fun of it by writing an article that is fictitious. The purpose is to entertain readers by making them laugh.

ACTIVITY 5   DIRECTIONS: *Write a short essay dealing with a contemporary issue that has entertainment as its purpose.*

ACTIVITY 6   DIRECTIONS: *Bring to class an example an article that was written to entertain readers.*

Combination of Purposes

Sometimes a writer has more than one purpose, as illustrated in the passage dealing with Eric Morse in the article "The Littlest Killers." As you recall, the writer provided factual information but also tried to persuade readers to accept his viewpoint and take action. The previous passage about dinner forks was designed to entertain. These examples are not at all unusual, especially when you are reading material that deals with controversial contemporary topics.

When there is a combination of purposes, try to uncover and concentrate on the writer's *overall* or *main purpose* by focusing on the most important messages and the information that lends direct support to them. Remember that recognizing the purpose (or purposes) helps you evaluate the reliability and objectivity of reading material. This is very important when dealing with issues that involve conflicting, debatable, and sometimes emotional viewpoints.

ACTIVITY 7

DIRECTIONS: *Write a short essay dealing with a contemporary issue that demonstrates a combination of purposes.*

ACTIVITY 8

DIRECTIONS: *Bring to class an example of a passage from your textbook or the Internet that has a combination of purposes.*

ACTIVITY 9

DIRECTIONS: *Read the following passages, and answer the questions. When reading each passage, keep in mind the writer's background or affiliation, the publication in which the writing appears, and how the most important information is presented, all of which should help you recognize the writer's overall or main purpose. Remember to use inference skills when appropriate.*

Eye on Vocabulary

When reading each passage, take note of any unfamiliar words you come across. List them and their definitions in your notebook or on note cards. Use the context, word parts, or the dictionary to determine their meanings. After the completion of each passage, your instructor will ask to see your notebook or note cards and may discuss key words in class.

1

Pornography

1   It is against the law to distribute pornography, "obscene," or sexually explicit materials in the media. The general public also opposes the distribution as well as the use of pornography. Yet pornography has become an enormous industry today. A major reason is that the demand for sexually explicit materials has soared over the last decade. The number of hard-core video rentals, for example, skyrocketed from only 75 million in 1985 to 665 million in 1996. Today, the United States has become by far the world's leading producer of hard-core videos, churning them out at the astonishing rate of about 150 new titles a week (Schlosser, 1997; Weber, 1997). Pornography has also gone online; whatever X-rated, hard-core material is

available in adult bookstores or video stores can be accessed via the Internet. But is pornography harmful?

2   According to some conservatives, pornography is harmful to society. The studies most often cited to support this view, conducted in laboratories, suggest that exposure to pornography increases aggression. In these studies, male subjects were first made to feel irritated, angry, or ready to behave aggressively. Then they were exposed to pornographic materials. In general, their level of aggression increased significantly (Soble, 1996; Linz and Malamuth, 1993). But the artificial laboratory setting is quite different from the real world. At home, pornography users may not become more aggressive because they can do something—such as masturbating or copulating—to satisfy their sexual arousal.

3   According to some liberals, pornography is harmless. To support this view, studies that fail to show a connection between pornography and rape are often cited. Cities with high circulation of sexually oriented magazines, for example, have largely the same rates of rape as cities with low circulation. But the pornography in such studies is mostly *nonviolent*, depicting merely nudity and consensual sex (Strossen, 1996; Linz and Malamuth, 1993).

4   Other studies suggest that *violent* pornography is harmful, as some feminists assert. For example, research often finds that men who see slasher movies, in which a female rape victim is cut up, show less sympathy for rape victims in general. Studies of rapists suggest that men who lack sympathy for rape victims are more likely to assault women (Kipnis, 1996; Cole, 1995; Linz and Malamuth, 1993). We may therefore conclude that nonviolent pornography may be harmless but that violent pornography is harmful.

Virtual World: The Proliferation of Cyberporn

5   Pornography in cyberspace is not new. Soon after the Internet came on the technological scene, people started to exchange dirty pictures on the Net. But amateur swapping has now given way to commercial ventures. By mid-1997, according to an online guide to cyberporn, there were already about 900 sex sites on the Web. Only 1 year later, this number had soared to somewhere between 20,000 and 30,000. These commercial sites vary in size from small outfits with just a few hundred paying members to major networks with thousands of subscribers.

6   Cyberporn has become big business, raking in some $700 million a year. Sex sites are comparable in popularity to sports or weather sites and have only slightly fewer visitors than business and travel sites. A onetime stripper's site brings in so much revenue that she has given up stripping for good. In her former profession, she made only $1,500 a month, but immediately

after going on the Web, her monthly earnings jumped to $10,000 to $15,000. A 23-year-old man formed a company called Internet Entertainment in 1997 and now makes $20 million annually by offering a wide range of online shows. One type, called "live video," features exotic nude dancers in full color on the computer screens of customers, who can chat on the phone with the gyrating performers. Customers can also click their way to different virtual rooms: in the "bedroom" the visitor can see a naked dancer rolling around on a giant mattress, and in the "health club" the performer works out on a step exerciser with no clothes on.

7   Cyberporn has become so popular primarily because customers can view racy material in the privacy of their homes. They no longer have to sneak into a sleazy adult bookstore or the back room of a video shop.

Alex Thio, *Sociology: A Brief Introduction*, 4th ed., pp. 154–155

COMPREHENSION QUESTIONS

1. What is the topic of the passage?
2. What is the central message of the passage?
3. Determine what is at issue. What is your initial personal viewpoint?
4. Distinguish among opposing viewpoints, and provide the rationale for each.
5. Think carefully about the viewpoints. Express a personal viewpoint, and give the reasons why you favor it. Does it differ from your initial personal viewpoint? Why or why not?
6. Write a few paragraphs *in support of the viewpoint that you do* not *favor.*

THOUGHT AND DISCUSSION QUESTIONS

1. In your view, should pornography be permitted in cyberspace? Why or why not?
2. Can you safely infer from the passage that the author is opposed to the use of pornography? Why or why not?
3. Have you ever used pornography? Why or why not?
4. In your view, did the studies that first made male subjects angry or ready to behave aggressively and then exposed them to pornographic materials prove that exposure to pornography increases aggression? Why or why not?
5. What is the author's *overall* or *main purpose*? Give specific reasons for your answer.
6. List any questions that came to mind while you were reading this selection, and be prepared to discuss possible answers to them.

2

March of the Penguins

1   Audiences of the popular documentary *March of the Penguins* could be forgiven for thinking that the biggest challenge facing Antarctica's Emperor penguins is their icy cold habitat. In fact, a significant threat to these denizens of the southernmost continent is that their home won't be icy enough for very much longer. Scientists studying Emperor penguins at the colony featured in the film found that their numbers have dropped by 70% since the 1960s. The likely culprit: global climate change.

2   In the 1970s, increasingly warm temperatures, in both the air and the ocean, descended on the penguins' Antarctic home. The Southern Ocean experiences natural shifts in weather from one decade to the next, but this warm spell has continued practically unabated. Warmer temperatures and stronger winds produce thinner sea ice, the frozen ocean water on which the penguins nest. The weakened ice is more likely to break apart and drift out to sea, taking the penguins' eggs and chicks with it. Emperor penguins are the only species of bird that can survive exclusively in or on the ocean—without ever touching land. But for the sea ice to be stable enough to nest on, it must be attached to land.

3   Scientists believe global warming is responsible for the rising temperatures and changes to sea ice, though they can't be certain. Sea ice has decreased only in certain parts of Antarctica, but the frozen freshwater that covers most of the land mass—called "land ice"—is thinning across the whole continent. A recent NASA study using satellite mapping technology found that Antarctica is losing land ice at a rate of 31 billion tons of water per year. The Emperor penguins, like other animals who rely on sea ice to breed and hunt for food, are feeling the impacts first.

From Al Gore, *An Inconvenient Truth*, 2006, p. 178

COMPREHENSION QUESTIONS

1. What is the topic of the passage?
2. What is the central message of the passage?
3. Determine what is at issue. What is your initial personal viewpoint?
4. What is an opposing viewpoint for this passage? Provide a rationale for your answer.
5. Think carefully about the viewpoints. Express a personal viewpoint, and give the reasons why you favor it. Does it differ from your initial personal viewpoint? Why or why not?
6. Write a few paragraphs *in support of the viewpoint that you do not favor.*

THOUGHT AND DISCUSSION QUESTIONS

1. In your view, is the loss of "land ice" a problem for other species, such as the polar bear? Why or why not?
2. If sea ice has decreased in only certain parts of Antarctica, would that still be a problem for the penguins? Why or why not?
3. In your view, is this passage biased? Why or why not?
4. A movie was made from the book in which the information for this selection was taken. In your opinion, is the author a reliable source? Why or why not?
5. What is the author's *overall* or *main purpose?* Give specific reasons for your answer.
6. List two questions that came to mind while you were reading the selection. Be prepared to discuss possible answers to them.

3

Waterboarding

1   (March 12)–Karl Rove, former senior political adviser to President George W. Bush, says he is "proud" the U.S. used waterboarding to gain information from terror suspects.

2   "I'm proud that we used techniques that broke the will of these terrorists," he said in a BBC interview, adding that he did not consider waterboarding to be torture.

3   The practice, considered by many to violate the terms of the Geneva Convention on the conduct of war, was sanctioned in a series of memos by white House lawyers in 2002. It involves pouring water into a captive's breathing passages, simulating a sensation of drowning.

4   President Barack Obama banned the practice in January 2009 and released documents that revealed the use of other techniques under Bush, including systematic sleep deprivation.

5   Though many view waterboarding as torture, Karl Rove told the BBC that he was "proud" that the United States used the interrogation technique on suspected terrorists.

6   Rove said waterboarding "gave us valuable information that allowed us to foil plots such as flying airplanes into Heathrow and into London, bringing down aircraft over the Pacific, flying an airplane into the tallest building in Los Angeles and other plots."

7   "Yes, I'm proud that we kept the world safer than it was, by the use of these techniques," he said in an interview from New York. "They're appropriate, they're in conformity with our international requirements and with U.S. law."

8   Asked if waterboarding was torture, he replied, "No, it's not."

9   He added: "People need to read the memos that outline what was permissible and not permissible before they make a judgment about these things.

10   "Every one of the people who were waterboarded had a doctor who had to ascertain that there had been no longstanding physical or mental damage to the individual."

11   Rove also said suspects were told they would not drown.

12   The Central Intelligence Agency publicly admitted using waterboarding for the first time in 2008, when Director Michael Hayden told Congress it had been applied on three al-Qaida suspects. These included Khalid Sheikh Mohammed, charged with masterminding the Sept. 11, 2001, attacks.

Terence Neilan, "Rove Says He's 'Proud' US Used Waterboarding," March 12, 2010, http://www.aolnews.com/world/article/karl-rove-says-hes-proud-us-used-waterboarding/19396354?sms ss=email

COMPREHENSION QUESTIONS

1. What is the topic of the passage?
2. What is the central message of the passage?
3. Determine what is at issue. What is your initial personal viewpoint?
4. Distinguish among opposing viewpoints, and provide the rationale for each.
5. Think carefully about the viewpoints. Express a personal viewpoint, and give the reasons why you favor it. Does it differ from your initial personal viewpoint? Why or why not?
6. Write a few paragraphs *in support of the viewpoint that you do* not *favor.*

THOUGHT AND DISCUSSION QUESTIONS

1. Do you agree with the author that waterboarding is not torture? Why or why not?
2. Can you infer from the passage that Karl Rove believes that the Geneva Convention does not prohibit waterboarding? What evidence from the article did you use to come to this conclusion?
3. In your view, will waterboarding be considered a criminal act in the future? Why or why not?
4. Do you think the information presented is mostly fact, mostly opinion, or a combination of both? Why? Cite examples.
5. What is the author's *overall* or *main purpose*? Give specific reasons for your answer.

■ The Importance of Recognizing Tone

A writer's **tone** or **mood** is *a reflection of the writer's attitude or feelings toward a given topic or issue.* Tone is expressed by the words and phrases used in the information presented. As with purpose, it is important for you to recognize the tone because it helps you determine a writer's motivations or reasons for writing, which can in turn make it easier to recognize bias and distinguish between facts and opinions. Furthermore, it is part of the whole evaluation process that you should use when considering not only what you read but also what you see and hear.

Thus, tone is an important consideration when you deal with contemporary issues and also when you gather information from people and written sources for problem-solving purposes. When interacting face-to-face, a person's *tone of voice* and *body language* will sometimes reveal the person's feelings on a given matter, so you may find yourself in a better position to assess the quality of the information the person is giving you. This, in turn, may help you solve a problem more efficiently. The same benefit applies when dealing with written sources for problem solving, when you want to weigh their objectivity.

As with purpose, writers don't always come right out and say what they are feeling about a particular topic or issue. In those instances, it becomes necessary to "read between the lines" and use inference skills to help determine tone. Thus, the words and phrases a writer uses will serve as the clues to the writer's attitude. As you will recall, it is often necessary to use those same clues to infer a writer's purpose when it is not explicit. In fact, tone and purpose are related, and therefore each can be used sometimes to help figure out the other. For example, if a writer's tone is humorous, it would probably indicate that the writer's purpose is to entertain and vice versa. On the other hand, if the tone is matter-of-fact, the purpose is likely to be informational.

When trying to recognize the tone, there are several possibilities to be considered. This is certainly the case when dealing with contemporary issues, where writers sometimes have more than one purpose. In addition, they may also express more than one attitude toward the subject matter. On those occasions, follow the same procedure that you used when dealing with a combination of purposes. Concentrate on the most important messages and the information that lends direct support to them. This should help you uncover the *overall tone*.

We will focus on five common tones or moods that are often expressed by writers: matter-of-fact, humorous, angry, sad, and ironic. Each one represents an overall feeling or attitude by a given writer toward a particular subject. Let us look at each of these.

Matter-of-Fact Tone

When adopting a matter-of-fact tone, which is common in textbooks, *the writer sticks to the facts and presents them in a straightforward, unemotional manner.* In other words, there is a concerted attempt to be evenhanded and objective. The purpose is informational. For example, read this paragraph:

> Although progress has been made with regard to women's rights in the United States, it appears that there is room for improvement. There are still

jobs not open to them, and they are sometimes paid less than men occupying the same or similar positions. Furthermore, some women have been the victims of out-and-out sexual harassment on the job. In short, it will take a while longer before we can safely say that there is equality between the sexes.

The paragraph expresses little emotion as the author attempts to present the information in a straightforward and unbiased way. For the most part, the words used are not extreme or slanted.

ACTIVITY 10   DIRECTIONS: *Write a paragraph with a matter-of-fact tone on any topic that interests you.*

ACTIVITY 11   DIRECTIONS: *Bring to class an example of a passage with a matter-of-fact tone.*

Humorous Tone

A humorous tone is one in which *a writer presents information in a lighthearted manner designed to entertain or make the reader laugh.* For instance, read the following paragraph, which deals with the same subject matter as the previous one:

> If you believe that there has been much progress with regard to women's rights in the United States, you probably also believe in the Tooth Fairy. Wake up and smell the aftershave lotion! Women are still excluded from some jobs as if they were suffering from some weird contagious disease. And just compare their pay scales to those of men in certain positions—you could die laughing. Not to mention that some males turn into cavemen when they are around women on the job. Equality between the sexes? Give me a break!

Although the paragraph makes basically the same points as the previous matter-of-fact one, it does so in a much more lighthearted way. The use of expressions such as "Tooth Fairy," "weird contagious disease," "you could die laughing," and "turn into cavemen" and the various exclamations are an attempt to be funny and make the reader laugh.

ACTIVITY 12   DIRECTIONS: *Write a paragraph with a humorous tone on the same topic that you used for Activity 10.*

ACTIVITY 13   DIRECTIONS: *Bring to class an example of a passage with a humorous tone.*

Angry Tone

An angry tone lets you know that *the writer is annoyed, irritated, or bothered in some way about the subject matter being presented.* For example, read the following paragraph, which deals with the same topic as the previous ones:

> I am sick and tired of hearing how much "progress" has been made with regard to women's rights in the United States. Women are prevented from filling some jobs and are paid ridiculously low wages in certain positions, compared to men. Furthermore, some men behave obnoxiously when they are around women on the job. It is absurd to say that we have achieved equality between the sexes.

Although the paragraph is similar to the other two in terms of the points being made, it presents them in a much more emotional manner. The use of the expressions "sick and tired," "ridiculously low," "behave obnoxiously," and "absurd" clearly express the writer's anger.

ACTIVITY 14   *DIRECTIONS: Write a paragraph with an angry tone on the same topic that you have been using.*

ACTIVITY 15   *DIRECTIONS: Bring to class an example of a passage with an angry tone.*

Sad Tone

A sad tone *presents information in a gloomy, melancholy, or sorrowful way.* For instance, read the following paragraph, which is on the same topic as the previous ones:

> Although some slight progress has been made with regard to women's rights in the United States, there is, regrettably, ample room for improvement. It is discouraging to realize that some jobs are still not open to women and that women are too often paid less than men occupying the same or similar positions. Furthermore, some women are still the unfortunate victims of sexual harassment on the job. In short, equality between the sexes at this point remains far beyond our grasp. What a sad state of affairs!

Once again, the points that are made in the paragraph are similar to those found in the others, but this time the points are presented in a downcast manner. The use of "regrettably," "discouraging," "unfortunate," and "sad state of affairs" and the generally negative approach to the material indicate that the writer is pessimistic about the situation.

ACTIVITY 16   *DIRECTIONS: Write a paragraph with a sad tone on the same topic that you have been using.*

ACTIVITY 17   *DIRECTIONS: Bring to class an example of a passage with a sad tone.*

Ironic Tone

The dictionary defines irony as "a method of humorous or sarcastic expression in which the intended meaning of the words used is the direct opposite of their usual sense" or "a combination of circumstances or a result that is the opposite of what might be expected or considered appropriate." Thus, an ironic message *conveys its meaning by using words to mean the opposite of what they usually mean,* and an ironic event is an occurrence that is *the opposite or reverse of what is normally expected.* We might describe a bad day in a sarcastic manner by saying "What a wonderful day I've had!" We also might observe the irony in the fact that the first ship specifically designed to be unsinkable, the *Titanic,* sank on its very first voyage. A writer generally uses irony to present messages in a catchy, unusual way so that readers will take notice and remember them. For instance, read the following paragraph, which deals once again with women's rights:

> Now that women are in business suits, why don't we just assume that no further progress needs to be made with regard to women's rights in the United States? We can simply ignore the fact that some jobs are still not open to them and that they are sometimes paid less than men occupying the same or similar positions. It really doesn't even matter that some women are still being subjected to sexual harassment on the job. Let's just proclaim equality between the sexes a *fait accompli* and get the whole issue behind us.

Notice how the writer takes what is essentially the same information but this time uses expressions that mean the *opposite* of the points he really wants to convey. By using this somewhat unusual technique, he hopes that the reader will be jolted into taking note of and remembering the *intended* messages.

Let us look at another example of irony, an occurrence that is the opposite of what is normally expected:

1   Earnest, lean Regilio Tuur, looking like a strip of copper wire with muscles, was no-nonsense as he shadowboxed outside the bloodstained ring at Gleason's Gym near the Brooklyn waterfront. But he permitted himself an ironic laugh when his workout was over and he talked about how his craft had changed.

2   He remembers when his big concern was how to keep from being cut badly. These days, he worries more when an opponent starts gushing blood. You never know anymore, said this young man.... Who can say where the other fellow has been?

3   "I've fought four times in the last year and had four H.I.V. tests, and my manager made sure that my opponents were tested, too," said Mr. Tuur, a Suriname-born Dutchman now living on Long Island. "This is a blood sport. You can't be careful enough. People talk about testing and the right to privacy, but that's a crock. We're talking about lives here. Going into the ring with someone who's tested positive, that's an act of suicide, isn't it?"

Here the irony involves how one circumstance has changed completely in the sport of boxing. In the past, the boxer discussed in the passage was concerned about sustaining a bad cut, whereas now, with the AIDS problem, he is more worried about an opponent getting cut. Thus, what is happening is the opposite of what normally has been expected. Notice that the writer explicitly lets the reader know that there is irony in this situation by calling the boxer's laugh "ironic."

ACTIVITY 18

DIRECTIONS: *Write two paragraphs in an ironic tone on any topics that are of interest to you. In one of the paragraphs, convey a message by using words to mean the opposite of what they usually mean, and in the other, discuss an occurrence that is the opposite or reverse of what is usually expected. Use the two examples in the text to guide you, and feel free to discuss your paragraphs with your classmates.*

ACTIVITY 19

DIRECTIONS: *Bring to class an example of a passage with an ironic tone.*

ACTIVITY 20

DIRECTIONS: *Read the following passages, and answer the questions. When reading each passage, concentrate on the most important messages and the information that lends direct support to them to help you uncover the overall tone. Remember to use inference skills when appropriate.*

Eye on Vocabulary

When reading each passage, take note of any unfamiliar words you come across. List them and their definitions in your notebook or on note cards. Use the context, word parts, or the dictionary to determine their meanings. After the completion of each passage, your instructor will ask to see your notebook or note cards and may discuss key words in class.

1

TWD Should Be the New Drunk Driving

1   Texting while driving (TWD) has been in the news a lot lately—most recently because of a new gone-viral video on YouTube that dramatizes its dangers. Although it's frequently lumped into the category of "distracted driving," TWD is a far cry from just talking on a cell phone. Talking basically translates to a phone and a crunched-up shoulder, leaving one hand free for steering. For the unskilled among us, TWD frequently requires the use of both hands—one to hold the device and the other to text. It also involves translating abstract thought into written language, no matter how truncated that language may be. Most importantly, TWD requires a driver to take his eyes off the road, making it both mentally and physically distracting.

2   While drunk driving is being driven into oblivion by a convergence of tougher policing and DUI Laws and social pressure from groups like MADD and the general public, TWD doesn't seem to have the same stigma. Drunk driving is bad in part because it suggests a lack of a self-control. Texting while driving frequently involves work—and in today's neo-Puritanical society where people are working longer and harder than ever, what could possibly be wrong with working constantly, even behind the wheel?

3   And guess what? Your peers are not only doing it, but admitting to it. We conduct a weekly "quick poll" on the *AA&B* Web site, with questions ranging from the silly (name your favorite fast food) to the serious (weighing in on the

health insurance reform debate). The question that has gotten the biggest response so far was, "Have you ever texted while driving?" —and almost a third of the respondents admitted that they had. If TWD levels are that significant among insurance people—who should really know better—the numbers are probably much higher in the general population.

4   While unscientific, our survey suggests that TWD isn't the exclusive domain of Gen Y-ers, who I don't think comprise much of *AA&B*'s readership. Text-intensive social networks like Twitter are peopled primarily by the 35-and-up demographic. Maybe it's just me, but the thought of a horde of aging drivers texting and hurtling down the expressway at 85 mph in their 5,000-pound SUVs beats the hell out of any Stephen King novel for scare value.

5   But the tide may be turning. Some states are passing laws prohibiting TWD, and federal legislation is on the table as well. A recent survey by Nationwide Insurance found that 80 percent of Americans favor a ban on texting while driving, while two thirds favor a ban on cell phone calls, and more than half say they would support a ban on cell phone use altogether.

6   It's unclear whether any laws will really stop the hard-core from texting while driving, but at least it might make them stop and think—even if they're only thinking about avoiding a costly ticket or better yet, a jail sentence.

7   And for those of you who are proud of your TWD ways—please let me know when you plan on being on the road so I can stay home.

Posted on September 3rd, 2009, by *Laura Toops,*
Editor of American Agent & Broker in *Gen Y, consumers, legislation,*
http://agent-for-change.com/2009/09/03/twd-should-be-the-new-drunk-driving/

COMPREHENSION QUESTIONS

1. What is the topic of the passage?
2. What is the central message of the passage?
3. Determine what is at issue. What is your initial personal viewpoint?
4. Distinguish among opposing viewpoints, and provide the rationale for each.
5. Think carefully about the viewpoints. Express a personal viewpoint, and give the reasons why you favor it. Does it differ from your initial personal viewpoint? Why or why not?
6. Write a few paragraphs *in support of the viewpoint that you do not favor*.

THOUGHT AND DISCUSSION QUESTIONS

1. Why did the author compare texting to drunk driving?
2. What words does the author use to let you know her opinion about texting while driving?
3. Do you think the information presented is mostly fact, mostly opinion, or a combination of both? Why? Cite specific examples.

4. What is the overall *tone* of the passage? Give specific reasons for your answer.

5. List any questions that came to mind while you were reading this selection, and be prepared to discuss possible answers to them.

2

You're in My Spot

SHARON WHITE TAYLOR

1   While my husband, Cliff, and I were sitting in our car outside a restaurant recently, a man pulled into a space clearly reserved for the handicapped. When he bounded out of his car and sprinted into the restaurant, all my senses stood at attention.

2   Since becoming disabled by a stroke three years ago, I've waged a campaign against the able-bodied who are too lazy to walk extra steps. In this case, the man had a choice of nearby parking spots, but he opted for the reserved space in front of the door.

3   This wasn't the first time I have challenged a parking cheat. Often, from my car, I've spotted a nonqualified person parked illegally and have called out: "Excuse me, you are parked in a handicapped zone." I have clumped after people with my walker and chased them down with my wheelchair to point out the errors of their ways.

4   While family members agree with my reasons for pursuing my mission, they worry about my methods. One winter's day my sister, Nancy, questioned my sanity when I forced her to push my wheelchair through an icy parking lot to confront a woman without a limp (or a parking sticker) walking away from a handicapped space. Later, Nancy was glad she had given me the chance to challenge the offender. The woman confessed: "I should know better. I'm a nurse." She moved her car. Not long ago, when I reminded another woman that she was parked in a handicapped zone, she retorted in a huff, "I know all about you people. I work in a convalescent home."

5   Most people don't apologize. Many are rude. Some offer nonsensical excuses. I confronted one man as he briskly headed into a grocery store. "My mother is handicapped," he snapped.

6   Before I joined the ranks of the disabled, I often eyed those coveted spots on rainy days or when I stopped for milk or bread after a long work day. I passed them by. After suffering a broken leg some years ago, I understood their importance. In my state, permits are not issued for temporary handicaps. When my husband pulled into a typical narrow parking space, he had great difficulty trying

to maneuver the wheelchair out of the car without hitting a neighboring vehicle. Pushing a wheelchair in the snow and rain or across a rutted parking lot can be hazardous.

7   The switch from temporary to permanent disability hasn't been easy. Following a brief bout with depression, I decided to accept what can't be changed. I have even learned to appreciate the perks. It is comforting to find a spot close to the store while other shoppers trek through snow or heat.

8   My adult children joke about taking me and my parking permit to concerts so they can have privileged parking. Of course, they quip, you have to wait in the car.

9   All kidding aside, others envy my parking status. One blistering hot summer day, a woman saw me getting out of my car at a crowded mall. She was obviously wilted after walking the length of the large lot. "You are so lucky," she said. "I'll trade places with you." I smiled. "Gladly," I answered. "I would love to walk."

10   Though I rarely feel sorry for myself these days, it would be nice to leave my house without wondering if my destination has stairs I can't negotiate or whether privileged parking will be available. In many places there are only one or two designated spots and they may be occupied. There have been times when being unable to find a space has meant we've had to forgo plans to attend an event. The frustration of finding the marked places filled by nondisabled drivers has spurred me to continue my battle against abusers.

11   Until recently, if I found a car illegally parked with no driver in sight, I would leave a hastily scribbled note on the windshield. Now I am armed with professionally printed, bright orange notices given to me by another family waging the same war. In large black letters the placards read: "This is not a ticket but a reminder. You are parked in a space that is reserved for the handicapped. These facilities are provided for individuals whose physical disabilities make their use a necessity."

12   Having left more than 50 handwritten notes and about a dozen printed notices, I was curious about their effect on the offenders. The very-abled man who had parked illegally in front of the restaurant would be a perfect gauge to test whether the placards made a difference.

13   I suggested to Cliff that we eat our sandwiches in the car and wait to see how the transgressor reacted. Cliff agreed, but he made me promise not to confront the man directly. Cliff is always conscious of my safety and blanches when I face off with scofflaws.

14   I'm sure he won't forget the day I spotted a burly oaf pulling a huge truck with monster tires into a reserved spot. Cliff refused to take my wheelchair out of the car and the guy was too far away to hear me shouting. I think of him as the big one that got away. I wasn't about to let that happen again.

15   So we munched our sandwiches, sipped coffee and discussed what the latest offender's reaction might be. Even though I'm an optimist, I didn't expect him to flagellate himself and cry *mea culpa*. Perhaps he would look sheepish and glance around to see if anyone had noticed the big orange flier under his windshield wiper. Maybe in the future he would be more considerate. My husband is a pessimist. His prediction proved more accurate.

16   After about 20 minutes, the man returned to his car. He saw the notice, pulled it off the windshield and quickly read it. Looking as if he had smelled something vile, he threw it down next to a trash container, spat on the ground and drove away.

17   We had our answer. People who illegally park in spaces for the handicapped also litter and spit.

18   Oh, dear, am I being politically incorrect? Have I stereotyped people who usurp handicapped parking? If you feel maligned, defend your position. Point out that you may selfishly inconvenience the disabled, but you never litter or spit in public.

Sharon White Taylor, "You're in My Spot," *Newsweek*, February 19, 1996, p. 20. Reprinted by permission of Clifford J. Taylor.

COMPREHENSION QUESTIONS

1. What is the topic of the passage?
2. What is the central message of the passage?
3. Determine what is at issue. What is your initial personal viewpoint?
4. Distinguish among opposing viewpoints, and provide the rationale for each.
5. Think carefully about the viewpoints. Express a personal viewpoint, and give the reasons why you favor it. Does it differ from your initial personal viewpoint? Why or why not?
6. Write a few paragraphs *in support of the viewpoint that you do* not *favor.*

THOUGHT AND DISCUSSION QUESTIONS

1. In your view, are handicapped parking spaces justified? Why or why not?
2. Do you ever park in handicapped parking spaces? Why or why not?
3. Is the writer on solid ground when she infers that "people who illegally park in spaces for the handicapped also litter and spit" (paragraph 17)? Why or why not?
4. What is the *overall tone* of the passage? Give specific reasons for your answer.
5. List any questions that came to mind while you were reading this selection, and be prepared to discuss possible answers to them.

LOOKING BACK...LOOKING FORWARD

To check your progress in meeting this chapter's learning objectives, log in to www.myreadinglab.com, go to your Study Plan, and click on the Reading Skills tab. Choose Purpose and Tone from the list of subtopics. Read and view the assets in the Review Materials section, then complete the Practices and Tests in the Activities section. You can check your scores by clicking on the Gradebook tab.

THINK AGAIN!

The following message, along with a picture of the local museum of art, appeared on the side of a bus in Atlanta, Georgia:

The real barrier between people and great art is not money. It is parking!

What is the purpose of the message? What is its tone?

CRITICAL READING

This chapter discussed the matter-of-fact tone which is common in academic textbooks. This chapter also discussed humorous, angry, sad, and ironic tones. Find a Web site passage that uses a humorous tone, an angry tone, a sad tone, or an ironic tone to get its point across. Write a paragraph citing the tone used, and include phrases used in the passage to support the tone. Attach an image or picture to your paragraph to support the paragraph's tone.

You may want to explore topics of your own choosing for this activity or some of the viewpoints expressed in the reading in this chapter:

- Global warming
- Crimes in housing projects
- Pornography or cyberporn
- Waterboarding
- Texting while driving

LISTENING SPRINGBOARD INQUIRY

Go to the National Public Radio Web site at http://www.npr.org/ and click on "listen" on the menu bar, then "24-Hour Program Stream." Select a topic to listen to.

Title of the selection: _____

Who is the individual speaking, and/or what is his or her title or position? What is the topic of this message?

_____

_____

_____

What are the key points of the message?

_____

_____

What is the purpose of the message or discussion?

_____

_____

Is the speaker's tone friendly? Belligerent? Matter-of-fact? Does the speaker's tone affect your response to the message? How?

_____

_____

_____

DROPOUT

Remember to follow these steps:

- first, read the narrative and all the questions
- second, examine the picture carefully
- third, answer the questions in the order they appear and come up with the solution

Have fun!

As the clock struck five, ninety-year-old Mrs. Mirabel Fallwell dropped out of the window of her spacious twelfth-floor apartment. On the fourth stroke she struck.

Detective Amos Shrewd investigated shortly afterwards and found the room as you see it. Jerry Jarvis, Mrs. Fallwell's nephew and heir, said that the portrait on the wall of his beloved aunt was one that he himself had painted. Under questioning, he claimed that he had been at the far end of the apartment at the time of the tragedy and that he knew nothing about it until informed by the police.

If you were Shrewd, would you charge Jarvis with homicide?

Questions

1. Is there a reason why Mirabel interrupted her phone call and went to the window? ☐ Yes ☐ No

2. Did Mirabel rush to the window?   ☐ Yes ☐ No

3. Is it likely that she brought a footstool to the window?   ☐ Yes ☐ No

4. Is it reasonable to suppose that Mirabel had a dizzy spell while at the window?   ☐ Yes ☐ No

5. Did she try to keep herself from falling out of the window?   ☐ Yes ☐ No

6. Do you think she committed suicide?   ☐ Yes ☐ No

7. What do you think was the cause of death?   ☐ Accident ☐ Murder

Text and illustration from Lawrence Treat, *Crime and Puzzlement: 24 Solve-Them-Yourself Picture Mysteries* (David R. Godine, Publisher, 1981), pp. 30–31

Dropout

Name _____   Date _____

MASTERY TEST 8-1

DIRECTIONS: Answer the questions.

1. Define the term *writer's purpose.*

   _____

2. Define the term *writer's tone.*

   _____

3. When a writer simply provides facts, data, or information about a subject so that we can learn more about it, the purpose is
   a. to persuade.
   b. to inform.
   c. to entertain.
   d. all of the above
   e. none of the above

4. When a writer is trying to get us to think in a certain way or take a particular action, the purpose is
   a. to inform.
   b. to entertain.
   c. to persuade.
   d. all of the above
   e. none of the above

5. When a writer sticks to the facts and presents them in a straightforward, unemotional manner, the tone is
   a. matter-of-fact.
   b. humorous.
   c. angry.
   d. sad.
   e. ironic.

6. When a writer is mad, annoyed, irritated, or bothered by the subject matter presented, the tone is
   a. sad.
   b. angry.

   c. humorous.

   d. matter-of-fact.

   e. ironic.

7. When a writer presents information in a lighthearted, funny manner, the tone is

   a. ironic.

   b. matter-of-fact.

   c. humorous.

   d. angry.

   e. sad.

8. When a writer presents information in a gloomy, melancholy, or sorrowful way, the tone is

   a. angry.

   b. ironic.

   c. sad.

   d. matter-of-fact.

   e. humorous.

9. When a writer uses words to mean the opposite of what those words usually mean, the tone is

   a. ironic.

   b. angry.

   c. sad.

   d. matter-of-fact.

   e. humorous.

10. What is the purpose and tone of the message on the sign in this photograph taken in Chicago?

Purpose: _____

Tone: _____

Name _____   Date _____

MASTERY TEST 8–2

DIRECTIONS: *Determine the purpose and tone for each of the passages.*

1

Happy National Apathy Day

WILL DURST

1   Don't vote. You don't have to. No one's going to make you. This isn't the Soviet Union in the 50's. You won't be forced from your bed and dragged to the polls against your will. Relax. None of your friends are voting. And things are pretty good the way they are, right? If it ain't broke, don't fix it. What do you care if some barren deserted beach does or doesn't get blanketed by a thick film of 30-weight because of offshore drilling? Find another beach. What's the big deal?

2   Don't vote; you know you don't want to. Parking is a pain, the print is so tiny, and it's always on a Tuesday—what's that all about, anyway? Besides, haven't the pollsters already told us who's going to win? Why beat your head against a wall? It's a done deal. Out of your hands. Don't even need to wash them. It'd be totally different if it actually mattered. But it's not as if we have any real choice. If voting were effective they would have made it illegal by now.

3   Don't vote. Everyone knows the big corporations have the politicians so deep in their pockets they've got to brush the lint out of their hair before photo ops. It's common knowledge. Conventional wisdom. You'll only end up encouraging them.

4   You must have better things to do. Jog on over to the library before it gets closed down and read up on other people who never voted. Or you could work on that extra room for Grandma when Medicare fails and she has to move in. Or take a farewell trip on your local mass transit and wave bye-bye to the neighborhood rec center. That would be fun.

5   Besides, what difference does it make? One lousy little vote. A spit in the ocean. Don't worry. Be happy. Stay home. This is still a free country, last time I looked. Who cares? Not you.

New York Times, November 2, 1998, p. A27

Purpose: _____

Tone: _____

2

As Demand for Donor Eggs Soars, High Prices Stir Ethical Concerns

RONI CARYN RABIN

1   Samantha Carolan was 23 and fresh out of graduate school when she decided to donate eggs to an infertile couple. Ms. Carolan concedes that she would never have done it if not for the money, $7,000 that she used to pay off some student loans. She has since had a second egg extraction, for which she was paid $8,000, and she is planning a third before taking a break. "The first time, it's frightening," said Ms. Carolan, now 24, of Winfield Park, N.J. "It is surgery, and I don't think I would have done it without compensation. But I had very limited pain, and it was a great experience for me. I would have done it the second time for less money or even no compensation."

2   Though many egg donors derive great satisfaction from knowing that they helped someone start a family, the price of eggs has soared in recent years as demand has increased, and the sizable payments raise controversy. A survey published this month in the journal *Fertility and Sterility*, "What Is Happening to the Price of Eggs?" found that the national average compensation for donors was $4,217. At least one center told the authors of the paper that it paid $15,000. Many centers did not respond.

3   Though laws prohibit the sale of transplant organs, sperm donors have always received small payments, and prospective parents in the United States are allowed to compensate women for their far greater expenditure of time and energy.

4   Meanwhile, advertisements recruiting students from elite universities to donate, promise tens of thousands of dollars, and donor agencies have sprung up, appealing to would-be parents with online videos and photo galleries of donors. According to the Centers for Disease Control and Prevention, 5,767 babies were born in 2003 from donor eggs; the number of actual egg donations is probably much higher, however, because the success rate is fairly low. Ethicists and some women's health advocates worry that lucrative payments are enticing young women with credit-card debt and steep tuition bills to sell eggs without seriously evaluating the risks.

5   "The real issue is whether the money can cloud someone's judgment," said Josephine Johnston, an associate for law and bioethics at the Hastings Center, a research group in Garrison, N.Y., that specializes in medical ethics. She does not oppose compensation, but she does worry about high prices. "We hear about egg donors being paid enormous amounts of money, $50,000 or $60,000," Ms. Johnston said. "How much is that person actually giving informed consent about the medical procedure and really listening and thinking as it's being described and its risks are explained?"

6   "One of the most striking facts about in vitro fertilization is just how little is known with certainty about the long-term health outcomes for the women who undergo the procedure," a recent report by the Institute of Medicine said.

7   The process of egg extraction is time consuming, and it is not comfortable. For some women, it can be painful. A woman first has to take medications to stop her menstrual cycle and then daily hormone injections for several weeks to stimulate her ovaries to produce a crop of mature eggs at once.

8   The drugs may cause bloating, weight gain, moodiness and irritability, and there is a risk of a rare condition called ovarian hyperstimulation syndrome that can cause life-threatening complications, blood clots and kidney failure. The egg extraction itself is a surgical procedure in which a thin needle is inserted through the vagina into the ovary to retrieve the eggs and liquid from the follicles. Risks include adverse responses to anesthesia, infection, bleeding or the inadvertent puncture of an organ.

9   It is the long-term risks, both physical and psychological, that are harder to assess. Questions have been raised about whether extraction may jeopardize the donor's fertility, and critics worry about the potential psychological harm to a donor of eggs as a young woman who later finds that she is unable to have children.

10   And since egg donors go through much the same process as women trying to conceive in vitro, there are concerns that they may be prone to the higher rates of certain cancers that some studies have found among the infertility patients. Still, said Dr. James A. Grifo, director of the division of reproductive endocrinology at the New York University School of Medicine, "There is no credible evidence of long-lasting effects or health consequences down the line." That does not necessarily mean that the procedures are safe.

11   When Ms. Carolan went to donate, the short-term risks were described to her in detail, but she said she did not recall any mention of possible long-term risks. Her family opposed her decision because they worried about her health, she said, and her friends did not understand. "They all think I'm crazy," she said. "If the topic comes up, and I tell friends I've done it, they're like: 'Why? Oh my God, aren't you afraid you have a baby out there?' They're so stunned and shocked." Then she tells them how much she was paid. "And then they go, 'O.K., I understand now, that's cool,'" she said. "People understand the money."

Purpose: _____

Tone: _____

Name _____   Date _____

DIRECTIONS: *Read the following article from* The Onion, *and discuss its ironies.*

White-Collar Prison Is a Great Networking Opportunity

LAWRENCE BEAN

1   This is turning into the best 6 to 10 years of my life. Serving a mandatory sentence at a federal prison is exactly the shot in the arm my career needed. No stress, no deadlines, no ongoing investigations. Just the freedom to learn and grow as a professional and—I'm not going to deny it—to have a little fun while I'm at it. This has got to be the best opportunity available for people in my line of work.

2   I am loving it here!

3   First of all, I can't say enough about the contacts I've already made between these walls. They are, bar none, some of the most skill-diverse colleagues I've ever had the pleasure of doing business with. We've got every kind of specialty man: the tech guys, the administrative types, the slick one-on-one cats, the gonzo all-in go-getters. The best of the best. In my cell block alone I could set up one of the best creative accounting teams American free enterprise has ever seen. And to think, they're here 24–7, always ready to share their expert advice.

4   I've made so many contacts, I've had to start keeping track of them by scratching the numbers on my cell wall. I've got 17 new contacts so far! This kind of access is invaluable.

5   It's amazing how quickly you get to know people once you're removed from the cut-throat competition of the business world, and realize that everyone in here is working toward a common goal.

6   I know I've accomplished a lot in life—and I've seen it all laid out ad nauseam in some of the finest courts of law in the land. Still, this experience has really made me rethink my priorities. It's amazing to be able to absorb the wisdom of those hardened veterans who have been around longer than me, to learn the lessons they've learned. It's made me realize that I'm capable of so much more. I see how important it is to take care, watch the little things, and be passionate about the work you do.

7   My roommate, Bill Halpert, is a perfect example of the kind of take-charge, no-nonsense, clear-thinking businessman I'm talking about. One time, on laundry detail, he slipped me a little tip about how important it is to make sure, when using deceased people's names and Social Security numbers to collect a couple dozen extra paychecks, that the CFO's grandmother doesn't end up on the payroll. Or to be careful not to use purchase-order numbers that could be traced back to your department when earning hundreds of thousands of dollars in false invoices.

8   This is stuff I could never pick up at some team-building exercise. This is the kind of gold you can only get from real insiders. These are the lessons you find in the most unexpected places, but wind up carrying with you for the rest of your life.

9   I don't have to tell you that dealing with S.E.C. regulations is enough to drive any average junior VP crazy. In here, I've learned how to channel that rage into other outlets. "But what about all those infuriating applications that make it harder for people like us to do an honest day's work?" you might ask. And I might answer, "What if I spot a guy at the bench-press who happens to work for the Feds, and what if he happens to have some pretty ingenious ideas for streamlining our bottom line?"

10   Brainstorming sessions can happen at anytime. There are just so many people here at the top of their game that the energy can sometimes be hard to contain. Still, nothing gets things done like a good old-fashioned lunch meeting. The stuff we come up with over Salisbury steak or chicken patties in the mess hall is so brilliant that I'm scared to tell you about it—and that's not just because one of the guys involved could arrange for someone completely unconnected to him but still on one of his tax-shelter company's payrolls to put a bullet in my brain!

11   But it's not all business in here. Outdoor activities provide some of the best opportunities for working on camaraderie with potential associates. Shooting hoops or playing softball really breaks down those barriers. The atmosphere is so natural and relaxed that there's never any reason to be shy. I've found that if you get in there and have a good sense of humor about yourself, people will respect you for it. The fact is, I've made so many new friends here that I know I'll have people I can turn to for support once I get on the outside. And when it comes to any professional relationship, isn't trust the key ingredient?

12   Sign me up for another stint anytime!

From *The Onion*, September 14, 2006, pp. 8-9. Reprinted with permission of THE ONION. Copyright © 2006, by ONION, INC. www.theonion.com.

Ironies: _____

_____

_____

9

Looking at Advertisements and the Internet with a Critical Eye

CHAPTER OUTCOMES

After completing Chapter 9, you should be able to:

- Continue to apply the basic method for personal problem solving.

- Evaluate an advertisement by determining how it tries to catch the interest of readers; to whom it is designed to appeal; what it is trying to persuade readers to buy, do, or think; the benefit to readers that it is stressing; and how convincing it is.

- Evaluate an e-mail to determine if it is trustworthy.

- Evaluate an Internet Web site for authority, accuracy, currency, purpose, and bias.

- Continue to find topics and central messages in contemporary-issue passages to determine what is at issue, distinguish among opposing viewpoints, and express personal viewpoints.

Think About It!

What is advertisement 1 trying to get readers to do? What is the tone? Discuss your answers with your classmates.

To whom is advertisement 2 appealing? What is it trying to get readers to do? What is its tone? Discuss your answers with your classmates.

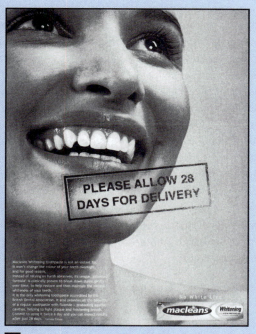

1

2

PROBLEM-SOLVING EXERCISE

Apply the first four steps of the basic method for personal problem solving to the following hypothetical situation. Your instructor will divide the class into four groups for purposes of dealing with the problem from the different perspectives of José, Maria, Carlotta, and Pedro. In other words, Group 1 will tackle the problem from José's point of view, Group 2 from Maria's point of view, Group 3 from Carlotta's point of view, and Group 4 from Pedro's point of view. After all four groups have completed their work, a person from each group will speak on behalf of the other members as the entire class attempts to come up with a possible solution acceptable to all groups.

Hypothetical Situation

José and Maria have been married for many years and have three children two years apart. Their oldest son is now residing in another state, while their 23-year-old daughter, Carlotta, and their 21-year-old son, Pedro, still live at home.

Pedro, as the youngest child, has been somewhat spoiled through the years to the extent that his siblings feel a certain amount of resentment toward him. To them, Pedro has always seemed to demand and receive more attention, time, and money.

In recent years, the situation has gotten very tense at home, particularly between José and Pedro. It seems that they clash about everything and are constantly shouting at each other, which is causing much stress for the entire family. José, who gets very angry, feels that Pedro is selfish and much too demanding. As head of the family, José has decided to draw the line. Otherwise, he fears that he will lose control of the household to Pedro. In fact, on several occasions, they have almost come to blows.

Maria believes that her husband is being much too firm with Pedro, and she really does not like the way José talks to him. She has told José many times that he is using insulting, degrading language in his arguments with their son. Pedro also gets very mad at his father and always tends to go to his mother as an ally who is more receptive to his wishes. José interprets Maria's actions as a lack of support for him, and as a result, he is losing his self-respect and has become very resentful.

Consequently, José and Maria have had some very heated arguments, which have affected the stability of their marriage. Carlotta, feeling the tension, has withdrawn from the situation and tends to stay in her room much of the time. She has become totally disgusted with the entire household!

■ Advertisements and Critical Thinking

Pretend that you are a skier, and read the following advertisement in the newspaper:

Every item in every Princeton Ski Shop has been reduced to the lowest price ever. Guaranteed.

Would you rush right out to the nearest Princeton Ski Shop and buy everything in sight? One hopes not! At the very least, you would first want to know if the advertisement is referring to the lowest prices ever at the Princeton Ski Shop or at all stores that sell those items. Furthermore, you would wonder how Princeton Ski Shop can prove to customers that the prices are indeed the lowest ever or, for that matter, how *you* would be able to find out that information for yourself. Finally, you would be interested in what the guarantee involves. For example, if you could prove to Princeton that it once sold a particular item at a cheaper price than it is now or that you can find it for less at a competing ski shop, what is the store prepared to do under the terms of its guarantee?

As a critical thinker and reader, you are very aware of the importance of evaluating what you see, hear, and read so that you are in a better position to make the best possible decisions. This is particularly important when dealing with advertisements, which are designed specifically to influence your thinking, which of course in turn has an effect on your purchasing, political, and philosophical decisions. In fact, in today's world, you are overwhelmed with advertisements that attempt to persuade you to *buy* something, *do* something, or *think* something. You are urged to buy certain products, including foods, drinks, automobiles, and clothing; to take advantage of particular services, such as tax-return preparation, cleaning, or pest control; to attend social affairs, workshops, or classes; to vote or not to vote for certain candidates or political issues; and to support or oppose particular viewpoints regarding such issues as abortion, health care, and school prayer. There is no end to the stream of claims and counterclaims, all designed to sell you something.

If you do not pick and choose among the products, services, and ideas pushed by advertisers, you could soon go broke, become confused about whom and what to vote for, or perhaps not even know what to think. You can avoid those unattractive possibilities by taking the time to think critically about advertisements so that you can evaluate the information *before* acting. In short, critical thinking can help you sift through all the information thrown your way. How, then, should you think critically about advertisements? You do this by answering a series of questions designed to uncover their purposes and strategies.

■ Evaluating an Advertisement

One way to evaluate an advertisement is to ask and answer the following questions:

- How does it try to catch the interest of readers?
- To whom is it designed to appeal?
- What is it trying to persuade readers to buy, do, or think?
- What benefit to readers is it stressing?
- How convincing is it?

As you know, looking at the world with a questioning mind to find answers to questions like these is an important aspect of critical thinking. This certainly applies when dealing with advertisements, which are often very clever in their attempts to sway our minds.

Although we will be concerned only with advertisements in print, the same questions are relevant to all forms of advertising. These questions should enable you to evaluate advertising claims more effectively so that you can make informed decisions regarding what to buy, what to do, and what to think. Let's look at each of the questions in turn.

How Does It Try to Catch the Interest of Readers?

Advertisers have numerous ways to catch your interest to persuade you to purchase something. One way is to build a whole experience around the product. For example, when you see this ad from Porsche, it promises freedom and excitement, "What a dog feels when the leash breaks."

To Whom Is It Designed to Appeal?

Advertisers always have intended audiences targeted for their messages—men, women, or children of specific ages, from various ethnic groups, and

**What a dog feels
when the leash breaks.**

Instant freedom, courtesy of the Boxster S. The 250 horsepower boxer engine launches you forward with its distinctive growl. Any memory of life on a leash evaporates in the wind rushing overhead. It's time to run free. Contact us at 1-800-PORSCHE or porsche.com.

PORSCHE

with certain interests. It is important that you know to whom an advertisement is designed to appeal so that you can decide whether you should spend your time giving serious consideration to what it has to say.

How does the following ad use gender as an appeal? In what specific ways does it get the attention of its intended audience?

If you answered that the ad is designed to appeal to women, you are correct. This advertisement for a new paint container shows how it makes painting easier for women because of its features. The color pink accentuates the ad's appeal to women in the original ad.

What Is It Trying to Persuade Readers to Buy, Do, or Think?

Obviously, the whole point of a given advertisement is to get you to purchase a product, take a certain action, or think a certain way. It is important that you recognize the point of an advertisement so that you can determine if it has relevance to your life and is therefore worthy of your time.

What are the ads on the following pages trying to get you to do? What technique do they use to persuade?

What Benefit to Readers Is It Stressing?

An effective advertisement is very specific about the benefit to readers as a result of their buying, doing, or thinking whatever is being urged by the ad. Buying the Dutch Boy brand of paint in its new container will make it easier and less messy for you to paint your home. It is extremely important that you recognize the benefit stressed by an advertisement so that you can make a sound decision as to whether to follow its advice. Look at the following advertisements, and determine what benefit they are stressing.

Choose electricity that's **100%** pollution-free

Want an easy way to help clean the air we breathe? Choose clean electricity from Green Mountain Energy Company.

Green Mountain's electricity is 100% pollution-free, because it's produced solely from Texas wind. In fact, by choosing Green Mountain, you can prevent as much carbon dioxide as your car makes in more than 22,000 miles of driving.

And since all that's changing is how your electricity is generated, not how it comes to your home, your electric service will be just as reliable as always.

Green Mountain Energy®

www.greenmountain.com

You may obtain important standardized information that will allow you to compare this product with other offers. Call Green Mountain Energy Company (Texas Certificate No. 10009) at 866-572-1312 or visit our website at www.greenmountain.com.

© 2007 Green Mountain Energy Company. All Rights Reserved. Green Mountain Energy and the Green Mountain Energy logo are registered service marks and Pollution Free is a service mark of Green Mountain Energy Company.

EVERYONE DESERVES A SECOND CHANCE.
NOT TO MENTION A FIRST.

A child comes into this world with nothing. And for some, sadly, that never changes. But your donations to The Salvation Army make a difference. With your support, our youth programs will continue to give poverty-stricken children something they would never otherwise have: Opportunity. To give, call 1-800-SAL-ARMY or visit salvationarmyusa.org

THE SALVATION ARMY

DISASTER RELIEF EMERGENCY RESPONSE HOUSING COUNSELING   REHABILITATION YOUTH SERVICES SOCIAL WORK EVANGELISM

DOING THE MOST GOOD®

To combat our dependence on the oil industry, many ads are now appealing to the concept of "green." This ad for electricity pledges to protect the environment and appeals to the reader's sense of civic duty to do his or her part to reduce greenhouse gas emissions. This is an example of a **moral appeal.**

See the ad above. What is the moral appeal in the Salvation Army ad?

How Convincing Is It?

From your perspective as a critical thinker, the most important consideration concerning the evaluation of a given advertisement involves how convincing it is in terms of the benefit stressed. In short, your decision as to whether to buy, do, or think what an ad is suggesting is based on the degree to which you become convinced that the benefit to you is both relevant and valid.

The "Got Milk" ads with their popular milk moustaches use well-known actors and sports figures to persuade you to drink milk. To emulate them, you should do the same thing. If they drink milk, it must be a healthy thing! This technique of using famous people to influence the reader is called a **testimonial**.

The photos at the top of page 411 are testimonials to sell Nike products and Ray-Ban sunglasses. Mia Hamm endorses Nike products, and NASCAR superstar Jeff Gordon is wearing Ray-Ban sunglasses. Why might these stars convince you to be "more like them"?

DIRECTIONS: Advertisements sometimes try to create a positive change in society. Do you remember the phrases, "Friends don't let friends drive drunk," and "Only you can prevent forest fires!"? The ads below are examples of the Ad Council's campaign to change social behavior. What would you say are the messages of these ads?

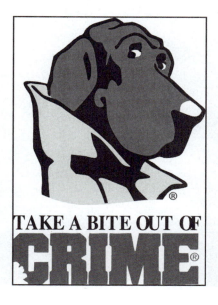

DIRECTIONS: Marketers are sometimes accused of deceptive practices in mailings. The tobacco industry is an example of marketing to young not giving out enough information about the dangers of smoking. To nies had to settle lawsuits and received hefty fines because of Medica treat people sick from diseases caused by smoking. Restrictions on ad marketing were part of the settlement. You may have received an env mail claiming that you have won money or products, or you may have pop-up screens promising free goods or discounted prices. Sweepstak

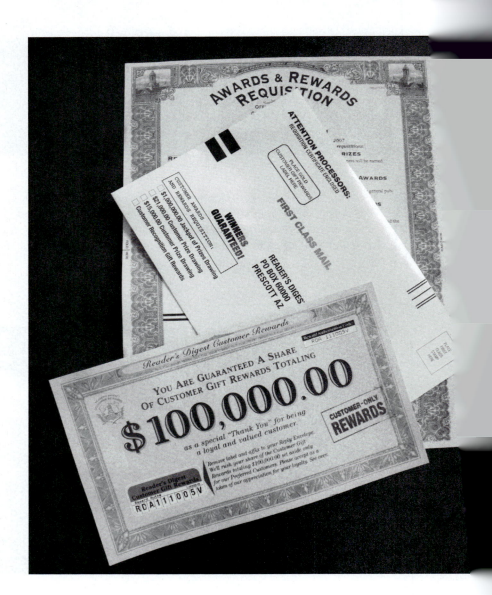

Publishers Clearing House recently paid fines to settle claims that its high-pressure marketing tactics misled customers into believing that they had won prizes when in fact they had not.

Look at the examples on pages 412 and 413. What claims or statements do these two ads make that are misleading?

ACTIVITY 3 *DIRECTIONS: For this activity, your instructor will divide the class into groups of three. Evaluate each of the following advertisements within your group by asking and answering these five questions:*

- How does it try to catch the interest of readers?
- To whom is it designed to appeal?
- What is it trying to persuade readers to buy, do, or think?
- What benefit to readers is it stressing?
- How convincing is it?

Be prepared to discuss your answers with the rest of the class.

TV is Good.

For years the pundits, moralists and self-righteous, self-appointed preservers of our culture have told us that television is bad. They've stood high on their soapbox and looked condescendingly on our innocuous pleasure. They've sought to wean us from our harmless habit by derisively referring to television as the Boob Tube or the Idiot Box.

Well, television is not the evil destroyer of all that is right in this world. In fact, and we say this with all the disdain we can muster for the elitists who purport otherwise – TV is good.

TV binds us together. It makes us laugh. Makes us cry. Why, in the span of ten years, TV brought us the downfall of an American president, one giant step for mankind and the introduction of Farrah Fawcett as one of "Charlie's Angels." Can any other medium match TV for its immediacy, its impact, its capacity to entertain? Who among us hasn't spent an entire weekend on the couch, bathed in the cool glow of a Sony Trinitron, only to return to work recuperated and completely refreshed? And who would dispute that the greatest advancement in aviation over the last ten years was the decision to air sitcoms during the in-flight service?

Why then should we cower behind our remote controls? Let us rejoice in our fully adjustable, leather-upholstered recliners. Let us celebrate our cerebral-free non-activity. Let us climb the highest figurative mountaintop and proclaim, with all the vigor and shrillness that made Roseanne a household name, that TV is good.

abc

Sony and Trinitron are trademarks of Sony.

1

This is my brother Omar.

He had a hole in his tummy.

A bullet hit him.

I saw red grass.

A gun was in the garage.

I didn't mean to shoot daddy's gun.

I didn't mean to shoot daddy's gun.

An unlocked gun could be the death of your family.
Please lock up your gun.

Ad Council

www.unloadandlock.com

NATIONAL CRIME
PREVENTION COUNCIL

2

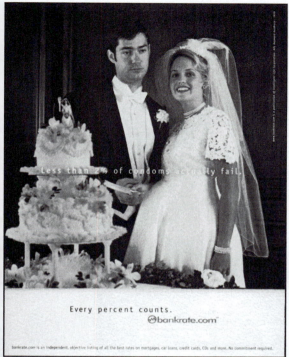

Less than 2% of condoms actually fail.

Every percent counts.

ⓔbankrate.com™

bankrate.com is an independent, objective listing of all the best rates on mortgages, car loans, credit cards, CDs and more. No commitment required.

3

TomPaine.common sense
A Journal of Opinion

Eating
in the Dark

FDA Will Not Require Labeling of Genetically Engineered Foods

Americans have a right to know what's in our food.

So how come the Food and Drug Administration wants us eating in the dark?

The FDA has proposed new rules that would not require genetically engineered food to be labeled as such. The rules would also continue to allow these foods to be sold without any required safety testing.

Very little independent research has been published on the safety of genetically engineered (GE) foods. The FDA's own scientists have warned that there's not enough evidence to declare them safe. Yet, in what amounts to an uncontrolled human experiment, the FDA has already allowed GE foods to become part of our diet.

We don't know what these foods might do to people with allergies or weak immune systems, or if they have any long-term effect on children. Biotechnology companies might know, but in the name of protecting trade secrets they have kept most of their test results private and away from peer review.

We do know this: Credible polling shows consumers overwhelmingly support GE food labeling. Yet the FDA has ignored the public's desire, proposing rules that give the biotech industry just what it wants. And no wonder. Generous contributions to both political parties give the industry special access to FDA's overseers in Congress and the White House.

The new FDA rules are not yet final. **Consumers have one more week – until May 3 – to let the agency know what they think.** They can do so through the website **www.TrueFoodNow.org.**

The 15-nation European Union, Japan, Australia, New Zealand, South Korea and Russia all mandate the labeling of genetically engineered food.

But if the FDA's new rules go through as drafted, Americans will be left eating in the dark.

This Week at TomPaine.com –
Eating in the Dark
Featuring a detailed critique of the FDA's proposed rules..."The A-B-C's of GE Food" by Rachel Massey... and "Common Sense on Biotech" by Michael F. Jacobson.

■ **TomPaine.com. Money and Politics. Environment. Media Criticism. History.**

© 2001 The Florence Fund, PO Box 53003, Washington, DC 20009

4

5

ADVERTISEMENTS

Investigate a Web site advertisement that tries to convince you to purchase a product, do something, or think a certain way. Is the ad misleading? Does the ad use inference to relay its message? Print the ad, and write an explanation of its appeal to share with the rest of the class.

■ Evaluating E-Mails

Critical reading of incoming e-mail has become an important skill in this technological age. Fraudulent messages try to scam the reader to give money, buy products, or collect free money and merchandise from "so-called reputable" retail stores and banks. Often the senders *phish*, or try to get your personal data.

Be aware that fraudulent e-mails often:

- appear to come from a legitimate source (i.e., your personal banking institution).

- request personal information (i.e., account numbers, usernames, credit card numbers, passwords).
- contain fraudulent offers (i.e., prizes or gift certificates).
- combine real and fraudulent information to create a message that is legitimate looking.

If you get suspicious-looking e-mail, you should:

- not give out any personal information.
- not click on any of the links or attachments within the e-mail.
- report the message on a security system purchased for the computer.

Look at the following example. What makes you think this e-mail may be suspicious?

From: Ticket Confirmation[ConfirmationDept@boywonder.com]
Sent: Monday, January 08, 2011 11:41 AM
To: Smith, Lori
Subject: All Expense Paid Trip to See OPRAH Live!

http://boywonder.com/x/iyd1/yh Congratulations 18duckie@yahoo.com

CLICK HERE for Your ALL EXPENSE PAID TRIP to CHICAGO

Get Your O Today!

*See Terms and Gift Rules Powered by Rewards Today. Rewards Today is an independent rewards program for consumers and is not affiliated with any of the companies mentioned above. Rewards Today is solely responsible for all gift fulfillment. To receive your gift, simply 1)Participate in the survey 2) Qualify for the sponsor offer(s) (see Gift Rules) and 3) Follow redemption instructions. By continuing, you certify that you agree to the terms and conditions. Copyright 2011 Rewards Today. All rights reserved. You can unsubscribe from promotions here http://optout.as3pub.com/pub.phy/pid+25. Mailing address: Rewards Today Customer Care, 151 Park Avenue South #1895 New York, NY 10076.

If the offer of a trip and free tickets is from an address that has nothing to do with the show in Chicago and does not reveal the terms and conditions, you would be correct to be suspicious. And who knows what would happen if you clicked on the link for the "all expense paid trip."

ACTIVITY 4   *Directions: Review the following e-mails and determine what would make them authentic or scams.*

1. What would make you think that the following e-mail might be a scam? Be specific and provide details. Share your ideas with your classmates.

From: HongKongPresent@aol.com
Sent: Friday, September 22, 2010 8:06 AM
To: Lori Smith
Subject: Re: Invitation To Treat

Dear Friend,

Top of the day to you, I hope this correspondence reach you in good health.

I must first crave your indulgence as the contents of this correspondence may not meet your personal or business ethics. I apologize in advance.

I am David Johnson, I presently head the investment division of Bank of America, Hong Kong. The main purpose of this correspondence is to intimate you of a possible joint business venture.

In the course of our yearly audit, we came across a fixed deposit account of US17,6000,000.00 (Seventeen Million, Six Hundred Thousand United States Dollars) only that has been rolled over for the past four years.

Further investigation revealed that the said fixed deposit belonged to an expatriate (Name with-held for the time being) who was a consultant/contractor with the Chinese Ministry of Agriculture

Going through his bio-data form, we discovered that the only contact written by him was that of his personal lawyer. Correspondence between both of me revealed that the depositor had passed on and the lawyer is the executor of his will. Further prodding from me also revealed that the will made no mention of the deposit being help in our bank.

After careful deliberations, the lawyer and I have decided to find a means of keeping this fund for ourselves. The lawyer proposed that he write a letter to our bank in his official capacity as the lawyer and executor of the will to have our bank transfer the funds a third party we will both nominate.

The lawyer has agreed I should look for the third party and he will facilitate the paperwork for this claim with your active participation. All I need is your consent to act as the third party and I will put all relevant information at your disposal and discuss your renumeration for this endeavour.

Should this proposal be of interest to you, please indicate your interest via a return mail to enable me put more information at your disposal.

I remain obliged.

Yours Truly,
David Johnson

2. If you owned a small business and received this e-mail, what would make you think twice about following through with the request? Share your ideas with your classmates.

From: VITTORIO FOUNDATION [b_xyz@walla.com]
Sent: Saturday, August 06, 2010 6:00 AM
Subject: Grant

You are by all means advised to keep this whole information confidential until you have collected your donation, to avoid double and unqualified claim, due to beneficiaries informing third parties on cash grant donation.

On behalf of the Board, kindly accept our warmest congratulations!

Yours faithfully,
Mr. Boitti Xelot
(Foundation officer)

3. Provide an example of an e-mail that is suspicious to you. Indicate why the e-mail might be suspicious. Share your ideas with your classmates.

Evaluating Web Sites

Caution is suggested when reading information from the Internet. The Internet is not owned by anyone and is thus not regulated. Many Web sites are not evaluated before they are published. Because of this, the reader cannot assume that every Web site has reliable and accurate information.

When using information from a Web site, a critical reader must evaluate the site's

1. authority
2. accuracy
3. currency
4. purpose or bias

Is the Authority Trustworthy?

The author or authors of Web sites need to be reliable. Questions to ask are:

- Is the author identified on the site?
- Does the author have the education, expertise, or experience to be a trustworthy source for the subject of the site?
- What is the affiliation of the author or organization of the site?
- Is the site a legitimate source for the subject?

A medical site, for instance, should be written by a reputable professional who is affiliated with a credible organization such as a hospital, medical

California's Velcro Crop under Challenge (1993)

by Ken Umbach

California's important Velcro crop, vital to the clothing, footwear, and sporting goods industries, has been severely stressed by drought, disease, and pests.

Background

Velcro®, an engineered crop, consists of two distinct strains: hooks and loops. As any user of Velcro knows, a strip of hooks clings to a strip of loops as the springy hook-shaped fibers latch through tiny but firm loops. Gentle pressure allows the hook strip to be pulled from the loop strip. The user may repeat the process time and again, making this product a convenient, versatile replacement for zippers, buttons, snaps, laces, and other forms of fastener in wide-ranging applications.

California's climate and soil conditions make the state an ideal venue for and successful producer of both strains of Velcro. For obvious reasons, of course, the hook strain must be grown in fields separated from those with the loop strain. This is often accommodated by widely spacing separate fields of the two strains among large expanses of cotton, alfalfa, or other crops.

For competitive and industrial confidentiality reasons, of course, the crop is not widely highlighted in crop reports. A little Velcro goes a long way, as both strains are densely packed on their respective mature plants, and the entire crop is dwarfed by other field crops, most notably cotton. Nonetheless, the crop is of high value and can be a substantial profit builder for the successful grower.

The Issues

Three issues have conspired to threaten and diminish the crop in California's southern San Joaquin Valley, especially drought-affected Kern County.

- Dry and windy conditions have caused hook and loop spores to commingle even across widely spaced fields, resulting in tangled Velcro bolls combining both strains and unprocessable by any known means.

- Invasions of disease and pests have damaged the crop. Specifically (1) the flaccidity virus has resulted in weakened hooks, unable to hold adequately or even to snap through the corresponding loops, and (2) the pest *millipedus minisculus*, or 'tiny thousand-footed creature', has multiplied in the Velcro fields, frequently becoming so ensnared in the developing loops as to make the crop unharvestable.

- Drought has both limited water for the westside Velcro fields and exacerbated crop-stunting salinity.

Crop management for Velcro is made especially difficult by the need to outfit field workers head-to-toe in Teflon® jumpsuits. (The Teflon crop is another issue, to be tackled in a future report in this series.) Absent such protection, field workers are in danger of becoming enmeshed in the Velcro bolls while working the fields. Clothing and even body hair may become entangled with the hooks or loops, requiring difficult extraction procedures. The Teflon jumpsuits in turn require personal cooling equipment and expensive maintenance. When available, it is preferable to hire a crew composed entirely of professional body builders, who are both strong and hairless from head to toe.

All in all, cultivation is a demanding and costly process, making profit margins unusually vulnerable to price swings and crop productivity losses.

Status

As the chart and table below so starkly show, the combined assaults on the Velcro crop have had marked effects.

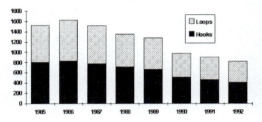

California Velcro Crop Acreage (Successful Harvest)

	1985	1986	1987	1988	1989	1990	1991	1992
Hooks	795	824	766	700	655	500	455	400
Loops	734	802	750	650	625	480	450	425

Recommendations

In view of the singular nature of this specialized crop and its high contribution, when successful, to the financial well-being of the farmers who have the tenacity to grow it:

The respective agricultural commissioners and extension personnel should emphasize proper spacing requirements for fields of the hook and loop strains. Research, training, and inspection are all necessary.

Responsible officials should redouble efforts to eradicate flaccidity virus and *millipedus minisculus*.

Water officials should accommodate the special needs of this high value crop in determining allocations, especially in years of water shortage.

By these means, it should be possible to restore the vigor, productivity, and profitability of this specialized but significant crop.

Postscript (December 1996). The return of relatively normal rainfall patterns, together with sunspot conditions that have decimated flaccidity virus and millipedus minisculus, have contributed to a strengthened Velcro crop, but no one knows what the future might bring. Consider investing in zippers and buttons.

school, or research facility. You can use a search engine to search for the other publications the author has written to give you a clue as to the author's reliability. Authoritative Web sites have links to information about the author or sponsor.

The Web site on the opposite page is about a supposedly lucrative crop in California. What do you think about the authority of this site? Is the site trustworthy? Why or why not?

Because it is a far-fetched idea that Velcro can be grown, you can immediately see the site is untrustworthy. If you were viewing the article online, you could click on the link for information about the author and be directed to a "totally bogus biography." This site and its authority are unreliable.

Now check the site by the Mayo clinic. Why would the authors be trustworthy? Various authors are identified, and they are reputable doctors. The clinic itself is well known throughout the world.

Is the Site Accurate?

The information on a Web site should be accurate and the facts documented. The Web site on page 423 from the city of Mankato, Minnesota, drew a lot of criticism, especially from the local tourist bureau. Some people from other states, who did not know a lot about Minnesota, actually visited in the wintertime expecting to have a beach vacation. The first page of the site should have clued the reader that there was something amiss. Does it sound credible to you that the Web site has been hijacked by terrorists? Does it seem plausible that Martha Stewart and Hillary Clinton are sponsoring the site? And finally, how is it possible that Mankato can have summer all year when it is in a northern state? What are some other details from the links that would make you suspicious of this site? How would you go about checking on these details?

If you were to actually access this site, you would see many more "unbelievable" photos and links. None of the facts are documented. However, the site has a *disclaimer* at the end indicating that the information is not sponsored by any organization and that the writers take no responsibility for its contents. The text on the Web site reads:

LET'S "MAKE IT IN MANKATO"!!

Mankato, Minnesota is truly a wonderland. Tucked into the Emerald Green Valley in Southern Minnesota, it is the hidden vacation Mecca of scores of knowing Midwesterners. Mankato has everything thanks to a freak of nature: the Sclare/Far Fissure. This fissure in the earth's crust takes water seeping through the earth, heats it to well over 165 degrees, and sends it back up to the surface in stream pits and boil holes. The heat from these pits and holes heats the valley air to such an extent that *the winter temperature in many Mankato neighborhoods has never dropped below a balmy 70 degrees!!!!* Come enjoy *our* winters! Let's "Make It Mankato"!!

Is the Site Current?

A Web site's information should be up-to-date. Determine if the site been revised or updated recently. For most Web sites, publication within the past five years is considered current. The links from the site to other sites should also be current.

What Is the Purpose of the Web Site? Is the Site Biased?

A reader should determine what the author's (or organization's) purpose is in publishing the Web site. Who is the intended audience? Web sites fall into one or more categories:

- Advocacy—champions a specific point of view of the authors or organization
- Commercial—tries to sell something

ATTENTION: This site has been hijacked by Sheikh Yarbouti. We are trying to resecure it. Because of this the proper Web address may not appear in your browser address window above.

NEW! **Web Address: http://city-mankato.us**

The Official City-Mankato.US Home Page

Its natural wonders, history, and culture.
Visit us soon!

`91 F`

Let's "Make It In Mankato" ! !

      Mankato, Minnesota is truly a wonderland. Tucked into the Emerald Green Valley in Southern Minnesota, it is the hidden vacation Mecca of scores of knowing Midwesterners. Mankato has everything thanks to a freak of nature: the Sclare/Far Fissure. This fissure in the earth's crust takes water seeping through the earth, heats it to well over 165 degrees, and sends it back up to the surface in steam pits and boil holes. The heat from these pits and holes heats the valley air to such an extent that *the winter temperature in many Mankato neighborhoods has never dropped below a balmy 70 degrees!!!!* Come enjoy *our* winters! Let's "Make It Mankato" ! !
We are real, we are warm and we would love to see you!

Let's visit:

1. Mankato Map. Showing points of interest!
2. Mankato's History.
3. Sibley Park Hot Springs with the DeScy Hot Falls and Johnson Sauna.
4. The Underwater City, and
5. Blue Rurht Underwater World Park.
6. The great Mankato Pyramid.
7. Mankato's Riverfront.
8. The great Stoddard/Milet expeditionary digs of 1907 and the mysterious Silver Disks! *Were they alien spacecraft or a communist plot?*
9. The Führer Putz Underbot Verks Submarine Docks and *"Submarine Days!"*,
10. The Presidents Bush enjoy fishing in Mankato ... the Venice of the north!
11. NEW! Do you know the legends of Haunted Mankato? You may wish that you did not!
12. Whale watching on the Minnesota River.
13. Enjoy tuna and swordfish? *Try* deep-sea fishing on the Minnesota River.
14. Enjoy the Ski-Cruise to 10 months of skiing on Mt. Kroto!
15. A Girl.
16. Celebrate the Winter Solenoid in Mankato: "Hurt Me, Hurt Me Mistress Zeta!",
17. Visit the Great Castle Leed on Mount Mankato. A thrilling mountain view! "All Hail Great Leeder Douglas!",

- Entertainment—amuses and often is humorous
- Informational—imparts documented information such as independent and scholarly research, reference sources, and fact sheets
- News—reports recent events (These sites include news wire services, electronic journals, and online magazines and newspapers.)
- Personal—allows people to publish personal profiles, résumés, and interests (MySpace and Facebook are two such sites used by many students today.)

Look at the following two Web sites. Can you tell immediately what the purpose is of each? Can you tell whether the sites endorse a particular political position? If not, how might you go about evaluating the content?

http://www.ellabakercenter.org/page.php?pageid=1

Whenever you use a Web site as a source for a research paper, you must make sure the site's purpose is appropriate. You will want to use only objective, authoritative sites. One way to determine bias or objectivity is to ask:

- Are only facts presented, or are opinions also included?
- Who benefits from the information on this Web site?
- What groups, individuals, political interests, or commercial interests stand to gain?

ACTIVITY 5

DIRECTIONS: *There are five Web sites featured in this section. Tell what type or types of Web sites they are and why they fit into that category or categories.*

1. California's Velcro Crop

   _____

   _____

2. Mayo Clinic

   _____

   _____

3. City of Mankato, Minnesota

   _____

   _____

4. Ella Baker Human Rights

   _____

   _____

5. Federation for American Immigration Reform (FAIR)

   _____

   _____

ACTIVITY 6

DIRECTIONS: *Visit the following Web sites, and follow the specific directions for each section.*

1. Visit the following Web sites, and evaluate their content. Briefly explain why you either trust or distrust each site for reliable content.
   a. http://www.doctoryourself.com
   b. http://www.improbable.com
   c. http://www.youtube.com
   d. http://factsnotfantasy.com

2. Visit the following Web sites, and evaluate their accuracy.

   a. http://www.wikipedia.org

   b. http://www.theonion.com (Click on "News Archive," and select
      a news story.)

3. Visit the following Web sites, and evaluate their timeliness.

   a. http://www.state.gov/r/pa/ei/bgn (Choose a geographical region, and
      evaluate whether the information is up-to-date.)

   b. http://www.nasa.gov

4. Visit the following informational Web sites. Identify the purpose of
   each site.

   a. http://www.about.com

   b. http://www.pcwebopedia.com

   c. http://www.ehow.com

   d. http://www.answers.com

5. Visit the following advocacy Web sites. Identify the issue and the organization's position on the issue. Check the site's home page, or search the
   organization's mission statement if the position is not clear.

   a. http://www.scorecard.org

   b. http://www.amnestyusa.org/home.html

   c. http://www.bannermoments.com/

   d. http://www.ifaw.org/splash.php

ACTIVITY 7

DIRECTIONS: Visit each site, and view the contents of the site. What is the purpose and tone of each Web site?

1. http://walmartwatch.com/

2. http://www.adbusters.org/

3. http://home.nra.org/#/home

4. http://www.bradycampaign.org

5. http://antifashionblog.blogspot.com/

ACTIVITY 8

DIRECTIONS: Read the following passages, and answer the questions. Remember to use inference skills when appropriate.

Eye on Vocabulary

When reading each passage, take note of any unfamiliar words you come across. List them and their definitions in your notebook or on note cards. Use the context, word parts, or the dictionary to determine their meanings. After the completion of each passage, your instructor will ask to see your notebook or note cards and may discuss key words in class.

1

Obedience to Authority

Harmful Consequences

1   In September of 1987, a protest against the shipment of military equipment to Nicaragua occurred outside of the Naval Weapons Station in Concord, California. Three of the protestors stretched their bodies across the railroad tracks leading out of the Naval Weapons Station to prevent a train from passing. *The civilian crew of the train had been given orders not to stop. In spite of being able to see the protestors 600 feet ahead, they never even slowed the train.* Two of the men managed to get out of the way; a third was not fast enough and had two legs severed below the knee. Naval medical corpsmen at the scene refused to treat him or allow him to be taken to the hospital in their ambulance. Onlookers tried to stop the flow of blood for 45 minutes until a private ambulance arrived. (Kelman and Hamilton, 1989)

Embarrassing Moments

2   A colleague sent a graduate student to be the "substitute teacher" in an introductory psychology class. The undergraduate students had never seen her before. The substitute began the class by saying, "I'm in charge today, and I want to get this session started by asking each of you to stand. Fine, now I want you to clap your hands three times and pat the person standing next to you on the shoulder five times. Now jump up and down for ten seconds. OK, sit down and put your pencils and notebooks on the floor." *Each of the 240 students in the class followed the commands of the teacher without questioning them.* My colleague then entered the room and began a well-listened-to presentation on obedience to authority.

Doing What I'm Told Versus What's Right for Me

3   I was once hired by a company to be part of a workshop on making effective personal decisions. The company maintained and repaired electronic equipment used to monitor radiation levels in nuclear facilities. Some technicians balked at entering an abandoned facility, fearing that it was dangerous to do so.

4   The company decided it only wanted to use technicians who had made an informed choice to maintain and repair the equipment. Experts in the area of radiation as well as those familiar with the site presented information and showed that the site was safe. I was asked to provide some principles of personal decision making that would help the employees decide whether or not they wanted to volunteer for the work.

5   Afterwards, I rode in an elevator with five of the technicians. One of them broke the silence by saying, *"You know, every one of us would have agreed to enter the facility if our boss had simply ordered us to do it. Having all of you experts brought in to talk to us only made us suspicious that the site was, in fact, dangerous."*

Anthony F. Grasha, *Practical Applications of Psychology*, p. 357

COMPREHENSION QUESTIONS

1. What is the topic of the passage?
2. What is the central message of the passage?
3. Determine what is at issue. What is your initial personal viewpoint?
4. Distinguish among opposing viewpoints, and provide the rationale for each.
5. Think carefully about the viewpoints. Express a personal viewpoint, and give the reasons why you favor it. Does it differ from your initial personal viewpoint? Why or why not?
6. Write a few paragraphs *in support of the viewpoint that you do* not *favor.*

THOUGHT AND DISCUSSION QUESTIONS

1. What would you have done if you had been a member of the civilian crew of the train? Why? What would you have done if you had been one of the undergraduate students? Why?
2. Do you agree with what the naval medical corpsmen did? Why or why not?
3. Under the circumstances, would you have felt confident that the nuclear site was safe? Why or why not?
4. Is there any connection between "obedience to authority" and advertising? Why or why not?
5. List any questions that came to mind while you were reading this selection, and be prepared to discuss possible answers to them.

2

Choosing a College with Help from the Web

KATE STONE LOMBARDI

1   Annie was valedictorian of her high school class, and everyone expected her to apply to Ivy League colleges. Annie had other ideas. "I knew I wanted a small liberal arts school comparable in academics to the Ivy League, but without the name-brand ultra-competitiveness that goes along with Princeton, Harvard and Yale," she said. Her mother bought her a thick college view book and Annie visited the counseling center at her high school. Ultimately, though, an Internet search engine helped Annie narrow her choices.

2   As the college application process has become increasingly available through the Web, many companies are offering search engines that help students put together a list of colleges to consider. Some of the sites are like a computer dating service, matching students with potentially compatible colleges.

3   Annie visited Counselor-O-Matic. After entering information about the kind of school she was looking for, along with her grades, class rank and SAT scores, the site generated a list that included an institution she had never heard of, Pomona College in Claremont, California. The more Annie researched Pomona, the better a fit she thought it would be. She is a freshman there.

4   Counselor-O-Matic and similar sites make money from advertising, fees paid by colleges and by selling the names of prospective students to colleges. Companies that sell products such as test-preparation materials also use these sites.

5   Search engines can be especially helpful for students at large high schools, where the ratio of students to counselors can be as high as 800 to 1, or for a student who has extremely specific criteria: the girl who wants a Christian college in the Southeast that offers cheerleading and a biochemistry major.

6   But critics say students must realize that search engines are not guidance counselors. They reduce the search to a numbers game and cannot factor in the culture of a campus, the personality of a student, or the more elusive concept of a fit. Bari Norman, an independent college counselor in Miami warned, "I tell them (students) that it's a good first draft, but you need a human being to contextualize this stuff."

7   Another drawback to the search engines is that they do not weigh factors that college officials consider when they are putting together their classes, like geographic distribution, the reputations of various high schools and sports prowess.

8   Most companies that offer search-engine services say they are meant to be only the beginning of a search process, and also offer related products. For example, most sites offer online college planners, so students can save their searches, take notes or receive automatic feeds from colleges on their list.

9   Still, despite these resources, few guidance counselors embrace the tool wholeheartedly. Thomas Hanley, director of College Guidance at Loyola School in Manhattan, says, "Fear, self-doubt, anxiety, and self-esteem are all at play in the college search. The authentic human interaction is still, thankfully, one of the best ways to reflect with another on one's choices in life."

COMPREHENSION QUESTIONS

1. What is the topic of the passage?
2. What is the central message of the passage?
3. Determine what is at issue. What is your initial personal viewpoint?
4. Distinguish among opposing viewpoints, and provide the rationale for each.

5. Think carefully about the viewpoints. Express a personal viewpoint, and give the reasons why you favor it. Does it differ from your initial personal viewpoint? Why or why not?

6. Write a few paragraphs *in support of the viewpoint that you do* not *favor.*

THOUGHT AND DISCUSSION QUESTIONS

1. List the supporting details for using the Web to search for a college. Are these details fact or opinion? Be prepared to discuss your conclusion with your classmates.

2. List the supporting details for not using the Web to search for a college. Are these details fact or opinion? Be prepared to discuss your conclusion with your classmates.

3. For what other topics could you use Web sites to find information to make a decision? Research some of these sites, and be prepared to share them with the class.

4. What would you say is the purpose of this selection? What is the tone?

5. List any questions that came to mind while you were reading this selection, and be prepared to discuss possible answers to them.

3

Deceptive Practices

1   Marketers are sometimes accused of deceptive practices that lead consumers to believe they will get more value than they actually do. Deceptive practices fall into three groups: pricing, promotion, and packaging. *Deceptive pricing* includes practices such as falsely advertising "factory" or "wholesale" prices or a large price reduction from a phony high retail list price. *Deceptive promotion* includes practices such as misrepresenting the product's features or performance or luring the customers to the store for a bargain that is out of stock. *Deceptive packaging* includes exaggerating package contents through subtle design, using misleading labeling, or describing size in misleading terms.

2   To be sure, questionable marketing practices do occur. For example, at one time or another, we've all gotten an envelope in the mail screaming something like "You have won $10,000,000!" Or a pop-up Web screen promises free goods or discounted prices. In recent years, sweepstakes companies have come under the gun for their deceptive communication practices. Sweepstakes promoter Publishers Clearing House recently paid heavily to settle claims that its high-pressure tactics had misled consumers into believing that they had won prizes when they hadn't. The Wisconsin Attorney General asserted that "there are older consumers who send [sweepstakes companies] checks and money orders on a weekly basis with a note that says they were very upset that the prize patrol did not come."

3   Deceptive practices have led to legislation and other consumer protection actions. For example, in 1938 Congress reacted to such blatant deceptions as Fleischmann's Yeast's claim to straighten crooked teeth by enacting the Wheeler-Lea Act giving the Federal Trade Commission (FTC) power to regulate "unfair or deceptive acts or practices." The FTC has published several guidelines listing deceptive practices. Despite new regulations, some critics argue that deceptive claims are still the norm.

4   The toughest problem is defining what is "deceptive." For instance, an advertiser's claim that its powerful laundry detergent "makes your washing machine 10 feet tall," showing a surprised homemaker watching her appliance burst through her laundry room ceiling, isn't intended to be taken literally. Instead, the advertiser might claim, it is "puffery"—innocent exaggeration for effect. One noted marketing thinker, Theodore Levitt, once claimed that advertising puffery and alluring imagery are bound to occur—and that they may even be desirable: "There is hardly a company that would not go down in ruin if it refused to provide fluff, because nobody will buy pure functionality....Worse, it denies...people's honest needs and values. Without distortion, embellishment, and elaboration, life would be drab, dull, anguished, and at its existential worst."

5   However, others claim that puffery and alluring imagery can harm consumers in subtle ways, and that consumers must be protected through education:

> The real danger to the public...comes not from outright lies—in most cases facts can ultimately be proven and mistakes corrected. But...advertising uses [the power of images and] emotional appeals to shift the viewer's focus away from facts. Viewers who do not take the trouble to distinguish between provable claims and pleasant but meaningless word play end up buying "the sizzle, not the steak" and often paying high. The best defense against misleading ads...is not tighter controls on [advertisers], but more education and more critical judgment among...consumers. Just as we train children to be wary of strangers offering candy, to count change at a store, and to kick the tires before buying a used car, we must make the effort to step back and judge the value of...advertisements, and then master the skills required to separate spin from substance.

6   Marketers argue that most companies avoid deceptive practices because such practices harm their business in the long run. Profitable customer relationships are built upon a foundation of value and trust. If consumers do not get what they expect, they will switch to more reliable products. In addition, consumers usually protect themselves from deception. Most consumers recognize a marketer's selling intent and are careful when they buy, sometimes to the point of not believing completely true product claims.

From Philip Kotler and Gary Armstrong, *Principles of Marketing*, 11th Edition, © 2006, pp. 323–324. Reprinted by permission of Pearson Education, Inc., Upper Saddle River, New Jersey.

COMPREHENSION QUESTIONS

1. What is the topic of the passage?
2. What is the central message of the passage?
3. Determine what is at issue. What is your initial personal viewpoint?
4. Distinguish among opposing viewpoints, and provide the rationale for each.
5. Think carefully about the viewpoints. Express a personal viewpoint, and give the reasons why you favor it. Does it differ from your initial personal viewpoint? Why or why not?
6. Write a few paragraphs *in support of the viewpoint that you do* not *favor.*

THOUGHT AND DISCUSION QUESTIONS

1. Give an example of a deceptive practice in marketing that you have encountered. Does it come under the practice of deceptive pricing, promotion, or packaging? Explain your answer.
2. Give an example of "puffery" in marketing that you have seen from your experience. Explain how you feel about this technique in this situation.
3. Analyze your current e-mails. Give an example of an e-mail that used deceptive practices in advertising. How did you determine it was deceptive?
4. Describe an advertisement on television, and analyze it for any deceptive practices. Explain your conclusion with examples from the advertisement.
5. List any questions that came to mind while you were reading this selection, and be prepared to discuss possible answers to them.

4

Bag-teria Alert: Germ of Truth or Yet Another Urban Legend?

1   Ladies, watch where you put your purses—no, not because of theft, but because of the nasty bacteria that could give you hepatitis and other diseases. That's the gist of a new e-mail getting wide circulation this month. Delete it as junk? Not so fast, according to Snopes.com, a Web site that vets urban legends. There's a germ of truth here.

2   The e-mail describes a TV news report about a study out of the University of Arizona. "A health team went to a local mall and took samples," states the e-mail. "The purses were swabbed with cotton swabs along the entire bottom of the purses and placed into special containers." One in four purses had traces of the E.coli bacterium, which can be a source of illness; other tests found hepatitis and other bugs.

3   To avoid illness, the e-mail advises, "Women should DAILY wipe their purses (particularly the bottom) with a disinfectant wipe and ... be extremely careful where you set your purse. Most important, do NOT place your purse on a table (anywhere) where you will eat or on a kitchen counter and do not put it anywhere close to a toilet" because "the spray goes a distance that is unrecognizable to the human eye."

4   The reality is, you may not want to view your toothbrush or your telephone under the microscope, either. "I am not surprised that women's purses—and probably shoes and other items around us—can be contaminated with organisms," said Shmuel Shoham, an infectious disease specialist at Washington Hospital Center. "But to make the leap from the presence of those organisms to ... disease is a big leap."

5   Washing your hands regularly is key to avoiding illness, Shoham advised. But unless you have a compromised immune system, he said, wiping your purse down daily with anti-microbial preparations is probably overkill.

6   On the Web: www.snopes.com/medical/disease/purse.asp

COMPREHENSION QEUESTIONS

1. What is the topic of the passage?
2. What is the central message of the passage?
3. Determine what is at issue. What is your initial personal viewpoint?
4. Distinguish among opposing viewpoints, and provide the rationale for each.
5. Think carefully about the viewpoints. Express a personal viewpoint, and give the reasons why you favor it. Does it differ from your initial personal viewpoint? Why or why not?
6. Write a few paragraphs *in support of the viewpoint that you do* not *favor.*

THOUGHT AND DISCUSSION QUESTIONS

1. Visit the Web site that goes along with this article. According to the site, this is a true story. List the supporting details from this site that are used to support that viewpoint.
2. If you were evaluating the truthfulness of this article, what topics would you search on the Internet? Search these topics, and relate what you find.
3. What other health-related topics and issues along the lines of this article come to mind? What are your opinions of these topics and issues?
4. In your experience, what are some other ways people can pick up bacteria without even realizing it?
5. List some questions that came to mind while you were reading this selection, and be prepared to discuss possible answers to them.

CRITICAL READING

Find six different Web sites that show the six different purposes/types: advocacy, commercial, entertainment, informational, news, and personal. Some of the sites you find may have a combination of purposes. Write a short paragraph explaining why they demonstrate the purpose(s) you have listed. Be prepared to share your sites with your classmates.

LISTENING SPRINGBOARD INQUIRY

Go to http://www.themoth.org and learn about this organization. What is the Moth? Go to http://www.themoth.org/listen and listen to a story that interests you.

Title: _____

Storyteller: _____

What is the central idea of this message? _____

_____

LOOKING BACK...LOOKING FORWARD

To check your progress in meeting this chapter's learning objectives, log in to www.myreadinglab.com, go to your Study Plan, and click on the Reading Skills tab. Choose Graphics and Visuals from the list of subtopics. Read and view the assets in the Review Materials section, then complete the Practices and Tests in the Activities section. You can check your scores by clicking on the Gradebook tab.

AN 8¢ STORY

Remember to follow these steps:

- first, read the narrative and all the questions
- second, examine the letter carefully
- third, answer the questions in the order they appear, and come up with the solution

Have fun!

The day after Georgio Erysipelas lost fifteen dollars and eight cents to Hans Liverwurst in their weekly poker game, Georgio entered Hans's High Class Delicatessen. Both men were known to be short tempered and had previously come close to fighting over poker hands, but this time the fight was to the death, as Hans's body attests.

All that Detective Sharpeye could learn from witnesses who had heard the argument leading to the tragedy was that Georgio had shouted out in English, "That's all you'll get!" Hans had responded angrily in German, whereupon Georgio had switched into high gear, but in Greek.

Can you guess what they accused each other of?

Questions

1. Was Hans apparently eating when Georgio came into the store?   ☐ Yes   ☐ No

2. Whose footprints are shown?   ☐ Hans's   ☐ Georgio's

3. Did Hans stop at the pickle barrel?   ☐ Yes   ☐ No

4. Do you think Hans offered Georgio a pickle?   ☐ Yes   ☐ No

5. Do you think Hans and Georgio were on friendly terms when Georgio entered the store?
   ☐ Yes   ☐ No

6. Did Hans return to his table at any time after leaving it?   ☐ Yes   ☐ No

7. Do you think that Georgio came to pay his debt?   ☐ Yes   ☐ No

8. Do you think that Georgio came to the store with malice aforethought?   ☐ Yes   ☐ No

9. Is there any evidence to show that Georgio may have acted in self-defense?   ☐ Yes   ☐ No

10. Where did the murder weapon come from? _____

11. Do you think Hans objected to the fact that the five dollar bill was torn?   ☐ Yes   ☐ No

12. What do you think the argument was about?   ☐ The 8¢   ☐ The pickles   ☐ The $10.00

Text and illustration from Lawerence Treat, *Crime and Puzzlement: 24 Solve-Them-Yourself Picture Mysteries* (David R. Godine, Publisher, 1981), pp. 46–47

An 8¢ Story

THINK AGAIN!

Evaluate your survival skills by taking the following "self-discovery test." Be prepared to discuss your responses in class.

Rate Your Survival Skills

LAURA BILLINGS

Most of us have mastered everyday safety basics: Always wear a seat belt. Don't let strangers into your home. Look both ways before you cross the street. But what if you were faced with a more immediate threat to your health and your life? Say a thug demands your car keys. Or a riptide carries you out to sea. Or the earth suddenly shakes beneath you. Would you know what to do—and what not to do? We've picked several high-pressure, panic-inducing situations and asked how you'd react in each case. See how many times you select the best strategy, or the worst.

1. The rain is coming down in sheets on the curvy country road ahead. You lose control of your car and steer yourself right off the pavement and into a river. How do you get out alive?
   a. Get out of the car any way you can.
   b. Stay in the car until help arrives—river currents are too dangerous for the average swimmer.
   c. Wait until the car sinks to the bottom and water pressure equalizes before you open the door to swim out.

2. On a hike, you stumble upon a mother bear and her cubs. She doesn't seem happy. What now?
   a. Run and climb up the nearest tree.
   b. Stand your ground and don't move.
   c. Charge at the bear and wave your arms to scare her and the cubs away.

3. It's been a record snowfall, and you're trapped on the side of the road. The radio says that even the tow trucks are spinning their wheels in the snow and ice, so you:
   a. hike off to find a service station.
   b. put the car in neutral and push until your tires find some traction.
   c. huddle up for warmth inside the car, turn on your dome light and check occasionally to make sure that your tailpipe isn't clogged.

4. You and your surfboard are not alone—a shark is in the neighborhood. Any way to reduce the chance that you'll end up as its afternoon snack?
   a. Leave the board and swim to shore.
   b. Pull your arms and legs on top of the board and remain still.
   c. Float face up in the water, with your limbs at your side—a shark won't attack if you look dead.

5. You hiked solo up a mountainside and are feeling very Maria Von Trapp. But now it's getting dark, and you don't remember how to get back down. You:
   a. find your way out by following flowing water downhill.
   b. build a fire and wait for rescue.
   c. spend the night retracing your tracks—you might have a hard time finding them the next day.

6. On your way out of a fast-food drive-through, a young thug asks you for your money and your car. He and his gun seem very insistent, so you:
   a. hand over your car keys and your wallet and step away from the car.
   b. lock the doors, floor the accelerator and peel out of there.
   c. scream "Help!" to attract the attention of passersby.

7. You wake up in the middle of the night to the sound of a fire alarm and the smell of smoke. Best plan:
   a. Hang a sheet from your window and jump out if the fire comes too close.
   b. Gather up important belongings and race for the door as fast as you can.
   c. Crawl to the door, check the conditions on the other side and proceed if it's safe. If not, retreat and wait for rescue.

8. You're in a Los Angeles parking lot when the Big One finally hits. You:
   a. run to your car and hop in.
   b. stop where you are, crouch into a squat and cover your head.
   c. rush to the doorway of a building, where it's structurally sound; you don't want to be in a wide-open space.

9. It's a Saturday night and you're all by yourself, tossing grapes in the air and catching them in your mouth when, suddenly, one goes down the wrong way. It's getting hard to breathe. How do you save yourself?
   a. Try sticking your fingers in your throat to pull out the offending fruit.
   b. Give yourself the Heimlich maneuver with your fists wrapped together in a ball.
   c. Throw yourself over the top of a high-backed chair with enough force to expel the grape.

10. You and three coworkers are in the office elevator when it gets stuck between floors. The lights dim, the alarm goes off and everyone is starting to panic. How to deal?
    a. Help each other climb out of the ceiling vent and up the cable to the nearest elevator landing.
    b. Take shallow breaths until help arrives—air flow may be limited.
    c. Hit the emergency button, use the elevator phone to call building security or 911, and wait for rescue.

11. You wake at night and hear a prowler. The safest strategy:
    a. Get out of the house and call 911 from a pay phone or neighbor's place.
    b. Grab your baseball bat and stand behind the door, ready to surprise him when he enters.
    c. Call the police, barricade your bedroom door and hide.

12. A rattlesnake clamped its fangs into your leg, then slithered away. Now what?
    a. Use a sharp knife or rock to cut into the site of the bite and suck the venom out, making sure not to swallow it.
    b. Wrap a tourniquet above the bite.
    c. Immobilize the leg and get medical attention immediately.

13. You planned on a dip, but a riptide has carried you far from shore. How do you stay afloat?
    a. Turn straight toward the beach and paddle as hard as you can.
    b. Swim parallel to shore, or at a 45-degree angle to it, until the wave action starts carrying you back to land.
    c. Wave while you're riding the rip out to the calmer waters behind the waves and hope a lifeguard sees you.

Name _____　Date _____

MASTERY TEST 9-1

Directions: Choose one of the options below to complete this statement.

Advertisements require critical reading and critical thinking because they:

    a. affect our purchasing decisions.

    b. affect our political decisions.

    c. affect our philosophical decisions.

    d. influence our thinking.

    e. all of the above.

Directions: Read and think critically about the following advertisements. Then answer these questions for each ad.

1. How does it try to catch the interest of readers?

2. To whom is it designed to appeal?

3. What is it trying to persuade readers to buy, do, or think?

4. What benefit to readers is it stressing?

5. How convincing is it?

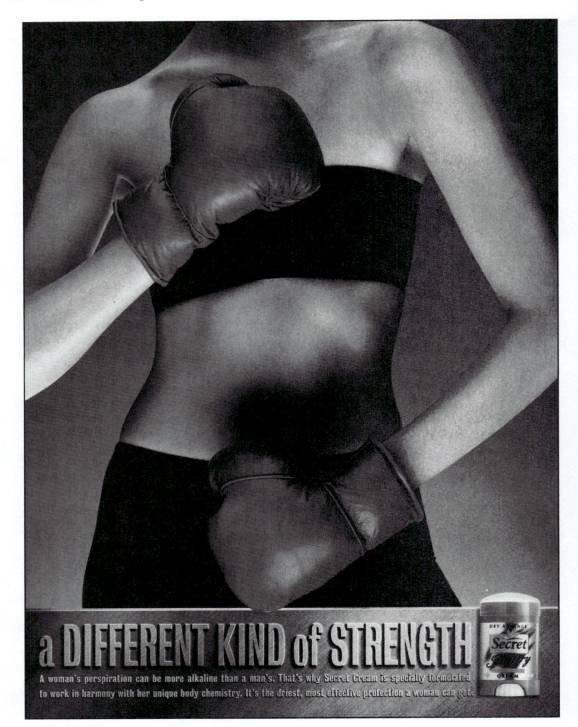

Name _____ Date _____

MASTERY TEST 9–2

DIRECTIONS: In the space below, create a convincing advertisement that catches the interest of readers, appeals to a certain audience, and, by stressing the benefits to readers, tries to persuade them to buy, do, or think something.

_____

_____

_____

_____

_____

_____

_____

_____

_____

_____

_____

_____

_____

_____

_____

_____

_____

_____

_____

Name _____   Date _____

DIRECTIONS: *Read and think about the passages below, and answer the questions that follow.*

1

Dead Body Photo

1   John Harte was the only photographer working on Sunday, July 28, at the Bakersfield *Californian*. After some routine assignments, he heard on the police scanner about a drowning at a lake twenty-five miles northeast of Bakersfield. When he arrived on the scene, divers were still searching for the body of five-year-old Edward Romero, who had drowned while swimming with his brothers.

2   The divers finally brought up the dead boy, and the sheriff kept onlookers at bay while the family and officials gathered around the open body bag. The television crew did not film that moment, but Harte ducked under the sheriff's arms and shot eight quick frames with his motor-driven camera.

3   The *Californian* had a policy of not running pictures of dead bodies. So managing editor Robert Bentley was called into the office on Sunday evening for a decision. Concluding that the picture would remind readers to be careful when kids are swimming, Bentley gave his approval. On Monday, Harte transmitted the picture over the Associated Press wire "after a 20-minute argument with an editor who was furious we ran the picture...and accused [Harte] of seeking glory and an AP award."

4   Readers bombarded the 80,000 circulation daily with 400 phone calls, 500 letters, and 80 cancellations. The *Californian* even received a bomb threat, forcing evacuation of the building for ninety minutes.

5   Distraught by the intensity of the reaction, Bentley sent around a newsroom memo admitting that "a serious error of editorial judgment was made....We make mistakes—and this clearly was a big one." He concluded that their most important lesson was "the stark validation of what readers—and former readers—are saying not just locally but across the country: that the news media are seriously out of touch with their audiences."

6   For photographer John Harte, Bentley's contrition was "disappointing to me and many of my co-workers." And editorial page editor Ed Clendaniel of the *Walla Walla* (Washington) *Union Bulletin* was not apologetic either about running it in his paper, even though it was out of context. "First, the foremost duty of any paper is to report the news," he argued. "One of the hard facts of life is that the world is filled with tragic moments as well as happy moments....Second, we believe the photograph does more to promote water safety than 10,000 words could ever hope to accomplish."

7   Later Bentley entered Harte's photo in the Pulitzer Prize competition. "I really don't see any contradiction," he explained. "I think the photograph should never have been published....But the Pulitzer Prize is given for journalistic and technical excellence. It is not given for reader approval."

8   Michael J. Ogden, executive director of the *Providence Journal-Bulletin*, condemns photographs that capitalize on human grief:

> I can understand the printing of an auto accident picture as an object lesson. What I can't understand is the printing of sobbing wives, mothers, children....What is the value of showing a mother who has just lost her child in a fire? Is this supposed to have a restraining effect on arsonists? I am sure that those who don't hesitate to print such pictures will use the pious pretense of quoting Charles A. Dana's famous *dictum* that "whatever the Divine Providence permitted to occur I was not too proud to print." Which is as peachy a shibboleth to permit pandering as I can image.

9   But Ogden is a rare editor. Every day in newspapers and on television, photographs and film footage emphasize grief and tragedy. Though Harte's photo did not win the Pulitzer, in fact, professional awards are regularly given to grisly pictures regardless of whether they pander to morbid tastes.

10   Defending photos of this type usually centers on newsworthiness. The broken-hearted father whose child was just run over, a shocked eight-year-old boy watching his teenage brother gunned down by police, the would-be suicide on a bridge—all pitiful scenes that communicate something of human tragedy and are therefore to be considered news. Photojournalists sum up a news event in a manner the mind can hold, capturing that portrayal "rich in meaning because it is a trigger image of all the emotions aroused by the subject." Harte in this case acted as an undaunted professional, fulfilling his role as reporter on everyday affairs—including the unpleasantries. From the photographer's perspective, to capture the newsworthy moment is an important self-discipline. Photographers are trained not to panic but to bring forth the truth as events dictate. They are schooled to be visual historians and not freelance medics or family counselors.

11   On what grounds, however, can the photographer's behavior be condoned in the Bakersfield drowning? The principals at the scene tried to prevent him from intruding, though, it should be granted, the authorities' judgment is not always correct. The warning bell thesis was generally used by the picture's proponents, asserting that the photo could make other parents more safety conscious. However, this utilitarian appeal to possible consequences has no factual basis. Perhaps in the name of reporting news, the photojournalist in this case was actually caught in those opportunistic professional values that build circulation by playing on the human penchant for morbidity.

12   No overarching purpose emerges that can ameliorate the direct invasion of privacy and insensitivity for these innocent victims of tragedy. In all jurisdictions, the reporting of events of public concern involves no legal issue of privacy invasion. But it is here that the photographer should consider the moral guideline: that suffering

individuals are entitled to dignity and respect, despite the fact that events may have made them part of the news.

13   Photojournalism is an extremely significant window on our humanity and inhumanity. In pursuing its mission, the ethical conflict typically revolves around the need for honest visual information and for respecting a person's privacy. Bob Greene of the *Chicago Tribune* is exaggerating only slightly in calling the Harte picture "pornography." "Because of journalistic factors they could not control," he wrote, "at the most terrible moment of their lives" the Romeros were exposed to the entire country. The older brother's hysteria for not watching his little brother closely enough is presented without compassion before an audience who had no right to become a participant in this traumatizing event for a suffering family. And even those who find the photo acceptable are upset by the context: The *Californian* printing the photo right next to a headline about teen killings by a satanic cult.

Clifford G. Christians et al., *Media Ethics*, 6th ed., pp. 123–126

COMPREHENSION QUESTIONS

1. What is the topic of the passage?
2. What is the central message of the passage?
3. Determine what is at issue. What is your initial personal viewpoint?
4. Distinguish among opposing viewpoints, and provide the rationale for each.
5. Think carefully about the viewpoints. Express a personal viewpoint, and give the reasons you favor it. Does it differ from your initial personal viewpoint? Why or why not?
6. Write a few paragraphs *in support of the viewpoint that you do* not *favor.*

THOUGHT AND DISCUSSION QUESTIONS

1. If you were John Harte, would you have taken the photograph? Why or why not?
2. Do you agree with Robert Bentley "that the news media are seriously out of touch with their audiences"? Why or why not?
3. Do you support "the warning bells thesis"? Why or why not?
4. "Every day in newspapers and on television, photographs and film footage emphasize grief and tragedy." Do you agree with this statement? Why or why not?
5. Do you think the information presented in the passage is mostly fact, mostly opinion, or a combination of both? Why? Provide specific examples.
6. Do you think the passage is unbiased? Why or why not?

2

Foxtrot

Can the Web be Trusted for Research?

FOXTROT © 2006 Bill Amend. Reprinted with permission of UNIVERSAL UCLICK. All rights reserved.

1   Most Web users are familiar with the huge and immensely popular Wikipedia, the online encyclopedia. What makes Wikipedia so different from traditional, print encyclopedias is that entries can be contributed or edited by anyone.

2   In a recent edition of the *Wall Street Journal*, Jimmy Wales, president of Wikimedia and one of its founders, debated the legitimacy of Wikipedia with Dale Hoiberg, editor-in-chief of *Encyclopedia Britannica.* Hoiberg's main criticism of Wikipedia is that its structure—an open-source wiki without the formal editorial control that shapes traditional, print encyclopedias—allows for inaccurate entries.

3   In response, Wales argues that *Britannica* and newspaper also contain errors, but Wikipedia has the advantage that they are easily corrected. Furthermore, he asserts that Wikipedia's policy of using volunteer administrators to delete irrelevant entries and requiring authors of entries to cite reliable, published sources ensures quality. Nonetheless, some universities including UCLA and the University of Pennsylvania along with many instructors strongly discourage and even ban students from citing Wikipedia in their work. (Wikipedia also cautions against using its entries as a primary source for serious research.)

COMPREHENSION QUESTIONS

1. What is the topic of the passage?
2. What is the central message of the passage?
3. Determine what is at issue. What is your initial personal viewpoint?

4. Distinguish among opposing viewpoints, and provide the rationale for each.
5. Think carefully about the viewpoints. Express a personal viewpoint, and give the reasons why you favor it. Does it differ from your initial personal viewpoint? Why or why not?
6. Write a few paragraphs *in support of the viewpoint that you do* not *favor.*

THOUGHT AND DISCUSSION QUESTIONS

1. Where do you see technology in the future at your school? Support your thoughts with specific examples. Include social-networking Web sites and research devices not mentioned in the reading selection.
2. What do you see as a disadvantage of using Wikipedia at your school? As a counterpoint, what do you see as an advantage? Support your thoughts with specific examples.
3. If your school decided to ban the use of Wikipedia, would you agree or disagree with this decision? Why or why not?
4. Do you think this reading selection is biased? Why or why not?
5. List some questions that came to mind while you were reading this selection, and be prepared to discuss possible answers to them.
6. What is the message of this cartoon?

Name _____   Date _____

1

DIRECTIONS: This problem confronted a non-traditional college student. Place yourself in her position as you proceed through the steps.

You are the mother of three young children who live with you and your boyfriend, who is not their father. Your two daughters are 4- and 2-years-old respectively, and your son has just turned 5. Although the children's biological father lives in the vicinity, he does not see them much nor does he provide any financial assistance. For those reasons, your relationship with him has been so strained that you barely talk to each other.

Your boyfriend and you plan on getting married in about two years. You are a full-time college student, while he attends only part-time because he holds two jobs. As a result, he is usually extremely tired. In addition, both money and living space in your two-bedroom apartment are very limited. Furthermore, your children demand much attention, which you are not always able to give. Although you feel guilty, you are simply too exhausted and overextended. In short, the situation has become very stressful.

To make matters even worse, two weeks ago you found out that you are pregnant with your boyfriend's child, and you are beside yourself as to what to do. As it stands now, there's not enough money or space in your apartment for the five of you, no less for a new baby. Your parents have lost patience with you and are not very sympathetic to your predicament.

_____

_____

_____

_____

_____

_____

_____

SHERLOCK HOLMES AND DR. WATSON

*DIRECTIONS: These questions refer to the first two readings of Sherlock Holmes and Dr. Watson. With your partner, refer to your notes from these previous readings, and answer the questions that follow. **After you have discussed your answers and conclusions with the rest of the class, your instructor will distribute the last part of the short story** so that you can determine if you are have successfully solved the mystery.*

1. Why did Holmes look through the window into the tutor's room?

2. Why did Holmes draw in his notebook, break his pencil, and borrow a pencil and knife from two of the students?

3. Why did Holmes want to know Miles McLaren's exact height?

4. After thinking critically about this case, who do you believe is the culprit? How did you and your partner come to that conclusion?

THE RETURN OF SHERLOCK HOLMES AND DR. WATSON

DIRECTIONS: Read The Adventure of the Three students: Part Three *by A. Conan Doyle distributed by your instructor to find out the identity of the guilty party. Write a different ending to the mystery using the same clues.*

SOLVING ONE MORE MYSTERY

DIRECTIONS: Read and think very carefully about the following passage. Now that the two of you are successful critical thinkers and accomplished detectives, what would you advise the poor merchant's daughter to do? Be prepared to discuss your solution to her predicament with your classmates.

Many years ago when a person who owed money could be thrown into jail, a merchant in London had the misfortune to owe a huge sum to a money-lender. The money-lender, who was old and ugly, fancied the merchant's beautiful teenage daughter. He proposed a bargain. He said he would cancel the merchant's debt if he could have the girl instead.

Both the merchant and his daughter were horrified at the proposal. So the cunning money-lender proposed that they let Providence decide the matter. He told them that he would put a black pebble and a white pebble into an empty money-bag and then the girl would have to pick out one of the pebbles. If she chose the black pebble she would become his wife and her father's debt would be cancelled. If she chose the white pebble she would stay with her father and the debt would still be cancelled. But if she refused to pick out a pebble her father would be thrown into jail and she would starve.

Reluctantly the merchant agreed. They were standing on a pebble-strewn path in the merchant's garden as they talked and the money-lender stooped down to pick up the two pebbles. As he picked up the pebbles the girl, sharp-eyed with fright, noticed that he picked up two black pebbles and put them into the money-bag. He then asked the girl to pick out the pebble that was to decide her fate and that of her father.

Edward de Bono, *Newthink,* p. 11

FURTHER INVESTIGATION

For your own information, research Sherlock Holmes and Dr. Watson online at http://www.sherlockholmes.org or the Sir Arthur Conan Doyle site at http://www.siracd.com for more information on Arthur Conan Doyle.

Glossary

abstract thinking thinking that is "outside the box" or apart from a literal meaning

aids to understanding elements that make a book easier to use

antonyms words that have opposite meanings

appendix section of a book containing supplementary information

asking questions and finding answers engaging in *critical thinking*

bias lack of impartiality or objectivity

bibliography list of works consulted while researching a book or an article

caption explanation of a *graphic aid*

cause and effect *pattern of organization* based on explaining why something happened

central message the *main idea* of a piece of writing longer than one paragraph

clear purpose a specific objective of *critical thinking*, such as an explanation, a solution, or a decision

clue words words that emphasize a value, judgment, feeling, or tone that an individual has toward a subject. Also called *value words*

communication skills creating meaning using listening, speaking, reading, writing, and/or nonverbal skills

comparison and contrast *pattern of organization* for presenting *details* by pointing out similarities and differences

concept cards cards that are similar to flash cards in the way they look and are also used to learn and review new terms or concepts

concept mapping a textbook reading strategy using categorization and organization of material in a visual picture. Diagrams, or maps, can take different forms and are drawn to show the relationship of ideas.

connotation other meanings or suggestions of a word that usually portray a specific tone or feeling

contemporary issues current topics of interest and debate

context the surrounding words in a sentence that make the specific meaning of a word clear

credits list of sources of material appearing in a book that are not original to the book

critical reading high-level comprehension of written material requiring interpretation and evaluation

skills that enable the reader to separate important information, use inference to come to logical conclusions, distinguish between facts and opinions, and determine a writer's purpose and tone

critical thinking a very careful and thoughtful way of dealing with events, issues, problems, decisions, or situations

denotation the literal or dictionary definition of a word

details bits of information that flesh out the *main idea* of a paragraph

fact a piece of knowledge that can be confirmed as accurate in a reliable and unbiased manner

figurative language language that is a symbolic representation of a concept. "She sings like a bird" means the person has a melodious voice, not that she sounds like a real bird like a robin or meadowlark.

finding answers part of engaging in *critical thinking*

flexible thinking considering various possibilities before coming to a conclusion

glossary list of relevant terms and their definitions, arranged alphabetically

graphic aids illustrative *aids to understanding* such as charts, graphs, maps, pictures, and tables

highlighting using a marker to stress and focus on the most important information in a passage

index list of cross-references, arranged alphabetically by topic

inference an "educated guess" based on knowledge, experience, and circumstantial evidence or clues

informed opinion the *opinion* of an expert who is well versed in the relevant *facts*

irony the use of words to mean their opposite for humorous or sarcastic effect

KWL (What I **K**now, What I **W**ant to Know, What I **L**earned) requires students to access their prior knowledge, by establishing a purpose for reading as they determine what information they want to know about the topic, and by identifying what they learned while reading

learning aids see *aids to understanding*

listening comprehension a receptive process whereby one hears, thinks about, and draws understanding from the spoken word

logical conclusions determinations based on rational consideration of all the *facts*

main idea   a sentence (stated or not) that summarizes the sense of an entire paragraph

major details   bits of information that explain the *main idea* of a paragraph

minor details   bits of information that make *major details* more specific

mood   see *tone*

notes   additional information or source identification, usually collected at the end of a chapter or book

objective   exhibiting ideas that are unbiased or impartial; factual

opinion   a personal judgment

opposing viewpoints   conflicting *opinions* regarding the same issue

organization   making the most productive use of limited time

overviewing   *skimming* a text to get acquainted with it

paraphrasing   shortening or condensing information or the main points of a passage by rewording or substituting your own words for those of the author

patterns of organization   arrangements of *facts* to clarify *details* and *main ideas*

preface   introductory chapter in a book

prefix   a word part added before a root or word to change its meaning or create a new word

prejudice   viewpoint adopted without consideration of all the *facts* or other possible viewpoints

previewing   *skimming* to familiarize oneself with the material

problem   any question or matter involving doubt, uncertainty, or difficulty

productive language   the ability to construct meaning by speaking and writing

purpose   reasons for writing

random thinking   thinking with no clear purpose in mind

rationale   specific reason or reasons supporting a viewpoint

receptive language   the ability to understand by reading and listening

reciprocal language   communication skills that have a return or reciprocal relation such as listening and speaking, and reading and writing

reference sources   works recommended for further reading on a given subject

research   process of gathering information to increase knowledge of a topic

root   the basic part or stem from which words are derived

simple listing of facts   lists of *details* used as a *pattern of organization*

skimming   glancing over a text quickly

solution   means by which we rid ourselves of problems

SQ4R   (Survey, Question, Read, Record, Recall, Review) a study-reading strategy that requires students to develop questions to be answered during the reading process and then used for reviewing the material

subjective   exhibiting an opinion, a view, a biased thought, or a personal judgment

suffix   a word part added after a root or word to create a new word or affect the way a word is used

suggested readings   see *reference sources*

summarizing   shortening or condensing information or the main points of a passage by using many of the writer's own words

synonyms   words that have the same or almost the same meaning

table of contents   list of the parts, chapters, and subheadings of a book

testimonial   involves the endorsement of a product or idea by a famous person. Many testimonials use athletes or movie celebrities to sell their merchandise.

thinking and viewing   nonverbal communication skills

time and effort   essential requirements of *critical thinking*

time sequence   *pattern of organization* in which events are recounted chronologically

title   formal name given to a book, article, chapter, *graphic aid*, or other book element

title page   page indicating title, author, publisher, and edition of a book

tone   a writer's attitude or feeling toward the *topic* being written about

topic   the subject of a paragraph

topic sentence   a sentence in a paragraph stating the *main idea* of that paragraph

transition words   words used to introduce *patterns of organization*

unbiased   evenhanded, objective, impartial, or without prejudice; factual

unstated main idea   a statement not appearing in a paragraph that summarizes the *main idea* of that paragraph

value words   words that emphasize a value, judgment, feeling, or tone that an individual has toward a subject. Also called *clue* words

word part   a root, prefix, or *suffix*

Credits

Photo Credits

Page 3 left: Roberto Schmidt/AFP/Getty Images;
3 right: Jim Hayes; **51:** © 2007 Girl Scouts of the
USA. Teen recruitment campaign "It's a Girls Life.
Lead It." Used by permission.; **55:** Earth Share/
The Advertising Council; **111:** Adbusters; **120:**
BEND IT FILMS/FILM COUNCIL/THE KOBAL
COLLECTION/PARRY, CHRISTINE; **175 left:**
Copyright © 2010 The Fresno Bee. Reprinted
with permission. All rights reserved; **175 right:**
"Deseret News; Salt Lake City, Utah"; **184:** Shawn
Baldwin/AP Images; **185:** Good Salt/PunchStock;
232 left: Eyewire/Photodisc/Punchstock;
232 right: Dallas and John Heaton/Free Agents
Limited/Corbis; **232b:** age fotostock/SuperStock;
289 left: Bill Aron/Photo Edit; **289 right:** Rudi Von
Briel/PhotoEdit; **295:** © Peter Steiner/The New
Yorker Collection/www.cartoonbank.com; **296:**
Brian Crane © 2005 The Washington Post Writer's
Group, Reprinted with Permission.; **297:**
© Columbus Dispatch/Dist. by United Feature
Syndicate, Inc.; **299:** Image Source/SuperStock;
330: Lars Leetaru; **339 right:** David Young-
Wolff/Photo Edit, Inc.; **367 left:** Michael Newman/
PhotoEdit, Inc.; **385:** © Emir Shabashvili/Alamy;
403 left: The Advertising Archives; **403 right:** Bill
Aron/Photo Edit, Inc.; **406:** Porsche Cars North
America, Inc.; **407:** Dutch Boy Paints; **408:** Green
Mountain Energy; **409:** The Salvation Army;
411 left: Mike Blake/Reuters; **411 right:** Paul
Sancya/AP Images; **411B left:** The Advertising
Council; **411B right:** J. Howard Miller/The
National Archives, Still Pictures Unit; **412:** Beryl
Goldberg; **413:** Beryl Goldberg; **414 left:** American
Broadcasting Company; **414 right:** Courtesy of the
National Crime Prevention Council; **415 right:**
The Florence Fund; **415 left:** The Pew Charitable
Trusts and the Tides Center; **416:** Reprinted with
permission from the publisher. © 2002 by
Merriam-Webster, Incorporated.; **442:** The
Advertising Archives; **443:** The Advertising
Archives; **444:** The Advertising Archives

Text Credits

Gary Armstrong and Philip Kotler, *Marketing: An
Introduction*, 9th ed., © 2009. Reprinted by per-
mission of Pearson Education, Inc., Upper Saddle
River, New Jersey.

Ella Baker Center for Human Rights. http://www
.ellabakercenter.org. http://creativecommons.org/
licenses /by/3.0/us/

Eugene V. Beresin, "Impact of Media Violence
on Children and Adolescents," American
Academy of Child and Adolescent Psychiatry.
Copyright © 2009 American Academy of
Child & Adolescent Psychiatry. Reprinted
with permission.

Christine Biederman, "As a Lawyer, He's
Exemplary; as a Robber, an Enigma," *New York
Times*, January 20, 1996, p. 7.

Neil A. Campbell, Jane B. Reece, Martha R.
Taylor, and Eric J. Simon, *Biology: Concepts &
Connections*, 5th ed. Copyright © 2006 by
Pearson Education, Inc. Reprinted by permission
of Pearson Education, Inc.

Clifford G. Christians, et al., *Media Ethics*, 6th ed.,
pp. 123–126, © 2001. Reproduced by permission
of Pearson Education, Inc.

Jesús Colón. "Kipling and I" from *A Puerto Rican
in New York and Other Sketches*, 2nd ed., 1982.
Reprinted by permission of International
Publishers, New York.

Jennifer Conner. Table "Topic: Gravity" from
"KWL (What I *K*now, What I *W*ant to Know,
What I *L*earned)." http://www.indiana.
edu/~l517/KWL.htm. Copyright 2006
Jennifer Conner. Reprinted with
permission.

Lacy Cordell, screen shot of "Media Violence
Good for Kids," http://www.ac-ranger.com.
October 14, 2004; updated December 5, 2009.
Reprinted by permission of The Ranger, Amarillo
College, Amarillo, TX.

Index

Page numbers with an *f* indicate figures.